D1268522

THE AMERICAN PAST: *An Informal Series*

New Editions of Classic Commentaries

William Bradford—OF PLYMOUTH PLANTATION
with an introduction and notes by Samuel Eliot Morison

Richard Burton—THE CITY OF THE SAINTS
With an introduction and notes by Fawn M. Brodie

Dan De Quille (William Wright)—THE BIG BONANZA
with an introduction by Oscar Lewis

Louis Moreau Gottschalk—NOTES OF A PIANIST
with a prelude, a postlude, and explanatory notes by Jeanne Behrend

Horace Greeley—AN OVERLAND JOURNEY
with an introduction and notes by Charles T. Duncan

Frances A. Kemble—JOURNAL OF A RESIDENCE ON A GEORGIAN PLANTATION IN 1838–1839
with an introduction and notes by John A. Scott

Frederick Marryat—A DIARY IN AMERICA
With an introduction and notes by S. W. Jackman

Frederick Law Olmsted—THE COTTON KINGDOM
with an introduction by Arthur M. Schlesinger

"Dame Shirley" (Louise A. K. S. Clappe)—
THE SHIRLEY LETTERS
with an introduction and notes by Carl I. Wheat

Susan Dabney Smedes—MEMORIALS OF A SOUTHERN PLANTER
with an introduction and notes by Fletcher M. Green

Alexis de Tocqueville—DEMOCRACY IN AMERICA
with an introduction, notes, and bibliographies by Phillips Bradley

Anthony Trollope—NORTH AMERICA
with an introduction and notes by Donald Smalley and Bradford Allen Booth

Mrs. Frances Trollope—DOMESTIC MANNERS OF THE AMERICANS
with an introduction and notes by Donald Smalley

These are BORZOI BOOKS, *published in New York by* ALFRED A. KNOPF

OF

Plymouth Plantation

OF Plymouth Plantation

1620–1647

by WILLIAM BRADFORD

SOMETIME GOVERNOR THEREOF

A NEW EDITION

The Complete Text, with Notes and an INTRODUCTION

by SAMUEL ELIOT MORISON

NEW YORK ALFRED A. KNOPF

2004

L. C. CATALOG CARD NUMBER: 51-13222

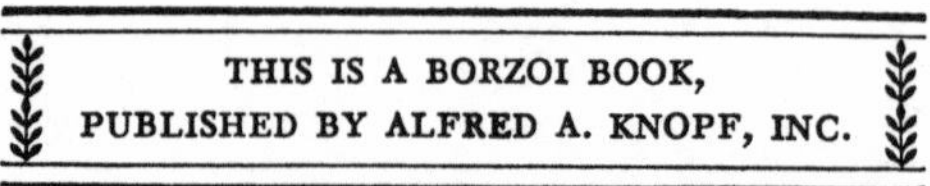

Published September 19, 1952
Reprinted Twenty-one Times
Twenty-third Printing, October 2004

For My Own Priscilla

PREFACE

Almost every American is familiar with the story of the Pilgrim Fathers, of whom Governor William Bradford's History is the official chronicle. The substance of it has entered into American folklore. Many English and American historians and literary critics have praised it as one of the greatest books of the seventeenth century, and have declared that the Governor's name should rank little lower than those of Milton, Bunyan and of King James's translators of the Bible. Yet hitherto there has been no edition of Bradford that the ordinary reader might peruse with pleasure as well as profit. The History has been treated as an ancient document or sacred palimpsest, rather than as a book for people to read. It has been printed with all the abbreviations and contractions in the original manuscript, or with the archaic and variant spellings used by Bradford, which make it so difficult to follow that few people other than students and specialists have done so. Nor are all the existing editions complete.

What I have done is to treat Bradford as a modern editor treats Shakespere or the English Bible. Nobody thinks of printing a sixteenth- or seventeenth-century book exactly as the manuscript was originally written. I do not imagine that many people would now read *Romeo and Juliet* if every modern editor insisted on following literally the First Quarto of 1597, which has Romeo say (Act III sc. v. 6–10):

See Loue what enuious ſtrakes
Doo lace the ſeurering clowdes in yonder Eaſt.
Nights candles are burnt out, and iocond Day
Stands tiptoes on the mystie mountaine tops.
I muſt be gone and liue, or ſtay and dye.

And the readers of the King James version of the Bible would certainly not be increased if every modern edition faithfully followed the original of 1611, in which Matthew xvi.12 is printed thus, spelling *she* two different ways in the same verse:

"For in that ſhe hath powred this ointment on my body, ſhee did it for my buriall."

Now, the case for a modern (*not* modernized) text of Bradford's History is even stronger, because Bradford's work was never printed in any form in his own day. None of Shakespere's manuscripts have been preserved, but we may be certain that those which he sent to the printer were at least as full of abbreviations, contractions and wild spellings as Bradford's. In the seventeenth century, and even down to the age of Linotype, an author counted on his printer to bring spelling, capitalization and punctuation into some order and consistency, and to expand contractions. And the author expected to do a great deal of revision in proof, as printing was cheap. But the complete text of Bradford came to light at a period and under circumstances which caused it to be printed as near as might be to the manuscript. Later editors did expand manuscript abbreviations such as y^e, y^t, y^m, *&*, w^{ch}, but respected Bradford's extraordinary spelling and odd punctuation. Worthington C. Ford's edition, now out of print, is a monument of scholarship, providing abundant notes and illustrations; every scholar should be grateful to it, and I am indebted to Mr. Ford for many of my notes. But even he did not provide a text which the ordinary intelligent reader can peruse with ease and pleasure. My first motive for editing a new edition is to do just that: to introduce a very great book to a much wider public.

My principle in preparing this text is to spell out all contractions and abbreviations in the manuscript, to adopt modern usage as to capitalization, punctuation and spelling, but *scrupulously to respect Bradford's language*. Probably there is no editor who does not think he could "improve" an author's language, even Shakespere's, in spots; but I have not succumbed to that temptation. I have not tried to correct Bradford's grammar, which is occasionally bad, or his syntax, which is sometimes obscure, or to replace an obsolete word by the modern equivalent, or to correct one of his persistent oddities, the use of *as* for *that*. I have, however, taken what some may consider a liberty with Bradford's order. For the record, Bradford inserted in his text letters and even long official documents. Some of these are essential to the narrative but others are not; and they are tedious too. Such letters and documents have been consigned to the Appendices. And I have added, in square brackets, subheadings to break up the longer chapters. But I have omitted nothing. Every word that Bradford wrote in his History, whether text, note, gloss or document, is here. And that is not true of some earlier editions, from which matters violating mid-nineteenth-century notions of propriety were expunged. I have, however, omitted items in the manuscript that are extraneous to the History. These are (1) the Governor's Hebrew vocabulary; (2) the very bad verses to his second wife, written in by someone else at a later date; (3) juvenile scribblings of some of his descendants; and (4) manuscript notes and underlinings added by the Rev. Thomas Prince in the early eighteenth century.

The business of bringing Bradford's spelling and punctuation up to date is not always easy. Many will differ from my opinion as to where a sentence or paragraph should properly end. Where variants exist in modern spelling, I follow the one that is nearest to Bradford's. Thus I use the English forms *honour* and *endeavour* because Bradford does; but as he inconsistently writes *harbor* and *Governor*, I follow him there. I call a certain type of vessel *bark* instead of *barque* because Bradford spells it *barke;* her capacity is called her *burthen*, not *burden*, and is stated in *tuns*, not *tons*, because Bradford spells each word the first way, more than nine times out of ten. Undoubtedly some flavor is lost in not printing *could* for *cold*, *powre* for *pour*, *catch* for *ketch* as Bradford writes these words because such (Bradford calls it *shuch*) spellings are a key to the way the Pilgrims and their contemporaries pronounced the language. But one cannot correct the spelling of some words and leave others as he wrote them. Proper names have been standardized in accordance with present usage; for Indian names the famous Frederick W. Hodge *Handbook* (1907) has been my guide.

I have followed the same principles with quotations from *Mourt's Relation*, the *Plymouth Colony Records* and other contemporary sources; only the titles of printed books are reproduced with complete accuracy. Annotations I have tried to keep down to the minimum necessary for a modern reader to understand contemporary allusions in the text, and to identify persons and places mentioned. Bradford was no inconsiderable annotator of his own History; his notes are always followed by his name, and may be so identified.

Readers may wish to know how this text was established. My

secretary, Miss Antha E. Card, who has worked with me on it at intervals during a period of five years, first made a typewritten text from the Commonwealth edition of 1897, expanding the abbreviations and modernizing the spelling according to the principles decided on. Secondly (as Bradford would say) she compared this typewritten text, word for word, with the original manuscript in the Massachusetts State Library at Boston. Thirdly, we collated it together; she following the typewritten copy which went to the printer while I read aloud to her the entire history from the manuscript, dictating corrections as I went along and deciding how the text should be punctuated. Finally, she and I collated the galley proof with the corrected typewritten copy, referring to the original manuscript in cases of doubt.

Miss Card and I do not pretend that our work is impeccable, but we do insist that this is the first edition of Bradford which has been compared word for word with the original manuscript. All others are based on the edition of 1856, the editors contenting themselves by comparing their text with the Doyle facsimile of 1896. Now, the Doyle facsimile, although very valuable, is not a perfect facsimile. In places it shaves off the edge of a page; and nowhere does it show the different colors of ink or the more subtle pen marks which indicate whether a given correction or underlining was made by Bradford or by Prince or by some other person who tampered with the manuscript.

For instance, the eloquent sentence: "Thus out of small beginnings . . ." which closes Chapter xxi (1630), part of which reads "and as one small candle may light a thousand, so the light here kindled hath shone unto many," has always been misprinted "hath shone to many," because the Doyle facsimile seemed to support the 1856 copyist's belief that Bradford crossed out the *un* of *unto*. A close examination of the manuscript, however, shows that the alleged erasure is merely an inadvertent blot from the Governor's quill pen.

Not all parts of Bradford will be equally interesting to the modern reader. I would advise those who are not concerned with the religious controversies of the Protestant Reformation to begin with Chapter iv "Showing the Reasons and Causes of Their

Removal" and read at least through the eloquent and moving Chapter ix. After that, either you will decide you do not care for Bradford and the Pilgrim Fathers or you will wish to read to the end; and Bradford retains his good story-telling ability to the very end: witness the tale of the pirates' visit to Plymouth in 1646. There are some arid bits, such as the prolonged account of the trickery of Allerton and the London partners, and the theological aspects of the crime wave, as related in Appendix X. But there are plenty of high and even humorous spots, as the account of Thomas Morton the gay blade of Merrymount, of Lyford the lewd parson, and of "Mad Jack" Oldham getting the Pilgrims' equivalent of a modern "bum's rush." Moving passages, too, relating the emotions of these people when they were landed on an inhospitable shore at the beginning of a New England winter (Chapter ix), and the story of that first terrible winter (Chapter x).

Bradford was the historian of a very small colony. About 100 persons reached Plymouth in the *Mayflower* in December 1620. Ten years later, after new arrivals by the *Anne*, the *Fortune*, the *Little James* and the *Talbot*, the total population was about 300. In 1650, when Governor Bradford stopped writing, there were less than a thousand people under his jurisdiction. Yet there is, I think you will admit, a certain timelessness about the Pilgrim story. More than once to this little band, as to people of free nations in our own time, came the awful question: "Can we possibly survive?" In the discussion over building the fort (Chapter xiii) we seem to see, as through a glass, the great debate of our own time, the balance of military security against preserving a certain way of life. As I was looking up the precedents for the legal maxim *nemo tenetur prodere seipsum* in Appendix X, an article in the *New York Times Magazine*, 22 April 1951, reminded me that this was the original form of Article V of the Federal Bill of Rights, very much to the fore in Senator Kefauver's crime investigation. In the debates in the New England Confederation over the Narragansetts, we are confronted with the United Nations in miniature–shall we start a "preventive" war now and risk losing all, or wait yet a little while, hoping that we, not they, will grow stronger? In their handling of these Indian relations, as with the dissidents in their midst, Bradford made no claim of omniscience for himself and his equally inexperienced assistants; but he had a constant sense of an unseen hand, and on one occasion (Chapter xiv) a mysterious voice, that seemed to be guiding the Pilgrim policy. One can say of these men and women what one of their descendants, Henry Adams, said of the Virginia ruling class at the birth of the Republic: "They were equal to any standard of excellence known to history. Their range was narrow, but within it they were supreme."

Bradford's History is a story of a simple people inspired by an ardent faith to a dauntless courage in danger, a resourcefulness in dealing with new problems, an impregnable fortitude in adversity that exalts and heartens one in an age of uncertainty, when courage falters and faith grows dim. It is this story, told by a great human being, that has made the Pilgrim Fathers in a sense the spiritual ancestors of all Americans, all pioneers.

S. E. Morison

Harvard University
March 1952

ACKNOWLEDGMENTS

First of the several persons to whom I am grateful for assistance and advice in preparing this edition is my secretary, Miss Antha E. Card, who prepared the trial text, collated it with me, supplied the Biblical and other references, and made the index. Mr. Dennis A. Dooley, Massachusetts State Librarian, and his assistant Mrs. Evelyn M. Campbell accorded us every facility for working from the precious original manuscript in their custody. My colleague Professor Johannes A. C. F. Auer established the short bit of Dutch text, and Professor Mark A. DeWolfe Howe gave me some leads on legal matters. Mr. Warren P. Strong, director of Pilgrim Hall, Plymouth, has been generous with photographs and maps, and Captain W. Sears Nickerson, author of *Land Ho!—1620*, has been most kind in allowing me to use material from his book and in supplying me with additional background information. Mr. Sidney V. James provided the historical data for some of the maps, which were drawn by Dr. Erwin Raisz.

CONTENTS

APPENDICES

LIST OF MAPS

Drawn by Erwin Raisz

PART OF CAPE COD 1620–1626 [67]

With the coastline of that era, as worked out by the researches of Captain W. Sears Nickerson, and by his kind permission based on the map in his *Land Ho!–1620.* Routes of exploring expeditions from Henry Martyn Dexter's notes and map in his edition of *Mourt's Relation*, 1865.

PLYMOUTH BAY 1620–1650 [91]

Soundings and channels based on the chart in Des Barres's *Atlantic Neptune*, London, 1780. This in turn is based on the oldest detailed chart of Plymouth Bay, the survey made by Charles Blaskowitz for the Royal Navy in July 1774, of which the original is in Pilgrim Hall, Plymouth. Land data from U. S. Geographical Surveys of 1853–1934.

NEW ENGLAND 1620–1650 [201]

Showing the principal settlements, fishing stations, and trading posts mentioned by Bradford.

THE COLONY OF NEW PLYMOUTH 1620–1650 [306–7]

With adjacent settlements. Based on research by Sidney James, A.M. The dates are those of first settlement. Only the general locality of Indian villages is indicated.

INTRODUCTION

1. *The Author*

William Bradford, the author of this History, was born at Austerfield, Yorkshire, in the early spring of 1590.[1] He was the third child and only son of William Bradford, a yeoman farmer of the parish, and Alice Hanson, daughter of the village shopkeeper. His father died when William was only a year old, his mother married again, and his grandfather and uncles then took him in hand to be trained as a farmer. At the age of twelve he became a constant reader of the Bible—the Geneva version that he generally quotes—and when still a lad he was so moved by the Word as to join a group of Puritans who met for prayer and discussion at the house of William Brewster in the nearby village of Scrooby. When this group, inspired by the Rev. Richard Clyfton, organized itself as a separate Congregational church in 1606, Bradford joined it despite "the wrath of his uncles" and the "scoff of his neighbors." [2]

From that date until his death half a century later, Bradford's life revolved around that of this church or congregation, first in Scrooby, next in the Low Countries and finally in New England. In his own words one may read of their escape to the Netherlands, their short sojourn at Amsterdam, and long one at Leyden, under a remarkable pastor, the Rev. John Robinson. Bradford, upon coming of age in 1611, received an inheritance from his parents, which apparently he expended in some sort of mercantile venture; but he saved enough to buy a house in Leyden, where he followed the trade of weaver. Largely through his own efforts he learned Dutch and a certain amount of Latin and Hebrew, and acquired a wide knowledge of general literature and a fair-sized library, which he brought with him to the New World.

[1] Baptized 19 March; the date of his birth, presumably not earlier than 15 March, was not recorded.

[2] Cotton Mather's biography of him in *Magnalia Christi* (1702) lib. ii p. 3. For bibliography of Bradford, see my article on him in *Dictionary of American Biography*. The first biography of Bradford to appear since Cotton Mather's is Bradford Smith *Bradford of Plymouth* (1951), an excellent work which came out as I was sending this manuscript to the printer.

In 1617 when the preparations began for the removal of this band of brothers to America, Bradford was twenty-seven years old; but his ability had evidently so impressed the elders of the congregation that he was chosen one of the committee to make the practical arrangements. He sailed in the *Mayflower* with his first wife, Dorothy May, whom he had married at Amsterdam in 1613. He took part in the boat expedition that explored Cape Cod, including the one that scudded into Plymouth Bay before a snowstorm and landed, traditionally on Plymouth Rock, on 11 December 1620. On returning to the *Mayflower* at Cape Cod (now Provincetown) Harbor, he learned that his "dearest consort, accidentally falling overboard, was drowned in the harbor." His failure to mention this in the History is consistent with his modest reticence about his own rôle of leadership in the colony; but it may be that he suspected (as do we) that Dorothy Bradford took her own life, after gazing for six weeks at the barren sand dunes of Cape Cod. For we have it from other tenderhearted women who came to New England among the pioneers, that their hearts grew faint and sick when they first beheld that wild-looking northern land, so different from the green and cultivated England they had left. Three years later, when a former member of the Leyden church, the widow Alice Southworth, came out to Plymouth with her two small boys, Bradford married her and she bore him three children.

In May 1621, after the death of Governor John Carver, William Bradford, just turned thirty-one, was unanimously chosen to that office, "the difficulties whereof were such that, if he had not been a person of more than ordinary piety, wisdom and courage, he must have sunk under them." And he was re-elected to the same office no less than thirty times, for a total term of 33 years—every year from 1622.[3] In other words, he was Governor of Plymouth Colony continuously from 1627 to 1656 inclusive, excepting for five years when he "by importunity gat off," according to Governor Winthrop; and in those years he was chosen an assistant to Governor Winslow or Governor Prence.

[3] An apparent error in this count is due to the fact that in two years, 1646 and 1649, no election was held; the Governor simply carried on. Checked from W. H. Whitmore *The Massachusetts Civil List* pp. 35–40.

So, from 1621 to his death, Bradford was the principal leader of the Pilgrim Fathers. William Brewster, who had had a university education, was elder of the church; Edward Winslow, more a man of the world than Bradford, did the Pilgrims' diplomatic business; Myles Standish provided the power to their politics. But Bradford, who never left New England after he had once landed there, was the man who made the major decisions. He exercised more plenary authority than any governor of an English colony in his day, with the possible exception of Sir William Berkeley in Virginia.

If Bradford had been moved by love of power or ambition for wealth, he had an opportunity in 1630 when the Warwick Patent from the Council for New England was made out in his name. He might then, had he wished, have become the sole lord and proprietor of Plymouth Colony; like Lord Baltimore in Maryland. Instead, he promptly shared his proprietary right with the "Old Comers," as the Pilgrim Fathers were called in their own day; and in 1640 he persuaded the "Old Comers" to surrender the patent to the whole body of Freemen. He was one of the small group known as the Undertakers, who were given by the Freemen a monopoly of offshore fishing and fur trading in order to pay off their debt to the merchant adventurers who financed the *Mayflower's* voyage. It is true that we have never heard the Adventurers' side of the story, except in their own letters that Bradford incorporated in his History; but even on their showing they treated the Pilgrims much as a loan shark treats a man in financial difficulties; the more beaver and other commodities they sent to England, the more the debt grew. Finally it was paid off in 1648 after Bradford, Alden, Standish, Winslow and Prence had sold houses and large parcels of land to make up the balance.

Thereafter, Bradford continued the Indian trade on his own account, through trading posts on Buzzard's Bay and the Kennebec. At his death at the age of sixty-seven on 9 May 1657 he owned a house in Plymouth valued only at £45, an orchard and several parcels of land at Plymouth; a "great beer bowle" and two smaller ones, six leather chairs, three "carved chairs," a "great chair," and a court cupboard, ten and a half pairs of sheets, a large quantity of table linen, about five dozen pewter dishes and vessels, a red Turkey grogram suit of clothes, a red waistcoat and a "sad colored" suit, a "stuff suit with silver buttons," an "old violet colored cloak" and "two hats—a black one and a colored one."

"He was a person for study as well as action," records Cotton Mather; and this may be seen not only by his literary skill,[4] but by the fact that he had at his death a library of about 400 volumes, including John Speed's *Prospect of the Most Famous Part of the World*, Peter Martyr *de Orbe Novo*, Jean Bodin *de Republica*, Pierre de la Primaudaye's *French Academy*, and "divers Dutch books." [5]

It is a pity that the Governor did not continue his History through 1650, for we would like to have known his opinion of Father Gabriel Druillettes, a Jesuit from Canada who visited him at the end of the year in order to come to some arrangement about the Abnaki Indians on the Kennebec. The Governor (whom Druillettes calls "Jehan Brentford") received him with courtesy and invited him to dine, taking care to serve a fish dinner because it was Friday, although Puritans made rather a point of not eating fish on Fridays.[6]

In his later years the Governor wrote out three "Dialogues" between "Ancient Men" of Plymouth, explaining to "Young Men born in New England" the principles of their religion and their church organization. He wrote a good deal of indifferent verse, some of which is appealing from its very simplicity and sincerity: [7]

> From my years young in days of youth,
> God did make known to me his truth,
> And call'd me from my native place
> For to enjoy the means of grace.

[4] E. F. Bradford "Conscious Art in Bradford's History," *New England Quarterly* I (1928) 133–57.

[5] The will and detailed inventory are printed in *The Mayflower Descendant* II (1900) 228–34 and described in Bradford Smith *Bradford of Plymouth* pp. 268–70, 314–15.

[6] R. G. Thwaites ed. *Jesuit Relations* XXXVI 91.

[7] Most of the Dialogues and poetry are printed in Massachusetts Historical Society *Proceedings* XI (1870) 396–482. These verses are given in Nathaniel Morton *New Englands Memoriall* for the year 1657.

In wilderness he did me guide,
And in strange lands for me provide.
In fears and wants, through weal and woe,
A Pilgrim passed I to and fro.

In his later years the Governor felt that the glory had departed from Plymouth; the town declining in numbers, population dispersed, young people indifferent to religion and heedless of their fathers' sacrifices, luxury coming in with prosperity, Indians growing insolent.

Unfortunately we have no contemporary biographical sketch of Bradford; not even a portrait or description of his person. But it will not be difficult for anyone to infer his character from this History; as fair a permanent monument as any man could wish.

2. *History of a History*

The book in which Bradford's History is written is a vellum-bound volume, measuring 11½" x 7¾", containing about 270 leaves, most of which Bradford numbered himself, very inaccurately. He skipped from 79 to 91, occasionally he left a number out; he went back to the 100's when he was in the 200's, and so forth. Mostly he writes on the obverse only, but sometimes on the reverse. His numbers, such as they are, I have placed in the text enclosed in vertical rules at the beginning of each folio, to facilitate reference to the original, the facsimile, or to other editions. Bradford, as he states in Appendix I, started to write in 1630, finished through Chapter x that year, did the rest "in pieces" until 1646, and added a few items as late as 1650.

The first folios, unnumbered, are occupied by Bradford's Hebrew exercises,[8] in the middle of which comes this statement which, judging from the ink and handwriting, was written by Bradford in 1650:

[8] Isidore S. Meyer "The Hebrew Preface to Bradford's History," American Jewish Historical Society *Publications* No. xxxviii Part 4 (June 1949) reproduces these exercises in facsimile with annotations. It is not correct, however, to call them a Preface to the History; they were written after the History, in his old age

Though I am grown aged, yet I have had a longing desire to see with my own eyes something of that most ancient language and holy tongue in which the Law and Oracles of God were writ, and in which God and Angels spake to the holy patriarchs of old time; and what names were given to things from the Creation. And though I cannot attain to much herein, yet I am refreshed to have seen some glimpse hereof, as Moses saw the land of Canaan afar off. My aim and desire is to see how the words and phrases lie in the holy text, and to discern somewhat of the same, for my own content.

According to a manuscript note by his great-grandson Samuel Bradford, recorded on one of the flyleaves on 20 March 1705, the manuscript book descended first to the Governor's eldest son, Major William Bradford, then to his son Major John Bradford, and then to his son Samuel. In the meantime Nathaniel Morton, the old Governor's nephew, later Secretary of the Colony of New Plymouth, had used the manuscript in writing his *New Englands Memoriall* (Cambridge 1669), the first published history of a New England colony. A large part of Morton is a mere paraphrase of Bradford. Not content with this, however, and (by his own confession) somewhat spurred by fellow Plymotheans who thought he had not done well by Uncle William, the pious Nathaniel faithfully copied into the Plymouth church records most of the Bradford History through Chapter ix of the First Book, together with extracts from the rest.[9]

Increase Mather had already borrowed the manuscript as a source for his own history of the Indian wars. Before he got around to returning it, Increase Mather lost his house by fire on 27 November 1676. Fortunately the History was not involved, and the manuscript does not show any sign of having been subjected to undue heat.

[9] This copy through Chapter ix was first printed in Alexander Young *Chronicles of the Pilgrim Fathers* (1841) pp. 1–108. The whole of Morton's copy was printed as part of the *Plymouth Church Records* in Colonial Society of Massachusetts *Publications* XXII (1920).

Increase Mather's son Cotton used the manuscript in his account of the Plymouth Colony in the *Magnalia Christi Americana*, completed before the end of the century and printed at London in 1702. William Hubbard used it in his *History of New England*, finished before 1683 but not printed until 1815. And, at some time between 1705 and 1728, Judge Samuel Sewall, author of a famous Diary, borrowed the manuscript; for what purpose we know not.

We do know that the book was in Sewall's possession in 1728, from a note in the manuscript itself made by the next borrower, the Rev. Thomas Prince, minister of the Old South Church in Boston. One of the first collectors of Americana, Prince began to accumulate books when he was in Harvard College; and by 1718, when he became colleague minister of the Old South Church, his library was so large that he fitted up the "steeple room" of the meeting house as "The New England Library." A few years later Prince decided to write a New England history of his own. The one document he needed for the Plymouth Colony was the Bradford History. He called on Major John Bradford at Plymouth in 1728 and apparently offered to buy it. According to Prince's own note in the manuscript itself, the Major said "he would never part with the property, but would lend it to me and desired me to get it"—of Judge Sewall, which he promptly did. Prince then jotted down, on a flyleaf of the manuscript: "I write down this that Major Bradford and his heirs may be known to be the right owners." Yet Prince's own New England Library book label is pasted on the same page! Major Bradford, according to another note by Prince, consented that the manuscript be deposited in the New England Library on condition that "he might have the perusal of it while he lived," and the Major's son Samuel regarded himself as the owner. But Prince undoubtedly regarded the loan as one of that indefinite sort which librarians and bibliophiles are apt to convert into complete ownership.

Thomas Prince made good use of the Bradford History in his *Chronological History of New England* (Boston 1736), and the manuscript bears much evidence of his earnest perusal. Not only did the reverend borrower make notes of his own on blank pages; he went right through the text underlining passages that he deemed important, even in some instances correcting the Governor's spelling. And when Prince died in 1758, he left the manuscript, together with his entire New England Library, to the Old South Church.[1]

Governor Thomas Hutchinson used the Bradford manuscript in the second volume of his *History of Massachusetts Bay* (Boston 1767). But after the War of Independence had been fought and won, the manuscript was no longer to be found in the New England Library. What had become of it? Naturally the finger of suspicion pointed to Governor Hutchinson. He was a Tory. He went to England in 1774. The book was not on the shelf in 1780. Very suspicious!

But there are other circumstances to be considered. Within a year of the Governor's departure for England, a British army was being besieged by that of the United Colonies in Boston. The Old South Meeting House, which still stands at the corner of Washington and Milk Streets, was used by the British garrison as a riding school. After the siege was raised, Thomas Prince's valuable library in the tower was found to be somewhat dilapidated, and the Bradford manuscript was not the only book that had disappeared. Fortunately the Bradford text through Chapter ix had been copied into the Plymouth church records, and that version was published by Alexander Young in *Chronicles of the Pilgrim Fathers,* 1841. But the entire Book II of the History had never been copied, and every New England historian and antiquarian bewailed the loss.

Enough has been said here to show that the contention of a recent writer, George F. Willison, that the Pilgrim story (or "saga" as he calls it) "was wholly the creation of the nineteenth century," is nonsense.[2] All the essential parts of the Pilgrim story had been in print since 1669; the Mayflower Compact since 1622. Captain John Smith in his *General History* of 1624, and all eighteenth-century historians of the English colonies, mention the Plymouth Colony in its right place and give it the proper empha-

1 The Old South Church still owns the Prince Library, but keeps it in the Boston Public Library, which has published a catalogue of it.

2 *Saints and Strangers* (1945) p. 2.

sis. The centenary of the *Mayflower's* voyage was celebrated at Plymouth in 1720, and Forefathers' Day was annually celebrated —on the wrong date to be sure—from 1769. The term *Pilgrim Fathers* was first applied exclusively to the *Mayflower* passengers in the celebration of 1799, but it was Bradford himself who called himself and his companions *Pilgrims.*[3] Naturally, as the shadow of American history lengthened, Americans became more and more interested in their origins, and more and more eager to obtain the full story of the Pilgrim colony.

They did not have long to wait after Young's publication of Book I. In 1844 Samuel Wilberforce, Bishop of Oxford, known to his contemporaries as "Soapy Sam," published an exceedingly dull work, *A History of the Protestant Episcopal Church in America, by Samuel, Lord Bishop of Oxford.* Therein, in Chapter iii, he makes an unmistakable quotation from the Bradford History, with a revealing footnote: "Fulham MS. History." (Fulham Palace was the residence of the Bishop of London.) Four years later the Rev. James S. M. Anderson published a three-volume *History of the Colonial Church.* He not only used the manuscript but distinctly stated that Governor Bradford wrote it. The following year, 1849, Wilberforce's *History* was reprinted in New York. That same year, Joseph Hunter, Vice President of the Society of Antiquaries in London, who was interested in the history of the Pilgrim Fathers, published in London a pamphlet on their origin without making any reference to the manuscript, despite the fact that he lived within a stone's throw of Fulham Palace, where it reposed. One can excuse an Englishman for not running down every clue to Bradford; but it passes one's comprehension how American scholars remained completely oblivious of these clues for eleven years.

For it was only in 1855 that John T. Thornton of Boston, when browsing in Burnham's Antique Bookstore on Cornhill, noted the reference in Wilberforce. He at once brought the book to the Rev. John S. Barry, who was writing a History of Massachusetts, with the important passage marked. There ensued an unseemly and absurd squabble between these two learned gentle-

[3] Albert Matthews in Colonial Society of Massachusetts *Publications* XVII 331.

men as to who had "discovered" Bradford. The upshot, however, was that Barry called the matter to the attention of Charles Deane, who at that time was editing the publications of the Massachusetts Historical Society. Deane promptly wrote to Joseph Hunter, begging him to look up the manuscript and get it copied. The Bishop amiably lent the manuscript to Hunter, who found "a gentleman who would undertake to . . . execute it in a scholar-like and business-like manner." This gentleman, whose name has not been preserved, made a remarkably accurate transcript, for which he received the modest compensation of £40. This longhand copy has been the basis of every text of Bradford published before 1912.[4] Charles Deane, adding numerous scholarly and interesting footnotes, sent the longhand copy to the printer and it was published as Volume III of the Fourth Series of the *Collections* of the Massachusetts Historical Society in 1856. The same year, Little, Brown & Company published an edition for the public from the same plates. This full publication of the Bradford History was a literary sensation.

The question at once arose, how did the manuscript get into the Bishop of London's library in Fulham Palace? Neither the Bishop nor anyone else knew. The manuscript had never been catalogued. Wilberforce had been the first Bishop to notice its existence. On Prince's New England Library bookplate someone had written: "It now belongs to the Bishop of London's Library," but nobody could, or at least admitted he could, recognize the handwriting. One theory is that Governor Hutchinson suffered pangs of conscience after purloining the manuscript from the Old South and, not wishing to return it to ungrateful rebels, presented it to the then Bishop of London. But there is no evidence of this in Hutchinson's writings or in the Fulham archives; a meticulously honest gentleman, Hutchinson left Boston several years after he had used the manuscript for his *History of Massachusetts Bay* and there is every reason to believe that he would have returned the manuscript to the New England Library before his departure.

[4] As proof of this, a sentence of Bradford's in his memoir of Elder Brewster (page 255 of the manuscript), which the English copyist carelessly omitted, was omitted in every printed edition before Worthington C. Ford's.

Much more probable it is that some British officer or soldier, straying into the steeple room of the Old South before or after his morning ride in 1775–6, decided to exercise the military prerogative once called by its proper name of looting; but now—at least when performed by Americans—known by the euphemism of souvenir-collecting. There is also reason to believe that the Bradford History was not the only bit of literary loot that this unknown thief carried off. A portion of one of the Governor's Letter-Books, which had also been deposited in the New England Library, was recovered shortly after 1783 at Halifax, whither the British garrison went after evacuating Boston. The Letter-Book was promptly returned to Massachusetts. Two other manuscript books from the Prince Library, the one a dictionary of authors and the other a commonplace book, both compiled by Thomas Prince's brother Nathan, also turned up at the Fulham Palace library; and there could be no mistake about their source, as each bore the New England Library book label.[5]

It seems very probable, therefore, that these four manuscript books were taken as loot during the war; that the Letter-Book was mislaid or left behind at Halifax, and that the other three, possibly sold for a song to an ignorant bookseller in London, were picked up by a man of some intelligence—perhaps a Bishop of London—and deposited in the Fulham Palace library.

There was no doubt whatsoever that the manuscript entitled "Of Plymouth Plantation" was the long-missing Bradford History. Under the circumstances, it would seem that the return of this volume to New England would have been a normal and proper act of restitution. As precedent, the Emperor Napoleon's will, made at St. Helena and therefore deposited in the Archbishop of Canterbury's probate records, had already been re-

[5] Letter of Charles Deane in Massachusetts Historical Society *Proceedings 1866–7*, pp. 345–6; Justin Winsor "The Bradford Manuscript," ibid., 2nd ser. XI (1897) 299–304; Introduction to Commonwealth ed. Bradford; E. G. Sandford *Memoirs of Archbishop Temple by Seven Friends* II (1906) 112; Louise Creighton *Life and Letters of Mandell Creighton* II (1904) 232. One of the Nathan Prince mss., the dictionary of authors, was given by the Bishop of London to the Harvard College Library in 1907; the other, so the present Bishop's secretary informs me, has disappeared from the Fulham Library. A second commonplace book by Nathan Prince, now in the Prince Library, had apparently never been removed from it.

turned to France by the British government. An Englishman, the Rev. John Waddington, proposed as early as 1855 that the Bradford manuscript be returned to New England. But to accomplish that required many petitions, much diplomacy, and the exercise of legal ingenuity, spread over a period of some forty years.

Robert C. Winthrop, president of the Massachusetts Historical Society, made a formal proposal to that end in 1860, with the added suggestion that the Prince of Wales as a good-will gesture might bring the manuscript with him on his visit to America that year. But the future Edward VII was not afforded the opportunity to peruse the original History of the Pilgrims on his voyage. In 1867 a parallel act of courtesy was performed by the Philadelphia Library in returning to the Public Records Office in London some official manuscripts of the reign of James I which had been presented to them by Charles Hamilton Cox, and later recognized as having been abstracted from government archives by an English historian. Justin Winsor, at that time head of the Boston Public Library and as such responsible for the Prince collection, deemed this a good occasion to strike again for the Bradford History, especially since John Lothrop Motley was about to sail for England as the American Ambassador. Motley saw the then Bishop of London, who said he was perfectly willing to return the manuscript but that an Act of Parliament would be necessary; it was thought that such an act could more easily be obtained at some other time since Mr. Disraeli was then in power, and neither he nor his Tory followers liked Americans; there would be a far better chance with Mr. Gladstone and the Liberals. Although the "G.O.M." succeeded "Dizzy" in 1869, Motley had accomplished nothing when he was unceremoniously recalled by President Grant in November 1870.

Every one of these attempts ran afoul of ecclesiastical red tape and official stuffiness. It was said that the Bishop of London had no right to return the manuscript, that either the Queen's permission or an Act of Parliament would be required. There seemed to be a deep-rooted reluctance to do anything about it.

In 1881 Benjamin Scott, Chamberlain of the City of London, proposed that Bradford's History be returned as palpable evidence of English sympathy on the occasion of the assassination of President Garfield. He pointed out the precedent of Napoleon's will, but nothing came of his suggestion.

In the final and successful effort it was the Honorable George Frisbie Hoar, United States Senator from Massachusetts, who took the initiative. In the introduction to the Commonwealth edition, he relates how he reached the conviction, after reading the printed edition through, that the manuscript was "the most precious on earth," with the possible exception of those of the Four Gospels. He describes his voyage to England in 1896, his difficulty in even getting a look at the manuscript, his interview at Fulham with the then Bishop of London, Frederick Temple; the Bishop's astonishment that Americans "cared anything about it," the Bishop's willingness to return it, yet caution that he must consult the Archbishop of Canterbury and the Queen. For, he said, "We should not do such a thing behind her Majesty's back." One wishes that the late Max Beerbohm might have done a cartoon of the Lord Bishop of London slipping the manuscript to the United States Senator behind Queen Victoria's back. But progress had been made; the Bishop promised to support Senator Hoar if he made a formal application.

Upon returning home, Senator Hoar persuaded the American Antiquarian Society, the Pilgrim Society of Plymouth, and the New England Society of New York, to make a joint application, dated 21 December 1896. The letter was signed, among others, by Edward Everett Hale, Samuel A. Green, Charles Francis Adams, Bishop William Lawrence, President Charles W. Eliot of Harvard, Arthur Lord, Joseph H. Choate, J. Pierpont Morgan and Governor Roger Wolcott. Senator Hoar then persuaded the Secretary of State, Richard Olney, to instruct the American Ambassador to the Court of St. James's, Thomas F. Bayard, to put his shoulder to the wheel; and he did.

Circumstances favored this effort. Anglo-American relations, after the nasty flare-up of the Venezuela episode, had resumed their normal course of friendly family bickering. Throughout that unpleasantness, Mr. Bayard had kept his head, and won golden opinions in England. Bishop Temple had been elevated to the archiepiscopal see of Canterbury, and Mandell Creighton, an historian who had many friends in America (and an LL.D. from Harvard), was now Bishop of London.

Bishop Creighton, on being approached by Mr. Bayard, appealed to the Prime Minister for an opinion. Lord Salisbury waived responsibility and told the Bishop that he must decide. Apparently one obstacle all along had been the conviction of certain ecclesiastical officials in the Diocese of London that the list of *Mayflower* passengers in an appendix to the History constituted a valuable section of vital records by virtue of which *Mayflower* descendants might put in a claim to property in England and embarrass the Bishop if he lost the volume. In rebuttal it was pointed out that Bradford's list was no official record, that it had nothing to do with the Diocese, that the names had all been printed in the edition of 1856 and in John H. Doyle's facsimile of the manuscript in 1896. Even so the ecclesiastical lawyers could only be placated by the fiction that the manuscript was a mere ship's log with a list of passengers attached. For at this point it occurred to some genius at legal prevarication that if the History were called by the idiotic title "The Log of the Mayflower," the ecclesiastical lawyers might consent to let it go.

The Chancellor of the Diocese, on Bishop Creighton's order, now summoned a Consistory Court which met in St. Paul's Cathedral on 25 March 1897, under the presidency of the Right Worshipful Thomas Hutchinson Tristram LL.D., Q.C. That fixed it. The decree of this court, copied in a neat clerical hand on the first two leaves of the manuscript, describes it as "A certain book known as and entitled 'The Log of the Mayflower,' containing an account as narrated by Captain William Bradford, who was one of the Company of Englishmen who left England in April 1620 in the ship known as 'The Mayflower.' And, whereas, the American Ambassador has prayed that the Honourable Court would deliver to him said manuscript book" on undertaking to use every means in his power "for the safe transmission of the said book to the United States of America, and to secure deposit and custody in the Pilgrim Hall at New Plymouth, or in such other place as may be selected by the President and Senate of the said United States," the Court decrees:

1. That the manuscript shall be delivered to Ambassador Bayard on his undertaking that he will "with all due care and diligence" deliver it to the Governor of Massachusetts "at his official office in the State House in the City of Boston";

2. That the book will "with all convenient speed" be finally deposited either in the Massachusetts Archives or in the Library of the Historical Society as the Governor shall determine;

3. That the Governors of Massachusetts for all time will be officially responsible for the safe custody of it, no matter where deposited, and for the performance of the following conditions: (a) All persons shall have access to it under reasonable regulations; (b) All persons desirous of searching it to establish a pedigree be permitted to search the same under suitable safeguards; (c) Certified copies of any entries on marriages, births or deaths be furnished; (d) Upon delivery of it to the Governor of Massachusetts, the Governor shall transmit to the Registrar of the Court a certificate of the delivery of the same by Mr. Bayard and that he accept the same, subject to the conditions, and terms here named. The Bishop of London confirmed this decree of his Consistorial Court on 12 April 1897.

The confusion of language in this decree is extraordinary. The Ambassador has requested that the manuscript be deposited in Pilgrim Hall at "New Plymouth" (a name obsolete since 1691), or at a place selected by the President and Senate of the United States. But it is delivered to him to hand over to the Governor of Massachusetts, for deposit in one of two places other than Pilgrim Hall, Plymouth, bypassing the President and Senate of the United States. Claims of the New England Library, from which it was stolen, and of the Bradford family, to which Prince stated it still belonged while in his custody, were not even considered. Finally, the manuscript is called "The Log of the Mayflower," of which Governor Bradford apparently is assumed to have been the skipper. An amazing misnomer, considering that there is no log of the *Mayflower* contained in the manuscript; that the name of that famous vessel is never even mentioned in it; that the name of her master, Christopher Jones, is clearly stated; and that the account of her voyage occupies only a part of one chapter out of thirty-six!

Massachusetts was glad enough to receive the manuscript, by whatever name; but this imbecile title, "The Log of the Mayflower," has never been shaken off. Newspapers of the time blossomed out with headlines, "MAYFLOWER'S LOG RETURNED"; and to this day many visitors to the State House ask to see the "Log of the Mayflower," and school children are apt to be disappointed because no log of wood from the structure of the ship is in evidence.

Ambassador Bayard, a Democrat, knew after the election of William McKinley to the Presidency that his term was up. Accordingly he sent in his resignation and returned to the United States in the spring of 1897, carrying the precious manuscript with him. On the morning of 26 May 1897, a Joint Convention of both houses of the Great and General Court was held in the Representatives' Chamber of the State House in Boston. His Excellency Governor Roger Wolcott, His Honor Lieutenant Governor Winthrop Murray Crane, the Honorable Council of the Commonwealth, the Honorable Thomas F. Bayard, late Ambassador of the United States at the Court of St. James's, the Honorable George F. Hoar, Senator from Massachusetts in the Congress of the United States, and invited guests, entered the Chamber. The decree of the Consistorial Court was read. The Honorable George P. Lawrence, President of the Senate, introduced Senator Hoar, who made a lengthy oration describing the manuscript and his efforts to procure its return. He made an eloquent tribute to Queen Victoria, declared that there was nothing like the Bradford History "in human annals since the Story of Bethlehem," and concluded with a promise that "Massachusetts will preserve it until the time shall come that her children are unworthy of it; and that time shall come,—never!" Ambassador Bayard presented the book to Governor Wolcott, who, in the graceful manner of which he was a master, alluded to the achievements of the Pilgrim Fathers, and pledged the faith of the Commonwealth that the History *of Plymouth Plantation* would forever be guarded in accordance with the terms of the decree. He ventured the prophecy that "for countless years to come . . . these mute pages shall eloquently speak of high resolve, great suffering and heroic endurance made possible by an absolute faith in the overruling providence of Almighty God."

That evening the American Antiquarian Society, which had initiated the successful movement for the restitution, gave a banquet at the Parker House, Boston, to celebrate the return. Thirty-four members of the Society (who paid ten dollars each) and ten invited guests, including the Governor, the Lieutenant Governor, Ambassador Bayard, the British Consul General (Sir Dominic Colnaghi), Bishop Lawrence, the Rev. George A. Gordon of the Old South Church, and representatives of the Bradford and Winslow families, were present. The menu seems worth preserving since it is almost as far removed from the austerity of our day as from that of the Pilgrims:

THE AMERICAN ANTIQUARIAN SOCIETY
On the Presentation of the Bradford Manuscript
to the Commonwealth of Massachusetts
May 26, 1897

MENU

LITTLE NECK CLAMS AND OYSTERS

SOUP

Clear Green Turtle   Cream of Lobster

FISH

Boiled Salmon, Hollandaise Sauce
Fried Soft Shell Crabs, Tartare Sauce

REMOVES

Roast Spring Lamb, Mint Sauce
Fillet of Beef, Sauce Bernaise
Boiled Philadelphia Capon

ENTREES

Sweetbreads Larded, Sauté Fresh Mushrooms
Patties of Lobster, Newburg
Fried Bananas Glacé, Benedictine

RELEVE

Frozen Tom and Jerry

GAME

English Snipe   Plover

SWEETS

Frozen Pudding   Sultana Roll
Strawberry Shortcake   Maraschino Jelly

DESSERT

Strawberries   Ice Cream   Sherbert
Pineapples   Olives   Cake
Coffee

PARKER HOUSE, BOSTON

Governor Wolcott decided to deposit the Manuscript History in the State Library in the State House, Boston; and there in a specially constructed bronze and glass case, it is carefully preserved to this day. It is still in superb condition, every word and almost every letter of Governor Bradford's script as easily discernible as when he wrote it over three centuries ago.

3. *Editions of the History*

1. The Deane edition of 1856, *editio princeps. History of Plymouth Plantation. By William Bradford, the Second Governor of the Colony. Now First Printed from the Original Manuscript for the Massachusetts Historical Society*. Boston, Little Brown and Company, 1856. 476 pages; preface, xix pp., signed by Charles Deane, who provided many learned and interesting notes.

   Also printed from the same plates as Massachusetts Historical Society *Collections*, 4th Series, Volume III, 1856.

2. Facsimile Edition of 1896. *History of the Plimoth Plantation, Containing an Account of the Voyage of the 'Mayflower,' written by William Bradford, One of the Founders and Second Governor of the Colony. Now reproduced in facsimile*

from the original Manuscript with an Introduction by John A. Doyle, Fellow of All Souls College, Oxford. London: Ward and Downey Ltd.; Boston: Houghton Mifflin & Co., 1896. 17 pp. printed Introduction followed by 535 pp. facsimile. Folio.

This facsimile was made by a photographic process, with zinc plates. It is exact and reliable, except that it does not show the different colors of ink used, occasionally blurs some of the finer writing, or shaves off the edge of a page.

3. Commonwealth Edition, 1897 and later printings. *Bradford's History "Of Plimoth Plantation."* From the Original Manuscript. With a Report of the Proceedings Incident to the Return of the Manuscript to Massachusetts. Printed Under the Direction of the Secretary of the Commonwealth, by Order of the General Court. Boston: Wright & Potter. First published in 1897 and still (1951) in print, the latest imprint being 1928. lxxxvii + 555 pp.

The editor of this edition was William M. Olin, Secretary of the Commonwealth. He followed the first edition very closely, making some corrections from Doyle's facsimile, but reproducing most of the mistakes made in the longhand copy of 1855. All manuscript abbreviations are printed as written; spelling and italicization inconsistent. The notes are few and the index is inadequate.

4. Original Narratives Edition, 1908. *Bradford's History of Plymouth Plantation, 1606–1646. Edited by William T. Davis, Formerly President of the Pilgrim Society. With a Map and Three Facsimiles.* New York: Charles Scribner's Sons, 1908. xv + 437 pp.

This edition appeared as one of the *Original Narratives of Early American History*, under the general editorship of Dr. J. Franklin Jameson. Many common manuscript abbreviations are spelled out, but others like *bp̃s* for *bishops* (p. 61) and *m*[r] for *master* (p. 109) are not, and the Governor's spelling is not changed. This text is a partially expanded reprint of the 1856 edition, reproducing several of the original copyist's errors, and deleting both text and letters on the crime wave of 1642.

Interesting notes on localities and personalities, and a good biographical introduction on Bradford.

5. Massachusetts Historical Society Edition of 1912. *History of Plymouth Plantation 1620–1647. By William Bradford.* The Massachusetts Historical Society, 1912. Volume I, xvi + 452 pp.; Volume II, xiii + 462 pp.

 This, the best edition of Bradford, was edited by Worthington C. Ford and is a monument to the work of that indefatigable historiographer. It is amply illustrated by photographs of contemporary documents, maps, title pages and other illustrations, coins, medals, signatures and ship pictures. Very full and scholarly notes. Manuscript abbreviations are expanded, but spelling, capitalization and punctuation are unchanged.

These are the only editions of the *History* with any pretence to fullness. Extracts in anthologies or printed in pamphlet form are too numerous to mention. An attempt by one Harold Paget in 1920 to get out an expurgated edition "Rendered into Modern English" was a lamentable failure, since this editor, in endeavoring to bring the Governor's language as well as his spelling up to date, succeeded in spoiling the charm of the language, much as the notorious Bowdler did with Shakespere.

The Seal of Plymouth Colony, reproduced on the cover and on the two-page map of New Plymouth, was sent over to the Colony by the London Adventurers as early as 1624; but it may not have been used before the issuance of the Warwick Patent in January 1630. It remained in use as long as the Colony maintained its independence and was used on official documents and, in outline, on the second edition of the Colony Laws published in 1685.[6] Attempts by several antiquarians to read significance into the meaning of the four naked kneeling figures and the doubtful object (bouquet, bunch of tobacco leaves, plumed heart?) that they are holding have been unconvincing. If the Pilgrims had been consulted, they would certainly not have used kneeling figures; and if they had wished to represent one

[6] Percival Hall Lombard "The Seal of the Plymouth Colony," *Mayflower Descendant* XXIX (January 1931) 1–9.

of themselves presenting something, it would have been a codfish or beaver. In my opinion, the Seal had been prepared by a die-cutter in London for an individual or corporation who did not pay up, and was then bought cheap by the Adventurers and fitted with a new date and inscription.

Of Plymouth Plantation

THE FIRST BOOK

OF
Plymouth
PLANTATION

And first of the occasion and inducements thereunto; the which, that I may truly unfold, I must begin at the very root and rise of the same. The which I shall endeavour to manifest in a plain style, with singular regard unto the simple truth in all things; at least as near as my slender judgment can attain the same.

CHAPTER I

[*The Separatist Interpretation of the Reformation in England*, 1550–1607]

It is well known unto the godly and judicious, how ever since the first breaking out of the light of the gospel in our honourable nation of England, (which was the first of nations whom the Lord adorned therewith after the gross darkness of popery which had covered and overspread the Christian world), what wars and oppositions ever since, Satan hath raised, maintained and continued against the Saints,[1] from time to time, in one sort or other. Sometimes by bloody death and cruel torments; other whiles imprisonments, banishments and other hard usages; as being loath his kingdom should go down, the truth prevail and the churches of God revert to their ancient purity and recover their primitive order, liberty and beauty.

But when he could not prevail by these means against the main truths of the gospel, but that they began to take rooting in many places, being watered with the blood of the martyrs and

[1] Bradford uses the word *Saint* in the Biblical sense, as one of God's chosen people, or a church member, not one of those canonized by the Roman Catholic Church.

blessed from Heaven with a gracious increase; he then began to take him to his ancient stratagems, used of old against the first Christians. That when by the bloody and barbarous persecutions of the heathen emperors he could not stop and subvert the course of the gospel, but that it speedily overspread, with a wonderful celerity, the then best known parts of the world; he then began to sow errours, heresies and wonderful dissensions amongst the professors [2] themselves, working upon their pride and ambition, with other corrupt passions incident to all mortal men, yea to the saints themselves in some measure, by which woeful effects followed. As not only bitter contentions and heartburnings, schisms, with other horrible confusions; but Satan took occasion and advantage thereby to foist in a number of vile ceremonies, with many unprofitable canons and decrees, which have since been as snares to many poor and peaceable souls even to this day.

So as in the ancient times, the persecutions |2| by the heathen and their emperors was not greater than of the Christians one against other:—the Arians and other their complices against the orthodox and true Christians. As witnesseth Socrates in his second book.[3] His words are these:

> The violence truly (saith he) was no less than that of old practiced towards the Christians when they were compelled and drawn to sacrifice to idols; for many endured sundry kinds of torment, often rackings and dismembering of their joints, confiscating of their goods; some bereaved of their native soil, others departed this life under the hands of the tormentor, and some died in banishment and never saw their country again, etc.

The like method Satan hath seemed to hold in these later times, since the truth began to spring and spread after the great defection made by Antichrist, that man of sin.[4]

[2] *Professor,* as used by Bradford and by Puritans generally, had no educational connotation; it merely meant one who professed Christianity.

[3] Socrates Scholasticus, Greek historian of the 5th century A.D. His Ecclesiastical History translated by Meredith Hanmer was printed in London in 1577. Bradford's quotation is from lib. ii chap. 22.

[4] 2 Thessalonians ii.3.

For to let pass the infinite examples in sundry nations and several places of the world, and instance in our own, when as that old serpent could not prevail by those fiery flames and other his cruel tragedies, which he by his instruments put in ure [5] everywhere in the days of Queen Mary and before, he then began another kind of war and went more closely to work; not only to oppugn but even to ruinate and destroy the kingdom of Christ by more secret and subtle means, by kindling the flames of contention and sowing the seeds of discord and bitter enmity amongst the professors and, seeming reformed, themselves. For when he could not prevail by the former means against the principal doctrines of faith, he bent his force against the holy discipline and outward regiment of the kingdom of Christ, by which those holy doctrines should be conserved, and true piety maintained amongst the saints and people of God.

Mr. Fox [6] recordeth how that besides those worthy martyrs and confessors which were burned in Queen Mary's days and otherwise tormented, "Many (both students and others) fled out of the land to the number of 800, and became several congregations, at Wesel, Frankfort, Basel, Emden, Markpurge, Strasburg and Geneva, etc." Amongst whom (but especially those at Frankfort) began that bitter war of contention and persecution about the ceremonies and service book, and other popish and antichristian stuff, the plague of England to this day, which are like the high places in Israel which the prophets cried out against, and were their ruin. |3| Which the better part sought, according to the purity of the gospel, to root out and utterly to abandon. And the other part (under veiled pretences) for their own ends and advancements, sought as stiffly to continue, maintain and defend. As appeareth by the discourse thereof published in print, anno 1575; a book that deserves better to be known and considered.[7]

[5] I.e., into practice.

[6] Acts and Mon[uments]: pag. 1587 edition 2 (Bradford). His reference is to John Fox *Acts and Monuments* (familiarly known as the *Book of Martyrs*) p. 1587 of 2nd edition.

[7] William Whittingham *Brieff Discours of the Troubles begonne at Franckford,* printed at Zurich or Geneva in 1575. The row was between the Marian exiles who wished to abolish "service books" altogether (which Bradford and the entire left wing of English Protestantism believed should have been done),

The one side laboured to have the right worship of God and discipline of Christ established in the church, according to the simplicity of the gospel, without the mixture of men's inventions; and to have and to be ruled by the laws of God's Word, dispensed in those offices, and by those officers of Pastors, Teachers and Elders, etc. according to the Scriptures. The other party, though under many colours and pretences, endeavoured to have the episcopal dignity (after the popish manner) with their large power and jurisdiction still retained; with all those courts, canons and ceremonies, together with all such livings, revenues and subordinate officers, with other such means as formerly upheld their antichristian greatness and enabled them with lordly and tyrannous power to persecute the poor servants of God. This contention was so great, as neither the honour of God, the common persecution, nor the mediation of Mr. Calvin and other worthies of the Lord in those places, could prevail with those thus episcopally minded; but they proceeded by all means to disturb the peace of this poor persecuted church, even so far as to charge (very unjustly and ungodlily yet prelatelike) some of their chief opposers with rebellion and high treason against the Emperor, and other such crimes.

And this contention died not with Queen Mary, nor was left beyond the seas. But at her death these people returning into England under gracious Queen Elizabeth, many of them being preferred to bishoprics and other promotions according to their aims and desires, that inveterate hatred against the holy discipline of Christ in His church [8] hath continued to this day. Insomuch that for fear |4| it should prevail, all plots and devices have been used to keep it out, incensing the Queen and State against it as dangerous for the commonwealth; and that it was most needful that the fundamental points of religion should be preached in those ignorant and superstitious times. And to win the weak and

---

and those who adopted the typically English compromise of a Book of Common Prayer. The Marian exiles, or some of them, wished to reorganize the church on congregational principles which they believed alone to be sanctioned by the New Testament.

[8] Bradford means the Congregational discipline. His account of church history during Elizabeth's reign is of course a partisan one, unfair to the acts and the motives of everyone not in the left wing of Protestantism.

ignorant they might retain divers harmless ceremonies; and though it were to be wished that divers things were reformed, yet this was not a season for it. And many the like, to stop the mouths of the more godly, to bring them on to yield to one ceremony after another, and one corruption after another; by these wiles beguiling some and corrupting others till at length they began to persecute all the zealous professors in the land (though they knew little what this discipline meant) both by word and deed, if they would not submit to their ceremonies and become slaves to them and their popish trash, which have no ground in the Word of God, but are relics of that man of sin. And the more the light of the gospel grew, the more they urged their subscriptions to these corruptions. So as (notwithstanding all their former pretences and fair colours) they whose eyes God had not justly blinded might easily see whereto these things tended. And to cast contempt the more upon the sincere servants of God, they opprobriously and most injuriously gave unto and imposed upon them that name of Puritans, which is said the Novatians out of pride did assume and take unto themselves.[9] And lamentable it is to see the effects which have followed. Religion hath been disgraced, the godly grieved, afflicted, persecuted, and many exiled; sundry have lost their lives in prisons and other ways. On the other hand, sin hath been countenanced; ignorance, profaneness and atheism increased, and the papists encouraged to hope again for a day.[1]

This made that holy man Mr. Perkins cry out in [2] his exhortation to repentance, upon Zephaniah ii:

Religion (saith he) hath been amongst us this thirty-five years; but the more it is published, the more it is contemned and reproached

[9] Eusebius lib. vi chap. 42 (Bradford). The Novatians were an obscure sect of the 3rd century. The term *Puritan*, like *Quaker*, was originally one of reproach, not accepted until nearly the close of the 17th century by the people to whom it was applied. The Puritans called themselves "God's people."

[1] On the blank page [4 v.] opposite, Bradford in 1646 added what he called *A late observation, as it were by the way, to be noted*, which will be found in Appendix I.

[2] William ("Painful") Perkins, a graduate of Emmanuel College, Cambridge, whose works were much esteemed by all branches of Puritans. The quotation is from his *Exposition of Christ's Sermon Upon the Mount* (1618) p. 421.

of many, etc. Thus not profaneness nor wickedness but religion itself is a byword, a mockingstock, and a matter of reproach; so that in England at this day the man or woman that begins to profess religion and to serve God, must resolve with himself to sustain |5| mocks and injuries even as though he lived amongst the enemies of religion.

And this, common experience hath confirmed and made too apparent. But that I may come more near my intendment.

When as by the travail and diligence of some godly and zealous preachers, and God's blessing on their labours, as in other places of the land, so in the North parts, many became enlightened by the Word of God and had their ignorance and sins discovered unto them, and began by His grace to reform their lives and make conscience of their ways; the work of God was no sooner manifest in them but presently they were both scoffed and scorned by the profane multitude; and the ministers urged with the yoke of subscription, or else must be silenced. And the poor people were so vexed with apparitors and pursuivants [3] and the commissary courts, as truly their affliction was not small. Which, notwithstanding, they bore sundry years with much patience, till they were occasioned by the continuance and increase of these troubles, and other means which the Lord raised up in those days, to see further into things by the light of the Word of God. How not only these base and beggarly ceremonies were unlawful, but also that the lordly and tyrannous power of the prelates ought not to be submitted unto; which thus, contrary to the freedom of the gospel, would load and burden men's consciences and by their compulsive power make a profane mixture of persons and things in the worship of God. And that their offices and callings, courts and canons, etc. were unlawful and antichristian; being such as have no warrant in the Word of God, but the same that were used in popery and still retained. Of which a famous author thus writeth in his Dutch commentaries,[4] at the coming of King James into England:

[3] Officers of the Church of England whose duty was to enforce conformity.

[4] Emanuel van Meteren *General History of the Netherlands* (London 1608) xxv.119. Bradford's reference, to which he adds this remark: "The reformed churches shapen much near[er] the primitive pattern than England,

The new king (saith he) found there established the reformed religion according to the reformed religion of King Edward VI, retaining or keeping still the spiritual state of the bishops, etc. after the old manner, much varying and differing from the reformed churches in Scotland, France and the Netherlands, Emden, Geneva, etc., whose reformation is cut, or shapen much nearer the first Christian churches, as it was used in the Apostles' times.

|6| So many, therefore, of these professors as saw the evil of these things in these parts, and whose hearts the Lord had touched with heavenly zeal for His truth, they shook off this yoke of antichristian bondage, and as the Lord's free people joined themselves (by a covenant of the Lord) into a church estate, in the fellowship of the gospel, to walk in all His ways made known, or to be made known unto them, according to their best endeavours, whatsoever it should cost them, the Lord assisting them.[5] And that it cost them something this ensuing history will declare.

These people became two distinct bodies or churches, and in regard of distance of place did congregate severally; for they were of sundry towns and villages, some in Nottinghamshire, some of Lincolnshire, and some of Yorkshire where they border nearest together. In one of these churches (besides others of note) was Mr. John Smith,[6] a man of able gifts and a good preacher, who afterwards was chosen their pastor. But these afterwards falling into some errours in the Low Countries, there (for the most part) buried themselves and their names.

But in this other church (which must be the subject of our discourse) besides other worthy men, was Mr. Richard Clyfton,

---

for they cashiered the Bishops with all their courts, canons, and ceremonies, at the first; and left them amongst the popish tr[ash] to which they per[tained]." Bradford passes over the fact that James I at the Hampton Court Conference in 1604 gave full opportunity of self-expression to the Puritans, who so exasperated him with their demands that he declared he would make them conform to the Church of England, "or . . . harry them out of the land, or else do worse."

[5] A paraphrase of the words of the covenant that people made when they formed a Separatist (later called Congregational) church.

[6] An alumnus of Christ's College, Cambridge, who seceded from the Church of England in 1605 and preached to the Separatist church at Gainsborough. This congregation emigrated in 1608 to Amsterdam, where Smith embraced a number of strange opinions and his church broke up.

a grave and reverend preacher, who by his pains and diligence had done much good, and under God had been a means of the conversion of many. And also that famous and worthy man Mr. John Robinson, who afterwards was their pastor for many years, till the Lord took him away by death. Also Mr. William Brewster a reverend man, who afterwards was chosen an elder of the church and lived with them till old age.[7]

But after these things they could not long continue in any peaceable condition, but were hunted and persecuted on every side, so as their former afflictions were but as flea-bitings in comparison of these which now came upon them. For some were taken and clapped up in prison, others had their houses beset and watched night and day, and hardly escaped their hands; and the most were fain to flee and leave their houses and habitations, and the means of their livelihood.

Yet these and many other sharper things which afterward befell them, were no other than they looked for, and therefore were the better prepared to bear them by the assistance of God's grace and Spirit.

Yet seeing themselves thus molested, |7| and that there was no hope of their continuance there, by a joint consent they resolved to go into the Low Countries, where they heard was freedom of religion for all men; as also how sundry from London and other parts of the land had been exiled and persecuted for the same cause, and were gone thither, and lived at Amsterdam and in other places of the land. So after they had continued together about a year, and kept their meetings every Sabbath in one place or other, exercising the worship of God amongst themselves, notwithstanding all the diligence and malice of their adversaries, they seeing they could no longer continue in that condition, they resolved to get over into Holland as they could. Which was in the year 1607 and 1608; of which more at large in the next chapter.

[7] Richard Clyfton and John Robinson also were Cambridge alumni in holy orders who separated. Clyfton and William Brewster organized the Separatist congregation at Scrooby, Nottinghamshire, which Bradford joined as a young man. The sentence on Brewster is written in a different ink from the rest of the chapter, having been inserted after the Elder's death in 1643.

CHAPTER II

Of their Departure into Holland and their Troubles thereabout, with some of the many Difficulties they found and met withal. Anno 1608

Being thus constrained to leave their native soil and country, their lands and livings, and all their friends and familiar acquaintance, it was much; and thought marvelous by many. But to go into a country they knew not but by hearsay, where they must learn a new language and get their livings they knew not how, it being a dear place and subject to the miseries of war, it was by many thought an adventure almost desperate; a case intolerable and a misery worse than death. Especially seeing they were not acquainted with trades nor traffic (by which that country doth subsist) but had only been used to a plain country life and the innocent trade of husbandry. But these things did not dismay them, though they did sometimes trouble them; for their desires were set on the ways of God and to enjoy His ordinances; but they rested on His providence, and knew Whom they had believed. Yet |8| this was not all, for though they could not stay, yet were they not suffered to go; but the ports and havens were shut against them, so as they were fain to seek secret means of conveyance, and to bribe and fee the mariners, and give extraordinary rates for their passages.[1] And yet were they often times betrayed, many of them; and both they and their goods intercepted and surprised, and thereby put to great trouble and charge, of which I will give an instance or two and omit the rest.

There was a large company of them purposed to get passage at Boston in Lincolnshire, and for that end had hired a ship wholly to themselves and made agreement with the master to be ready at a certain day, and take them and their goods in at a convenient place, where they accordingly would all attend in readiness. So after long waiting and large expenses, though he kept not day

[1] In England, as in other European nations at the time, a license was required to go abroad, and such licenses were commonly refused to Roman Catholics and dissenters. This first attempt of the Scrooby congregation to flee was in the fall of 1607.

with them, yet he came at length and took them in, in the night. But when he had them and their goods aboard, he betrayed them, having beforehand complotted with the searchers and other officers so to do; who took them, and put them into open boats, and there rifled and ransacked them, searching to their shirts for money, yea even the women further than became modesty; and then carried them back into the town and made them a spectacle and wonder to the multitude which came flocking on all sides to behold them. Being thus first, by these catchpoll officers rifled and stripped of their money, books and much other goods, they were presented to the magistrates, and messengers sent to inform the Lords of the Council of them; and so they were committed to ward. Indeed the magistrates used them courteously and showed them what favour they could; but could not deliver them till order came from the Council table. But the issue was that after a month's imprisonment the greatest part were dismissed and sent to the places from whence they came; but seven of the principal were still kept in prison and bound over to the assizes.

The next spring [2] after, there was another attempt made by some of these and others to get over at another place. And it so fell out that they light of [3] a Dutchman at Hull, having a ship of his own belonging to Zealand. They made agreement with him, and |9| acquainted him with their condition, hoping to find more faithfulness in him than in the former of their own nation; he bade them not fear, for he would do well enough. He was by appointment to take them in between Grimsby and Hull, where was a large common a good way distant from any town. Now against the prefixed time, the women and children with the goods were sent to the place in a small bark which they had hired for that end; and the men were to meet them by land. But it so fell out that they were there a day before the ship came, and the sea being rough and the women very sick, prevailed with the seamen to put into a creek hard by where they lay on ground at low water. The next morning the ship came but they were fast and could not stir until about noon. In the meantime, the shipmaster, perceiving how the matter was, sent his boat to be getting the

[2] Of 1608.

[3] Happened upon.

men aboard whom he saw ready, walking about the shore. But after the first boatful was got aboard and she was ready to go for more, the master espied a great company, both horse and foot, with bills and guns and other weapons, for the country was raised to take them. The Dutchman, seeing that, swore his country's oath *sacremente*, and having the wind fair, weighed his anchor, hoised sails, and away.

But the poor men which were got aboard were in great distress for their wives and children which they saw thus to be taken, and were left destitute of their helps; and themselves also, not having a cloth to shift them with, more than they had on their backs, and some scarce a penny about them, all they had being aboard the bark. It drew tears from their eyes, and anything they had they would have given to have been ashore again; but all in vain, there was no remedy, they must thus sadly part. And afterward endured a fearful storm at sea, being fourteen days or more before they arrived at their port; in seven whereof they neither saw sun, moon nor stars, and were driven near the coast of Norway; the mariners themselves often despairing of life, and once with shrieks and cries gave over all, as if the ship had been foundered in the sea and they sinking without recovery. But when man's hope and help wholly failed, the Lord's power and mercy appeared in their recovery; for the ship rose again and gave the mariners courage again to manage her. And if modesty would suffer me, I might declare with what fervent |10| prayers they cried unto the Lord in this great distress (especially some of them) even without any great distraction. When the water ran into their mouths and ears and the mariners cried out, "We sink, we sink!" they cried (if not with miraculous, yet with a great height or degree of divine faith), "Yet Lord Thou canst save! Yet Lord Thou canst save!" with such other expressions as I will forbear. Upon which the ship did not only recover, but shortly after the violence of the storm began to abate, and the Lord filled their afflicted minds with such comforts as everyone cannot understand, and in the end brought them to their desired haven, where the people came flocking, admiring their deliverance; the storm having been so long and sore, in which much hurt had been done, as the master's friends related unto him in their congratulations.

But to return to the others where we left. The rest of the men that were in greatest danger made shift to escape away before the troop could surprise them, those only staying that best might be assistant unto the women. But pitiful it was to see the heavy case of these poor women in this distress; what weeping and crying on every side, some for their husbands that were carried away in the ship as is before related; others not knowing what should become of them and their little ones; others again melted in tears, seeing their poor little ones hanging about them, crying for fear and quaking with cold. Being thus apprehended, they were hurried from one place to another and from one justice to another, till in the end they knew not what to do with them; for to imprison so many women and innocent children for no other cause (many of them) but that they must go with their husbands, seemed to be unreasonable and all would cry out of them. And to send them home again was as difficult; for they alleged, as the truth was, they had no homes to go to, for they had either sold or otherwise disposed of their houses and livings. To be short, after they had been thus turmoiled a good while and conveyed from one constable to another, they were glad to be rid of them in the end upon any terms, for all were wearied and tired with them. Though in the meantime they (poor souls) endured misery enough; and thus in the end necessity forced a way for them.

But that I be not tedious in these things, I will omit the rest, though I might relate many other notable passages and troubles which they endured and underwent in these their wanderings and travels both at land and sea; but I haste |11| to other things. Yet I may not omit the fruit that came hereby, for by these so public troubles in so many eminent places their cause became famous and occasioned many to look into the same, and their godly carriage and Christian behaviour was such as left a deep impression in the minds of many. And though some few shrunk at these first conflicts and sharp beginnings (as it was no marvel) yet many more came on with fresh courage and greatly animated others. And in the end, notwithstanding all these storms of opposition, they all gat over at length, some at one time and some at another, and some in one place and some in another, and met together again according to their desires, with no small rejoicing.[4]

[4] About 125 members of the Scrooby congregation "gat over" to Amsterdam, including the two ministers Clyfton and Robinson, William Brewster and Bradford himself.

CHAPTER III

Of their Settling in Holland, and their Manner of Living, and Entertainment there

Being now come into the Low Countries, they saw many goodly and fortified cities, strongly walled and guarded with troops of armed men. Also, they heard a strange and uncouth language, and beheld the different manners and customs of the people, with their strange fashions and attires; all so far differing from that of their plain country villages (wherein they were bred and had so long lived) as it seemed they were come into a new world. But these were not the things they much looked on, or long took up their thoughts, for they had other work in hand and another kind of war to wage and maintain. For although they saw fair and beautiful cities, flowing with abundance of all sorts of wealth and riches, yet it was not long before they saw the grim and grisly face of poverty coming upon them like an armed man,[1] with whom they must buckle and encounter, and from whom they could not fly. But they were armed with faith and patience against him and all his encounters; and though they were sometimes foiled, yet by God's assistance they prevailed and got the victory.

Now when Mr. Robinson, Mr. Brewster and other principal members were come over (for they were of the last and stayed to help the weakest over before them) such things were |12| thought on as were necessary for their settling and best ordering of the church affairs.

And when they had lived at Amsterdam about a year, Mr. Robinson their pastor and some others of best discerning, seeing how Mr. John Smith and his company was already fallen into contention with the church that was there before them, and no means they could use would do any good to cure the same, and also that the flames of contention were like to break out in that ancient church itself (as afterwards lamentably came to pass); which things they prudently foreseeing thought it was best to remove before they were any way engaged with the same, though they well knew it would be much to the prejudice of their out-

[1] Proverbs xxiv.34.

ward estates, both at present and in likelihood in the future; as indeed it proved to be.

Their Removal to Leyden

For these and some other reasons they removed to Leyden,[2] a fair and beautiful city and of a sweet situation, but made more famous by the university wherewith it is adorned, in which of late had been so many learned men.[3] But wanting that traffic by sea which Amsterdam enjoys, it was not so beneficial for their outward means of living and estate. But being now here pitch[ed], they fell to such trades and employments as they best could, valuing peace and their spiritual comfort above any other riches whatsoever. And at length they came to raise a competent and comfortable living, but with hard and continual labour.[4]

Being thus settled (after many difficulties) they continued many years in a comfortable condition, enjoying much sweet and delightful society and spiritual comfort together in the ways of God, under the able ministry and prudent government of Mr. John Robinson and Mr. William Brewster who was an assistant unto him in the place of an Elder, unto which he was now called and chosen by the church.[5] So as they grew in knowledge and

[2] A formal application was made to the Burgomasters of Leyden by the Pilgrims, to settle in that city, and was granted 12 Feb. 1609. Text in 1912 ed. Bradford I 39–40.

[3] The University of Leyden, founded in 1575, had in the space of a single generation become one of the first in Christendom, with scholars such as Scaliger, Heinsius, Arminius, Vorstius, Golius and Cluvier on its several faculties.

[4] D. Plooij *The Pilgrim Fathers from a Dutch Point of View* (1932) is the principal authority on the Pilgrim Fathers in Leyden; but Henry Martyn Dexter *England and Holland of the Pilgrims* had already made extensive researches into their life there. He found that of 131 English in the city at that time, 86 of which belonged to the Pilgrim company, 57 occupations were represented, most of them having something to do with cloth making. Bradford himself is described in the local records as a fustian maker. Brewster and Winslow ran a printing press where Puritan tracts that could not get a license in England were published.

[5] Not only the Separatists, but all Puritans called the principal officers of their churches Elders. The two clerical ones, ordained by laying on of hands, were the Preaching Elder or Pastor and the Teaching Elder or Teacher; the other two, laymen both, were the Ruling Elders.

other gifts and graces of the Spirit of God, and lived together in peace and love and holiness and many came unto them from divers parts of England, so as they grew a great congregation. And if at any time any differences arose or offenses broke |13| out (as it cannot be but some time there will, even amongst the best of men) they were ever so met with and nipped in the head betimes, or otherwise so well composed as still love, peace, and communion was continued. Or else the church purged off those that were incurable and incorrigible when, after much patience used, no other means would serve, which seldom came to pass.

Yea, such was the mutual love and reciprocal respect that this worthy man had to his flock, and his flock to him, that it might be said of them as it once was of that famous Emperor Marcus Aurelius,[6] and the people of Rome, that it was hard to judge whether he delighted more in having such a people, or they in having such a pastor. His love was great towards them, and his care was always bent for their best good, both for soul and body. For besides his singular abilities in divine things (wherein he excelled) he was also very able to give directions in civil affairs and to foresee dangers and inconveniences, by which means he was very helpful to their outward estates and so was every way as a common father unto them. And none did more offend him than those that were close and cleaving to themselves and retired from the common good; as also such as would be stiff and rigid in matters of outward order and inveigh against the evils of others, and yet be remiss in themselves, and not so careful to express a virtuous conversation. They in like manner had ever a reverent regard unto him and had him in precious estimation, as his worth and wisdom did deserve. And though they esteemed him highly whilst he lived and laboured amongst them, yet much more after his death, when they came to feel the want of his help and saw (by woeful experience) what a treasure they had lost, to the grief of their hearts and wounding of their souls. Yea, such a loss as they saw could not be repaired; for it was as hard for them to

[6] Golden Book, etc. (Bradford). *The Golden Book of Marcus Aurelius, or, the Dial of Princes,* translated from the Spanish of Antonio de Guevara, was one of the most popular books of Bradford's time.

find such another leader and feeder in all respects as for the Taborites to find another Ziska.[7] And though they did not call themselves orphans (as the other did) after his death, yet they had cause as much to lament in another regard, their present condition, and after usage.

But to return; I know not but it may be spoken to the honour of God and without prejudice |14| to any, that such was the true piety, the humble zeal and fervent love of this people (whilst they thus lived together) towards God and His ways, and the singleheartedness and sincere affection one towards another, that they came as near the primitive pattern of the first churches as any other church of these later times have done, according to their rank and quality.[8]

But seeing it is not my purpose to treat of the several passages that befell this people whilst they thus lived in the Low Countries (which might worthily require a large treatise of itself) but to make way to show the beginning of this plantation, which is that I aim at; yet because some of their adversaries did, upon the rumor of their removal, cast out slanders against them, as if that state had been weary of them, and had rather driven them out (as the heathen historians did feign of Moses and the Israelites when they went out of Egypt) than that it was their own free choice and motion. I will therefore mention a particular or two to show the contrary, and the good acceptation they had in the place where they lived.

And first, though many of them were poor, yet there was none so poor but if they were known to be of that congregation the Dutch (either bakers or others) would trust them in any reasonable matter when they wanted money, because they had found by experience how careful they were to keep their word, and

[7] Tabor, a town in Czechoslovakia founded in 1420 by Hussites, who became known as Taborites. John Zizka was the greatest of the Taborite leaders. H. M. Dexter's researches show that the Pilgrim church numbered between 400 and 500 English in 1620; the Pilgrim Fathers who left for America were, therefore, a small minority.

[8] Bradford's picture of the Pilgrim church at Leyden and of their pastor is not overdrawn. Unlike the other English churches in exile in the Netherlands, the congregation was free of factionalism; and Robinson's own writings show him to have been a clergyman of relatively broad views, catholic spirit and human sympathy.

saw them so painful and diligent in their callings. Yea, they would strive to get their custom and to employ them above others in their work, for their honesty and diligence.

Again, the magistrates of the city, about the time of their coming away or a little before, in the public place of justice gave this commendable testimony of them, in the reproof of the Walloons[9] who were of the French church in that city. These English, said they, have lived amongst us now these twelve years, and yet we never had any suit or accusation come against any of them; but your strifes and quarrels are continual, etc.

In these times also were the great troubles raised by the Arminians,[1] who, as they greatly molested the whole state, so this city in particular in which was the chief university; so as there were daily and hot disputes in the schools[2] thereabout. And as the students and other learned were divided in their opinions

[9] After that part of the Low Countries which is now Belgium had been reduced to obedience by the Spaniards, many thousand Protestants among the French-speaking Walloons emigrated across the border to the United Netherlands. Some of them joined the Pilgrim church in Leyden; one of these, Philippe de la Noye, came to Plymouth in the *Fortune* in 1621. This name, Englished as Delano, has descended to a host of Americans, including the late President Franklin Delano Roosevelt. Many Walloons later emigrated to New Amsterdam, where they enjoyed an influence even greater than their numbers. See Mrs. Emily J. DeForest *A Walloon Family in America.*

[1] Jacobus Arminius, professor of theology at the University of Leyden from 1603 until his death in 1609, was a learned Dutchman whose mild and liberal spirit revolted against the rigid and gloomy dogmatism of Calvin. He sought to make election dependent on faith and repentance rather than on God's absolute decree; declared that the sovereignty of God is so exercised as to be compatible with the freedom of man, and that every believer could be assured of his own salvation. His successor, Simon Episcopius, and other disciples, presented to the governments of Holland and Friesland in 1610 a remonstrance formulating their points of departure from Calvinism. Their adversaries, led by Arminius's colleague Gomarus and his successor Polyander, made a counter-remonstrance. The States General issued an edict tolerating both parties and ordering the dispute to cease; but it went on, as Bradford relates. In 1619 the Synod of Dort refused seats to the Arminians or Remonstrants, and for about ten years ministers who preached that doctrine were persecuted in the Netherlands. Historically, the Arminian tenets influenced several systems of liberal Protestant theology, and sundry liberal churches in America such as the Dutch Reformed and the Unitarian.

[2] The public rooms of the University which were used for lectures and other exercises; the word is still used in that sense at Oxford and Cambridge.

herein, so were the two professors or divinity readers themselves, the one daily teaching for it, the other against it. Which grew to that pass, that few of the disciples of the one would hear the other teach. But Mr. Robinson, though he taught [3] thrice a week himself, and wrote sundry books besides his manifold pains otherwise, yet he went constantly to hear their readings and heard the one as well as the other; by which means he was so well grounded in the controversy and saw the force of all their arguments and knew the shifts of the adversary. And being himself very able, none was fitter to buckle with them than himself, as appeared by sundry disputes, so as he began to be terrible to the Arminians. Which made Episcopius (the Arminian professor) to put forth his best strength and set forth sundry theses [4] which by public dispute he would defend against all men.

Now Polyander, the other professor, and the chief preacher of the city, desired Mr. Robinson to dispute against him; but he was loath, being a stranger. Yet the other did importune him and told him that such was the ability and nimbleness of the adversary that the truth would suffer if he did not help them. So as he condescended and prepared himself against the time; and when the day came, the Lord did so help him to defend the truth and foil this adversary, as he put him to an apparent nonplus in this great and public audience. And the like he did a second or third time uoon such like occasions. The which as it caused many to praise God that the truth had so famous victory, so it procured him much honour and respect from those learned men and others which loved the truth. Yea, so far were they from being weary of him and his people or desiring their absence, as it was said by some of no mean note that were it not for giving offense to the state of England they would have preferred him otherwise if he would, and allowed them some public favour. Yea, when there was speech of their removal into these parts, sundry of note and eminency of that nation would have had them come under them,

[3] Lectured to his own congregation.

[4] Theses in the original meaning of the word: propositions which would be posted up on a university bulletin board as a challenge to others to dispute if they would.

and for that end made them large offers.[5] Now, though I might allege many other particulars and examples of the like kind, to show the untruth and unlikelihood of this slander, yet these shall suffice, seeing it was believed of few, being only raised by the malice of some who laboured their disgrace.

[5] Presumably to settle in the colony of New Netherland, which was just being organized.

CHAPTER IV

Showing the Reasons and Causes of Their Removal

After they had lived in this city about some eleven or twelve years (which is the more observable being the whole time of that famous truce between that state and the Spaniards) [1] and sundry of them were taken away by death and many others began to be well stricken in years (the grave mistress of Experience having taught them many things), |15| those prudent governors with sundry of the sagest members began both deeply to apprehend their present dangers and wisely to foresee the future and think of timely remedy. In the agitation of their thoughts, and much discourse of things hereabout, at length they began to incline to this conclusion: of removal to some other place. Not out of any newfangledness or other such like giddy humor by which men are oftentimes transported to their great hurt and danger, but for sundry weighty and solid reasons, some of the chief of which I will here briefly touch.

And first, they saw and found by experience the hardness of the place and country to be such as few in comparison would come to them, and fewer that would bide it out and continue with them. For many that came to them, and many more that desired to be with them, could not endure that great labour and hard fare, with other inconveniences which they underwent and were contented with. But though they loved their persons, approved their cause and honoured their sufferings, yet they left them as it were weeping, as Orpah did her mother-in-law Naomi,[2] or as those Romans did Cato in Utica who desired to be excused and borne with, though they could not all be Catos. For many, though they desired to enjoy the ordinances of God in their purity and the liberty of the gospel with them, yet (alas) they admitted of bondage with danger of conscience, rather than to

[1] The twelve years' truce was signed on 30 March 1609, and therefore was due to end in 1621. Although war was then renewed, the Netherlands had powerful allies such as France, Sweden and several German States already engaged with Spain in the Thirty Years' War, at the end of which, in the Treaty of Westphalia (1648), Spain recognized the independence of the United Netherlands.

[2] Ruth i.14.

endure these hardships. Yea, some preferred and chose the prisons in England rather than this liberty in Holland with these afflictions.[3] But it was thought that if a better and easier place of living could be had, it would draw many and take away these discouragements. Yea, their pastor would often say that many of those who both wrote and preached now against them, if they were in a place where they might have liberty and live comfortably, they would then practice as they did.

Secondly. They saw that though the people generally bore all these difficulties very cheerfully and with a resolute courage, being in the best and strength of their years; yet old age began to steal on many of them; and their great and continual labours, with other crosses and sorrows, hastened it before the time. So as it was not only probably thought, but apparently seen, that within a few years more they would be in danger to scatter, by necessities pressing them, or sink under their burdens, or both. And therefore according to the divine proverb, that a wise man seeth the plague when it cometh, and hideth himself, Proverbs xxii.3, so they like skillful and beaten soldiers were fearful either to be entrapped or surrounded by their enemies so as they should neither be able to fight nor fly. And therefore thought it better to dislodge betimes to some place of better advantage and less danger, if any such could be found. |16|

Thirdly. As necessity was a taskmaster over them so they were forced to be such, not only to their servants but in a sort to their dearest children, the which as it did not a little wound the tender hearts of many a loving father and mother, so it produced likewise sundry sad and sorrowful effects. For many of their children that were of best dispositions and gracious inclinations, having learned[4] to bear the yoke in their youth and willing to bear part of their parents' burden, were oftentimes so oppressed with their heavy labours that though their minds were free and willing, yet their bodies bowed under the weight of the same, and became decrepit in their early youth, the vigour of nature being

[3] It may seem strange that it should seem easier to emigrate to the American wilderness than to a Dutch city; but the Netherlands were overpopulated in relation to the economic system of that day, and the standard of living in the handicrafts, the only occupations open to English immigrants, was low.

[4] Lamentations iii.27.

consumed in the very bud as it were. But that which was more lamentable, and of all sorrows most heavy to be borne, was that many of their children, by these occasions and the great licentiousness of youth in that country,[5] and the manifold temptations of the place, were drawn away by evil examples into extravagant and dangerous courses, getting the reins off their necks and departing from their parents. Some became soldiers, others took upon them far voyages by sea, and others some worse courses tending to dissoluteness and the danger of their souls, to the great grief of their parents and dishonour of God. So that they saw their posterity would be in danger to degenerate and be corrupted.[6]

Lastly (and which was not least), a great hope and inward zeal they had of laying some good foundation, or at least to make some way thereunto, for the propagating and advancing the gospel of the kingdom of Christ in those remote parts of the world; yea, though they should be but even as stepping-stones unto others for the performing of so great a work.

These and some other like reasons moved them to undertake this resolution of their removal; the which they afterward prosecuted with so great difficulties, as by the sequel will appear.

The place they had thoughts on was some of those vast and unpeopled countries of America, which are fruitful and fit for habitation, being devoid of all civil inhabitants, where there are only savage and brutish men which range up and down, little otherwise than the wild beasts of the same. This proposition being made public and coming to the scanning of all, it raised many variable opinions amongst men and caused many fears and doubts amongst themselves. Some, from their reasons and hopes conceived, laboured to stir up and encourage the rest to undertake

5 The Dutch, curiously enough, did not "remember the Sabbath Day to keep it holy" in the strict sense that other Calvinists did. Sunday after church was a day of feasting and merrymaking, especially for children. This was one of the conditions that the English community found most obnoxious.

6 Both Nathaniel Morton in *New Englands Memoriall* p. 3, and Edward Winslow in *Hypocrisie Unmasked* p. 89 stressed the fear of the Pilgrims lest their children lose their language and nationality. And their fear of the Dutch "melting pot" was well taken; for the offspring of those English Puritans who did not emigrate to New England or return to England became completely amalgamated with the local population by 1660.

and prosecute the same; others again, out of their fears, objected against it and sought to divert from it; alleging many things, and those neither unreasonable nor unprobable; as that it was a great design and subject to many unconceivable perils and dangers; as, besides the casualties of the sea (which none can be freed from), the length of the voyage was such as the weak bodies of women and other persons worn out with age and travail (as many of them were) could never be able to endure. And yet if they should, the miseries of the land which they should be |17| exposed unto, would be too hard to be borne and likely, some or all of them together, to consume and utterly to ruinate them. For there they should be liable to famine and nakedness and the want, in a manner, of all things. The change of air, diet and drinking of water [7] would infect their bodies with sore sicknesses and grievous diseases. And also those which should escape or overcome these difficulties should yet be in continual danger of the savage people, who are cruel, barbarous and most treacherous, being most furious in their rage and merciless where they overcome; not being content only to kill and take away life, but delight to torment men in the most bloody manner that may be; flaying some alive with the shells of fishes, cutting off the members and joints of others by piecemeal and broiling on the coals, eat the collops of their flesh in their sight whilst they live, with other cruelties horrible to be related.[8]

And surely it could not be thought but the very hearing of these things could not but move the very bowels of men to grate within them and make the weak to quake and tremble. It was further objected that it would require greater sums of money to furnish such a voyage and to fit them with necessaries, than their consumed estates would amount to; and yet they must as well

[7] It was a general opinion of the time, which Bradford on sundry occasions shows that he shared, that water was an unwholesome beverage, as indeed it was when drawn from a contaminated well in a city or farmyard. The common table beverages of poor families in England and Holland were beer and cider.

[8] As the Netherlands was then the principal center for the publication of illustrated narratives of voyages, the Pilgrims had a wide choice of literature from which to acquire a healthy respect for the Indians and an aversion to taking up a new abode within reach of the Spaniards.

look to be seconded with supplies as presently to be transported. Also many precedents of ill success and lamentable miseries befallen others in the like designs were easy to be found, and not forgotten to be alleged; besides their own experience, in their former troubles and hardships in their removal into Holland, and how hard a thing it was for them to live in that strange place, though it was a neighbour country and a civil and rich commonwealth.

It was answered, that all great and honourable actions are accompanied with great difficulties and must be both enterprised and overcome with answerable courages. It was granted the dangers were great, but not desperate. The difficulties were many, but not invincible. For though there were many of them likely, yet they were not certain. It might be sundry of the things feared might never befall; others by provident care and the use of good means might in a great measure be prevented; and all of them, through the help of God, by fortitude and patience, might either be borne or overcome. True it was that such attempts were not to be made and undertaken without good ground and reason, not rashly or lightly as many have done for curiosity or hope of gain, etc. But their condition was not ordinary, their ends were good and honourable, their calling lawful and urgent; and therefore they might expect the blessing of God in their proceeding. Yea, though they should lose their lives in this action, yet might they have comfort in the same and their endeavours would be honourable. They lived here but as men in exile and in a poor condition, and as great miseries might possibly befall them in this place; for the twelve years of truce were now out and there was nothing but beating of drums and preparing for war, the events whereof are always uncertain. The Spaniard might prove as cruel as |18| the savages of America, and the famine and pestilence as sore here as there, and their liberty less to look out for remedy.

After many other particular things answered and alleged on both sides, it was fully concluded by the major part to put this design in execution and to prosecute it by the best means they could.

CHAPTER V

Showing What Means They Used for Preparation to This Weighty Voyage

And first after their humble prayers unto God for His direction and assistance, and a general conference held hereabout, they consulted what particular place to pitch upon and prepare for. Some (and none of the meanest) had thoughts and were earnest for Guiana, or some of those fertile places in those hot climates. Others were for some parts of Virginia, where the English had already made entrance and beginning. Those for Guiana alleged that the country was rich, fruitful, and blessed with a perpetual spring and a flourishing greenness, where vigorous nature brought forth all things in abundance and plenty without any great labour or art of man.[1] So as it must needs make the inhabitants rich, seeing less provisions of clothing and other things would serve, than in more colder and less fruitful countries must be had. As also that the Spaniards (having much more than they could possess) had not yet planted there nor anywhere very near the same. But to this it was answered that out of question the country was both fruitful and pleasant, and might yield riches and maintenance to the possessors more easily than the other; yet, other things considered, it would not be so fit for them. And first, that such hot countries are subject to grievous diseases and many noisome impediments which other more temperate places are freer from, and would not so well agree with our English bodies. Again, if they should there live and do well, the jealous Spaniard would never suffer them long, but would displant or overthrow them as he did the French in Florida, who were seated further from his richest countries; and the sooner because they

[1] Guiana at that time meant the region between the Orinoco and the Amazon. Both Sir Walter Raleigh's *Discoverie of the Large, Rich and Bewtifull Empyre of Guiana* and Lawrence Keymis's *Relation of the Second Voyage to Guiana* came out in 1596; Robert Harcourt's *Relation of a Voyage to Guiana* was printed in 1613. There had been several illustrated editions and translations of Thomas Hariot's *Briefe and True Report* of the Raleigh colony at Roanoke since its first appearance in 1588, and a number of pamphlets about the Jamestown colony, which were the main sources of the Pilgrims' information about those countries.

should have none to protect them, and their own strength would be too small to resist so potent an enemy and so near a neighbour.

On the other hand, for Virginia it was objected that if they lived among the English which were there planted, or so near them as to be under their government, they should be in as great danger to be troubled and persecuted for the cause of religion as if they lived in England; and it might be worse. And if they lived too far off, they should neither have succour nor defense from them.

But at length the conclusion was to live as a distinct body by themselves under the general Government of Virginia; and by their friends to sue to His Majesty that he would be pleased to grant them freedom of religion. And that this might be obtained they were put in good hope by some great persons of good rank and quality that were made their friends. Whereupon two were chosen |19| and sent into England (at the charge of the rest) to solicit this matter, who found the Virginia Company very desirous to have them go thither and willing to grant them a patent, with as ample privileges as they had or could grant to any; and to give them the best furtherance they could.[2] And some of the chief of that Company doubted not to obtain their suit of the King for liberty in religion, and to have it confirmed under the

[2] The Virginia Company of London, whose third charter, of 1612 (William MacDonald *Select Charters* p. 18), extended its northern boundary to lat. 41° N (which would include Manhattan and most of Long Island), began about 1617 the practice of granting large tracts of land, up to 80,000 acres, to groups of individuals who would undertake to people and cultivate them. Such grants, known in Virginia as "Hundreds" or "Particular Plantations," carried special privileges such as local self-government, jurisdiction, fishing rights or permission to trade with the Indians. Some 44 such grants were made before 1624, and a number of these colonies within a colony were actually established. The best known were Martin's Hundred, Southampton Hundred, Berkeley's Hundred and Fleur de Hundred. See P. A. Bruce *Institutional History of Virginia* II 290–4 and 327; and C. M. Andrews *Colonial Period of American History* I 128–33. The Pilgrims sought and were actually granted two such patents, neither of which, as we shall see, they were able to use. Their means of access to the Virginia Company of London was through William Brewster's father, the bailiff of the manor of Scrooby, whose lord was Edwin Sandys, an "obstinate and conscientious Puritan"; his son Samuel held the lease of the manor and so was Brewster's landlord, and another son, Sir Edwin Sandys, was a leading promoter and from 1619 Treasurer of the Virginia Company and a Puritan sympathizer. Edward Channing *History of the United States* I 190.

King's broad seal, according to their desires. But it proved a harder piece of work than they took it for; for though many means were used to bring it about, yet it could not be effected. For there were divers of good worth laboured with the King to obtain it, amongst whom was one of his chief secretaries, Sir Robert Naunton.[8] And some others wrought with the Archbishop to give way thereunto, but it proved all in vain. Yet thus far they prevailed, in sounding His Majesty's mind, that he would connive at them and not molest them, provided they carried themselves peaceably. But to allow or tolerate them by his public authority, under his seal, they found it would not be. And this was all the chief of the Virginia Company or any other of their best friends could do in the case. Yet they persuaded them to go on, for they presumed they should not be troubled. And with this answer the messengers returned and signified what diligence had been used and to what issue things were come.

But this made a damp in the business and caused some distraction, for many were afraid that if they should unsettle themselves and put off their estates and go upon these hopes, it might prove dangerous and prove but a sandy foundation. Yea it was thought they might better have presumed hereupon without making any suit at all than, having made it, to be thus rejected. But some of the chiefest thought otherwise and that they might well proceed hereupon, and that the King's Majesty was willing enough to suffer them without molestation, though for other reasons he would not confirm it by any public act. And furthermore, if there was no security in this promise intimated, there would be no great certainty in a further confirmation of the same; for if afterwards there should be a purpose or desire to wrong them, though they had a seal as broad as the house floor it would not serve the turn; for there would be means enow found to recall or

[8] The name inserted by Bradford in the margin. A Puritan sympathizer, he became Secretary of State to James I in January 1618. Edward Winslow wrote in *Hypocrisie Unmasked* (1646) p. 89 that Sandys persuaded Naunton to go to the King with the proposition; that James I asked how his clients intended to earn their living; Naunton said: "By fishing," to which the King replied: "So God have my soul, 'tis an honest trade, 'twas the apostles' own calling." But (says Winslow) the King would not grant them religious liberty without consulting the Archbishop of Canterbury, George Abbot.

reverse it. Seeing therefore the course was probable, they must rest herein on God's providence as they had done in other things.

Upon this resolution, other messengers were dispatched, to end with the Virginia Company as well as they could. And to procure |20| a patent with as good and ample conditions as they might by any good means obtain. As also to treat and conclude with such merchants and other friends as had manifested their forwardness to provoke to and adventure in this voyage. For which end they had instructions given them upon what conditions they should proceed with them, or else to conclude nothing without further advice. And here it will be requisite to insert a letter or two that may give light to these proceedings.

A Copy of Letter from Sir Edwin Sandys, directed to Mr. John Robinson and Mr. William Brewster.

After my hearty salutations. The agents of your congregation, Robert Cushman and John Carver, have been in communication with divers select gentlemen of His Majesty's Council for Virginia; and by the writing of seven Articles [4] subscribed with your names, have given them that good degree of satisfaction, which hath carried them on with a resolution to set forward your desire in the best sort that may be, for your own and the public good. Divers particulars whereof we leave to their faithful report; having carried themselves here with that good discretion, as is both to their own and their credit from whence they came. And whereas being to treat for a multitude of people, they have requested further time to confer with them that are to be interested in this action, about the several particularities which in the prosecution thereof will fall out

[4] These Seven Articles which the Church of Leyden sent to the Virginia Council in 1617, signed by Robinson and Brewster, are not in Bradford's History. The original manuscript is in the Public Records Office. They have frequently been printed, most recently in the 1912 edition Bradford I 72 footnote. In sum they are: 1. Acknowledge the XXXIX Articles of Religion. 2. Wish to keep spiritual Communion with the Church of England and "will practise on our parts all lawful things." 3. Acknowledge obedience to the King unless he commands them "against God's Word." 4 and 5, a somewhat qualified admission of the legality of bishops. 6. Admit that no synod or other body can have ecclesiastical jurisdiction except by the King's authority. 7. Will give "unto all superiors due honour." This was not a frank statement of the Pilgrims' position; but they doubtless felt that once in America they could do as they liked.

considerable, it hath been very willingly assented to. And so they do now return unto you. If therefore it may please God so to direct your desires as that on your parts there fall out no just impediments, I trust by the same direction it shall likewise appear that on our part all forwardness to set you forward shall be found in the best sort which with reason may be expected. And so I betake [5] you with this design (which I hope verily is the work of God), to the gracious protection and blessing of the Highest.

London, November 12 Your very loving friend,
Anno: 1617 EDWIN SANDYS

Their answer was as followeth.

RIGHT WORSHIPFUL:

Our humble duties remembered, in our own, our messengers, and our church's name, with all thankful acknowledgment of your singular love, |21| expressing itself, as otherwise, so more specially in your great care and earnest endeavour of our good in this weighty business about Virginia, which the less able we are to requite, we shall think ourselves the more bound to commend in our prayers unto God for recompense; Whom, as for the present you rightly behold in our endeavours, so shall we not be wanting on our parts (the same God assisting us) to return all answerable fruit and respect unto the labour of your love bestowed upon us. We have with the best speed and consideration withal that we could, set down our requests in writing, subscribed as you willed, with the hands of the greatest part of our congregation, and have sent the same unto the Council by our agent and a deacon of our church, John Carver, unto whom we have also requested a gentleman of our company to adjoin himself. To the care and discretion of which two we do refer the prosecuting of the business. Now we persuade ourselves, Right Worshipful, that we need not provoke your godly and loving mind to any further or more tender care of us, since you have pleased so far to interest us in yourself that, under God, above all persons and things in the world, we rely upon you, expecting the care of your love, counsel of your wisdom and the help and countenance of your authority. Notwithstanding, for your encouragement in the work, so far as probabilities may lead, we will not forbear to mention these instances of inducement.

1. We verily believe and trust the Lord is with us, unto whom

[5] Commit, command.

and whose service we have given ourselves in many trials; and that He will graciously prosper our endeavours according to the simplicity of our hearts therein.

2. We are well weaned from the delicate milk of our mother country, and inured to the difficulties of a strange and hard land, which yet in a great part we have by patience overcome.

3. The people are, for the body of them, industrious and frugal, we think we may safely say, as any company of people in the world.

4. We are knit together as a body in a most strict and sacred bond and covenant of the Lord,[6] of the violation whereof we make great conscience, and by virtue whereof we do hold ourselves straitly tied to all care of each other's good and of the whole, by every one and so mutually.

5. Lastly, it is not with us as with other men, whom small things can discourage, or small discontentments cause to wish themselves at home again. We know our entertainment in England and in Holland. We shall much prejudice both our arts and means by removal; who, if we should be driven to return, we should not hope to recover our present helps and comforts, neither indeed look ever, for ourselves, to attain unto the like in any other place during our lives, which are now drawing towards their periods.

|22| These motives we have been bold to tender unto you, which you in your wisdom may also impart to any other our worshipful friends of the Council with you; of all whose godly disposition and loving towards our despised persons we are most glad, and shall not fail by all good means to continue and increase the same. We will not be further troublesome, but do, with the renewed remembrance

[6] Bradford wrote the following in his aged hand on the blank page opposite:

"O sacred bond, whilst inviolaby preserved! How sweet and precious were the fruits that flowed from the same! But when this fidelity decayed, then their ruin approached. O that these ancient members had not died or been dissipated (if it had been the will of God) or else that this holy care and constant faithfulness had still lived, and remained with those that survived, and were in times afterwards added unto them. But (alas) that subtle serpent hath slyly wound in himself under fair pretences of necessity and the like, to untwist these sacred bonds and tied, and as it were insensibly by degrees to dissolve, or in a great measure to weaken, the same. I have been happy, in my first times, to see, and with much comfort to enjoy, the blessed fruits of this sweet communion, but it is now a part of my misery in old age, to find and feel the decay and want thereof (in a great measure) and with grief and sorrow of heart to lament and bewail the same. And for others' warning and admonition, and my own humiliation, do I here note the same."

of our humble duties to your Worship and (so far as in modesty we may be bold) to any other of our wellwillers of the Council with you, we take our leaves, committing your persons and counsels to the guidance and direction of the Almighty.

Yours much bounden in all duty,

Leyden, December 15
Anno: 1617

JOHN ROBINSON,
WILLIAM BREWSTER

For further light in these proceedings see some other letters and notes as followeth.[7]

|26| But at last, after all these things and their long attendance, they had a patent granted them, and confirmed under the Company's seal. But these divisions and distractions had shaken off many of their pretended friends, and disappointed them of much of their hoped-for and proffered means. By the advice of some friends this Patent was not taken in the name of any of their own but in the name of Mr. John Wincop (a religious gentleman then belonging to the Countess of Lincoln) [8] who intended to go with them. But God so disposed that he never went, nor they ever made use of this Patent which had cost them so much labour and charge, as by the sequel will appear. This Patent being sent over

[7] This correspondence with members of the Virginia Company, in which the Pilgrims state their religious beliefs and practices much more frankly than in the Seven Articles, will be found in Appendix II below, together with the account of Francis Blackwell's tragic voyage.

[8] John Wincop, one of three clergymen brothers, was a tutor or chaplain in the household of Thomas Fiennes-Clinton, third Earl of Lincoln, who died 15 January 1619. The Earl's daughters, Lady Arbella Johnson and Lady Susan Humfry, were among the earliest settlers of the Massachusetts Bay Company, and Thomas Dudley, who served both the third and the fourth Earls as steward, became Governor of the Bay Colony. Wincop was evidently the "window dressing" for this patent to a Particular Plantation in Virginia (see p. 29 above, footnote 2), no copy of which has survived, although the granting of it is recorded in *Records of the Virginia Company* I 221, 228 on 9 June 1619. There has been endless speculation as to its terms. Charles M. Andrews (*Colonial Period* I 133) thinks it "impossible to believe" that the patent could have allowed Wincop's associates to settle as far away from Jamestown as the Hudson, which Bradford later states to have been the *Mayflower's* destination. But these patents for "particular plantations" never did specify where the plantation was to be located; the leaders were supposed to report at Jamestown and select a tract of land not already granted. It is certainly not inconceivable that the local authorities in Virginia would have welcomed an outpost against Dutch or French encroachments to the north. Cf. p. 60 note 6, below.

for them to view and consider, as also the passages about the propositions between them and such merchants and friends as should either go or adventure with them, and especially with those [9] on whom they did chiefly depend for shipping and means, whose proffers had been large, they were requested to fit and prepare themselves with all speed. A right emblem, it may be, of the uncertain things of this world, that when men have toiled themselves for them, they vanish into smoke.[1]

[9] Mr. Thomas Weston, etc. (Bradford).

[1] This last sentence was written later than the rest of the chapter; Bradford evidently decided, on reading it over, to point the moral.

CHAPTER VI

Concerning the Agreements and Articles between them and such Merchants and Others as Adventured Moneys; with Other Things Falling out about Making their Provisions

Upon the receipt of these things by one of their messengers, they had a solemn meeting and a day of humiliation to seek the Lord for His direction; and their pastor took this text: 1 Samuel xxiii.3,4: "And David's men said unto him, see we be afraid here in Judah, how much more if we come to Keilah against the host of the Philistines? Then David asked counsel of the Lord again," etc. From which text he taught many things very aptly and befitting their present occasion and condition, strengthening them against their fears and perplexities and encouraging them in their resolutions. |27|

After which they concluded both what number and what persons should prepare themselves to go with the first; for all that were willing to have gone could not get ready for their other affairs in so short a time; neither, if all could have been ready, had there been means to have transported them all together. Those that stayed, being the greater number, required the pastor to stay with them; and indeed for other reasons he could not then well go, and so it was the more easily yielded unto. The other then desired the elder, Mr. Brewster, to go with them, which was also condescended unto. It was also agreed on by mutual consent and covenant that those that went should be an absolute church of themselves, as well as those that stayed, seeing in such a dangerous voyage, and a removal to such a distance, it might come to pass they should (for the body of them) never meet again in this world. Yet with this proviso, that as any of the rest came over to them, or of the other returned upon occasion, they should be reputed as members without any further dismission or testimonial. It was also promised to those that went first, by the body of the rest, that if the Lord gave them life and means, and opportunity, they would come to them as soon as they could.

About this time, whilst they were perplexed with the proceedings of the Virginia Company and the ill news from thence about Mr. Blackwell and his company, and making inquiry about the hiring and buying of shipping for their voyage, some Dutchmen [1] made them fair offers about going with them. Also one Mr. Thomas Weston,[2] a merchant of London, came to Leyden about the same time (who was well acquainted with some of them and a furtherer of them in their former proceedings), having much conference with Mr. Robinson and others of the chief of them, persuaded them to go on (as it seems) and not to meddle with the Dutch or too much to depend on the Virginia Company. For if that failed, if they came to resolution, he and such merchants as were his friends, together with their own means, would set them forth; and they should make ready and neither fear want of shipping nor money; for what they wanted should be provided. And, not so much for himself as for the satisfying of such friends as he should procure to adventure in this business,

[1] The New Netherland Company, which was exploiting the future State of New York, petitioned the Prince of Orange to sanction a settlement of the Leyden congregation on their territory, but was turned down. 1912 ed. Bradford I 99. For Blackwell's fate see Appendix II.

[2] Thomas Weston, citizen and ironmonger of London, was an "Adventurer" (promoter and capitalist) somewhat below the great men of the Virginia and Massachusetts Bay companies; a man of enterprise, eager to reap quick profits from the new world, and not very scrupulous as to means. For several years he had been the head of a group of likeminded men who had fouled the hawse of the incorporated Merchants Adventurers of London, on whose complaint they had been haled before the Privy Council and ordered to stop unlicensed trade with the Netherlands. The need of the Pilgrims and other groups for money to finance emigration gave Weston and his associates a new opportunity for speculative investment. He and his group, which we shall encounter frequently in the course of this history, are, according to the usage of the day, called by Bradford the Adventurers, in contrast to the Colonists or Planters. According to Captain John Smith's *Generall Historie of Virginia, New England* etc. (Arber ed. of his *Travels and Works* II 783), about 70 men, "some Gentlemen, some Merchants, some handy-crafts men," were associated with Weston in this enterprise, and their total investment was about £7000. But, judging by facts in this History, especially the price for which the Adventurers sold out in 1627 (see chap. xviii below), the cost of the *Mayflower's* voyage, including ship hire, victuals and outfit, can hardly have exceeded £1500. Weston, after squeezing all he could out of the Pilgrims, became a planter and burgess in Virginia, whence he made fishing and trading voyages to the Maine coast. After being arrested more than once for breaking the Colony's laws, he went to Maryland, acquired new property, returned to England and died there in 1646, heavily in debt. C. M. Andrews *Colonial Period* I 261, 330–1.

they were to draw such articles of agreement and make such propositions as might the better induce his friends to venture. Upon which, after the former conclusion, articles were drawn and agreed unto and were shown unto him and approved by him. And afterwards by their messenger (Mr. John Carver) sent into England who, together with Robert Cushman,[3] were to receive the moneys and make provision both for shipping and other things for the voyage; with this charge, not to exceed their commission but to proceed according to the former articles. Also some were chosen to do the like for such things as were to be prepared there.[4] So those that were to go prepared themselves with all speed and sold off their estates and (such as were able) put in their moneys into the common stock, which was disposed by those appointed, for the making of general provisions.

About this time also they had heard, both by Mr. Weston and others, that sundry Honourable Lords had obtained a large grant from the King for the more northerly parts of that country, derived out of the Virginia patent and wholly secluded from their Government, and to be called by another name, viz., New England.[5] Unto which Mr. Weston and the chief of them began to

[3] Robert Cushman had been a member of the Leyden church since 1609. Possessed of some private means, he was one of the leading organizers of the voyage but did not sail in the *Mayflower*, probably because of the controversy over altering the terms with Weston & Co. He came to Plymouth later and was one of the staunchest supporters of the Colony. His letter gives an interesting account of Virginia Company politics, and of the unfortunate voyage of Francis Blackwell, who tried to found a Puritan colony in Virginia in 1619.

[4] Readers who like the minutiae of history may be amused by a controversy between the late Dr. Charles E. Banks and myself, in Massachusetts Historical Society *Proceedings* LXI (1928) as to whether this *there* means Leyden or London, and whether Bradford did or did not leave Leyden in 1619.

[5] New England was first so called by Capt. John Smith in his *Description of New England* (London 1616) following his voyage of 1614. The Northern (or Plymouth) Virginia Company had begun a settlement at the mouth of the Kennebec in 1607 but it failed, and no second attempt was made. The fisheries, however, were profitable and in March 1620 Sir Ferdinando Gorges and "sundry honourable lords" who had been members of the Northern Virginia Company petitioned for a new charter to the region, with a fishing monopoly. The charter, which passed the seals 3 Nov. 1620, created a new corporation called "The Council established at Plymouth in the County of Devon for the planting, ruling, ordering and governing of New-England in America," commonly called for short the Council for New England. It was granted jurisdiction over all America between lats. 40° and 48° N (roughly Philadelphia to the Bay de

incline it was |28| best for them to go; as for other reasons, so chiefly for the hope of present profit to be made by the fishing that was found in that country.[6]

But as in all businesses the acting part is most difficult, especially where the work of many agents must concur, so was it found in this. For some of those that should have gone in England fell off and would not go; other merchants and friends that had offered to adventure their moneys withdrew and pretended many excuses; some disliking they went not to Guiana; others again would adventure nothing except they went to Virginia. Some again (and those that were most relied on) fell in utter dislike with Virginia and would do nothing if they went thither. In the midst of these distractions, they of Leyden who had put off their estates and laid out their moneys were brought into a great strait, fearing what issue these things would come to. But at length the generality was swayed to this latter opinion.[7]

Chaleur), and from sea to sea. Text in William MacDonald *Select Charters* p. 23. This corporation never effected a settlement itself, but granted land patents to its own members and others who proposed to do so. The patents which legalized the Plymouth Colony and many others, including those whence Maine, New Hampshire and, in part, Connecticut, are derived, were issued by the Council during the 15 years of its existence; see the list in Massachusetts Historical Society *Lectures on Early History of Massachusetts* (1869) pp. 129–62.

[6] Bradford does not explain why they did not forthwith decide to go to New England rather than Virginia. I suggest that the reasons were these: (1) On 2 Feb. 1620 the Virginia Company issued a patent for a "Particular Plantation" to John Peirce, citizen and clothier of London, a close associate of Thomas Weston and brother to Abraham Peirce, cape merchant in Virginia. The text of this patent has not survived, but it was probably more liberal than the Wincop Patent and so was substituted for it as the basic grant for the Pilgrim Fathers. (2) On the same day the Virginia Company (*Records* I 303) passed a very liberal ordinance for Particular Plantations, giving their captains or leaders, associating with themselves "divers of the gravest and discreetest of their companies," almost complete autonomy within the Virginia Colony. (3) The charter of the Council for New England, owing to the dispute about the fishing monopoly, did not pass the seals until 3 Nov. 1620, when the Pilgrims were already at sea, and until it did so, no patent for a Particular Plantation could be obtained from them.

[7] I.e., to go to New England. Bradford Smith *Bradford of Plymouth* pp. 108–9 relies on this passage to prove that the *Mayflower* was really headed for New England, not Virginia; to me it seems merely to indicate that a majority of the would-be emigrants at this point preferred New England if they could get a patent, which they could not. See p. 60 below, footnote 6.

But now another difficulty arose, for Mr. Weston and some other that were for this course, either for their better advantage or rather for the drawing on of others, as they pretended, would have some of those conditions altered that were first agreed on at Leyden. To which the two agents sent from Leyden (or at least one of them who is most charged with it) did consent, seeing else that all was like to be dashed and the opportunity lost, and that they which had put off their estates and paid in their moneys were in hazard to be undone.[8] They presumed to conclude with the merchants on those terms, in some things contrary to their order and commission and without giving them notice of the same; yea, it was concealed lest it should make any further delay. Which was the cause afterward of much trouble and contention.

It will be meet I here insert these conditions, which are as followeth:

Anno: 1620. July 1.

1. The Adventurers and Planters do agree, that every person that goeth being aged 16 years and upward, be rated at £10, and £10 to be accounted a single share.

2. That he that goeth in person, and furnisheth himself out with £10 either in money or other provisions, be accounted as having £20 in stock, and in the division shall receive a double share.

3. The persons transported and the Adventurers shall continue their joint stock and partnership together, the space of seven years, (except some unexpected impediment do cause the whole company to agree otherwise) during which time all profits and benefits that are got by trade, traffic, trucking, working, fishing, or any other means of any person or persons, remain still in the common stock until the division.

4. That at their coming there, they choose out such a number of fit persons as may furnish their ships and boats for fishing upon the sea, employing the rest in their several faculties upon the land, as

[8] Bradford himself had sold his house in Leyden in 1619. In justice to Weston it should be said that he had been counting on giving the Pilgrims a monopoly of fishing off the New England coast; but the movement against monopolies was then so strong in England that the Council for New England could not obtain a fishing monopoly and so could not grant it. This lack made their investment in the Pilgrims much less attractive to the Adventurers.

building houses, tilling and planting the ground, and making such commodities as shall be most useful for the colony.

5. That at the end of the seven years, the capital and profits, viz. the houses, lands, goods and chattels, be equally divided betwixt the Adventurers and Planters; which done, every man shall be free from other of them [9] of any debt or detriment concerning this adventure. |29|

6. Whosoever cometh to the colony hereafter or putteth any into the stock, shall at the end of the seven years be allowed proportionably to the time of his so doing.

7. He that shall carry his wife and children, or servants, shall be allowed for every person now aged 16 years and upward, a single share in the division; or, if he provide them necessaries, a double share; or, if they be between 10 year old and 16, then two of them to be reckoned for a person both in transportation and division.

8. That such children as now go, and are under the age of 10 years, have no other share in the division but 50 acres of unmanured land.

9. That such persons as die before the seven years be expired, their executors to have their part or share at the division, proportionably to the time of their life in the colony.

10. That all such persons as are of this colony are to have their meat, drink, apparel, and all provisions out of the common stock and goods of the said colony.[1]

The chief and principal differences between these and the former conditions, stood in those two points: that the houses, and lands improved, especially gardens and home lots, should remain undivided wholly to the planters at the seven years' end. Secondly, that they should have had two days in a week for their own private employment, for the more comfort of themselves and their families, especially such as had families. But because letters are by some wise men counted the best parts of histories, I shall show their grievances hereabout by their own letters, in which the passages of things will be more truly discerned.

[9] I.e., from each other.

[1] These conditions were almost identical with those under which the Council for Virginia settled Jamestown and the surrounding region except that in the case of Virginia an investment of £12 10*s* was accounted equivalent to one colonist's labor for seven years. The Pilgrims' objections were based on experience in Virginia, where concessions to private property had to be made.

A Letter of Mr. Robinson's to John Carver [2]

June 14, 1620
New Style [3]

My Dear Friend and Brother, whom with yours I always remember in my best affection, and whose welfare I shall never cease to commend to God by my best and most earnest prayers:

You do thoroughly understand by our general letters the estate of things here, which indeed is very pitiful, especially by want of shipping and not seeing means likely, much less certain, of having it provided; though withal there be great want of money and means to do needful things. Mr. Pickering, you know before this, will not defray a penny here, though Robert Cushman presumed of I know not how many hundred pounds from him and I know not whom. Yet it seems strange that we should be put to him to receive both his and his partner's adventure; and yet Mr. Weston writ unto him that in regard of it he hath drawn upon him £100 more. But there is in this some mystery, as indeed it seems there is in the whole course. Besides, whereas divers are to pay in some parts of their moneys yet behind, they refuse to do it till they see shipping provided, or a course taken for it. Neither do I think is there a man here would pay anything, if he had again his money in his purse.

You know right well we depended on Mr. Weston alone, and upon such means as he would procure for this common business; and when we had in hand another course with the Dutchmen, broke it off at his motion and upon the conditions by him shortly after propounded. He did this in his love I know, but things appear not answerable from him hitherto. That he should have first have put in his moneys is thought by many to have been but fit. But that I can well excuse, he being a merchant and having use of it to his benefit; whereas others, if it had been in their hands, would have consumed it. |30| But that he should not but have had either shipping ready before this time, or at least certain means and course and the same known to us for it; or have taken other order otherwise, cannot in my conscience be excused. I have heard that when he hath been

[2] John Carver, aged 44, was one of the oldest of the Pilgrims; he was a well-to-do London merchant who joined the Leyden congregation about 1610 and became a deacon of their church. Chief organizer of the London contingent, charterer of the *Mayflower,* and first Governor of the Colony.

[3] Date altered in the ms. from 24 to 14 June; the former is correct, as Prince observes in a note on the opposite page.

moved in the business he hath put it off from himself and referred it to the others; and would come to George Morton[4] and enquire news of him about things, as if he had scarce been some accessory unto it. Whether he failed of some helps from others which he expected, and so be not well able to go through with things, or whether he hath feared lest you should be ready too soon and so increase the charge of shipping above that is meet, or whether he have thought by withholding to put us upon straits, thinking that thereby Mr. Brewer and Mr. Pickering[5] would be drawn by importunity to do more, or what other mystery is in it we know not; but sure we are that things are not answerable to such an occasion.

Mr. Weston makes himself merry with our endeavours about buying a ship, but we have done nothing in this but with good reason, as I am persuaded, nor yet that I know in anything else, save in those two: the one, that we employed Robert Cushman who is known (though a good man and of special abilities in his kind) yet most unfit to deal for other men by reason of his singularity and too great indifferency for any conditions; and for (to speak truly) that we have had nothing from him but terms and presumptions. The other, that we have so much relied (by implicit faith, as it were) upon generalities without seeing the particular course and means for so weighty an affair set down unto us. For shipping, Mr. Weston, it should seem, is set upon hiring, which yet I wish he may presently effect; but I see little hope of help from hence if so it be. Of Mr. Brewer you know what to expect; I do not think Mr. Pickering will engage except in the course of buying, in former letters specified.

About the conditions, you have our reasons for our judgments of what is agreed. And let this specially be borne in minds, that the greatest part of the colony is like to be employed constantly, not upon dressing their particular land and building houses, but upon fishing, trading, etc. So as the land and house will be but a trifle for advantage to the Adventurers, and yet the division of it a great discouragement to the Planters, who would with singular care make it comfortable with borrowed hours from their sleep. The same con-

[4] George Morton, a merchant of York, was married to the sister of Alice Southworth, whom Bradford married as his second wife. The Mortons came to Plymouth in the *Anne* in 1623; the son, Nathaniel, became Secretary of the Colony and wrote *New Englands Memoriall* (1669).

[5] Thomas Brewer was a partner of Brewster in the printing business, and Thomas Pickering was another member of the Leyden congregation. Both joined the Weston Adventurers, but neither emigrated. 1912 ed. Bradford I 89, 107

sideration of common employment constantly by the most is a good reason not to have the two days in a week denied the few planters for private use, which yet is subordinate to common good. Consider also how much unfit that you and your likes must serve a new apprenticeship of seven years, and not a day's freedom from task.

Send me word what persons are to go, who of useful faculties and how many, and particularly of everything; I know you want not a mind. I am sorry you have not been at London all this while, but the provisions could not want you. Time will suffer me to write no more; fare you and yours well always in the Lord, in Whom I rest.

Yours to use,
JOHN ROBINSON [6]

Besides these things, there fell out a difference among those three that received |35| the moneys, and made the provisions in England; for besides these two formerly mentioned sent from Leyden for this end, viz, Mr. Carver and Robert Cushman, there was one chosen in England to be joined with them to make the provisions for the voyage.[7] His name was Mr. Martin,[8] he came from Billerica in Essex, from which parts came sundry others to go with them, as also from London and other places. And therefore it was thought meet and convenient by them in Holland that these strangers [9] that were to go with them should appoint one thus to be joined with them, not so much for any great need of their help as to avoid all suspicion or jealousy of any partiality. And indeed their care for giving offense, both in this and other things afterward, turned to great inconvenience unto them, as in the sequel will appear; but however it showed their equal and honest minds. The provisions were for the most part made at

[6] The rest of this correspondence between the Leyden committee and Carver and Cushman in London, about the conditions of the voyage, is printed as Appendix III.

[7] "Making provisions" meant salting down beef, baking hardtack, providing casks for beer and water, and preparing other victuals so they would last a long voyage. There were no ship chandlers in those days where such provisions could be bought; the cattle had to be purchased on the hoof and the wheat in the ear, and people hired to prepare them.

[8] Christopher Martin, one of the passengers in the *Mayflower*.

[9] Here first appear the "strangers," i.e., persons unknown to the Leyden Pilgrims or to their friends, who had to be taken along to please the Adventurers and increase the number of colonists.

Southampton, contrary to Mr. Weston's and Robert Cushman's mind whose counsels did most concur in all things. A touch of which things I shall give in a letter of his to Mr. Carver, and more will appear afterward.

To his loving friend Mr. John Carver, these, etc.

Loving Friend, I have received from you some letters, full of affection and complaints, and what it is you would have of me I know not; for your crying out, "Negligence, negligence, negligence," I marvel why so negligent a man was used in the business. Yet know you that all I have power to do here shall not be one hour behind, I warrant you. You have reference to Mr. Weston to help us with money, more than his adventure, when he protesteth but for his promise he would not have done anything. He saith we take a heady course, and is offended that our provisions are made so far off,[1] as also that he was not made acquainted with our quantity of things; and saith that in now being in three places so far remote, we will, with going up and down and wrangling and expostulating, pass over the summer before we will go. And to speak the truth, there is fallen already amongst us a flat schism, and we are readier to go to dispute than to set forward a voyage.

I have received from Leyden since you went, three or four letters directed to you; though they only concern me, I will not trouble you with them. I always feared the event of the Amsterdamers striking in with us. I trow you must excommunicate me or else you must go without their company, or we shall want no quarreling; but let them pass. We have reckoned, it should seem, without our host, and counting upon a 150 persons, there cannot be found above £1200 and odd moneys of all the ventures you can reckon, besides some cloth, stockings and shoes which are not counted, so we shall come short at least £300 or £400. I would have had something shortened at first of beer and other provisions, in hope of other adventures; and now we could, both in Amsterdam and Kent, have beer enough to serve our turn, but now we cannot accept it without prejudice. You fear we have begun to build and shall not be able to make an end. Indeed, our courses were never established by counsel; we may therefore justly fear their standing. Yea, there was a |36| schism amongst us three at the first. You wrote to Mr. Martin to prevent

[1] Apparently Cushman visited his home county of Kent to "make provisions"; both Weston and the Leyden committee were annoyed at the expense of bringing them to Southampton.

the making of the provisions in Kent, which he did, and set down his resolution, how much he would have of everything, without respect to any counsel or exception. Surely he that is in a society and yet regards not counsel may better be a king than a consort. To be short, if there be not some other disposition settled unto, than yet is, we that should be partners of humility and peace shall be examples of jangling and insulting. Yet your money which you there must have, we will get provided for you instantly. £500 you say will serve; for the rest which here and in Holland is to be used, we may go scratch for it. For Mr. Crabe,[2] of whom you write, he hath promised to go with us; yet I tell you I shall not be without fear till I see him shipped, for he is much opposed, yet I hope he will not fail. Think the best of all and bear with patience what is wanting, and the Lord guide us all.

London, June 10
Anno 1620

Your loving friend,
ROBERT CUSHMAN

|36| I have been the larger in these things, and so shall crave leave in some like passages following (though in other things I shall labour to be more contract) that their children may see with what difficulties their fathers wrestled in going through these things in their first beginnings; and how God brought them along, notwithstanding all their weaknesses and infirmities. As also that some use may be made hereof in after times by others in such like weighty employments. And herewith I will end this chapter.

[2] He was a minister (Bradford). But he did not sail.

CHAPTER VII

Of their Departure from Leyden, and other things thereabout; with their Arrival at Southampton, where they all met together and took in their Provisions

At length, after much travel and these debates, all things were got ready and provided. A small ship [1] was bought and fitted in Holland, which was intended as to serve to help to transport them, so to stay in the country and attend upon fishing and such other affairs as might be for the good and benefit of the colony when they came there. Another was hired at London, of burthen about 9 score,[2] and all other things got in readiness. So being ready to depart, they had a day of solemn humiliation, their pastor taking his text from Ezra viii.21: "And there at the river, by Ahava, I proclaimed a fast, that we might humble ourselves before our God, and seek of him a right way for us, and for our children, and for all our substance." Upon which he spent a good part of the day very profitably and suitable to their present occasion; the rest of the time was spent in pouring [3] out prayers to the Lord with great fervency, mixed with abundance of tears. And the time being come that they must depart, they were accompanied with most of their brethren out of the city, unto a town sundry miles off called Delftshaven, where the ship lay ready to receive them. So they left that goodly and pleasant city which had been their resting place near twelve years; but they knew they were pilgrims,[4] and looked not much on those things, but lift up their eyes to the heavens, their dearest country, and quieted their spirits. |37|

When they came to the place they found the ship and all

[1] Of some 60 tun (Bradford). This was the *Speedwell.*

[2] The *Mayflower,* 180 tons. See chap. viii note 1.

[3] Spelled *powering* by Bradford, which is the way *pour* was pronounced until the 19th century. "Mine eye powreth out tears unto God," says Job (xvi.20) in the Geneva Bible.

[4] Hebrews xi.13–16 (Bradford). It was owing to this passage, first printed in 1669, that the *Mayflower's* company came eventually to be called the Pilgrim Fathers. Albert Matthews's exhaustive history of the use of that term is in Colonial Society of Massachusetts *Publications* XVII (1915) 300–92.

things ready, and such of their friends as could not come with them followed after them, and sundry also came from Amsterdam to see them shipped and to take their leave of them. That night was spent with little sleep by the most, but with friendly entertainment and Christian discourse and other real expressions of true Christian love. The next day (the wind being fair) they went aboard and their friends with them, where truly doleful was the sight of that sad and mournful parting, to see what sighs and sobs and prayers did sound amongst them, what tears did gush from every eye, and pithy speeches pierced each heart; that sundry of the Dutch strangers that stood on the quay as spectators could not refrain from tears. Yet comfortable and sweet it was to see such lively and true expressions of dear and unfeigned love. But the tide, which stays for no man, calling them away that were thus loath to depart, their reverend pastor falling down on his knees (and they all with him) with watery cheeks commended them with most fervent prayers to the Lord and His blessing. And then with mutual embraces and many tears they took their leaves one of another, which proved to be the last leave to many of them.

Thus hoising sail,[5] with a prosperous wind they came in short time to Southampton, where they found the bigger ship come from London, lying ready, with all the rest of their company. After a joyful welcome and mutual congratulations, with other friendly entertainments, they fell to parley about their business, how to dispatch with the best expedition; as also with their agents about the alteration of the conditions. Mr. Carver pleaded he was employed here at Hampton, and knew not well what the other had done at London; Mr. Cushman answered he had done nothing but what he was urged to, partly by the grounds of equity and more especially by necessity, otherwise all had been dashed and many undone. And in the beginning he acquainted his fellow agents herewith, who consented unto him and left it to him to execute, and to receive the money at London and send it down to them at Hampton, where they made the provisions. The which he accordingly did, though it was against his mind and some of the merchants, that they were there made. And for giv-

[5] This was about 22 of July (Bradford), 1620.

ing them notice at Leyden of this change, he could not well in regard of the shortness of the time; again, he knew it would trouble them and hinder the business, which was already delayed overlong in regard of the season of the year, which he feared they would find to their cost.

Mr. Weston, likewise, came up from London to see them dispatched and to have the conditions confirmed. But they refused and answered him that he knew right well that these were not according to the first agreement, neither could they yield to them without the consent of the rest that were behind. And indeed they had special charge when they came away, from the chief of those that were behind, not to do it. At which he was much offended and told them they must then look to stand on their own legs. So he returned in displeasure and this was the first ground of discontent between them. And whereas there wanted well near £100 to clear things at their going away, he would not take order to disburse a penny but let them shift as they could. |38| So they were forced to sell off some of their provisions to stop this gap, which was some three or four-score firkins of butter,[6] which commodity they might best spare, having provided too large a quantity of that kind. Then they writ a letter to the merchants and Adventurers about the differences concerning the conditions, as followeth:

Southampton, Aug. 3, Anno 1620.

Beloved Friends,

Sorry we are that there should be occasion of writing at all unto you, partly because we ever expected to see the most of you here, but especially because there should any difference at all be conceived between us. But seeing it falleth out that we cannot confer together, we think it meet (though briefly) to show you the just cause and reason of our differing from those articles last made by Robert Cushman, without our commission or knowledge. And though he might propound good ends to himself, yet it no way justifies his doing it. Our main difference is in the fifth and ninth articles concerning the dividing or holding of house and lands; the enjoying whereof, some of yourselves well know, was one special motive amongst many other, to provoke us to go. This was thought so

[6] This would mean 3360 to 4720 lb. of butter.

reasonable that when the greatest of you in adventure (whom we have much cause to respect) when he propounded conditions to us freely of his own accord, he set this down for one. A copy whereof we have sent unto you, with some additions then added by us; which being liked on both sides, and a day set for the payment of moneys, those of Holland paid in theirs. After that, Robert Cushman, Mr. Peirce, and Mr. Martin, brought them into a better form and writ them in a book now extant; and upon Robert's showing them and delivering Mr. Mullins a copy thereof under his hand (which we have) he paid in his money. And we of Holland had never seen other before our coming to Hampton, but only as one got for himself a private copy of them. Upon sight whereof we manifested utter dislike but had put off our estates and were ready to come, and therefore was too late to reject the voyage.

Judge therefore, we beseech you, indifferently of things, and if a fault have been committed, lay it where it is, and not upon us who have more cause to stand for the one than you have for the other. We never gave Robert Cushman commission to make any one article for us, but only sent him to receive moneys upon articles before agreed on, and to further the provisions till John Carver came, and to assist him in it. Yet since you conceive yourselves wronged as well as we, we thought meet to add a branch to the end of our ninth article, as will almost heal that wound of itself, which you conceive to be in it. But that it may appear to all men that we are not lovers of ourselves only, but desire also the good and enriching of our friends who have adventured your moneys with our persons, we have added our last article to the rest, promising you again by letters in the behalf of the whole company, that if large profits should not arise within the seven years, that we will continue together longer with you, if the Lord give a blessing.[7] This we hope is sufficient to satisfy any in this case, especially friends; since we are assured that if the whole charge was divided into four parts, three of them will not stand upon it, neither do regard it, etc.

We are in such a strait at present, as we are forced to sell away £60 worth of our provisions to clear the haven, and withal to put ourselves upon great extremities, scarce having any butter, no oil, not a sole to mend a shoe, |39| nor every man a sword to his side, wanting many muskets, much armour, etc. And yet we are willing

[7] It was well for them that this was not accepted (Bradford). Several members of the Leyden congregation who did not emigrate contributed to the "adventure" or investment; hence this lengthy explanation.

to expose ourselves to such eminent dangers as are like to ensue, and trust to the good providence of God, rather than His name and truth should be evil spoken of, for us. Thus saluting all of you in love, and beseeching the Lord to give a blessing to our endeavour, and keep all our hearts in the bonds of peace and love, we take leave and rest,

Aug. 3, 1620 Yours, etc.

It was subscribed with many names of the chiefest of the company.

At their parting Mr. Robinson writ a letter to the whole company; which though it hath already been printed,[8] yet I thought good here likewise to insert it.[9] As also a brief letter writ at the same time to Mr. Carver, in which the tender love and godly care of a true pastor appears.

|41| All things being now ready, and every business dispatched, the company was called together and this letter read amongst them, which had good acceptation with all, and after fruit with many. Then they ordered and distributed their company for either ship, as they conceived for the best; and chose a Governor and two or three assistants for each ship, to order the people by the way, and see to the disposing of their provisions and such like affairs. All which was not only with the liking of the masters of the ships but according to their desires. Which being done, they set sail from thence about the 5th of August. But what befell them further upon the coast of England will appear in the next chapter.

[8] In the extracts from Bradford's and Winslow's Journals, published in London 1622 and generally called *Mourt's Relation.*

[9] This letter and the following will be found in Appendix IV, below.

CHAPTER VIII

Of the Troubles that befell them on the Coast, and at Sea, being forced after much Trouble to leave one of their Ships and some of their Company behind them. |42|

Being thus put to sea, they had not gone far but Mr. Reynolds, the master of the lesser ship, complained that he found his ship so leaky as he durst not put further to sea till she was mended. So the master of the bigger ship (called Mr. Jones) [1] being consulted with, they both resolved to put into Dartmouth and have her there searched and mended, which accordingly was done, to their great charge and loss of time and a fair wind. She was here thoroughly searched from stem to stern, some leaks were found and mended, and now it was conceived by the workmen and all, that she was sufficient, and they might proceed without either fear or danger. So with good hopes from hence, they put to sea again,

[1] Christopher Jones, master of the *Mayflower* (spelled *Jonas* by Bradford). A native of Rotherhithe, he had for several years been a quarter owner of the *Mayflower* as well as her master. The basic research on the *Mayflower* by R. G. Marsden is in *English Historical Review* XIX (1904) pp. 669–80. There are no pictures or plans of her extant, but Mr. R. C. Anderson, a learned marine archeologist, has made a very careful model of a ship of the period of her tonnage (180), which is in Pilgrim Hall, Plymouth. It is described, and the plans illustrated, in *Mariner's Mirror* XII (1926) p. 260. "A *Mayflower* Model" as Mr. Anderson properly calls it, is to the scale of 90 ft. over all, 64-ft. keel, 26-ft. beam and 11-ft. depth of hold; her sails were fore and main courses, fore and main topsails, spritsail on the bowsprit (these five being square), and a lateen mizzen. She was steered with a whipstaff attached to the tiller, and armed with 12 cannon—8 "minions" and 4 "sakers." The actual *Mayflower* of the Pilgrims (and it was a common ship's name) according to Mr. Marsden was at least 12 years old in 1620 and had been employed largely in the wine trade with Bordeaux and La Rochelle. The ullage from wine casks is known to have neutralized the filth that the sailors of that day left in the bilge and to have made a "sweet ship," which may explain why the *Mayflower* got all but one of her passengers across alive, despite a late season and tempestuous voyage. The best book on her and the voyage is Capt. W. Sears Nickerson *Land Ho!—1620* (1931). The Rev. J. Rendel Harris, the gentleman who argues for an Egyptian discovery of America, in an extraordinary pair of books *The Finding of the "Mayflower"* and *The Last of the "Mayflower"* (1920) demonstrates by a series of wild syllogisms that the *Mayflower's* bones came to their final resting place as the roof timbers of an old barn at Jordans, Buckinghamshire, which is preserved by the Society of Friends.

conceiving they should go comfortably on, not looking for any more lets of this kind; but it fell out otherwise. For after they were gone to sea again above 100 leagues without the Lands End, holding company together all this while, the master of the small ship complained his ship was so leaky as he must bear up or sink at sea, for they could scarce free her with much pumping. So they came to consultation again, and resolved both ships to bear up back again and put into Plymouth, which accordingly was done. But no special leak could be found, but it was judged to be the general weakness of the ship, and that she would not prove sufficient for the voyage. Upon which it was resolved to dismiss her and part of the company, and proceed with the other ship. The which (though it was grievous and caused great discouragement) was put into execution.

So after they had took out such provision as the other ship could well stow, and concluded both what number and what persons to send back, they made another sad parting; the one ship going back for London and the other was to proceed on her voyage. Those that went back were for the most part such as were willing so to do, either out of some discontent or fear they conceived of the ill success of the voyage, seeing so many crosses befall, and the year time so far spent. But others, in regard of their own weakness and charge of many young children were thought least useful and most unfit to bear the brunt of this hard adventure; unto which work of God, and judgment of their brethren, they were contented to submit. And thus, like Gideon's army, this small number was divided, as if the Lord by this work of His providence thought these few too many for the great work He had to do.[2]

But here by the way let me show how afterward it was found that the leakiness of this ship was partly by being over-masted and too much pressed with sails; for after she was sold and put into her old trim, she made many voyages and performed her service very sufficiently, to the great profit of her owners.[3] But

[2] Judges vii.4: "And the Lord said unto Gideon, The people are yet too many; bring them down to the water, . . . and it shall be that of whom I say unto thee, This shall go with thee, the same shall go with thee. . . ."

[3] This makes sense. Any wooden vessel, if overmasted and given more sail than she can carry, will labor in a seaway, open her seams and spew her oakum.

more especially, by the cunning and deceit of the master and his company, who were hired to stay a whole year in the country, and now fancying dislike and fearing want of victuals, they plotted this stratagem to free themselves; as afterwards was known and by some of them confessed. For they apprehended that the greater ship (being of force and in whom most of the provisions were stowed) she would retain enough for herself, whatsoever became of them or the passengers. And indeed such speeches had been cast out by some of them. And yet, besides other encouragements, the chief of them that came from Leyden went in this ship to give the master content. But so strong was self-love and his fears, as he forgot all duty and |43| former kindnesses, and dealt thus falsely with them, though he pretended otherwise.

Amongst those that returned was Mr. Cushman and his family, whose heart and courage was gone from them before (as it seems) though his body was with them till now he departed; as may appear by a passionate letter he writ to a friend in London from Dartmouth whilst the ship lay there a-mending. The which, besides the expressions of his own fears, it shows much of the providence of God working for their good beyond man's expectation, and other things concerning their condition in these straits. I will here relate it. And though it discover some infirmities in him (as who under temptation is free) yet after this he continued to be a special instrument for their good, and to do the offices of a loving friend and faithful brother unto them, and partaker of much comfort with them. The letter is as followeth.

To his loving friend Edward Southworth at Heneage House in the Duke's Place,[4] *these, etc.*

Dartmouth, Aug. 17.

LOVING FRIEND, my most kind remembrance to you and your wife, with loving E. M. etc., whom in this world I never look to see again. For besides the eminent dangers of this voyage, which are no less than deadly, an infirmity of body hath seized me, which will not in

[4] Edward Southworth, a member of the Leyden congregation who did not emigrate, died in 1623; his widow became Bradford's second wife. Heneage House, Duke's Place, was a sort of rabbit warren of tenements in Aldgate where many dissenters lived. Ironmonger's Hall, to which Weston belonged, was near by. Massachusetts Historical Society *Proceedings* LXI 55–63.

all likelihood leave me till death. What to call it I know not, but it is a bundle of lead, as it were, crushing my heart more and more these fourteen days; as that although I do the actions of a living man, yet I am but as dead, but the will of God be done.[5]

Our pinnace will not cease leaking, else I think we had been half-way at Virginia. Our voyage hither hath been as full of crosses as ourselves have been of crookedness. We put in here to trim her; and I think, as others also, if we had stayed at sea but three or four hours more, she would have sunk right down. And though she was twice trimmed at Hampton, yet now she is as open and leaky as a sieve; and there was a board a man might have pulled off with his fingers, two foot long, where the water came in as at a mole hole. We lay at Hampton seven days in fair weather, waiting for her, and now we lie here waiting for her in as fair a wind as can blow, and so have done these four days, and are like to lie four more, and by that time the wind will happily turn as it did at Hampton. Our victuals will be half eaten up, I think, before we go from the coast of England, and if our voyage last long, we shall not have a month's victuals when we come in the country.

Near £700 hath been bestowed at Hampton, upon what I know not; Mr. Martin[6] saith he neither can nor will give any account of it, and if he be called upon for accounts, he crieth out of unthankfulness for his pains and care, that we are suspicious of him, and flings away, and will end nothing. Also he so insulteth over our poor people, with such scorn and contempt, as if they were not good enough to wipe his shoes. It would break your heart to see his dealing, and the mourning of our people; they complain to me, and alas! I can do nothing for them. If I speak to him, he flies in my face as mutinous, and saith no complaints shall be heard or received but by himself, and saith they are froward and waspish, discontented people, and I do ill to hear them. There are others that would lose all they have put in, or make satisfaction for what they have had, that they might depart; but he will not hear them, nor suffer them to go ashore, lest they should run away. The sailors also are so offended at his ignorant boldness in meddling and controlling in things he knows not what belongs to, as that some threaten to mischief him; others say they will leave the ship and go their way. But at the best

[5] Cushman nevertheless managed to make a round voyage to Plymouth in 1621 and to live until 1625.

[6] He [Christopher Martin] was governor in the bigger ship and Mr. Cushman assistant (Bradford).

this cometh of it, that he makes himself a scorn and laughing stock unto them.

As for Mr. Weston, except grace do greatly sway him, he will hate us ten times more than ever he loved us, for not confirming the conditions. But now, since some pinches have taken them, they begin to revile the truth and say Mr. Robinson was in the fault who charged them never to consent to those conditions, nor choose me into office; but indeed appointed them to choose them they did choose.[7] But he and they will rue too late, they may |44| now see, and all be ashamed when it is too late, that they were so ignorant; yea and so inordinate in their courses. I am sure as they were resolved not to seal those conditions, I was not so resolute at Hampton to have left the whole business, except they would seal them, and better the voyage to have been broken off then than to have brought such misery to ourselves, dishonour to God and detriment to our loving friends, as now it is like to do. Four or five of the chief of them which came from Leyden, came resolved never to go on those conditions. And Mr. Martin, he said he never received no money on those conditions; he was not beholden to the merchants for a pin, they were bloodsuckers, and I know not what. Simple man, he indeed never made any conditions with the merchants, nor ever spake with them. But did all that money fly to Hampton, or was it his own? Who will go and lay out money so rashly and lavishly as he did, and never know how he comes by it or on what conditions? Secondly, I told him of the alteration long ago and he was content, but now he domineers and said I had betrayed them into the hands of slaves; he is not beholden to them, he can set out two ships himself to a voyage. When, good man? He hath but £50 in and if he should give up his accounts he would not have a penny left him, as I am persuaded, etc.[8]

Friend, if ever we make a plantation, God works a miracle, especially considering how scant we shall be of victuals, and most of all ununited amongst ourselves and devoid of good tutors and regiment.[9] Violence will break all. Where is the meek and humble spirit of Moses? and of Nehemiah who re-edified the walls of Jerusalem, and the state of Israel? Is not the sound of Rehoboam's brags daily here amongst us? [1] Have not the philosophers and all wise men observed

[7] I think he was deceived in these things (Bradford).

[8] This was found true afterward (Bradford).

[9] I.e., leaders and discipline.

[1] "My father . . . chastised you with whips . . . I will chastise you with scorpions." 1 Kings xii.14.

that, even in settled commonwealths, violent governors bring either themselves or people or both to ruin? How much more in the raising of commonwealths, when the mortar is yet scarce tempered that should bind the walls! If I should write to you of all things which promiscuously forerun our ruin, I should over-charge my weak head and grieve your tender heart. Only this, I pray you prepare for evil tidings of us every day. But pray for us instantly, it may be the Lord will be yet entreated one way or other to make for us. I see not in reason how we shall escape even the gasping of hunger-starved persons; but God can do much, and His will be done. It is better for me to die than now for me to bear it, which I do daily and expect it hourly, having received the sentence of death both within me and without me. Poor William Ring and myself do strive who shall be meat first for the fishes; but we look for a glorious resurrection, knowing Christ Jesus after the flesh no more, but looking unto the joy that is before us, we will endure all these things and account them light in comparison of that joy we hope for.

Remember me in all love to our friends as if I named them, whose prayers I desire earnestly and wish again to see, but not till I can with more comfort look them in the face. The Lord give us that true comfort which none can take from us. I had a desire to make a brief relation of our estate to some friend. I doubt not but your wisdom will teach you seasonably to utter things as hereafter you shall be called to it. That which I have written is true, and many things more which I have forborn. I write it as upon my life, and last confession in England. What is of use to be spoken |45| of presently, you may speak of it; and what is fit to conceal, conceal. Pass by my weak manner, for my head is weak, and my body feeble. The Lord make me strong in Him, and keep both you and yours.

Your loving friend,

Dartmouth, Aug. 17. 1620 ROBERT CUSHMAN

These being his conceptions and fears at Dartmouth, they must needs be much stronger now at Plymouth.

CHAPTER IX

Of their Voyage, and how they Passed the Sea; and of their Safe Arrival at Cape Cod

September 6. These troubles being blown over, and now all being compact together in one ship, they put to sea again with a prosperous wind, which continued divers days together, which was some encouragement unto them; yet, according to the usual manner, many were afflicted with seasickness. And I may not omit here a special work of God's providence. There was a proud and very profane young man, one of the seamen, of a lusty, able body, which made him the more haughty; he would alway be contemning the poor people in their sickness and cursing them daily with grievous execrations; and did not let to tell them that he hoped to help to cast half of them overboard before they came to their journey's end, and to make merry with what they had; and if he were by any gently reproved, he would curse and swear most bitterly. But it pleased God before they came half seas over, to smite this young man with a grievous disease, of which he died in a desperate manner, and so was himself the first that was thrown overboard. Thus his curses light on his own head, and it was an astonishment to all his fellows for they noted it to be the just hand of God upon him.

After they had enjoyed fair winds and weather for a season, they were encountered many times with cross winds and met with many fierce storms with which the ship was shroudly[1] shaken, and her upper works made very leaky; and one of the main beams in the midships was bowed and cracked, which put them in some fear that the ship could not be able to perform the voyage. So some of the chief of the company, perceiving the mariners to fear the sufficiency of the ship as appeared by their mutterings, they entered into serious consultation with the master and other officers of the ship, to consider in time of the danger, and rather to return than to cast themselves into a desperate and inevitable peril. And truly there was great distraction and difference of opinion amongst the mariners themselves; fain would they do what could be done for their wages' sake (being

[1] An old form of *shrewdly* in its original meaning *wickedly*.

now near half the seas over) and on the other hand they were loath to hazard their lives too desperately. But in examining of all opinions, the master and others affirmed they knew the ship to be strong and firm under water; and for the buckling of the main beam, there was a great iron screw the passengers brought out of Holland, which would raise the beam into his place; the which being done, the carpenter and master affirmed that with a post put under it, set firm in the lower deck and otherways bound, he would make it sufficient. And as for the decks and upper works, they would caulk them as well as they could, and though with the working of the ship they |46| would not long keep staunch, yet there would otherwise be no great danger, if they did not overpress her with sails. So they committed themselves to the will of God and resolved to proceed.

In sundry of these storms the winds were so fierce and the seas so high, as they could not bear a knot of sail, but were forced to hull [2] for divers days together. And in one of them, as they thus lay at hull in a mighty storm, a lusty [3] young man called John Howland, coming upon some occasion above the gratings was, with a seele [4] of the ship, thrown into sea; but it pleased God that he caught hold of the topsail halyards which hung overboard and ran out at length. Yet he held his hold (though he was sundry fathoms under water) till he was hauled up by the same rope to the brim of the water, and then with a boat hook and other means got into the ship again and his life saved. And though he was something ill with it, yet he lived many years after and became a profitable member both in church and commonwealth. In all this voyage there died but one of the passengers, which was William Butten, a youth, servant to Samuel Fuller, when they drew near the coast.

But to omit other things (that I may be brief) after long beating at sea they fell with that land which is called Cape Cod; [5] the which being made and certainly known to be it, they were not a

[2] To heave or lay-to under very short sail and drift with the wind.

[3] Lively, merry; no sexual connotation. Howland, a servant of Governor Carver, rose to be one of the leading men of the Colony.

[4] Roll or pitch.

[5] At daybreak 9/19 Nov. 1620, they sighted the Highlands of Cape Cod. Full discussion in W. Sears Nickerson *Land Ho!—1620* chap. iv.

little joyful. After some deliberation had amongst themselves and with the master of the ship, they tacked about and resolved to stand for the southward (the wind and weather being fair) to find some place about Hudson's River for their habitation.[6] But after they had sailed that course about half the day, they fell amongst dangerous shoals and roaring breakers, and they were so far entangled therewith as they conceived themselves in great danger; and the wind shrinking upon them withal, they resolved to bear up again for the Cape and thought themselves happy to get out of those dangers before night overtook them, as by God's good providence they did. And the next day [7] they got into the Cape Harbor [8] where they rid in safety.

A word or two by the way of this cape. It was thus first named

[6] This is the only direct statement in the *History* as to whither the *Mayflower* was bound. I see no reason to doubt its accuracy. It is borne out by Bradford's own journal in *Mourt's Relation* (see chap. x note 2, below): "We made our course south-southwest, purposing to go to a river ten leagues to the south of the Cape, but at night the wind being contrary, we put round again for the Bay of Cape Cod." Although the mouth of the Hudson is nearer 15 than 10 leagues south of the Cape in latitude, the Pilgrims' knowledge of New England geography was far from exact, and the Hudson was doubtless meant. The Virginia Company, which had granted the Peirce Patent which the Pilgrims brought with them, had a right to colonize up to lat. 41° N, which included Manhattan Island. The Dutch did not settle Manhattan (the famous $24 purchase) until 1626, although they claimed the region by virtue of Hudson's voyage in 1609; the English never admitted their claim, and the Pilgrims, who certainly had heard of the Hudson River and Long Island Sound from the several Dutch voyages thither before 1620, doubtless hoped to be first at that natural center for fur trade and fishing, and were glad to rely on their Patent from the Virginia Company both for local self-government and for protection from Dutch encroachment. John Pory, the Secretary of Virginia who visited Plymouth Colony in 1622 (see below, chap. xiii), reported that "their voyage was intended for Virginia." They carried letters, he says, from Sir Edwin Sandys and John Ferrar to Governor Sir George Yeardley recommending "that he should give them the best advice he could for trading in Hudson's River." Champlin Burrage *John Pory's Lost Description of Plymouth* (1918) p. 35. The theory that Master Jones of the *Mayflower* was bribed by the Dutch to set the Pilgrims ashore at a safe distance from Manhattan has a respectable antiquity but no basis in fact. No seaman who has weathered Cape Cod needs any better explanation than a head wind on unbuoyed Pollock Rip to explain why the *Mayflower* turned back.

[7] Nov. 11/21, 1620. Thus the *Mayflower's* passage from Plymouth took 65 days.

[8] Now Provincetown Harbor.

by Captain Gosnold and his company,[9] Anno 1602, and after by Captain Smith was called Cape James; but it retains the former name amongst seamen. Also, that point which first showed those dangerous shoals unto them they called Point Care, and Tucker's Terrour; but the French and Dutch to this day call it Malabar by reason of those perilous shoals and the losses they have suffered there.[1]

Being thus arrived in a good harbor, and brought safe to land, they fell upon their knees and blessed the God of Heaven [2] who had brought them over the vast and furious ocean, and delivered them from all the perils and miseries thereof, again to set their feet on the firm and stable earth, their proper element. And no marvel if they were thus joyful, seeing wise Seneca was so affected with sailing a few miles on the coast of his own Italy, as he affirmed, that he had rather remain twenty years on his way by land than pass by sea to any place in a short time, so tedious and dreadful was the same unto him.[3]

But here I cannot but stay and make a pause, and stand half amazed at this poor people's present condition; and so I think will the reader, too, when he well considers |47| the same. Being thus passed the vast ocean, and a sea of troubles before in their preparation (as may be remembered by that which went before), they had now no friends to welcome them nor inns to entertain or refresh their weatherbeaten bodies; no houses or much less towns to repair to, to seek for succour. It is recorded in Scripture [4] as a mercy to the Apostle and his shipwrecked company,

[9] Because they took much of that fish there (Bradford).

[1] The location of these places is discussed by W. Sears Nickerson chap. iii. He believes that the original Point Care and Tucker's Terror (so named by Gosnold) and Mallebarre (named by Champlain) were at Nauset Harbor. The name Mallebarre later became transferred to Monomoy, which is called Cape Malabar in the *Atlantic Neptune* (1774), Anthony Finley's *New General Atlas* (1832), U. S. Coast Survey Chart No. 11 (1860), *Black's General Atlas American Edition* (1879), and E. G. Perry *A Trip Around Cape Cod* (1898) p. 206. Thereafter it drops out, except as a name for John Alden's yachts.

[2] Daniel ii.19.

[3] Epistle 53 (Bradford). The sentence is in Seneca *ad Lucilium Epistulae Morales* liii §5: *Et ego quocumque navigare debuero, vicesimo anno perveniam.*

[4] Acts xxviii (Bradford); verse 2.

that the barbarians showed them no small kindness in refreshing them, but these savage barbarians, when they met with them (as after will appear) were readier to fill their sides full of arrows than otherwise. And for the season it was winter, and they that know the winters of that country know them to be sharp and violent, and subject to cruel and fierce storms, dangerous to travel to known places, much more to search an unknown coast. Besides, what could they see but a hideous and desolate wilderness, full of wild beasts and wild men—and what multitudes there might be of them they knew not. Neither could they, as it were, go up to the top of Pisgah to view from this wilderness a more goodly country to feed their hopes; for which way soever they turned their eyes (save upward to the heavens) they could have little solace or content in respect of any outward objects. For summer being done, all things stand upon them with a weather-beaten face, and the whole country, full of woods and thickets, represented a wild and savage hue. If they looked behind them, there was the mighty ocean which they had passed and was now as a main bar and gulf to separate them from all the civil parts of the world. If it be said they had a ship to succour them, it is true; but what heard they daily from the master and company? But that with speed they should look out a place (with their shallop) where they would be, at some near distance; for the season was such as he would not stir from thence till a safe harbor was discovered by them, where they would be, and he might go without danger; and that victuals consumed apace but he must and would keep sufficient for themselves and their return. Yea, it was muttered by some that if they got not a place in time, they would turn them and their goods ashore and leave them. Let it also be considered what weak hopes of supply and succour they left behind them, that might bear up their minds in this sad condition and trials they were under; and they could not but be very small. It is true, indeed, the affections and love of their brethren at Leyden was cordial and entire towards them, but they had little power to help them or themselves; and how the case stood between them and the merchants at their coming away hath already been declared.

What could now sustain them but the Spirit of God and His

grace? May not and ought not the children of these fathers rightly say: "Our fathers were Englishmen which came over this great ocean, and were ready to perish in this wilderness; but they cried unto the Lord, and He heard their voice and looked on their adversity," [5] etc. "Let them therefore praise the Lord, because He is good: and His mercies endure forever." "Yea, let them which have been redeemed of the Lord, shew how He hath delivered them from the hand of the oppressor. When they wandered in the desert wilderness out of the way, and found no city to dwell in, both hungry and thirsty, their soul was overwhelmed in them. Let them confess before the Lord His lovingkindness and His wonderful works before the sons of men." [6]

[5] Deuteronomy xxvi.5, 7 (Bradford).
[6] Psalm cvii.1–5, 8 (Bradford).

CHAPTER X

Showing How they Sought out a place of Habitation; and What Befell them Thereabout |48|

Being thus arrived at Cape Cod the 11th of November, and necessity calling them to look out a place for habitation (as well as the master's and mariners' importunity); they having brought a large shallop with them out of England, stowed in quarters in the ship, they now got her out and set their carpenters to work to trim her up; but being much bruised and shattered in the ship with foul weather, they saw she would be long in mending. Whereupon a few of them tendered themselves to go by land and discover those nearest places, whilst the shallop was in mending; and the rather because as they went into that harbor there seemed to be an opening some two or three leagues off, which the master judged to be a river.[1] It was conceived there might be some danger in the attempt, yet seeing them resolute, they were permitted to go, being sixteen of them well armed under the conduct of Captain Standish,[2] having such instructions given them as was thought meet.

They set forth the 15th of November; and when they had marched about the space of a mile by the seaside, they espied five or six persons with a dog coming towards them, who were savages; but they fled from them and ran up into the woods, and

[1] Looking south from Provincetown Harbor where the Pilgrims then were, the high land near Plymouth looks like an island on clear days, suggesting that there is a river or arm of the sea between it and Cape Cod.

[2] Myles Standish, scion of an old Lancashire family, was now about 36 years old. A soldier of fortune in the wars of the Netherlands, he was engaged either by Weston or the Carver-Cushman committee to go with the colonists and handle their military affairs. Though a "stranger" to the Leyden Pilgrims, Standish, like John Alden the hired cooper, became one of their staunchest supporters. Bradford, Hopkins and Tilley accompanied Standish. More details on these exploring expeditions will be found in the extracts from Bradford's and Winslow's Journals which were published in London in 1622 as *A Relation or Iournall of the beginning and proceedings of the English Plantation setled at Plimoth in New England, by certain English Aduenturers both Merchants and others.* As the authors' names did not appear, and the preface was signed "G. Mourt," this is generally called *Mourt's Relation* (although who Mourt was, nobody knows). Several times reprinted, it is included in Alexander Young *Chronicles of the Pilgrim Fathers* (1841).

the English followed them, partly to see if they could speak with them, and partly to discover if there might not be more of them lying in ambush. But the Indians seeing themselves thus followed, they again forsook the woods and ran away on the sands as hard as they could, so as they could not come near them but followed them by the track of their feet sundry miles and saw that they had come the same way. So, night coming on, they made their rendezvous and set out their sentinels, and rested in quiet that night; and the next morning followed their track till they had headed a great creek and so left the sands, and turned another way into the woods. But they still followed them by guess, hoping to find their dwellings; but they soon lost both them and themselves, falling into such thickets as were ready to tear their clothes and armor in pieces; but were most distressed for want of drink. But at length they found water and refreshed themselves, being the first New England water they drunk of, and was now in great thirst as pleasant unto them as wine or beer had been in foretimes.

Afterwards they directed their course to come to the other |49| shore, for they knew it was a neck of land they were to cross over, and so at length got to the seaside and marched to this supposed river, and by the way found a pond [3] of clear, fresh water, and shortly after a good quantity of clear ground where the Indians had formerly set corn, and some of their graves. And proceeding further they saw new stubble where corn had been set the same year; also they found where lately a house had been, where some planks and a great kettle was remaining, and heaps of sand newly paddled with their hands. Which, they digging up, found in them divers fair Indian baskets filled with corn, and some in ears, fair and good, of divers colours, which seemed to them a very goodly sight (having never seen any such before). This was near the place of that supposed river they came to seek, unto which they went and found it to open itself into two arms with a high cliff of sand in the entrance [4] but more like to be

[3] The pond that gives its name to Pond Village, Truro.

[4] Pamet River, a salt creek that almost bisects the Cape in Truro. The place where they found the corn is still called Corn Hill. It runs along the Bay side, just north of Little Pamet River.

creeks of salt water than any fresh, for aught they saw; and that there was good harborage for their shallop, leaving it further to be discovered by their shallop, when she was ready. So, their time limited them being expired, they returned to the ship lest they should be in fear of their safety; and took with them part of the corn and buried up the rest. And so, like the men from Eshcol, carried with them of the fruits of the land and showed their brethren; [5] of which, and their return, they were marvelously glad and their hearts encouraged.

After this, the shallop being got ready, they set out again for the better discovery of this place, and the master of the ship desired to go himself. So there went some thirty men but found it to be no harbor for ships but only for boats.[6] There was also found two of their houses covered with mats, and sundry of their implements in them, but the people were run away and could not be seen. Also there was found more of their corn and of their beans of various colours; the corn and beans they brought away, purposing to give them full satisfaction when they should meet with any of them as, about some six months afterward they did, to their good content.

And here is to be noted a special providence of God, and a great mercy to this poor people, that here they got seed to plant them corn the next year, or else they might have starved, for they had none nor any likelihood to get any |50| till the season had been past, as the sequel did manifest. Neither is it likely they had had this, if the first voyage had not been made, for the ground was now all covered with snow and hard frozen; but the Lord is never wanting unto His in their greatest needs; let His holy name have all the praise.

[5] Numbers xiii.23–6.

[6] This second exploring expedition, which started by boat, 28 Nov., made for the mouth of the Pamet River (later called Cold Harbor), which still is good for boats only. Readers interested in further details may profitably consult *Mourt's Relation*, the 1865 edition of which, edited by Henry Martyn Dexter, has an excellent map with details of the routes. This second expedition ranged up and down the valleys of the Pamet and Little Pamet Rivers, and returned to Cape Cod Harbor on 30 Nov. by the shallop. The Indians who lived in this region were the Nauset; they built arborlike wigwams of boughs bent over and stuck in the ground at both ends, woven by smaller boughs into a stout frame and covered with woven mats or strips of bark. Descendants of the Nauset still survive in the village of Mashpee on Cape Cod.

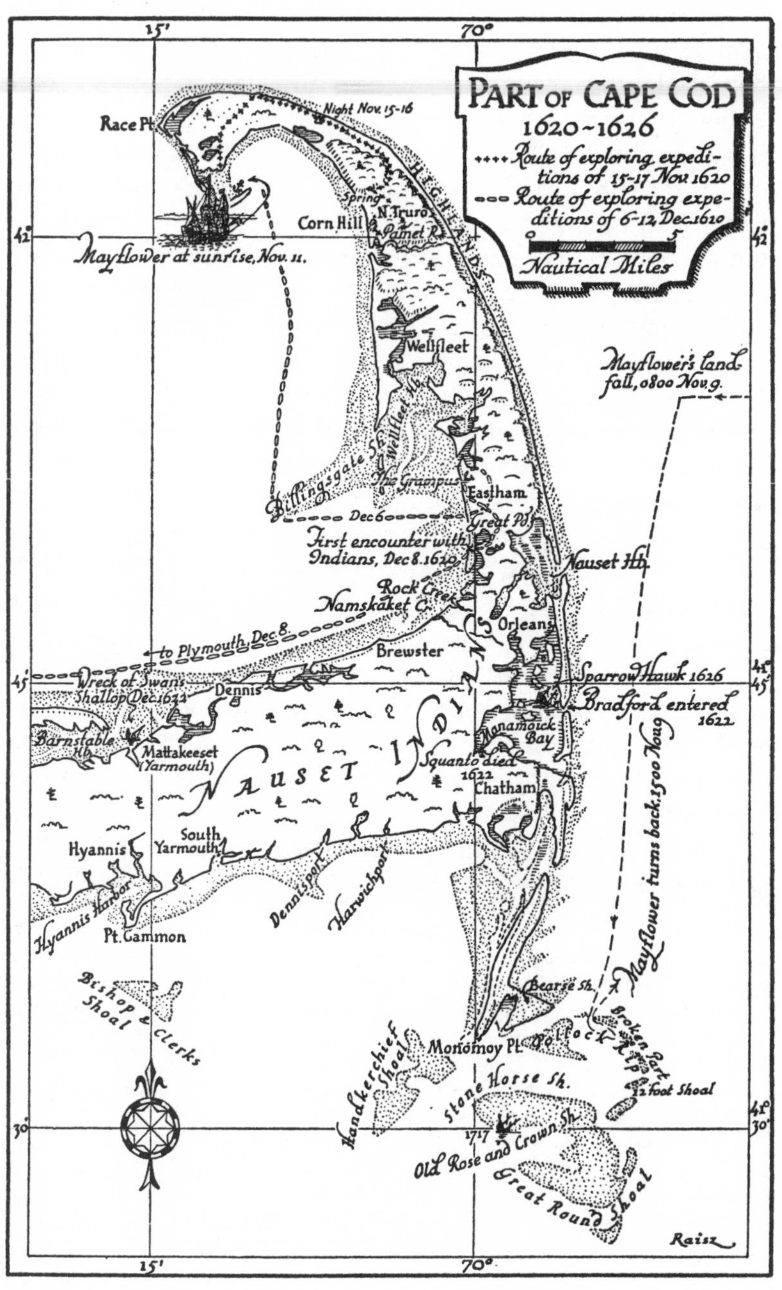

PART OF CAPE COD
1620~1626
Route of exploring expeditions of 15-17 Nov. 1620
Route of exploring expeditions of 6-12 Dec. 1620
Nautical Miles
Race Pt.
Night Nov. 15-16
HIGHLANDS
Spring
Corn Hill
N. Truro
Pamet R.
Mayflower at sunrise, Nov. 11.
Wellfleet
Mayflower's landfall, 0800 Nov. 9.
Billingsgate Sh.
Wellfleet Hb.
The Grampus
Eastham
Dec 6
Great Pd.
First encounter with Indians, Dec 8. 1620
Nauset Hb.
Rock Creek
Namskaket C.
Orleans
to Plymouth, Dec. 8.
Brewster
Wreck of Swan's Shallop Dec. 1622
Dennis
Sparrow Hawk 1626
Bradford entered 1622
Barnstable Hb.
Mattakeeset (Yarmouth)
NAUSET INDIANS
Monamoick Bay
Squanto died 1622
Chatham
Mayflower turns back. 1500 Nov. 9
Hyannis
South Yarmouth
Hyannis Harbor
Pt. Gammon
Dennisport
Harwichport
Bishop & Clerks Shoal
Bearse Sh.
Broken Part
Pollock Rip
Monomoy Pt.
Handkerchief Shoal
Stone Horse Sh.
12 foot Shoal
1717
Old Rose and Crown Sh.
Great Round Shoal
Raisz

The month of November being spent in these affairs, and much foul weather falling in, the 6th of December they sent out their shallop again with ten of their principal men[7] and some seamen, upon further discovery, intending to circulate that deep bay of Cape Cod. The weather was very cold and it froze so hard as the spray of the sea lighting on their coats, they were as if they had been glazed. Yet that night betimes they got down into the bottom of the bay, and as they drew near the shore they saw some ten or twelve Indians very busy about something. They landed about a league or two from them,[8] and had much ado to put ashore anywhere—it lay so full of flats. Being landed, it grew late and they made themselves a barricado with logs and boughs as well as they could in the time, and set out their sentinel and betook them to rest, and saw the smoke of the fire the savages made that night. When morning was come they divided their company, some to coast along the shore in the boat, and the rest marched through the woods to see the land, if any fit place might be for their dwelling. They came also to the place where they saw the Indians the night before, and found they had been cutting up a great fish like a grampus,[9] being some two inches thick of fat like a hog, some pieces whereof they had left by the way. And the shallop found two more of these fishes dead on the sands, a thing usual after storms in that place, by reason of the great flats of sand that lie off.

[7] The names of the ten (from *Mourt's Relation*) are Standish, Carver and his servant Howland, Bradford, Winslow, John and Edward Tilley, Richard Warren, Stephen Hopkins and his servant Doten; also the pilots, John Clarke and Robert Coppin, and the master gunner and three sailors, whose names are unknown. *Mourt's Relation* states that after the return of the second exploring expedition there was much debate on board the *Mayflower* whether they should settle at Pamet River, at Agawam (the later Ipswich), which looked good on Captain John Smith's map, at Cape Ann, or at Plymouth. On the strength of the recommendations of Coppin, who had been to Plymouth on a previous voyage and offered to pilot them thither, they decided to investigate that place before deciding.

[8] Somewhere in the present Eastham, at one of the several beaches (Kingsbury, Campground, Silver Spring), north of the Great Pond. The tide along this shore runs out very far. The barricade where they passed the night was (according to H. M. Dexter's researches) a few hundred yards northwest of the Great Pond.

[9] This was probably one of the blackfish (*Globicephala melæna*) that frequently get stranded on Cape Cod.

So they ranged up and down all that day, but found no people, nor any place they liked. When the sun grew low, they hasted out of the woods to meet with their shallop, to whom they made signs to come to them into a creek hard by,[1] the which they did at high water; of which they were very glad, for they had not seen each other all that day since the morning. So they made them a barricado as usually they did every night, with logs, stakes and thick pine boughs, the height of a man, leaving it open to leeward, partly to shelter them from the cold and wind (making their fire in the middle and lying round about it) and partly to defend them from any sudden assaults of the savages, if they should surround them; so being very weary, they betook them to rest. But about midnight |51| they heard a hideous and great cry, and their sentinel called "Arm! arm!" So they bestirred them and stood to their arms and shot off a couple of muskets, and then the noise ceased. They concluded it was a company of wolves or such like wild beasts, for one of the seamen told them he had often heard such a noise in Newfoundland.

So they rested till about five of the clock in the morning; for the tide, and their purpose to go from thence, made them be stirring betimes. So after prayer they prepared for breakfast, and it being day dawning it was thought best to be carrying things down to the boat. But some said it was not best to carry the arms down, others said they would be the readier, for they had lapped them up in their coats from the dew; but some three or four would not carry theirs till they went themselves. Yet as it fell out, the water being not high enough, they laid them down on the bank side and came up to breakfast.

But presently, all on the sudden, they heard a great and strange cry, which they knew to be the same voices they heard in the night, though they varied their notes; and one of their company being abroad came running in and cried, "Men, Indians! Indians!" And withal, their arrows came flying amongst them. Their men ran with all speed to recover their arms, as by the good providence of God they did. In the meantime, of those that were there

[1] The mouth of Herring River, in the present Eastham. The beach north of the river mouth, where the action about to be described took place, is still called First Encounter Beach.

ready, two muskets were discharged at them, and two more stood ready in the entrance of their rendezvous but were commanded not to shoot till they could take full aim at them. And the other two charged again with all speed, for there were only four had arms there, and defended the barricado, which was first assaulted. The cry of the Indians was dreadful, especially when they saw their men run out of the rendezvous toward the shallop to recover their arms, the Indians wheeling about upon them. But some running out with coats of mail on, and cutlasses in their hands, they soon got their arms and let fly amongst them and quickly stopped their violence. Yet there was a lusty man, and no less valiant, stood behind a tree within half a musket shot, and let his arrows fly at them; he was seen [to] shoot three arrows, which were all avoided. He stood three shots of a musket, till one taking full aim at him and made the bark or splinters of the tree fly about his ears, after which he gave an extraordinary shriek and away they went, all of them. They [2] left some to keep the shallop and followed them about a quarter of a mile and shouted once or twice, and shot off two or three pieces, and so returned. This they did that they might conceive that they were not |52| afraid of them or any way discouraged.

Thus it pleased God to vanquish their enemies and give them deliverance; and by His special providence so to dispose that not any one of them were either hurt or hit, though their arrows came close by them and on every side [of] them; and sundry of their coats, which hung up in the barricado, were shot through and through. Afterwards they gave God solemn thanks and praise for their deliverance, and gathered up a bundle of their arrows and sent them into England afterward by the master of the ship, and called that place the First Encounter.

From hence they departed and coasted all along but discerned no place likely for harbor; and therefore hasted to a place that their pilot (one Mr. Coppin who had been in the country before) did assure them was a good harbor, which he had been in, and they might fetch it before night; of which they were glad for it began to be foul weather.

After some hours' sailing it began to snow and rain, and about

[2] I.e., the English.

the middle of the afternoon the wind increased and the sea became very rough, and they broke their rudder, and it was as much as two men could do to steer her with a couple of oars. But their pilot bade them be of good cheer for he saw the harbor; but the storm increasing, and night drawing on, they bore what sail they could to get in, while they could see. But herewith they broke their mast in three pieces and their sail fell overboard in a very grown sea, so as they had like to have been cast away. Yet by God's mercy they recovered themselves, and having the flood [3] with them, struck into the harbor. But when it came to, the pilot was deceived in the place, and said the Lord be merciful unto them for his eyes never saw that place before; and he and the master's mate would have run her ashore in a cove full of breakers before the wind. But a lusty seaman which steered bade those which rowed, if they were men, about with her or else they were all cast away; the which they did with speed. So he bid them be of good cheer and row lustily, for there was a fair sound before them, and he doubted not but they should find one place or other where they might ride in safety. And though it was very dark and rained sore, yet in the end they got under the lee of a small island and remained there all that night in safety. But they knew not this to be an island till morning, but were divided in their minds; some would keep the boat for fear they might be amongst the Indians, others were so wet and cold they could not endure but got ashore, and with much ado got fire (all things being so

[3] I.e., the flood tide. The mean rise and fall of tide there is about 9 ft. Plymouth Bay, even today when well buoyed, is a bad place to enter in thick weather with a sea running and night coming on. For if you do not steer for the Gurnet, the high point that marks the northern entrance to Plymouth Bay, you run afoul of Browns Bank, which breaks all over in heavy weather or at low tide; in 1620 a part of this bank was dry at all tides. Coppin, I believe, mistook the Gurnet for Saquish Head; and Saquish for Goose Point; steering between them so as to enter the harbor, he was unnerved by seeing the breakers in Saquish Cove. Mr. Gershom Bradford, late of the U. S. Hydrographic Survey, has a different interpretation: that the storm blew from the NE, not the SE, that the shallop clung to the shoreline and worked through the boat channel between Browns Bank and Long Beach, and that the cove full of breakers was Warrens Cove east of Long Beach. In either case, it is clear that the rowers, encouraged by the "lusty seaman" at the steering oar, managed to weather Saquish Head, behind which they found shelter and good anchorage late in the night of Friday 8 Dec. 1620. They spent Saturday and Sunday 9 and 10 Dec. on Clarks Island, and made the famous "landing" on the 11th.

wet); and the rest were glad to come to them, for after midnight the wind shifted to the |53| northwest and it froze hard.

But though this had been a day and night of much trouble and danger unto them, yet God gave them a morning of comfort and refreshing (as usually He doth to His children) for the next day was a fair, sunshining day, and they found themselves to be on an island secure from the Indians, where they might dry their stuff, fix their pieces and rest themselves; and gave God thanks for His mercies in their manifold deliverances. And this being the last day of the week, they prepared there to keep the Sabbath.

On Monday they sounded the harbor and found it fit for shipping, and marched into the land and found divers cornfields and little running brooks, a place (as they supposed) fit for situation.[4] At least it was the best they could find, and the season and their present necessity made them glad to accept of it. So they returned to their ship again with this news to the rest of their people, which did much comfort their hearts.

On the 15th of December they weighed anchor to go to the place they had discovered, and came within two leagues of it, but were fain to bear up again; but the 16th day, the wind came fair, and they arrived safe in this harbor. And afterwards took better view of the place, and resolved where to pitch their dwelling; and the 25th day began to erect the first house for common use to receive them and their goods.[5]

[4] Here is the only contemporary authority for the "Landing of the Pilgrims on Plymouth Rock" on Monday, 11/21 Dec. 1620. It is clear that the landing took place from the shallop, not the *Mayflower*, which was then moored in Provincetown Harbor; that no women were involved in it, and no Indians or anyone else were on the receiving end. Nor is it clear that they landed on the large boulder since called Plymouth Rock. That boulder was identified in 1741 by Elder John Faunce, aged 95, as the "place where the forefathers landed," and although he probably only meant to say that they used it as a landing place, for it would have been very convenient for that purpose at half tide, everyone seems to have assumed that they "first" landed there. The exploring party may have landed anywhere between Captain's Hill and the Rock.

[5] *Mourt's Relation* p. 23 says that after the *Mayflower's* arrival in Plymouth Bay on 16/26 Dec. the men explored the bay again and debated whether to settle at Plymouth, the mouth of Jones River (the present Kingston) or on Clark's Island. They decided on the first because much of the land was already cleared and a fort on the hill—now Burial Hill—could command the surrounding country; and because "a very sweet brook"—the Town Brook—"runs under the hillside."

THE SECOND BOOK

The rest of this history (if God give me life and opportunity) I shall, for brevity's sake, handle by way of annals, noting only the heads of principal things, and passages as they fell in order of time, and may seem to be profitable to know or to make use of. And this may be as the Second Book.[1]

[1] I have added chapter numbers for the reader's convenience (Bradford started to do so but crossed out "the 11 chapter"); and I have broken up some of the longer chapters with subheadings in square brackets. It must be remembered that Bradford's year begins 25 March and extends through 24 March of the following year; and he often extends his narrative into the following summer before starting another chapter.

CHAPTER XI

The Remainder of Anno 1620
[The Mayflower Compact]

I shall a little return back, and begin with a combination made by them before they came ashore; being the first foundation of their government in this place. Occasioned partly by the discontented and mutinous speeches that some of the strangers amongst them had let fall from them in the ship: That when they came ashore they would use their own liberty, for none had power to command them, the patent they had being for Virginia and not for New England, which belonged to another government, with which the Virginia Company had nothing to do.[1] And partly that such an |54| act by them done, this their condition considered, might be as firm as any patent, and in some respects more sure.

The form was as followeth: [2]

IN THE NAME OF GOD, AMEN.

We whose names are underwritten, the loyal subjects of our dread Sovereign Lord King James, by the Grace of God of

[1] This, as we have seen, was correct; the Pilgrims were now in New England, as the "Northern Parts of Virginia" had just been renamed, and the patent that they brought with them was invalid. With mutiny threatened, something had to be done; and the church covenants, or compacts, with which all Puritans were familiar, suggested this Compact. Moreover, John Robinson had suggested (see Appendix IV) that they broaden the base of their local government; and the Virginia Company of London, immediately after sealing the Pilgrims' patent and those of other Particular Plantations on 2 Feb. 1620, voted "that such Captains and Leaders of Particular Plantations that shall go there to inhabit by virtue of their Grants, and plant themselves, their tenants and servants in Virginia, shall have liberty, till a form of Government be here settled for them, associating with them divers of the gravest and discreetest of their Companies, to make Orders, Ordinances and Constitutions for the better ordering and directing of their servants and business, provided they be not repugnant to the Laws of England." (*Records of Virginia Company* I 303.) Thus, the Pilgrims would have had a right to form a government even if they had settled within the boundaries of Virginia and had been encouraged to do so.

[2] The original document has disappeared, so this may be regarded as the most authentic text of the Compact. It was first printed in *Mourt's Relation* (1622) and that text differs from this only by the dropping of an occasional *the, and* and *at.* Nathaniel Morton printed it in *New Englands Memoriall* (1669), together with the names of the 41 signers. See Appendix XIII below, where signers' names are distinguished by an asterisk.

Great Britain, France, and Ireland King, Defender of the Faith, etc.

Having undertaken, for the Glory of God and advancement of the Christian Faith and Honour of our King and Country, a Voyage to plant the First Colony in the Northern Parts of Virginia, do by these presents solemnly and mutually in the presence of God and one of another, Covenant and Combine ourselves together into a Civil Body Politic, for our [3] better ordering and preservation and furtherance of the ends aforesaid; and by virtue hereof to enact, constitute and frame such just and equal Laws, Ordinances, Acts, Constitutions and Offices, from time to time, as shall be thought most meet and convenient for the general good of the Colony, unto which we promise all due submission and obedience. In witness whereof we have hereunder subscribed our names at Cape Cod, the 11th of November, in the year of the reign of our Sovereign Lord King James, of England, France and Ireland the eighteenth, and of Scotland the fifty-fourth. Anno Domini 1620.

After this they chose, or rather confirmed, Mr. John Carver (a man godly and well approved amongst them) their Governor for that year. And after they had provided a place for their goods, or common store (which were long in unlading for want of boats, foulness of the winter weather and sickness of divers) and begun some small cottages [4] for their habitation; as time would admit, they met and consulted of laws and orders, both for their civil and military government as the necessity of their condition did require, still adding thereunto as urgent occasion in several times, and as cases did require.

In these hard and difficult beginnings they found some discontents and murmurings arise amongst some, and mutinous speeches and carriages in other; but they were soon quelled and overcome

[3] Bradford scratched out *y^e^* and substituted *our*. This and other corrections suggest that he collated his own text with the original document.

[4] The subject of early housing at Plymouth has been covered exhaustively in Harold R. Shurtleff *The Log Cabin Myth* (1939) chap. v. On the basis of this and other researches a one-room frame house with a thatched roof, representing one of these first cottages, has been constructed by Plimoth Plantation, Inc. on the Plymouth waterfront, near the Rock.

by the wisdom, patience, and just and equal carriage of things, by the Governor and better part, which clave faithfully together in the main.

[*The Starving Time*]

But that which was most sad and lamentable was, that in two or three months' time half of their company died, especially in January and February, being the depth of winter, and wanting houses and other comforts; being infected with the scurvy and |55| other diseases which this long voyage and their inaccommodate condition had brought upon them. So as there died some times two or three of a day in the foresaid time, that of 100 and odd persons, scarce fifty remained.[5] And of these, in the time of most distress, there was but six or seven sound persons who to their great commendations, be it spoken, spared no pains night nor day, but with abundance of toil and hazard of their own health, fetched them wood, made them fires, dressed them meat, made their beds, washed their loathsome clothes, clothed and unclothed them. In a word, did all the homely and necessary offices for them which dainty and queasy stomachs cannot endure to hear named; and all this willingly and cheerfully, without any grudging in the least, showing herein their true love unto their friends and brethren; a rare example and worthy to be remembered. Two of these seven were Mr. William Brewster, their reverend Elder, and Myles Standish, their Captain and military commander, unto whom myself and many others were much beholden in our low and sick condition. And yet the Lord so upheld these persons as in this general calamity they were not at all infected either with sickness or lameness. And what I have said of these I may say of many others who died in this general visitation, and others yet living; that whilst they had health, yea, or any strength continuing, they were not wanting to any that had

[5] Of the 102 *Mayflower* passengers who reached Cape Cod, 4 died before she made Plymouth; and by the summer of 1621 the total deaths numbered 50. Only 12 of the original 26 heads of families and 4 of the original 12 unattached men or boys were left; and of the women who reached Plymouth, all but a few died. Doubtless many of the deaths took place on board the *Mayflower* at anchor, since there was not enough shelter ashore for all; and Plymouth Harbor is so shallow that she was moored about 1½ nautical miles from the Rock.

need of them. And I doubt not but their recompense is with the Lord.

But I may not here pass by another remarkable passage not to be forgotten. As this calamity fell among the passengers that were to be left here to plant, and were hasted ashore and made to drink water that the seamen might have the more beer, and one [6] in his sickness desiring but a small can of beer, it was answered that if he were their own father he should have none. The disease began to fall amongst them also, so as almost half of their company died before they went away, and many of their officers and lustiest men, as the boatswain, gunner, three quartermasters, the cook and others. At which the Master was something strucken and sent to the sick ashore and told the Governor he should send for beer for them that had need of it, though he drunk water homeward bound.

But now amongst his company |56| there was far another kind of carriage in this misery than amongst the passengers. For they that before had been boon companions in drinking and jollity in the time of their health and welfare, began now to desert one another in this calamity, saying they would not hazard their lives for them, they should be infected by coming to help them in their cabins; and so, after they came to lie by it, would do little or nothing for them but, "if they died, let them die." But such of the passengers as were yet aboard showed them what mercy they could, which made some of their hearts relent, as the boatswain (and some others) who was a proud young man and would often curse and scoff at the passengers. But when he grew weak, they had compassion on him and helped him; then he confessed he did not deserve it at their hands, he had abused them in word and deed. "Oh!" (saith he) "you, I now see, show your love like Christians indeed one to another, but we let one another lie and die like dogs." Another lay cursing his wife, saying if it had not been for her he had never come this unlucky voyage, and anon cursing his fellows, saying he had done this and that for some of them; he had spent so much and so much amongst them, and they were now weary of him and did not help him, having need. Another gave his companion all he had, if he died, to help him

[6] Which was this author himself (Bradford).

in his weakness; he went and got a little spice and made him a mess of meat once or twice. And because he died not so soon as he expected, he went amongst his fellows and swore the rogue would cozen him, he would see him choked before he made him any more meat; and yet the poor fellow died before morning.

[*Indian Relations*]

All this while the Indians came skulking about them, and would sometimes show themselves aloof off, but when any approached near them, they would run away; and once they stole away their tools where they had been at work and were gone to dinner.[7] But about the 16th of March, a certain Indian came boldly amongst them and spoke to them in broken English, which they could well understand but marveled at it. At length they understood by discourse with him, that he was not of these parts, but belonged to the eastern parts where some English ships came to fish, with whom he was acquainted and could name sundry of them by their names, amongst whom he had got his language. He became profitable to them |57| in acquainting them with many things concerning the state of the country in the east parts where he lived, which was afterwards profitable unto them; as also of the people here, of their names, number and strength, of their situation and distance from this place, and who was chief

[7] *Mourt's Relation* adds more details. On every fair day the men worked building houses. On 8 Jan. 1621 Master Jones and some of the men caught three seal and a codfish, and Francis Billington, the *Mayflower's* bad boy, sighted from a treetop "a great sea, as he thought," but found it to be a lake; it is still called Billington's Sea. On 9 Jan. the 20-foot-square common house for stores was completed except for the roof, and the house lots were laid out. On the 12th two men went afield to cut thatch, accompanied by a mastiff bitch and a spaniel. The dogs flushed a deer and the men gave chase, got lost and were benighted. Terrified at the howling of wolves, which they mistook for lions, they passed an unhappy night but got back next day. On the 14th the common house caught fire and the thatched roof was consumed; Bradford was lying sick abed inside but escaped. On the 19th John Goodman, one of the hunters, beat off two wolves that chased the spaniel. On 9 Feb. Master Jones shot five wild geese and found a deer killed by the Indians and being eaten by wolves. On the 16th a man out fowling saw twelve Indians; these were they who stole the tools. After that some of the ordnance from the *Mayflower* was mounted on the hill. On 3 March the wind turned south and "birds sang in the woods most pleasantly."

amongst them. His name was Samoset.[8] He told them also of another Indian whose name was Squanto, a native of this place, who had been in England and could speak better English than himself.

Being, after some time of entertainment and gifts dismissed, a while after he came again, and five more with him, and they brought again all the tools that were stolen away before, and made way for the coming of their great Sachem, called Massasoit. Who, about four or five days after, came with the chief of his friends and other attendance, with the aforesaid Squanto. With whom, after friendly entertainment and some gifts given him, they made a peace with him (which hath now continued this 24 years) [9] in these terms:

1. That neither he nor any of his should injure or do hurt to any of their people.

2. That if any of his did hurt to any of theirs, he should send the offender, that they might punish him.

3. That if anything were taken away from any of theirs, he should cause it to be restored; and they should do the like to his.

4. If any did unjustly war against him, they would aid him; if any did war against them, he should aid them.

[8] Samoset was an Algonkian sagamore of Pemaquid Point, Maine, a region much frequented by English fishermen. He probably shipped with Capt. Dermer from Monhegan to Cape Cod shortly before the Pilgrims landed and worked his way overland to Plymouth. He conveyed 12,000 acres of Pemaquid Point to one John Brown in 1625, and lived until about 1653. One of the best historical paintings of the Pilgrims is that of this scene by Charles Hoffbauer in the New England Mutual Life Insurance building, Boylston Street, Boston.

[9] This passage dates Bradford's writing of this chapter not earlier than 1644. Massasoit, chief of the Wampanoag, had his principal seat at Sowams in the present town of Barrington, R. I. On this first visit he was accompanied by his brother and 60 warriors. *Mourt's Relation*, p. 36, describes the meeting, the exchange of presents, and speeches interpreted by Squanto. The Pilgrims "conducted him to an house then in building, where we placed a green rug and three or four cushions. Then instantly came our Governor, with drum and trumpet after him, and some few musketeers. After salutations, our Governor kissing his hand, the King kissed him; and so they sat down. The Governor called for some strong water and drunk to him; and he drunk a great draught, that made him sweat all the while after." The treaty thus concluded was faithfully kept until the reign of Massasoit's son Metacom, better known as King Philip.

5. He should send to his neighbours confederates to certify them of this, that they might not wrong them, but might be likewise comprised in the conditions of peace.

6. That when their men came to them, they should leave their bows and arrows behind them.

After these things he returned to his place called Sowams,[1] some 40 miles from this place, but Squanto continued with them and was their interpreter and was a special instrument sent of God for their good beyond their expectation. He directed them how to set their corn, where to take fish, and to procure other commodities, and was also their pilot to bring them to unknown places for their profit, and never left them till he died. He was a native |58| of this place, and scarce any left alive besides himself. He was carried away with divers others by one Hunt, a master of a ship,[2] who thought to sell them for slaves in Spain. But he got away for England and was entertained by a merchant in London, and employed to Newfoundland and other parts, and lastly brought hither into these parts by one Mr. Dermer, a gentleman employed by Sir Ferdinando Gorges and others for discovery and other designs in these parts. Of whom I shall say something, because it is mentioned in a book set forth Anno 1622 by the President and Council for New England,[3] that he made the peace between the savages of these parts and the English, of which this plantation, as it is intimated, had the benefit; but what a peace it was may appear by what befell him and his men.

This Mr. Dermer was here the same year that these people came, as appears by a relation written by him and given me by a friend, bearing date June 30, Anno 1620. And they came in November following, so there was but four months difference. In

[1] For the history of this place see Thomas W. Bicknell *Sowams* (1908).

[2] Squanto or Tisquantum appears to have been the sole survivor of the Patuxet tribe. Kidnapped there by Capt. Thomas Hunt in 1614, he had the curious career that Bradford says; he jumped Capt. Dermer's ship in 1618 and made his way to the site of Plymouth, where he found himself to be the sole survivor of his tribe, wiped out in the pestilence of 1617.

[3] Page 17 (Bradford). This is a reference to *A Briefe Relation of the Discovery and Plantation of New England* (1622), reprinted in James Phinney Baxter *Sir Ferdinando Gorges and His Province of Maine* (Prince Society, 1890) I 199 ff; the Dermer-Squanto business is on pp. 211–12.

which relation to his honoured friend, he hath these passages of this very place:

I will first begin (saith he) with that place from whence Squanto or Tisquantum, was taken away; which in Captain Smith's map is called Plymouth; and I would that Plymouth had the like commodities. I would that the first plantation might here be seated, if there come to the number of 50 persons, or upward. Otherwise, Charlton,[4] because there the savages are less to be feared. The Pocanockets,[5] which live to the west of Plymouth, bear an inveterate malice to the English, and are of more strength than all the savages from thence to Penobscot. Their desire of revenge was occasioned by an Englishman, who having many of them on board, made a greater slaughter with their murderers[6] and small shot when as (they say) they offered no injury on their parts. Whether they were English or no it may be doubted; yet they believe they were, for the French have so possessed them. For which cause Squanto cannot deny but they would have killed me when I was at Namasket, had he not entreated hard for me.

The soil of the borders of |59| this great bay may be compared to most of the plantations which I have seen in Virginia. The land is of divers sorts, for Patuxet is a hardy but strong soil; Nauset and Satucket[7] are for the most part a blackish and deep mould much like that where groweth the best tobacco in Virginia. In the bottom of that great bay is store of cod and bass or mullet, etc. But above all he commends Pocanocket for the richest soil, and much open ground fit for English grain, etc.

Massachusetts is about nine leagues from Plymouth, and situated in the midst between both, is full of islands and peninsulas, very fertile for the most part.

[4] A place so designated on Capt. John Smith's Map of New England (1616) near the mouth of the Charles River.

[5] The Pocanockets were the same as the Wampanoags, Massasoit's tribe. Their country lay around Mount Hope and the Taunton and Dighton Rivers, which flow into Narragansett Bay.

[6] A ship's gun that used small bullets and slugs.

[7] Patuxet, meaning "at the little falls," was the Indian name of the site of Plymouth, as Samoset informed the Pilgrims (*Mourt's Relation*). Nauset, named after the Indian tribe, was the region roughly corresponding to Eastham on Cape Cod. Satucket, meaning "near the mouth of the stream," was a Nauset Indian village in the present town of Brewster, not far west of Orleans. Either Dermer grossly exaggerated the quality of the soil in that part of Cape Cod, or it has become depleted in the course of three centuries.

With sundry such relations which I forbear to transcribe, being now better known than they were to him.

He was taken prisoner by the Indians at Manamoyick,[8] a place not far from hence, now well known. He gave them what they demanded for his liberty, but when they had got what they desired, they kept him still, and endeavoured to kill his men. But he was freed by seizing on some of them and kept them bound till they gave him a canoe's load of corn. Of which, see *Purchas*, lib. 9, fol. 1778.[9] But this was Anno 1619.

After the writing of the former relation, he came to the Isle of Capawack [1] (which lies south of this place in the way to Virginia) and the aforesaid Squanto with him, where he going ashore amongst the Indians to trade, as he used to do, was betrayed and assaulted by them, and all his men slain, but one that kept the boat. But himself got aboard very sore wounded, and they had cut off his head upon the cuddy of the boat, had not the man rescued him with a sword. And so they got away and made shift to get into Virginia where he died, whether of his wounds or the diseases of the country, or both together, is uncertain. |60| By all which it may appear how far these people were from peace, and with what danger this plantation was begun, save as the powerful hand of the Lord did protect them.

These things were partly the reason why they [2] kept aloof and were so long before they came to the English. Another reason as after themselves made known was how about three years before, a French ship was cast away at Cape Cod, but the men got ashore and saved their lives, and much of their victuals and other goods. But after the Indians heard of it, they gathered together from these parts and never left watching and dogging them till they got advantage and killed them all but three or four which they kept, and sent from one sachem to another to make

[8] Manamoyick or Monomoit meant the region around Pleasant Bay in the present towns of Orleans and Harwich. It was then a harbor entered directly from the sea by a passage now closed up. It was the Nauset Indians who captured Dermer.

[9] *Purchas His Pilgrimes* (the continuation of Hakluyt's *Voyages*) IV p. 1778.

[1] Martha's Vineyard. See W. F. Gookin *Capawack alias Martha's Vineyard,* Dukes Co. Historical Society, Edgartown (1947).

[2] The Indians.

sport with, and used them worse than slaves. Of which the aforesaid Mr. Dermer redeemed two of them; and they conceived this ship was now come to revenge it.[3]

Also, as after was made known, before they came to the English to make friendship, they got all the Powachs [4] of the country, for three days together in a horrid and devilish manner, to curse and execrate them with their conjurations, which assembly and service they held in a dark and dismal swamp.

But to return. The spring now approaching, it pleased God the mortality began to cease amongst them, and the sick and lame recovered apace, which put as [it] were new life into them, though they had borne their sad affliction with much patience and contentedness as I think any people could do. But it was the Lord which upheld them, and had beforehand prepared them; many having long borne the yoke, yea from their youth.[5] Many other smaller matters I omit, sundry of them having been already published in a journal made by one of the company,[6] and some other passages of journeys and relations already published, to which I refer those that are willing to know them more particularly.

And being now come to the 25th of March, I shall begin the year 1621.

[3] "This ship" means the *Mayflower*. The sad plight of these shipwrecked Frenchmen is also told in Phineas Pratt's Narrative in Massachusetts Historical Society *Collections* 4th ser. IV 479.

[4] Powows, medicine men.

[5] Lamentations iii.26.

[6] *Mourt's Relation*—see Chap. x note 2, above.

CHAPTER XII

Anno 1621 |61| [Mayflower *Departs and Corn Planted*]

They now began to dispatch the ship away which brought them over, which lay till about this time, or the beginning of April.[1] The reason on their part why she stayed so long, was the necessity and danger that lay upon them; for it was well towards the end of December before she could land anything here, or they able to receive anything ashore. Afterwards, the 14th of January, the house which they had made for a general rendezvous by casualty fell afire, and some were fain to retire aboard for shelter; then the sickness began to fall sore amongst them, and the weather so bad as they could not make much sooner any dispatch. Again, the Governor and chief of them, seeing so many die and fall down sick daily, thought it no wisdom to send away the ship, their condition considered and the danger they stood in from the Indians, till they could procure some shelter; and therefore thought it better to draw some more charge upon themselves and friends than hazard all. The master and seamen likewise, though before they hasted the passengers ashore to be gone, now many of their men being dead, and of the ablest of them (as is before noted), and of the rest many lay sick and weak; the master durst not put to sea till he saw his men begin to recover, and the heart of winter over.

Afterwards they (as many as were able) began to plant their corn, in which service Squanto stood them in great stead, showing them both the manner how to set it, and after how to dress and tend it. Also he told them, except they got fish and set with it in these old grounds it would come to nothing. And he showed them that in the middle of April they should have store enough come up the brook by which they began to build, and taught them how to take it, and where to get other provisions necessary for them. All which they found true by trial and experience. Some English seed they sowed, as wheat and pease, but it came not to good, either by the badness of the seed or lateness of the season or both, or some other defect. |62|

[1] The *Mayflower* sailed 5 April and arrived in England 6 May.

[*Bradford Succeeds Carver; Civil Marriage*]

In this month of April, whilst they were busy about their seed, their Governor (Mr. John Carver) came out of the field very sick, it being a hot day. He complained greatly of his head and lay down, and within a few hours his senses failed, so as he never spake more till he died, which was within a few days after. Whose death was much lamented and caused great heaviness amongst them, as there was cause. He was buried in the best manner they could, with some volleys of shot by all that bore arms. And his wife, being a weak woman, died within five or six weeks after him.

Shortly after, William Bradford was chosen Governor in his stead, and being not recovered of his illness, in which he had been near the point of death, Isaac Allerton was chosen to be an assistant unto him who, by renewed election every year, continued sundry years together. Which I here note once for all.

May 12 was the first marriage in this place which, according to the laudable custom of the Low Countries, in which they had lived, was thought most requisite to be performed by the magistrate, as being a civil thing, upon which many questions about inheritances do depend, with other things most proper to their cognizance and most consonant to the Scriptures (Ruth iv) and nowhere found in the Gospel to be laid on the ministers as a part of their office. "This decree or law about marriage was published by the States of the Low Countries Anno 1590. That those of any religion (after lawful and open publication) coming before the magistrates in the Town, or State house, were to be orderly (by them) married one to another."—Petit's History, fol. 1029.[2] And this practice hath continued amongst not only them, but

[2] Jean F. Le Petit *La Grande Chronique Ancienne et Moderne de Hollande* (1601). The marriage was that of Edward Winslow, whose first wife died in the great sickness, to Susannah, widow of William White, another victim of the first winter. On the trusted emissary of the Pilgrims and later the Bay Colony, the late George G. Wolkins brought out some new facts in American Antiquarian Society *Proceedings* for Oct. 1950. He was born at Droitwich 18 Oct. 1595, grandson of Kenelm Winslow, yeoman, and son of Edward Winslow, a salt victualer. After five years as a scholar in the King's School, Worcester, Winslow probably entered the printing trade in London; in 1617 he was at Leyden, associated with William Brewster in the printing business.

hath been followed by all the famous churches of Christ in these parts to this time—Anno 1646.

[*Indian Diplomacy*]

Having in some sort ordered their business at home, it was thought meet to send some abroad to see their new friend Massasoit, and to bestow upon him some gratuity to bind him the faster unto them; as also that hereby they might view the country and see in what manner he lived, what strength he had about him, and how the ways were to his place, if at any time they should have occasion. So the second of July they sent Mr. Edward Winslow and Mr. Hopkins,[3] with the foresaid Squanto for their guide; who gave him a suit of clothes and a horseman's coat, with some other small things, which were kindly accepted; but they found but short commons and came both weary and hungry home. For the Indians used then to have nothing |63| so much corn as they have since the English have stored them with their hoes, and seen their industry in breaking up new grounds therewith.

They found his place to be forty miles from hence, the soil good and the people not many, being dead and abundantly wasted in the late great mortality, which fell in all these parts about three years before the coming of the English, wherein thousands of them died. They not being able to bury one another, their skulls and bones were found in many places lying still above the ground where their houses and dwellings had been, a very sad spectacle to behold. But they brought word that the Narragansetts lived but on the other side of that great bay, and were a strong people and many in number, living compact together, and had not been at all touched with this wasting plague.

About the latter end of this month, one John Billington lost himself in the woods, and wandered up and down some five days, living on berries and what he could find. At length he light on an Indian plantation twenty miles south of this place, called Manomet; they conveyed him further off, to Nauset among those peo-

[3] Stephen Hopkins, of London, is probably the same man of that name who was wrecked in Bermuda in 1609, proceeded to Virginia next year, but did not stay long. C. E. Banks *English Ancestry of the Pilgrim Fathers* pp. 61–4. This mission to the Indians is told in greater detail in *Mourt's Relation.*

ple that had before set upon the English when they were coasting whilst the ship lay at the Cape, as is before noted. But the Governor caused him to be inquired for among the Indians, and at length Massasoit sent word where he was, and the Governor sent a shallop for him and had him delivered. Those people also came and made their peace; and they gave full satisfaction to those whose corn they had found and taken when they were at Cape Cod.

Thus their peace and acquaintance was pretty well established with the natives about them. And there was another Indian called Hobomok come to live amongst them, a proper lusty man, and a man of account for his valour and parts amongst the Indians, and continued very faithful and constant to the English till he died. He and Squanto being gone upon business among the Indians, at their return (whether it was out of envy to them or malice to the English) there was a sachem called Corbitant, allied to Massasoit but never any good friend to the English to this day, met with them at an Indian town called Namasket, fourteen miles to the west of this place, and began to quarrel with |64| them and offered to stab Hobomok.[4] But being a lusty man, he cleared himself of him and came running away all sweating, and told the Governor what had befallen him. And he feared they had killed Squanto, for they threatened them both; and for no other cause but because they were friends to the English and serviceable unto them. Upon this the Governor taking counsel, it was conceived not fit to be borne; for if they should suffer their friends and messengers thus to be wronged, they should have none would cleave to them, or give them any intelligence, or do them service afterwards, but next they would fall upon themselves. Whereupon it was resolved to send the Captain and fourteen men well armed, and to go and fall upon them in the night. And if they found that Squanto was killed, to cut off Corbitant's head, but not to hurt any but those that had a hand in it.

Hobomok was asked if he would go and be their guide and bring them there before day. He said he would, and bring them

[4] Hobomok was a Wampanoag; Corbitant, sachem of the Pocasset but subject to Massasoit, lived on what is now Gardner's Neck, Swansea; Namasket was in the present township of Middleborough.

to the house where the man lay, and show them which was he. So they set forth the 14th of August, and beset the house round. The Captain, giving charge to let none pass out, entered the house to search for him. But he was gone away that day, so they missed him, but understood that Squanto was alive, and that he had only threatened to kill him and made an offer to stab him but did not. So they withheld and did no more hurt, and the people came trembling and brought them the best provisions they had, after they were acquainted by Hobomok what was only intended. There was three sore wounded which broke out of the house and assayed to pass through the guard. These they brought home with them, and they had their wounds dressed and cured, and sent home. After this they had many gratulations from divers sachems, and much firmer peace; yea, those of the Isles of Capawack sent to make friendship; and this Corbitant himself used the mediation of Massasoit to make his peace, but was shy to come near them a long while after.[5]

After this, the 18th of September they sent out their shallop to the Massachusetts, with ten men and Squanto for their guide and |65| interpreter, to discover and view that Bay and trade with the natives. The which they performed, and found kind entertainment. The people were much afraid of the Tarentines, a people to the eastward which used to come in harvest time and take away their corn, and many times kill their persons.[6] They returned in safety and brought home a good quantity of beaver, and made report of the place, wishing they had been there seated. But it seems the Lord, who assigns to all men the bounds of their habitations,[7] had appointed it for another use. And thus they found

[5] There is a more detailed account in *Mourt's Relation* chap. xiii of this episode, a typical instance of the Pilgrims' combination of justice, wisdom and mercy in dealing with the Indians.

[6] The submission of Chikataubut, sachem of the Massachusetts, and eight other sachems and sagamores to King James on 13 Sept. 1621 will be found in 1912 ed. Bradford I 227. *Tarentine* was the name then used for the Abnaki Indians, who occupied the shores of Maine from Casco Bay eastward and part of New Brunswick. They were the Vikings of New England, preferring to take corn from their neighbors than to grow it.

[7] Deuteronomy xxxii.8. The fur trade, economic salvation of the Colony, began in the summer of 1621 through Squanto acting as buyer. On this "voyage to the Massachusetts" he was impatient to "rifle the salvage women" of their beaver coats, but the Pilgrims wisely insisted on fair trade. The women "sold

the Lord to be with them in all their ways, and to bless their outgoings and incomings, for which let His holy name have the praise forever, to all posterity.

[*First Thanksgiving*]

They began now to gather in the small harvest they had, and to fit up their houses and dwellings against winter, being all well recovered in health and strength and had all things in good plenty. For as some were thus employed in affairs abroad, others were exercised in fishing, about cod and bass and other fish, of which they took good store, of which every family had their portion. All the summer there was no want; and now began to come in store of fowl, as winter approached, of which this place did abound when they came first (but afterward decreased by degrees). And besides waterfowl there was great store of wild turkeys, of which they took many, besides venison, etc. Besides they had about a peck a meal a week to a person, or now since harvest, Indian corn to that proportion. Which made many afterwards write so largely of their plenty here to their friends in England, which were not feigned but true reports.[8]

[*Arrival of the* Fortune]

In November, about that time twelvemonth that themselves came, there came in a small ship to them unexpected or looked

---

their coats from their backs, and tied boughs about them, but with great shamefacedness (for indeed they are more modest than some of our English women are)." *Mourt's Relation* p. 60.

[8] Edward Winslow's letter of 11 Dec. 1621 to a friend in England describing this "First Thanksgiving" is printed in *Mourt's Relation* pp. 60–5:

"Our harvest being gotten in, our Governor sent four men on fowling, that so we might after a more special manner rejoice together, after we had gathered the fruit of our labours. They four in one day killed as much fowl as, with a little help beside, served the Company almost a week. At which time, amongst other recreations, we exercised our arms, many of the Indians coming amongst us, and amongst the rest their greatest king, Massasoit with some 90 men, whom for three days we entertained and feasted. And they went out and killed five deer which they brought to the plantation and bestowed on our Governor and upon the Captain and others."

The actual date of this festival is nowhere related. See William De Loss Love *Fast and Thanksgiving Days of New England* (1895).

Sandy upland
Winslow House
Rouses Hummock
Duxbury R.
Powder Pt.
Blue R.
DUXBURY BEACH
High Pines
Eagles Nest
DUXBURY BAY
Captains Hill
Brewster Pt
Clark I.
Saquish Cove
The Gurnet
CAPE COD BAY
Saquish Head
BROWN'S BANK
Rocky Nook
Jones R.
Nathans Brook
Horse Race
Dotens Cliff
Goose Pt.
Goose Pt. Ch'l
LONG BEACH
PLYMOUTH HARBOR
Smelt Pond
The Rock
Plymouth
Town Br.
Warren's Cove
MANOMET HILL
Billington Sea
Eel R.
Hills
PLYMOUTH BAY 1620-1650
Soundings and Channels from Chart in The Atlantic Neptune, 1780
Land Data from U.S. Geological Surveys 1853-1934
Soundings in fathoms
Nautical Miles
Raisz

for,[9] in which came Mr. Cushman (so much spoken of before) and with him thirty-five persons to remain and live in the plantation; which did not a little rejoice them. And they when they came ashore and found all well and saw plenty of victuals in every house, were no less glad; for most of them were lusty young men, and many of them wild enough, who little considered whither or about what they went till they came into the harbor at Cape Cod and there saw nothing but a naked and barren place. They then began to think what should become of them, if the people here were dead or cut off by the Indians. They began to consult (upon some speeches that some of the seamen had cast out) to take the sails from the yard lest the ship |66| should get away and leave them there. But the master, hearing of it, gave them good words and told them if anything but well should have befallen the people here, he hoped he had victuals enough to carry them to Virginia; and whilst he had a bit they should have their part, which gave them good satisfaction.

So they were all landed; but there was not so much as biscuit-cake or any other victuals [1] for them, neither had they any bedding but some sorry things they had in their cabins; nor pot, or pan to dress any meat in; nor overmany clothes, for many of them had brushed away their coats and cloaks at Plymouth as they came. But there was sent over some Birching Lane [2] suits in the ship, out of which they were supplied. The plantation was glad of this addition of strength, but could have wished that many of them had been of better condition, and all of them better furnished with provisions. But that could not now be helped.

In this ship Mr. Weston sent a large letter to Mr. Carver, the late Governor, now deceased; full of complaints and expostulations about former passages at Hampton, and the keeping the ship so long in the country, and returning her without lading, etc., which for brevity I omit. The rest is as followeth:

[9] She came the 9th to the Cape (Bradford). This was the *Fortune*, 55 tons, which the Adventurers sent in July, but she made an even longer voyage than the *Mayflower's*. Among the 35 passengers were John Adams, Jonathan Brewster, Philip Delano and Thomas Prence.

[1] Nay, they were fain to spare the ship some to carry her home (Bradford). Apparently the *Fortune* tarried about three weeks at Provincetown Harbor before proceeding to Plymouth.

[2] A street in London where cheap ready-made clothes were sold.

Part of Mr. Weston's Letter

I durst never acquaint the Adventurers with the alterations of the conditions first agreed on between us, which I have since been very glad of, for I am well assured had they known as much as I do, they would not have adventured a halfpenny of what was necessary for this ship. That you sent no lading in the ship is wonderful, and worthily distasted. I know your weakness was the cause of it, and I believe more weakness of judgment than weakness of hands. A quarter of the time you spent in discoursing, arguing and consulting would have done much more; but that is past, etc. If you mean, bona fide, to perform the conditions agreed upon, do us the favour to copy them out fair and subscribe them with the principal of your names. And likewise give us account as particularly as you can, how our moneys were laid out. And then I shall be able to give them some satisfaction, whom I am now forced with good words to shift off. And consider that the life of the business depends on the lading of this ship, which if you do to any good purpose, that I may be freed from the great sums I have disbursed for the former and must do for the latter, I promise you I will never quit the business, though all the other Adventurers should. |67|

We have procured you a charter, the best we could, which is better than your former, and with less limitation.[8] For anything that is else worth writing Mr. Cushman can inform you. I pray write instantly for Mr. Robinson to come to you. And so praying God to bless you with all graces necessary both for this life and that to come, I rest

Your very loving friend,
London, July 6, 1621 THOMAS WESTON

[8] This was the Peirce Patent, second of that name, obtained 1 June 1621 from the Council for New England to take the place of the first Peirce Patent from the Virginia Company. The original document, signed and sealed by the Dukes of Lenox and Hamilton, the Earls of Warwick and Sheffield and Sir Ferdinando Gorges, is in Pilgrim Hall, Plymouth. Printed with facsimile in 1912 ed. Bradford I 246–51. It conveys to John Peirce and Associates 100 acres of ground for every colonist, in any uninhabited place, with liberty to fish and truck, and 1500 acres extra for each Adventurer; and promises that after proper survey within seven years this patent will be replaced by one with definite bounds and right of self-government. In the meantime all laws and ordinances by the "Associates, Undertakers and Planters" shall be legal. So this patent may be said to have confirmed the Mayflower Compact.

This ship (called the *Fortune*) was speedily dispatched away,[4] being laden with good clapboard as full as she could stow, and two hogsheads of beaver and otter skins which they got with a few trifling commodities brought with them at first, being altogether unprovided for trade. Neither was there any amongst them that ever saw a beaver skin till they came here and were informed by Squanto. The freight was estimated to be worth near £500. Mr. Cushman returned back also with this ship, for so Mr. Weston and the rest had appointed him, for their better information. And he doubted not, nor themselves neither, but they should have a speedy supply, considering also how by Mr. Cushman's persuasion and letters received from Leyden wherein they willed them so to do, they yielded to the aforesaid conditions and subscribed them with their hands.

But it proved otherwise, for Mr. Weston, who had made that large promise in his letter (as is before noted) that if all the rest should fall off, yet he would never quit the business but stick to them, if they yielded to the conditions, and sent some lading in the ship; and of this Mr. Cushman was confident, and confirmed the same from his mouth, and serious protestations to himself before he came. But all proved but wind, for he was the first and only man that forsook them, and that before he so much as heard of the return of this ship, or knew what was done. So vain is the confidence in man; but of this, more in its place.

[*Bradford's Reply to Weston*]

A letter in answer to his writ to Mr. Carver, was sent to him from the Governor, of which so much as is pertinent to the thing in hand, I shall here insert:

SIR:

Your large letter, written to Mr. Carver and dated the 6th of July 1621, I have received the 10th of November, wherein after the apol-

[4] On 13 Dec. 1621. The day before, Cushman, although a layman, delivered a sermon which was printed as *A Sermon preached at Plimmoth in New England . . . in an Assemblie of His Maiesties faithful Subiects there inhabiting . . . together with a Preface Shewing the state of the Country and Condition of the Savages* (London 1622). The latter part, which adds a little detail to *Mourt's Relation*, is printed in Alex. Young *Chronicles of the Pilgrim Fathers* (1841) chap. xvii.

ogy made for yourself you lay many heavy imputations upon him and us all. Touching him, he is departed this life and now is at rest |68| in the Lord from all those troubles and encumbrances with which we are yet to strive. He needs not my apology; for his care and pains was so great for the common good, both ours and yours, as that therewith (it is thought) he oppressed himself and shortened his days; of whose loss we cannot sufficiently complain.

At great charges in this adventure I confess you have been, and many losses may sustain; but the loss of his and many other honest and industrious men's lives cannot be valued at any price. Of the one there may be hope of recovery; but the other no recompense can make good. But I will not insist in generals, but come more particularly to the things themselves.

You greatly blame us for keeping the ship so long in the country, and then to send her away empty. She lay five weeks at Cape Cod whilst with many a weary step (after a long journey) and the endurance of many a hard brunt, we sought out in the foul winter a place of habitation. Then, we went in so tedious a time to make provision to shelter us and our goods; about which labour, many of our arms and legs can tell us to this day, we were not negligent. But it pleased God to visit us then with death daily, and with so general a disease that the living were scarce able to bury the dead, and the well not in any measure sufficient to tend the sick. And now to be so greatly blamed for not freighting the ship doth indeed go near us and much discourage us. But you say you know we will pretend weakness. And do you think we had not cause? Yes, you tell us you believe it, but it was more weakness of judgment than of hands. Our weakness herein is great we confess, therefore we will bear this check patiently amongst the rest, till God send us wiser men. But they which told you we spent so much time in discoursing and consulting, etc., their hearts can tell their tongues they lie. They cared not, so they might salve their own sores, how they wounded others. Indeed, it is our calamity that we are, beyond expectation, yoked with some ill-conditioned people who will never do good, but corrupt and abuse others, etc.

The rest of the letter declared how they had subscribed those conditions according to his desire, and sent him the former accounts very particularly; also how the ship was laden and in what condition their affairs stood; that the coming of these |69| people would bring famine upon them unavoidably if they had not supply in time, as Mr. Cushman could more fully inform him and the rest of the Adventurers. Also that seeing he was now satisfied in all his demands, that offenses would be forgotten and he remember his promise, etc.

After the departure of this ship, which stayed not above fourteen days,[5] the Governor and his assistant having disposed these late comers into several families as they best could, took an exact account of all their provisions in store and proportioned the same to the number of persons, and found that it would not hold out above six months at half allowance, and hardly that; and they could not well give less this winter time till fish came in again. So they were presently put to half allowance, one as well as another, which began to be hard, but they bore it patiently under hope of supply.

[*Narragansett Challenge*]

Soon after this ship's departure, that great people of the Narragansetts, in a braving manner, sent a messenger unto them with a bundle of arrows tied about with a great snakeskin, which their interpreters told them was a threatening and a challenge. Upon which the Governor, with the advice of others, sent them a round answer that if they had rather have war than peace, they might begin when they would; they had done them no wrong, neither did they fear them or should they find them unprovided. And by another messenger sent the snakeskin back with bullets in it. But they would not receive it, but sent it back again.[6] But these things I do but mention, because they are more at large already put forth in print by Mr. Winslow at the request of some friends.[7] And it is like the reason was their own ambition who (since the death of so many of the Indians) thought to domineer and lord it over the rest, and conceived the English would be a

[5] The *Fortune*, which sailed 13 Dec. 1621, according to Capt. John Smith *New Englands Trials* (1622; Arber ed. *Travels and Works*, 1910, p. 260).

[6] Canonicus, sachem of the Narragansett, sent the challenge; Squanto did the interpreting. This happened in Jan. 1622.

[7] Edward Winslow *Good Newes from New England* (London 1624). This too, is reprinted in Young's *Chronicles of the Pilgrim Fathers*, as "Winslow's Relation."

bar in their way, and saw that Massasoit took shelter already under their wings.

But this made them the more carefully to look to themselves, so as they agreed to enclose their dwellings with a good strong pale, and make flankers in convenient places with gates to shut, which were every night locked, and a watch kept; and when need required, there was also warding in the daytime. And the company was by the Captain's and the Governor's |70| advice divided into four squadrons, and everyone had their quarter appointed them unto which they were to repair upon any sudden alarm. And if there should be any cry of fire, a company were appointed for a guard, with muskets, whilst others quenched the same, to prevent Indian treachery. This was accomplished very cheerfully, and the town impaled round by the beginning of March, in which every family had a pretty garden plot secured.

And herewith I shall end this year. Only I shall remember one passage more, rather of mirth than of weight. On the day called Christmas Day, the Governor called them out to work as was used. But the most of this new company excused themselves and said it went against their consciences to work on that day. So the Governor told them that if they made it matter of conscience, he would spare them till they were better informed; so he led away the rest and left them. But when they came home at noon from their work, he found them in the street at play, openly; some pitching the bar, and some at stool-ball and such like sports. So he went to them and took away their implements and told them that was against his conscience, that they should play and others work. If they made the keeping of it matter of devotion, let them keep their houses; but there should be no gaming or reveling in the streets. Since which time nothing hath been attempted that way, at least openly.[8]

[8] All English and Scots Puritans objected to the celebration of Christmas as a pagan revelry, the excuse being that 25 Dec. was not the correct date of the Nativity. Stool-ball is an old country game something like cricket, in which a ball is batted about from stool to stool; said to be still played in Sussex.

CHAPTER XIII

Anno 1622 [*Squanto and Massasoit*]

At the spring of the year they had appointed the Massachusetts to come again and trade with them, and began now to prepare for that voyage about the latter end of March; but upon some rumors heard, Hobomok, their Indian, told them upon some jealousies [1] he had, he feared they were joined with the Narragansetts and might betray them if they were not careful. He intimated also some jealousy of Squanto, by what he gathered from some private whisperings between him and other Indians. |71| But they resolved to proceed, and sent out their shallop with ten of their chief men about the beginning of April, and both Squanto and Hobomok with them, in regard of the jealousy between them.

But they had not been gone long, but an Indian belonging to Squanto's family came running in seeming great fear and told them that many of the Narragansetts, with Corbitant and he thought also Massasoit, were coming against them, and he got away to tell them, not without danger; and being examined by the Governor, he made as if they were at hand, and would still be looking back as if they were at his heels. At which the Governor caused them to take arms and stand on their guard, and supposing the boat to be still within hearing (by reason it was calm) caused a warning piece or two to be shot off, the which they heard and came in. But no Indians appeared; watch was kept all night, but nothing was seen. Hobomok was confident for Massasoit, and thought all was false; yet the Governor caused him to send his wife privately, to see what she could observe (pretending other occasions), but there was nothing found, but

[1] I.e., apprehensions. Winslow in *Good Newes* (1624) p. 6 states that the Governor consulted with the Captain and the Assistants on this matter, and that they "came to this resolution, so it would not now stand with our safety to mew up ourselves in our new-enclosed town; partly because our store was almost empty, and therefore must seek out for our daily food, without which we could not long subsist; but especially for that thereby they would see us dismayed and be encouraged to prosecute their malicious purposes with more eagerness. . . ." The frequency with which the Pilgrims in their small colony had to meet the same sort of problems that 20th-century statesmen meet on a world basis is no less amazing than the resolution with which they accepted every challenge.

all was quiet. After this they proceeded on their voyage to the Massachusetts, and had good trade, and returned in safety, blessed be God.

But by the former passages, and other things of like nature, they began to see that Squanto sought his own ends and played his own game, by putting the Indians in fear and drawing gifts from them to enrich himself, making them believe he could stir up war against whom he would, and make peace for whom he would. Yea, he made them believe they kept the plague buried in the ground, and could send it amongst whom they would, which did much terrify the Indians and made them depend more on him, and seek more to him, than to Massasoit. Which procured him envy and had like to have cost him his life; for after the discovery of his practices, Massasoit sought it both privately and openly, which caused him to stick close to the English, and never durst go from them till he died.[2] They also made good use of the emulation that grew between Hobomok and him, which made them carry more squarely. And the Governor seemed to countenance the one, and the Captain the other, by which they had better intelligence, and made them both more diligent. |72|

Now in a manner their provisions were wholly spent, and they looked hard for supply but none came. But about the latter end of May, they spied a boat at sea (which at first they thought had been some Frenchman), but it proved a shallop which came from a ship which Mr. Weston and another had set out afishing,[3] at a place called Damariscove, forty leagues to the eastward of them, where were that year many more ships come afishing.[4] This boat

[2] Massasoit, incensed at Squanto's malicious gossip, sent emissaries with a peremptory demand that he be given up to Indian justice. This put Bradford on a spot, for the Colony depended on Massasoit's good will for its existence; the Governor hated to give Squanto up, but felt that he must. He was saved from the consequences of this weak decision by the appearance of Weston's shallop in the offing, which interrupted the transaction. Before he could get around to it again, Massasoit's messengers, "mad with rage . . . departed in great heat." Squanto was saved; yet Massasoit did nothing.

[3] The *Sparrow*, Rodgers master.

[4] Damariscove Island is off Boothbay, Maine; it is called Damerill's Isles on Capt. John Smith's map (1614) and was probably named after a fisherman who located there. The fishing along the Maine coast at this time was marvelous; 300 to 400 sail of various countries, of which 30 to 40 were English and some from

brought seven passengers and some letters, but no victuals nor any hope of any. Some part of which [letters] I shall set down.

[*Fair Words, no Food, but More Mouths to Feed*]

MR. CARVER, In my last letters by the *Fortune*, in whom Mr. Cushman went, and who I hope is with you, for we daily expect the ship back again. She departed hence, the beginning of July with 35 persons, though not over-well provided with necessaries, by reason of the parsimony of the Adventurers. I have solicited them to send you a supply of men and provisions before she come; they all answer they will do great matters when they hear good news, nothing before. So faithful, constant and careful of your good are your old and honest friends, that if they hear not from you, they are like to send you no supply, etc.

I am now to relate the occasion of sending this ship, hoping if you give credit to my words, you will have a more favourable opinion of it than some here, (whereof Pickering is one), who taxed me to mind my own ends, which is in part true, etc. Mr. Beauchamp [5] and myself bought this little ship and have set her out, partly if it may be, to uphold the Plantation, as well as to do others good as ourselves, and partly to get up what we are formerly out; though we are otherwise censured, etc. This is the occasion we have sent this ship, and these passengers, on our own account. Whom we desire you will friendly entertain and supply with such necessaries as you can spare, and they want, etc. And among other things, we pray you lend or sell them some seed corn, and if you have the salt remaining of the last year, that you will let them have it for their present use, and we will either pay you for it or give you more when we have set our salt-pan to work; which we desire may be set up in one of the little islands in your bay, etc. And because we intend, if God please, |73| (and the generality do it not) to send within a month another ship who, having discharged her passengers, shall go to Virginia, etc. And it may

---

Virginia, spent the early months of each year in Maine waters, returning to Europe in the summer.

[5] John Beauchamp, one of the Adventurers of whom more will be heard. This was the first of many such incidents which made things difficult for the Pilgrims: the Adventurers sending over groups of men "on their Particular" who had to be fed, but refused to take part in common labors, and at the same time diverted furs from the common stock to private purses. Well did Bradford annotate the word *uphold* in the next line: "I know not which way."

be we shall send a small ship to abide with you on the coast, which I conceive may be a great help to the Plantation. To the end our desire may be effected, which I assure myself will be also for your good, we pray you give them entertainment in your houses the time they shall be with you, that they may lose no time, but may presently go in hand to fell trees and cleave them, to the end lading may be ready and our ship stay not.

Some of the Adventurers have sent you herewithal some directions for your furtherance in the common business; who are like those St. James speaks of, that bid their brother eat, and warm him, but give him nothing,[6] so they bid you make salt, and uphold the Plantation, but send you no means wherewithal to do it, etc. By the next we purpose to send more people on our own account, and to take a patent; that if your people should be as unhuman as some of the Adventurers, not to admit us to dwell with them, which were extreme barbarism and which will never enter into my head, to think you have any such Pickerings amongst you. Yet to satisfy our passengers I must of force do it, and for some other reasons not necessary to be written, etc.

I find the general so backward, and your friends at Leyden so cold, that I fear you must stand on your legs and trust (as they say) to God and yourselves.

Subscribed,
Your loving friend,
Jan. 12, 1621 [22] THOMAS WESTON

Sundry other things I pass over, being tedious and impertinent.

All this was but cold comfort to fill their hungry bellies; and a slender performance of his former late promise; and as little did it either fill or warm them, as those the Apostle James spake of, by him before mentioned. And well might it make them remember what the Psalmist saith, Psalm cxviii.8, "It is better to trust in the Lord than to have confidence in man." And Psalm cxlvi, "Put not your trust in princes," (much less in merchants) "nor in the son of man, for there is no help in them." v. 5. "Blessed is he that hath the God of Jacob for his help, whose hope is in the Lord his God."

And as they were now failed of supply by him and others in

[6] James ii.15–16.

this their greatest need and wants, which was caused by him and the rest who put so great a company of men upon them as the former company were, without any food, and came at such a time, as they must live almost a whole year before any could |74| be raised, except they had sent some. So upon the point they never had any supply of victuals more afterwards (but what the Lord gave them otherwise), for all [that] the company sent at any time was always too short for those people that came with it.

There came also by the same ship other letters, but of later date, one from Mr. Weston, another from a part of the Adventurers as followeth:

MR. CARVER, Since my last, to the end we might the more readily proceed to help the general, at a meeting of some of the principal Adventurers, a proposition was put forth and allowed by all present (save Pickering) to adventure each man the third part of what he formerly had done, and there are some other that follow his example and will adventure no further. In regard whereof, the greater part of the Adventurers being willing to uphold the business, finding it no reason that those that are willing should uphold the business of those that are unwilling, whose backwardness doth discourage those that are forward, and hinder other new Adventurers from coming in. We having well considered thereof, have resolved, according to an article in the agreement ("that it may be lawful by a general consent of the Adventurers and planters, upon just occasion, to break off their joint stock") to break it off; and do pray you to ratify and confirm the same on your parts. Which being done, we shall the more willingly go forward for the upholding of you with all things necessary. But in any case you must agree to the articles, and send it by the first under your hands and seals. So I end

Your loving friend,

Jan. 17, 1621 [22] THOMAS WESTON

Another letter was writ from part of the Company of the Adventurers to the same purpose, and subscribed with nine of their names, whereof Mr. Weston's and Mr. Beauchamp's were two. These things seemed strange unto them, seeing this unconstancy and shuffling; it made them to think there was some mystery in the matter. And therefore the Governor concealed these letters from the public, only imparted them to some trusty friends for advice, who concluded with him that this tended to disband and scatter them (in regard of their straits); and if Mr. Weston and others, who seemed to run in a particular way, should come over with shipping so provided as his letters did intimate, the most would fall to him, to the prejudice of themselves and the rest of the Adventurers their friends, from whom as yet they heard nothing.

And it was doubted whether he had not sent |75| over such a company in the former ship,[7] for such an end. Yet they took compassion of those seven men which this ship, which fished to the eastward, had kept till planting time was over, and so could set no corn. And also wanting victuals, for they turned them off without any, and indeed wanted for themselves. Neither was their salt-pan come, so as they could not perform any of those things which Mr. Weston had appointed; and might have starved if the Plantation had not succoured them, who, in their wants, gave them as good as any of their own. The ship [8] went to Virginia, where they sold both ship and fish, of which (it was conceived) Mr. Weston had a very slender account.

[*Letters which came in the* Charity]

After this came another of his ships,[9] and brought letters dated the 10th of April, from Mr. Weston, as followeth:

MR. BRADFORD, these, etc. The *Fortune* is arrived, of whose good news touching your estate and proceedings I am very glad to hear. And howsoever he was robbed on the way by the Frenchmen, yet I hope your loss will not be great, for the conceit of so great a return doth

[7] The *Fortune*.

[8] The *Sparrow*, 30 tons, whose shallop brought the 7 unwanted passengers to Plymouth.

[9] The *Charity*, 100 tons, accompanied by the *Swan*, 30 tons. They departed London about 30 April and arrived Plymouth about 30 June. The Council for New England was very averse to these doings of Weston, and tried to get the Privy Council to order his ships seized for going to New England "in contempt of authority."

much animate the Adventurers, so that I hope some matter of importance will be done by them, etc. As for myself, I have sold my adventure and debts unto them, so as I am quit [1] of you, and you of me for that matter, etc.

Now, though I have nothing to pretend as an adventurer amongst you, yet I will advise you a little for your good, if you can apprehend it. I perceive and know as well as another, the dispositions of your Adventurers, whom the hope of gain hath drawn on to this they have done; and yet I fear that hope will not draw them much further. Besides, most of them are against the sending of them of Leyden, for whose cause this business was first begun, and some of the most religious (as Mr. Greene by name) excepts against them. So that my advice is (you may follow it if you please) that you forthwith break off your joint stock, which you have warrant to do both in law and conscience, for the most part of the Adventurers have given way unto it by a former letter. And the means you have there, which I hope will be to some purpose by the trade of this spring, may with the help of some friends here, bear the charge of transporting those of Leyden. And when they are with you, I make no question, but by God's help you will be able to subsist of yourselves; but I shall leave you to your discretion.

I desired divers of the Adventurers, as Mr. Peirce, Mr. Greene and others, if they had anything to send you, either victuals or letters, to send them by these ships; and, marveling they sent not so much as a letter, I asked our passengers what letters they had, and with some difficulty one of them told me he had one, which was delivered to him with |76| great charge of secrecy, and for more security to buy a pair of new shoes and sew it between the soles for fear of intercepting. I, taking the letter, wondering what mystery might be in it, broke it open and found this treacherous letter subscribed by the hands of Mr. Pickering and Mr. Greene. Which letter, had it come to your hands without answer, might have caused the hurt, if not the ruin, of us all. For assuredly if you had followed their instructions and showed us that unkindness which they advise you unto, to hold us in distrust as enemies, etc., it might have been an occasion to have set us together by the ears, to the destruction of us all; for I do believe that in such a case, they, knowing what business hath been between us, not only my brother but others also would have been violent and heady against you, etc.

I meant to have settled the people I before and now send, with or

[1] See how his promise is fulfilled (Bradford).

near you, as well for their as your more security and defense, as help on all occasions. But I find the Adventurers so jealous and suspicious, that I have altered my resolution and given order to my brother and those with him to do as they and himself shall find fit. Thus, etc.

Your loving friend,
THOMAS WESTON

April 10, 1621.[2]

Some Part of Mr. Pickering's Letter Before Mentioned

TO MR. BRADFORD AND MR. BREWSTER, etc.

My dear love remembered unto you all, etc. The company hath bought out Mr. Weston, and are very glad they are freed of him, he being judged a man that thought himself above the general, and not expressing so much the fear of God as was meet in a man to whom such trust should have been reposed in a matter of so great importance. I am sparing to be so plain as indeed is clear against him, but a few words to the wise.

Mr. Weston will not permit letters to be sent in his ships, nor anything for your good or ours, of which there is some reason in respect of himself, etc. His brother Andrew, whom he doth send as principal in one of these ships, is a heady young man and violent, and set against you there and the company here; plotting with Mr. Weston their own ends, which tend to your and our undoing in respect of our estates there, and prevention of our good ends.[3] For by credible testimony we are informed his purpose is to come to your colony, pretending he comes for and from the Adventurers, and will seek to get what you have in readiness |77| into his ships, as if they came from the Company; and possessing all, will be so much profit to himself. And further to inform themselves what special places or things you have discovered, to the end that they may suppress and deprive you, etc.

The Lord, who is the watchman of Israel and sleepeth not, preserve you and deliver you from unreasonable men. I am sorry that there is cause to admonish you of these things concerning this man. So I leave you to God, who bless and multiply you into thousands,

[2] Obviously a mistake for 1622.

[3] Andrew Weston, returning to England in the *Charity*, carried off an Indian boy of one of the Massachusetts sachems; the Council for New England, which disliked Weston only less than the Pilgrims did, ordered him to return the boy by the first ship.

to the advancement of the glorious gospel of our Lord Jesus, Amen. Fare well,

Your loving friends,
EDWARD PICKERING
WILLIAM GREENE

I pray conceal both the writing and delivery of this letter, but make the best use of it. We hope to set forth a ship ourselves within this month.

The Heads of his Answer [4]

MR. BRADFORD, this is the letter that I wrote unto you of; which to answer in every particular is needless and tedious. My own conscience and all our people can and I think will testify that my end in sending the ship *Sparrow* was your good, etc. Now I will not deny but there are many of our people rude fellows, as these men term them; yet I presume they will be governed by such as I set over them, and I hope not only to be able to reclaim them from that profaneness that may scandalize the voyage, but by degrees to draw them to God, etc. I am so far from sending rude fellows to deprive you either by fraud or violence of what is yours, as I have charged the master of the ship *Sparrow* not only to leave with you 2000 of bread, but also a good quantity of fish,[5] etc. But I will leave it to you to consider what evil this letter would or might have done, had it come to your hands and taken the effect the other desired.

Now if you be of the mind that these men are, deal plainly with us, and we will seek our residence elsewhere; if you are as friendly as we have thought you to be, give us the entertainment of friends; and we will take nothing from you, neither meat, drink nor lodging, but what we will in one kind or other pay you for, etc. I shall leave in the country a little ship (if God send her safe thither) with mariners and fishermen to stay there. Who shall coast and trade with the savages and the old plantation.[6] It may be we shall be as helpful to you as you will be to us. I think I shall see you the next spring, and so I commend you to the protection of God, who ever keep you.

Your loving friend,
THOMAS WESTON |78|

[4] I.e., Weston's comment on the intercepted letter above.

[5] But he left not his own men a bite of bread (Bradford).

[6] The little ship was the *Swan;* the "old plantation" probably means Virginia, for the *Records of the Virginia Company* (II 496) note a "pynnace of Mr. Weston's" bringing provisions to Jamestown in the summer of 1623.

Thus all their hopes in regard of Mr. Weston were laid in the dust; and all his promised help turned into an empty advice, which they apprehended was neither lawful nor profitable for them to follow. And they were not only thus left destitute of help in their extreme wants, having neither victuals nor anything to trade with; but others prepared and ready to glean up what the country might have afforded for their relief.

As for those harsh censures and suspicions intimated in the former and following letters; they desired to judge as charitably and wisely of them as they could, weighing them in the balance of love and reason; and though they (in part) came from godly and loving friends, yet they conceived many things might arise from over-deep jealousy and fear, together with unmeet provocations, though they well saw Mr. Weston pursued his own ends and was embittered in spirit. For after the receipt of the former letters, the Governor received one from Mr. Cushman (who went home in the ship) and was always intimate with Mr. Weston (as former passages declare) and it was much marveled that nothing was heard from him all this while. But it should seem it was the difficulty of sending, for this letter was directed as the letter of a wife to her husband, who was here, and brought by him to the Governor. It was as followeth:

Beloved Sir, I heartily salute you, with trust of your health and many thanks for your love. By God's providence we got well home the 17 of February, being robbed by the Frenchmen by the way, and carried by them into France, and were kept there 15 days, and lost all that we had that was worth taking; but thanks be to God, we escaped with our lives and ship.[7] I see not that it worketh any discouragement here; I purpose by God's grace to see you shortly, I hope in June next or before. In the mean space know these things, and I pray you be advertised a little. Mr. Weston hath quite broken off from

[7] This was the *Fortune*, Thomas Barton master, which took the first returns home in December 1621. A document in the Public Records Office, printed in Arber *Story of the Pilgrim Fathers* p. 506 and 1912 ed. Bradford I 268, tells how she was captured by a French warship and carried into the Ile de Dieu off the coast of Poitou and pillaged of cargo to the value of £400 and equipment worth £50, and the passengers' effects. The French Governor, after detaining them two weeks and feeding them only with "lights, livers and entrails," released them. Capt. John Smith mentions this in *New Englands Trials*.

our company, through some discontents that arose betwixt him and some of our Adventurers, and hath sold all his adventures, and hath now sent three small ships for his particular plantation. The greatest whereof, being 100 tons,[8] Mr. Reynolds goeth master, and he with the rest purposeth to come himself, for what end I know not.

The people which they carry are no men for us; wherefore I pray you entertain them not, neither exchange man for man with them, except it be some of your worst. He [9] hath taken a patent for himself; if they offer to buy anything of you, let it be such as you can spare, and let them give the worth of it. If they borrow anything of you, let them leave a good pawn, etc. It is like he |78 [2]| will plant to the southward of the Cape, for William Trevore hath lavishly told but what he knew or imagined of Capawack, Mohegan and the Narragansetts.[1] I fear these people will hardly deal so well with the savages as they should. I pray you therefore signify to Squanto that they are a distinct body from us, and we have nothing to do with them, neither must be blamed for their faults, much less can warrant their fidelity.

We are about to recover our losses in France. Our friends at Leyden are well and will come to you as many as can this time. I hope all will turn to the best. Wherefore I pray you be not discouraged, but gather up yourself, to go through these difficulties cheerfully and with courage in that place wherein God hath set you, until the day of refreshing come. And the Lord God of sea and land bring us comfortably together again, if it may stand with His glory.

Yours,
[March or April 1623] ROBERT CUSHMAN

On the other side of the leaf, in the same letter, came these few lines from Mr. John Peirce, in whose name the Patent was taken, and of whom more will follow, to be spoken in its place.

WORTHY SIR, I desire you to take into consideration that which is written on the other side, and not any way to damnify your own col-

[8] The *Charity;* the other two were the *Sparrow* and *Swan.*

[9] Weston; apparently he pretended to have obtained a patent for Wessagusset (the south side of Boston Bay) but he had none.

[1] Capawack is Martha's Vineyard; Mohegan, the Pequot country in eastern Connecticut. Trevore was a seaman engaged to stay in Plymouth a year, and who returned in the *Fortune.*

ony, whose strength is but weakness, and may thereby be more enfeebled. And for the letters of association, by the next ship we send I hope you shall receive satisfaction. In the meantime, whom you admit I will approve. But as for Mr. Weston's company, I think them so base in condition (for the most part) as in all appearance not fit for an honest man's company; I wish they prove otherwise. My purpose is not to enlarge myself, but cease in these few lines, and so rest

Your loving friend,
JOHN PEIRCE

[*Desperate Straits; Succour from Virginia*]

All these things they pondered and well considered; yet concluded to give his men friendly entertainment, partly in regard of Mr. Weston himself, considering what he had been unto them and done for them, and to some more especially; and partly in compassion to the people, who were now come into a wilderness (as themselves were) and were by the ship [2] to be presently put ashore (for she was to carry other passengers to Virginia, who lay at great charge); and they were altogether unacquainted and knew not what to do. So as they had received his former company of seven men and victualed them as their own hitherto, so they also received these (being about sixty lusty men) and gave |79| housing for themselves and their goods. And many being sick, they had the best means the place could afford them. They stayed here the most part of the summer till the ship came back again from Virginia. Then, by his direction or those whom he set over them, they removed into the Masachusetts Bay, he having got a patent for some part there (by light of their former discovery in letters sent home). Yet they left all their sick folk here till they were settled and housed; but of their victuals they had not any, though they were in great want, nor anything else in recompense of any courtesy done them; neither did they desire it, for they saw they were an unruly company and had no good government over them, and by disorder would soon fall into wants if Mr. Weston came not the sooner amongst them; and

[2] The *Charity*.

therefore, to prevent all after occasion, would have nothing of them.[3]

Amidst these straits, and the desertion of those from whom they had hoped for supply, and when famine began now to pinch them sore, they not knowing what to do, the Lord (who never fails His) presents them with an occasion beyond all expectation; this boat which came from the eastward brought them a letter from a stranger of whose name they had never heard before,[4] being a captain of a ship come there a-fishing. This letter was as followeth, being thus inscribed:

To all his good friends at Plymouth, these, etc.

FRIENDS, COUNTRYMEN, and NEIGHBOURS: I salute you, and wish you all health and happiness in the Lord. I make bold with these few lines to trouble you, because unless I were unhuman I can do no less. Bad news doth spread itself too far; yet I will so far inform you that myself, with many good friends in the south colony of Virginia have received such a blow that 400 persons large [5] will not make good our losses. Therefore I do intreat you (although not knowing you) that the old rule which I learned when I went to school may be sufficient; that is, Happy is he whom other men's harms doth make to beware. And now again and again, wishing all those that willingly would serve the Lord, all health and happiness in this world and everlasting peace in the world to come. And so I rest,

Yours,
JOHN HUDDLESTON

By this boat the Governor returned a thankful answer, as was meet, and sent a boat of their own with them, which was piloted by them, in which Mr. Winslow was sent to procure what provi-

[3] Weston's "60 lusty men" sponged on the Pilgrims until September 1622—the sick ones still longer—when they established a settlement in the present town of Weymouth, called by the Indians Wessagusset. Charles Francis Adams has told the story of Weston's colony entertainingly in *Three Episodes of Massachusetts History* (1892).

[4] Captain John Huddleston, master of the *Bona Nova* of 200 tons, is described in the *Records of the Virginia Company of London* I 370 as "one of the sufficientest masters that ever came thither." He was now on a fishing voyage to Maine. He writes of the terrible Indian massacre of 1622.

[5] I.e., taken together.

sions he could of the ships; who was kindly received by the foresaid gentleman, who not only spared what he |90 [6]| could, but writ to others to do the like. By which means he got some good quantity and returned in safety. By which the Plantation had a double benefit; first, a present refreshing by the food brought and, secondly, they knew the way to those parts for their benefit hereafter. But what was got, and this small boat brought, being divided among so many, came but to a little; yet by God's blessing it upheld them till harvest. It arose but to a quarter of a pound of bread a day to each person, and the Governor caused it to be daily given them; otherwise, had it been in their own custody, they would have ate it up and then starved; but thus, with what else they could get, they made pretty shift till corn was ripe.

[*The Fort Built; Visitors from Virginia Received*]

This summer they built a fort with good timber, both strong and comely, which was of good defense, made with a flat roof and battlements, on which their ordnance were mounted, and where they kept constant watch, especially in time of danger. It served them also for a meeting house and was fitted accordingly for that use. It was a great work for them in this weakness and time of wants, but the danger of the time required it; and both the continual rumors of the fears from the Indians here, especially the Narragansetts, and also the hearing of that great massacre in Virginia, made all hands willing to dispatch the same.[7]

Now the welcome time of harvest approached, in which all

[6] Bradford omits 80–89 in his numbering, but there is no hiatus in the text.

[7] Winslow, in *Good Newes* pp. 13, 39–40 says that the fort was begun in June 1622, after he had returned from Monhegan with the provisions, and that it required ten months to complete. He also indicates that the arguments for and against "preparedness" were about the same then as now: "Amongst us divers seeing the work prove tedious, would have dissuaded from proceeding, flattering themselves with peace and security, and accounting it rather a work of superfluity and vainglory than of simple necessity." The devil, he observes, will cause "reasonable men to reason against their own safety." This fort, on Burial Hill, was also used for divine worship. Isaack de Rasieres, secretary of New Netherland, visited Plymouth in 1627; his description of the fort, and of the Sabbath-day procession up the hill to worship, every man armed and marching three abreast, is classic. It is translated in J. F. Jameson ed. *Narratives of New Netherland* (1909) pp. 111–12.

had their hungry bellies filled. But it arose but to a little, in comparison of a full year's supply; partly because they were not yet well acquainted with the manner of Indian corn (and they had no other), also their many other employments; but chiefly their weakness for want of food, to tend it as they should have done. Also, much was stolen both by night and day before it became scarce eatable, and much more afterward. And though many were well whipped, when they were taken for a few ears of corn; yet hunger made others, whom conscience did not restrain, to venture. So as it well appeared that famine must still ensue, the next year also if not some way prevented, or supply should fail, to which they durst not trust. Markets there was none to go to, but only the Indians, and they had no trading commodities.

Behold, now, another providence of God. A ship comes into the |91| harbor, one Captain Jones being chief therein.[8] They were set out by some merchants to discover all the harbors between this and Virginia, and the shoals of Cape Cod, and to trade along the coast where they could. This ship had store of English beads (which were then good trade) and some knives; but would sell none but at dear rates and also a good quantity together. Yet they were glad of the occasion and fain to buy at any rate; they were fain to give after the rate of cento per cento,[9] if not more; and yet pay away coat-beaver at 3*s* per pound, which in a few years after yielded 20*s*. By this means they were fitted again to trade for beaver and other things, and intended to buy what corn they could.

But I will here take liberty to make a little digression. There was in this ship a gentleman, by name Mr. John Pory.[1] He had been secretary in Virginia and was now going home, passenger in

[8] Thomas Jones, who had been on voyages to the East Indies and Virginia, now commanded the *Discovery*, 60 tons, in the employ of the Virginia Company. He got into trouble both with his employers and with the Council for New England by taking furs forcibly and trying to kidnap Indians.

[9] I.e., 100 per cent.

[1] John Pory, an alumnus of Caius College, Cambridge, and a friend of Richard Hakluyt, was a learned and much traveled gentleman. His own account of his visit to Plymouth on this occasion, recently discovered, was published by Champlin Burrage as *John Pory's Lost Description of Plymouth Colony in the Earliest Days of the Pilgrim Fathers* (1918). He had nothing but praise for the Pilgrims, their hospitality, and their military preparedness.

this ship. After his departure he writ a letter to the Governor, in the postscript whereof he hath these lines:

To yourself and Mr. Brewster, I must acknowledge myself in many ways indebted; whose books I would have you think very well bestowed on him, who esteemeth them such jewels. My haste would not suffer me to remember, much less to beg, Mr. Ainsworth's elaborate work upon the five books of Moses.[2] Both his and Mr. Robinson's do highly commend the authors as being most conversant in the Scriptures, of all others. And what good (who knows) it may please God to work by them, through my hands (though most unworthy), who finds such high content in them. God have you all in his keeping.

Your unfeigned and firm friend,
August 28, 1622 JOHN PORY

These things I here insert for honour sake of the author's memory, which this gentleman doth thus ingeniously acknowledge. And himself, after his return, did this poor Plantation much credit amongst those of no mean rank. But to return. |92|

[*A Voyage in Search of Corn*]

Shortly after harvest Mr. Weston's people who were now seated at the Massachusetts, and by disorder (as it seems) had made havoc of their provisions, began now to perceive that want would come upon them. And hearing that they here had bought trading commodities and intended to trade for corn, they writ to the Governor and desired they might join with them, and they would employ their small ship [3] in the service; and further requested either to lend or sell them so much of their trading commodities as their part might come to, and they would undertake to make payment when Mr. Weston, or their supply, should come. The Governor condescended upon equal terms of agree-

[2] Henry Ainsworth *Annotations upon the Fourth Book of Moses, called Numbers* (London 1619). Pory's wish to borrow this book for light reading at sea is one of the many indications that learned Anglicans of that era were as much interested in theology as the Puritans.

[3] The *Swan*. Weston's men at Wessagusset, according to Winslow, were already in bad odor with the local Indians because of stealing corn.

ment, thinking to go about the Cape to the southward with the ship, where some store of corn might be got.

All things being provided, Captain Standish was appointed to go with them, and Squanto for a guide and interpreter, about the latter end of September; but the winds put them in again, and putting out the second time, he [4] fell sick of a fever, so the Governor went himself. But they could not get about the shoals of Cape Cod for flats and breakers, neither could Squanto direct them better nor the master durst venture any further. So they put into Manamoyick Bay and got with [5] they could there. In this place Squanto fell sick of an Indian fever, bleeding much at the nose (which the Indians take for a symptom of death) and within a few days died there; desiring the Governor to pray for him that he might go to the Englishmen's God in Heaven; and bequeathed sundry of his things to sundry of his English friends as remembrances of his love; of whom they had a great loss.

They got in this voyage, in one place and other,[6] about 26 or 28 hogsheads of corn and beans, which was more than the Indians could well spare in these parts, for they set but a little till they got English hoes. And so were fain to return, being sorry they could not get about the Cape, to have been better laden. Afterward the Governor took a few men and went to the inland places to get what he could, and to fetch it home at the spring, which did help them something. |93|

After these things, in February a messenger came from John Sanders, who was left chief over Mr. Weston's men in the Bay of

[4] Standish. Richard Green, Weston's brother-in-law and one of the few respectable characters in his settlement, died at Plymouth just before the voyage started. Winslow *Good Newes* has more details of this expedition.

[5] Bradford's *lapsus calami* for *what*. Manamoyick is the present Pleasant Bay, to which there were then two inlets practicable for deep-sea vessels, since closed up.

[6] They returned around the Cape, stretched across Boston Harbor, where no corn was to be had, then doubled back to the Bay side of the Cape, obtaining corn from Aspinet the Nauset sachem near the place of the first encounter, and at Mattakeeset. A northerly gale cast the *Swan's* shallop so far up on the beach near the present Yarmouthport that they could not float her; and as she had no other boat to lighter out the corn, Bradford kenched it and walked home some 50 miles, "receiving all respect that could be had from the Indians in his journey." Standish led a party back to Mattakeeset in January 1623 and recovered both shallop and corn. Winslow *Good Newes*.

Massachusetts, who brought a letter showing the great wants they were fallen into; and he would have borrowed a hogshead of corn of the Indians, but they would lend him none. He desired advice whether he might not take it from them by force to succour his men till he came from the eastward whither he was going. The Governor and rest dissuaded him by all means from it, for it might so exasperate the Indians as might endanger their safety, and all of us might smart for it; for they had already heard how they had so wronged the Indians by stealing their corn, etc. as they were much incensed against them. Yea, so base were some of their own company as they went and told the Indians that their Governor was purposed to come and take their corn by force. The which, with other things, made them enter into a conspiracy against the English, of which more in the next. Herewith I end this year.

CHAPTER XIV

Anno Dom: 1623 [*Sad Straits of Weston's Men, and the Great Indian Conspiracy*]

It may be thought strange that these people should fall to these extremities in so short a time; being left competently provided when the ship left them, and had an ambition by that moiety of corn that was got by trade, besides much they got of the Indians where they lived, by one means and other. It must needs be their great disorder, for they spent excessively whilst they had or could get it; and, it may be, wasted part away among the Indians; for he that was their chief was taxed by some amongst them for keeping Indian women, how truly I know not. And after they began to come into wants, many sold away their clothes and bed coverings; others (so base were they) became servants to the Indians, and would cut them wood and fetch them water for a capful of corn; others fell to plain stealing, both night and day, from the Indians, of which they grievously complained. In the end, they came to that misery that some starved and died with cold and hunger. One in gathering shellfish was so weak as he stuck fast in the mud and was found dead in the place. At last most of them left their dwellings and scattered up and down in the |94| woods and by the watersides, where they could find ground nuts [1] and clams, here six and there ten.

By which their carriages [2] they became contemned and scorned of the Indians, and they began greatly to insult over them in a most insolent manner. Insomuch that many times as they lay thus scattered abroad and had set on a pot with ground nuts or shellfish, when it was ready the Indians would come and eat it up; and when night came, whereas some of them had a sorry blanket or such like to lap themselves in, the Indians would take it and let the other lie all night in the cold, so as their condition was very lamentable. Yea, in the end they were fain to hang

[1] A low plant with edible tubers on its roots, once very common in New England.

[2] I.e., conduct.

one of their men whom they could not reclaim from stealing, to give the Indians content.[3]

Whilst things went in this manner with them, the Governor and people here had notice that Massasoit their friend was sick and near unto death. They sent to visit him, and withal sent him such comfortable things as gave him great content and was a means of his recovery. Upon which occasion he discovers the conspiracy of these Indians, how they were resolved to cut off Mr. Weston's people for the continual injuries they did them, and would now take opportunity of their weakness to do it, and for that end had conspired with other Indians their neighbours thereabout; and, thinking the people here would revenge their death, they therefore thought to do the like by them, and had solicited him to join with them. He advised them therefore to prevent it, and that speedily, by taking of some of the chief of them before it was too late, for he assured them of the truth hereof.[4]

This did much trouble them, and they took it into serious deliberation, and found upon examination other evidence to give light hereunto, too long here to relate. In the meantime, came one of them from the Massachusetts with a small pack at his back,

[3] Thomas Morton of Merrymount, in his *New English Canaan* (1637), spun a yarn about this execution, to the effect that Weston's men in order to placate the Indians, offered to hang a sickly member of their company, who was doomed to die anyway, instead of the thief. Samuel Butler picked this up and pinned it on the Pilgrims in Part ii Canto 2 of *Hudibras* (ed. 1710):

> "Our *Brethren* of *New England* use
> Choice *Malefactors* to excuse,
> And *Hang* the *Guiltless* in their stead,
> Of whom the *Churches* have less need."

A useful cobbler, having slain an Indian "Not out of *Malice* but meer *Zeal*, because he was an *Infidel*," the local chief "Tottipottymoy" demands his death; but the "Saints . . . maturely having weigh'd" that he was a useful citizen,

> "Yet to do
> The Indian *Hoghan Moghgan* too
> Impartial Justice, in his stead did
> Hang an old *Weaver* that was Bed-rid."

[4] Winslow, who was one of the delegation to visit Massasoit, tells of it in great detail in *Good Newes* (Young's *Chronicles* chap. xx). Massasoit, who was suffering from constipation following a bout of gluttony, was relieved by "physic" and chicken broth, and his life was saved.

and though he knew not a foot of the way, yet he got safe hither but lost his way; which was well for him for he was pursued, and so was missed. He told them here, how all things stood amongst them, and that he durst stay no longer; he apprehended they (by what he observed) would be all knocked in the head shortly.[5]

This made them make the more haste, and dispatched a boat away with Captain Standish and some men, who found them in a miserable condition, out of which he rescued them and helped them to some relief, cut off some few of the chief conspirators, and according to his order, offered to bring them all hither if they thought good, and they should fare no worse than themselves, till Mr. Weston or some supply came to them.[6] Or, if any other course liked them better, he was to do them any helpfulness he could. They thanked him and the rest, but most of them desired he would help them with some corn, and they would go with their small ship to the eastward, where haply they might hear of Mr. Weston or some supply from him, seeing the time of the year was for fishing ships to |95| be in the land; if not, they would work among the fishermen for their living and get their passage into England, if they heard nothing from Mr. Weston in time. So they shipped what they had of any worth, and he got them all the corn he could (scarce leaving to bring him home), and saw them well out of the bay, under sail at sea, and so came home, not taking the worth of a penny of anything that was theirs. I have but touched these things briefly, because they have already been published in print more at large.

This was the end of these, that some time boasted of their strength (being all able, lusty men) and what they would do and bring to pass in comparison of the people here, who had many women and children and weak ones amongst them. And said at their first arrival, when they saw the wants here, that they would take another course and not to fall into such a condition as this simple people were come to. But a man's way is not in his

[5] The messenger was Phineas Pratt, who wrote a narrative of it many years later when the sole survivor of Weston's colony. It is printed in *Collections* of the Massachusetts Historical Society, 4th ser. IV 472–6.

[6] Additional details are in Winslow (Young's *Chronicles* chap. xxi) and a letter of Bradford, 8 Sept. 1623, printed in *American Historical Review* VIII 295.

own power, God can make the weak to stand. Let him also that standeth take heed lest he fall.[7]

[*Weston Arrives, and Makes Trouble*]

Shortly after, Mr. Weston came over with some of the fishermen, under another name, and the disguise of a blacksmith, where he heard of the ruin and dissolution of his colony. He got a boat and with a man or two came to see how things were. But by the way, for want of skill, in a storm he cast away his shallop in the bottom of the bay between Merrimac River and Piscataqua, and hardly escaped with life. And afterwards fell into the hands of the Indians, who pillaged him of all he saved from the sea, and stripped him out of all his clothes to his shirt. At last he got to Piscataqua[8] and borrowed a suit of clothes, and got means to come to Plymouth. A strange alteration there was in him, to such as had seen and known him in his former flourishing condition; so uncertain are the mutable things of this unstable world. And yet men set their hearts upon them, though they daily see the vanity thereof.

After many passages, and much discourse (former things boiling in his mind but bit in as was discerned) so he desired to borrow some beaver of them; and told them he had hope of a ship and good supply to come to him, and then they should have anything for it they stood in need of. They gave little credit to his supply, but pitied his case and remembered former courtesies. They told him he saw their wants, and they knew not when they should have any supply, also how the case stood between them and their Adventurers he well knew; they had not much beaver, and if they should let him have it, it were enough to make a mutiny among the people, seeing there was no other means to procure them food which they so much wanted, and clothes also. Yet they told him they would help him, considering his necessity, but must do it secretly for the former reasons. So they let him have 100 beaver skins which weighed 170-odd pounds.

Thus they helped him when all the world failed him, and with

[7] Romans xiv.4 and 1 Corinthians x.12.

[8] The settlement then called Strawberry Bank, later Portsmouth, N H.

this means he went again to the ships, and stayed his small ship and some of his men, and bought provisions and fitted himself; and it was the only foundation |96| of his after course. But he requited them ill, for he proved after a bitter enemy unto them upon all occasions, and never repaid them anything for it to this day, but reproaches and evil words. Yea, he divulged it to some that were none of their best friends, whilst he yet had the beaver in his boat; that he could now set them altogether by the ears, because they had done more than they could answer in letting him have this beaver, and he did not spare to do what he could. But his malice could not prevail.

[*End of the "Common Course and Condition"*]

All this while no supply was heard of, neither knew they when they might expect any. So they began to think how they might raise as much corn as they could, and obtain a better crop than they had done, that they might not still thus languish in misery. At length, after much debate of things, the Governor (with the advice of the chiefest amongst them) gave way that they should set corn every man for his own particular, and in that regard trust to themselves; in all other things to go on in the general way as before. And so assigned to every family a parcel of land, according to the proportion of their number, for that end, only for present use (but made no division for inheritance) and ranged all boys and youth under some family. This had very good success, for it made all hands very industrious, so as much more corn was planted than otherwise would have been by any means the Governor or any other could use, and saved him a great deal of trouble, and gave far better content. The women now went willingly into the field, and took their little ones with them to set corn; which before would allege weakness and inability; whom to have compelled would have been thought great tyranny and oppression.

The experience that was had in this common course and condition, tried sundry years and that amongst godly and sober men, may well evince the vanity of that conceit of Plato's and other ancients applauded by some of later times; that the taking away of property and bringing in community into a commonwealth would make them happy and flourishing; as if they were wiser than God.[9] For this community (so far as it was) was found to breed much confusion and discontent and retard much employment that would have been to their benefit and comfort. For the young men, that were most able and fit for labour and service, did repine that they should spend their time and strength to work for other men's wives and children without any recompense. The strong, or man of parts, had no more in division of victuals and clothes than he that was weak and not able to do a quarter the other could; this was thought injustice. The aged and graver men to be ranked and |97| equalized in labours and victuals, clothes, etc., with the meaner and younger sort, thought it some indignity and disrespect unto them. And for men's wives to be commanded to do service for other men, as dressing their meat, washing their clothes, etc., they deemed it a kind of slavery, neither could many husbands well brook it. Upon the point all being to have alike, and all to do alike, they thought themselves in the like condition, and one as good as another; and so, if it did not cut off those relations that God hath set amongst men, yet it did at least much diminish and take off the mutual respects that should be preserved amongst them. And would have been worse if they had been men of another condition. Let none object this is men's corruption, and nothing to the course itself. I answer, seeing all men have this corruption in them, God in His wisdom saw another course fitter for them.

[*Short Rations and the ill-fated* Paragon]

But to return. After this course settled, and by that their corn was planted, all their victuals were spent and they were only to rest on God's providence; at night not many times knowing

[9] Presumably Bradford had read the gibes at Plato's *Republic* in Jean Bodin *de Republica* (1586), a copy of which is mentioned in the inventory of his estate. "But he [Plato] understood not that by making all things thus common, a Commonweal must needs perish: for nothing can be public, where nothing is private. . . . Albeit that such a Commonweal should also be against the law of God and nature . . . which expressly forbids us to . . . desire anything that another man's is." *The Six Bookes of a Commonweale . . . Done into English by Richard Knolles*, Book I p. 11 (London, 1606).

where to have a bit of anything the next day. And so, as one well observed, had need to pray that God would give them their daily bread, above all people in the world. Yet they bore these wants with great patience and alacrity of spirit; and that for so long a time as for the most part of two years. Which makes me remember what Peter Martyr writes (in magnifying the Spaniards) in his 5th Decade, page 208. "They" (saith he) "led a miserable life for five days together, with the parched grain of maize only, and that not to saturity"; and then concludes, "that such pains, such labours, and such hunger, he thought none living which is not a Spaniard could have endured." [1]

But alas! these, when they had maize (that is, Indian corn) they thought it as good as a feast and wanted not only for five days together, but some time two or three months together, and neither had bread nor any kind of corn. Indeed, in another place, in his 2nd Decade, page 94, he mentions how others of them were worse put to it, where they were fain to eat dogs, toads and dead men, and so died almost all. From these extremities the Lord in His goodness kept these His people, and in their great wants preserved both their lives and healths. Let His name have the praise. Yet let me here make use of his [2] conclusion, which in some sort may be applied to this people:

"That with their miseries they opened a way to these new lands, and after these storms, with what ease other men came to inhabit in them, in respect of the calamities these men suffered; so as they seem to go to a bride feast where all things are provided for them."

They having but one boat left and she not over-well fitted, they were divided into several companies, six or seven to a gang or company, and so went out, with a net they had bought, to take bass and such like fish by course, every company knowing their turn.[3] No sooner was the boat discharged |98| of what she

1 Peter Martyr d'Anghiera *de Nouo Orbe, or the Historie of the West Indies*, Englished by Richard Eden, 1612.

2 Peter Martyr's.

3 The Striped Bass (*Roccus lineatus*), now a favorite sporting fish along the New England coast, was then the favorite food fish, described by William Wood in *New Englands Prospect* (1634) as "a delicate fine, fat, fast fish . . .

brought, but the next company took her and went out with her. Neither did they return till they had caught something, though it were five or six days before, for they knew there was nothing at home, and to go home empty would be a great discouragement to the rest. Yea, they strive who should do best. If she stayed long or got little, then all went to seeking of shellfish, which at low water they digged out of the sands. And this was their living in the summer time, till God sent them better; and in winter they were helped with ground nuts and fowl. Also in the summer they got now and then a deer, for one or two of the fittest was appointed to range the woods for that end, and what was got that way was divided amongst them.

At length they received some letters from the Adventurers, too long and tedious here to record, by which they heard of their further crosses and frustrations; beginning in this manner (these letters were dated December 21, 1622).[4]

Loving Friends, As your sorrows and afflictions have been great, so our crosses and interceptions in our proceedings here have not been small. For after we had with much trouble and charge sent the *Paragon* away to sea, and thought all the pain past, within fourteen days after she came again hither, being dangerously leaked and bruised with tempestuous storms, so as she was fain to be had into the dock, and an £100 bestowed upon her. All the passengers lying upon our charge for six or seven weeks, and much discontent and distem-

---

and though men are soon wearied with other fish, yet are they never with bass." They swarmed around the mouths of streams and so could be taken easily from small boats with hook and line, or by netting in tidal estuaries when the tide went down. Bass disappeared from the New England coast in the 19th century but have since returned in limited numbers, and have recovered their popularity as a food fish when served fresh. William Hubbard's contemporary *History of New England* p. 80 notes that with their net the Pilgrims "took a multitude of bass, which was their livelihood all that summer. It is a fish not inferior to a salmon, that comes upon the coast every summer pressing into most of the great creeks every tide. Few countries have such an advantage. Sometimes 1500 of them have been stopped in a creek and taken in one tide." As early as 1639 bass were becoming scarce, so that Massachusetts Bay forbade the use of them for manure. Henry B. Bigelow and W. W. Welsh *Fishes of the Gulf of Maine* (*Bulletin* of U. S. Bureau of Fisheries, XI, 1924).

[4] Bradford's note in the margin.

per was occasioned hereby, so as some dangerous event had like to ensued. But we trust all shall be well and work for the best and your benefit, if yet with patience you can wait, and but have strength to hold in life. Whilst these things were doing, Mr. Weston's ship[5] came and brought divers letters from you, etc. It rejoiceth us much to hear of those good reports that divers have brought home from you, etc.

So far of this letter.

[*John Peirce cheats the Pilgrims*]

This ship was bought by Mr. John Peirce, and set out at his own charge, upon hope of great matters. These passengers, and the goods the company sent in her, he took in for freight, for which they agreed with him to be delivered here. This was he in whose name their first Patent was taken, by reason of acquaintance and some alliance that some of their friends had with him. But his name was only used in trust. But when he saw they were here hopefully thus seated, and by the success God gave them had obtained the favour of the Council of New England, he goes and sues to them for another patent of much larger extent, in their names, which was easily obtained.[6] But he meant to keep it to himself and allow them what he pleased, to hold of him as tenants and sue to his courts as chief lord, as will appear by that which follows. But the Lord marvelously crossed him; for after this first return, and the charge above mentioned, when she was again fitted he pesters himself and takes in more passengers, and those not very good, to help to bear his losses, and sets out the

[5] The *Charity*, which sailed for home about 1 Oct. 1622. The *Paragon* made two false starts in the fall of 1622, and on the third was wrecked.

[6] John Peirce, as we have seen, had already taken out two patents for the Pilgrims, the first from the Virginia Company in Feb. 1620 and the second from the Council for New England on 1 June 1621. The patent here referred to was dated 20 April 1622. It was in the form of a deed poll of the land to Peirce, as Bradford says. When the Council heard the complaint of the Pilgrims that they had not been consulted, they invalidated this patent and declared the one of 1 June 1621 to be still in force. *Lectures on the Early History of Massachusetts* (1869) p. 152.

second time. But |99| what the event was will appear from another letter from one of the chief of the company,[7] dated the 9th of April, 1623, writ to the Governor here, as followeth:

LOVING FRIEND, When I writ my last letter, I hoped to have received one from you well-nigh by this time. But when I writ in December I little thought to have seen Mr. John Peirce till he had brought some good tidings from you. But it pleased God, he brought us the woeful tidings of his return when he was half way over, by extreme tempest. Wherein the goodness and mercy of God appeared in sparing their lives, being 109 souls. The loss is so great to Mr. Peirce, etc., and the Company put upon so great charge, as verily, etc.

Now with great trouble and loss we have got Mr. John Peirce to assign over the grand Patent to the Company, which he had taken in his own name, and made quite void our former grant. I am sorry to write how many here think that the hand of God was justly against him, both the first and second time of his return. In regard he, whom you and we so confidently trusted, but only to use his name for the Company, should aspire to be lord over us all, and so make you and us tenants at his will and pleasure, our assurance or Patent being quite void, and disannulled by his means. I desire to judge charitably of him. But his unwillingness to part with his royal lordship, and the high rate he set it at, which was £500, which cost him but £50, makes many speak and judge hardly of him. The Company are out, for goods in his ship, with charge about the passengers, £640.

We have agreed with two merchants for a ship of 140 tuns, called the *Anne*, which is to be ready the last of this month, to bring 60 passengers, and 60 tun of goods, etc.

This was dated April 9, 1623.

These were their own words and judgment of this man's dealing and proceedings. For I thought it more meet to render them in theirs than my own words. And yet, though there was never got other recompense than the resignation of this Patent, and the shares he had in adventure for all the former great sums, he was never quiet, but sued them in most of the chief courts in England,

[7] Probably by Robert Cushman. The Company he refers to here is Weston's Adventurers and the Pilgrims; i.e., all £10 shareholders in the Plymouth enterprise.

and when he was still cast,[8] brought it to the Parliament. But he is now dead, and I will leave him to the Lord.

[*Important Personages Arrive*]

This ship [9] suffered the greatest extremity at sea at her second return, that one shall lightly hear of, to be saved, as I have been informed by Mr. William Peirce [1] who was then master of her, and many others that were passengers in her. It was about the middle of February; the storm was for the most part of fourteen days, but for two or three days and nights together in most violent extremity. After they had cut down their mast, the storm beat off their round house and all their upper works; three men had work enough at the helm, and he that conned the ship before the sea, was fain |100| to be bound fast for washing away. The seas did so over-rake them, as many times those upon the deck knew not whether they were within board or without; and once she was so foundered in the sea as they all thought she would never rise again. But yet the Lord preserved them and brought them at last safe to Portsmouth, to the wonder of all men that saw in what a case she was in, and heard what they had endured.

About the latter end of June came in a ship,[2] with Captain Francis West, who had a commission to be Admiral of New England, to restrain interlopers and such fishing ships as came to fish and trade without a license from the Council of New Eng-

[8] I.e., defeated. For this suit, and a more favorable view of Peirce than Bradford's, see C. M. Andrews *Colonial Period* I (1934) 281–3.

[9] The *Paragon.*

[1] Master William Peirce made many voyages to New England, and is frequently mentioned in the course of this History. He was the most highly esteemed of all shipmasters who served the Puritan colonies.

[2] The *Plantation,* built in Whitby for several principal members of the Council for New England, including the Duke of Lenox, the Earl of Arundel, Sir Ferdinando Gorges and his son and brother, at a cost of £1250. Her captain, Francis West, a brother of Lord de la Warr, had been a leading planter in Virginia since 1608. He was appointed Admiral–i.e., judge of admiralty–by the Council 2 Nov. 1622; one of his objectives being to take possession of the Island of Mount Desert, which had been rediscovered and renamed Mount Mansell by Sir Robert Mansell. A facsimile of the Royal Proclamation "prohibiting interloping and disorderly trading to New England," that he brought out, is printed in 1912 ed. Bradford I 313.

land, for which they should pay a round sum of money. But he could do no good of them, for they were too strong for him, and he found the fishermen to be stubborn fellows. And their owners, upon complaint made to the Parliament, procured an order that fishing should be free. He told the Governor they spoke with a ship at sea, and were aboard her, that was coming for this Plantation, in which were sundry passengers; and they marveled she was not arrived, fearing some miscarriage; for they lost her in a storm that fell shortly after they had been aboard. Which relation filled them full of fear, yet mixed with hope. The master of this ship had some two hogsheads of pease to sell, but seeing their wants, held them at £9 sterling a hogshead, and under £8 he would not take, and yet would have beaver at an under rate. But they told him they had lived so long without, and would do still, rather than give so unreasonably. So they went from hence to Virginia.

[*The* Anne *and* Little James]

About fourteen days after came in this ship, called the *Anne*, whereof Mr. William Peirce was master; and about a week or ten days after came in the pinnace which, in foul weather, they lost at sea, a fine, new vessel of about 44 tun,[3] which the Company had built to stay in the country. They brought about 60 persons for the General,[4] some of them being very useful persons and became good members to the body; and some were the wives and children of such as were here already. And some were so bad as they were fain to be at charge to send them home again the next year. Also, besides these there came a company that did not belong to the General Body but came on their Particular and were to have lands assigned them and be for themselves, yet to be subject to the general government; which caused some difference and disturbance |101| amongst them, as will after appear.

I shall here again take liberty to insert a few things out of such letters as came in this ship, desiring rather to manifest things in

[3] The *Little James*.

[4] I.e., to share and share alike with the Planters and Adventurers as distinct from bodies of men like Weston's who were "on their Particular."

their words and apprehensions, than in my own, as much as may be without tediousness.

BELOVED FRIENDS, I kindly salute you all, with trust of your healths and welfare, being right sorry that no supply hath been made to you all this while; for defense whereof, I must refer you to our general letters. Neither indeed have we now sent you many things which we should and would, for want of money. But persons more than enough (though not all we should) for people come flying in upon us, but moneys come creeping in to us. Some few of your old friends are come, as, etc. So they come dropping to you, and by degrees; I hope ere long you shall enjoy them all. And because people press so hard upon us to go, and often such as are none of the fittest, I pray you write earnestly to the Treasurer and direct what persons should be sent. It grieveth me to see so weak a company sent you; and yet had I not been here they had been weaker. You must still call upon the company here to see that honest men be sent you, and threaten to send them back if any other come, etc. We are not any way so much in danger as by corrupt and naughty persons. Such and such came without my consent, but the importunity of their friends got promise of our Treasurer in my absence. Neither is there need we should take any lewd men, for we may have honest men enow, etc.

Your assured friend,
ROBERT CUSHMAN

This following was from the general.[5]

LOVING FRIENDS, We most heartily salute you in all love and hearty affection. Being yet in hope that the same God which hath hitherto preserved you in a marvelous manner doth yet continue your lives and health, to His own praise and all our comforts. Being right sorry that you have not been sent unto all this time, etc. We have in this ship sent such women as were willing and ready to go to their husbands and friends, with their children, etc. We would not have you discontented because we have not sent you more of your old friends, and in special him [6] on whom you most depend. Far be it from us to neglect you or contemn him. But as the intent was at first, so the

[5] The general body of Adventurers. Their treasurer was James Sherley.

[6] J. R. (Bradford)—John Robinson. The eagerness of the Pilgrims to attract more of the Leyden congregation, especially their pastor, is very evident.

event at last shall show it, that we will deal fairly, and squarely answer your expectations to the full.

There are also come unto you some honest men to plant upon their own Particulars besides you. A thing which, if we should not give way unto, we should wrong both them and you; them, by putting them on things more inconvenient; and you, for that being honest men they will be a strengthening to the place, and good neighbours |102| unto you. Two things we would advise you of, which we have likewise signified to them here. First, the trade for skins to be retained for the general till the dividend;[7] secondly, that their settling by you be with such distance of place as is neither inconvenient for the lying of your lands, nor hurtful to your speedy and easy assembling together.

We have sent you divers fishermen with salt, etc. Divers other provisions we have sent you, as will appear in your bill of lading, and though we have not sent all we would (because our cash is small) yet it is that we could, etc.

And although it seemeth you have discovered many more rivers and fertile grounds than that where you are; yet seeing by God's providence that place fell to your lot, let it be accounted as your portion, and rather fix your eyes upon that which may be done there than languish in hopes after things elsewhere. If your place be not the best, it is better; you shall be the less envied and encroached upon; and such as are earthly minded will not settle too near your border. If the land afford you bread and the sea yield you fish, rest you a while contented; God will one day afford you better fare.[8] And all men shall know you are neither fugitives nor discontents, but can, if God so order it, take the worst to yourselves with content, and leave the best to your neighbours with cheerfulness.

Let it not be grievous unto you that you have been instruments to break the ice for others who come after with less difficulty; the honour shall be yours to the world's end, etc.

We bear you always in our breasts, and our hearty affection is towards you all, as are the hearts of hundreds, more which never saw your faces; who doubtless pray for your safety as their own, as we ourselves both do and ever shall, that the same God which hath so marvelously preserved you from seas, foes and famine, will still preserve you from all future dangers, and make you honourable amongst men, and glorious in bliss at the last day. And so the Lord be with

[7] The dividing up of assets scheduled for 1627.

[8] This proved rather a prophecy than advice (Bradford).

you all, and send us joyful news from you, and enable us with one shoulder so to accomplish and perfect this work as much glory may come to Him that confoundeth the mighty by the weak, and maketh small things great. To whose greatness be all glory for ever and ever.

This letter was subscribed with thirteen of their names.

[*More Semi-Starvation*]

These passengers, when they saw their low and poor condition ashore, were much daunted and dismayed, and according to their divers humors were diversely affected. Some wished themselves in England again; others fell a-weeping, fancying their own misery in what they saw now in others; other some pitying the distress they saw their friends had been long in, and still were under. In a word, all were full of sadness. Only some of their old friends rejoiced to see them, and that it was no worse with them, for they could not expect it should be better, and now hoped they should enjoy better days together. And truly it was |103| no marvel they should be thus affected, for they were in a very low condition; many were ragged in apparel and some little better than half naked, though some that were well stored before were well enough in this regard. But for food they were all alike, save some that had got a few pease of the ship that was last here. The best dish they could present their friends with was a lobster or a piece of fish without bread or anything else but a cup of fair spring water. And the long continuance of this diet, and their labours abroad, had something abated the freshness of their former complexion; but God gave them health and strength in a good measure, and showed them by experience the truth of that word, (Deuteronomy viii.3) "That man liveth not by bread only, but by every word that proceedeth out of the mouth of the Lord doth a man live."

When I think how sadly the Scripture speaks of the famine in Jacob's time, when he said to his sons, "Go buy us food, that we may live and not die," (Genesis xlii.2 and xliii.1) that the famine was great or heavy in the land. And yet they had such great herds and store of cattle of sundry kinds, which, besides flesh, must needs produce other food as milk, butter and cheese, etc. And yet it was counted a sore affliction. Theirs here must needs be very great, therefore, who not only wanted the staff of bread but all these things, and had no Egypt to go to. But God fed them out of the sea for the most part, so wonderful is His providence over His in all ages; for His mercy endureth for ever.[9]

I may not here omit how, notwithstand all their great pains and industry, and the great hopes of a large crop, the Lord seemed to blast, and take away the same, and to threaten further and more sore famine unto them. By a great drought which continued from the third week in May, till about the middle of July, without any rain and with great heat for the most part, insomuch as the corn began to wither away though it was set with fish, the moisture whereof helped it much. Yet at length it began to languish sore, and some of the drier grounds were parched like withered hay, part whereof was never recovered. Upon which they set apart a solemn day of humiliation, to seek the Lord by humble and fervent prayer, in this great distress. And He was pleased to give them a gracious and speedy answer, both to their own and the Indians' admiration that lived amongst them. For all the morning, and greatest part of the day, it was clear weather and very hot, and not a cloud or any sign of rain to be seen; yet toward evening it began to overcast, and shortly after to rain with such sweet and gentle showers as gave them cause of rejoicing and blessing God. It came without either wind or thunder or any violence, and by degrees in that abundance as that the earth was thoroughly wet and soaked and therewith. Which did so apparently revive and quicken the decayed corn and other fruits, as was wonderful to see, and made the Indians astonished to behold. And afterwards the Lord sent them such seasonable showers, with interchange of fair warm weather as, through His blessing, caused a fruitful and liberal harvest, to their no small

[9] The following paragraph is written on the verso of fol. 102. It was "overslipped in its place," noted Bradford, who at first wrote most of it on the verso of fol. 79 as of 1622; but discovering his error before completing the passage, drew his pen across it and noted beneath: "This is to be here rased out and is to be placed on page 103 where it is inserted."

comfort and rejoicing. For which mercy, in time convenient, they also set apart a day of thanksgiving.[1]

On the other hand, the Old Planters were afraid that their corn, when it was ripe, should be imparted to the newcomers, whose provisions which they brought with them they feared would fall short before the year went about, as indeed it did. They came to the Governor and besought him that as it was before agreed that they should set corn for their Particular (and accordingly they had taken extraordinary pains thereabout) that they might freely enjoy the same; and they would not have a bit of the victuals now come, but wait till harvest for their own and let the newcomers enjoy what they had brought; they would have none of it except they could purchase any of it of them by bargain or exchange. Their request was granted them, for it gave both sides good content; for the newcomers were as much afraid that the hungry Planters would have ate up the provisions brought, and they should have fallen into the like condition.

This ship was in a short time laden with clapboard by the help of many hands. Also they sent in her all the beaver and other furs they had, and Mr. Winslow was sent over with her to inform of all things and procure such things as were thought needful for their present condition. By this time harvest was come, and instead of famine now God gave them plenty, and the face of things was changed, to the rejoicing of the hearts of many, for which they blessed God. And the effect of their particular planting was well seen, for all had, one way and other, pretty well to bring the year about; and some of the abler sort and more |104| industrious had to spare, and sell to others; so as any general want or famine hath not been amongst them since to this day.

1 Love in *Fast and Thanksgiving Days of New England* pp. 84–5 argues that this Thanksgiving Day was celebrated 30 July 1623, the day before the *Anne* arrived. The Pilgrims never had a regular fall Thanksgiving Day. A law of 15 Nov. 1636 (*Plymouth Colony Records* XI 18) allows the Governor and Assistants "to command solemn days of humiliation by fasting, etc., and also for thanksgiving as occasion shall be offered."

[*Agreement with Newcomers*]

Those that came on their Particular looked for greater matters than they found or could attain unto, about building great houses and such pleasant situations for them as themselves had fancied; as if they would be great men and rich all of a sudden. But they proved castles in the air. These were the conditions agreed on between the Colony and them.

1. That the Governor, in the name and with the consent of the Company, doth in all love and friendship receive and embrace them, and is to allot them competent places for habitations within the town. And promiseth to show them all such other courtesies as shall be reasonable for them to desire or us to perform.

2. That they on their parts be subject to all such laws and orders as are already made, or hereafter shall be, for the public good.

3. That they be freed and exempt from the general employments of the said Company (which their present condition of community requireth) except common defense and such other employments as tend to the perpetual good of the Colony.

4. Towards the maintenance of government and public officers of the said Colony, every male above the age of sixteen years shall pay a bushel of Indian wheat, or the worth of it, into the common store.

5. That, according to the agreement the merchants made with them before they came, they are to be wholly debarred from all trade with the Indians, for all sorts of furs and such like commodities, till the time of the communality be ended.

[*The Robert Gorges Colony*]

About the middle of September arrived Captain Robert Gorges [2] in the Bay of the Massachusetts, with sundry passengers and

[2] Robert Gorges, second son of Sir Ferdinando, had a patent from the Council for New England, dated 30 Dec. 1622, to the entire North Shore of Massachusetts Bay, extending 30 miles inland. Wessagusset, deserted by Weston's beachcombers, lay outside his grant. See C. F. Adams *Three Episodes* and Raymond Gorges *A History of the Family of Gorges* (1944). Gorges's plans, like those of his father, were very grand; he was accompanied by six gentlemen and many servants.

families, intending there to begin a plantation; and pitched upon the place Mr. Weston's people had forsaken. He had a commission from the Council of New England to be general governor of the country, and they appointed for his counsel and assistance, Captain Francis West the aforesaid admiral, Christopher Levett, Esquire,[3] and the Governor of Plymouth for the time being, etc. Also they gave him authority to choose such other as he should find fit. Also they gave, by their commission, full power to him and his assistants or any three of them, whereof himself was alway to be one, to do and execute what to them should seem good, in all cases, capital, criminal and civil, etc., with divers other instructions. Of which, and his commission, it pleased him to suffer the Governor here to take a copy.

He gave them notice of his arrival by letter, but before they could visit him he went to the eastward with the ship he came in. But a storm arising, and they wanting a good pilot to harbor them in those parts, they bore up for this harbor. He and his men were here kindly entertained; he stayed here fourteen days.

In the meantime came in Mr. Weston with his small ship, which he had now recovered. |105 [4]| Captain Gorges took hold of the opportunity, and acquainted the Governor here that one occasion of his going to the eastward was to meet with Mr. Weston, and call him to account for some abuses he had to lay to his charge. Whereupon he called him before him and some other of his assistants, with the Governor of this place, and charged him first with the ill carriage of his men at the Massachusetts, by which means the peace of the country was disturbed; and himself and the people which he had brought over to plant in that bay were thereby much prejudiced. To this Mr. Weston easily answered, that what was that way done was in his absence, and might have befallen any man; he left them sufficiently provided, and conceived they would have been well governed, and for any

[3] Christopher Levett, author of *A Voyage into New England* (1628), was a traveler and master mariner who bought a £100 share in the Council for New England in 1623 and was granted 6000 acres of land; he conceived a plan of building a city, but wandered from the site of Portland, Maine, to the Piscataqua and returned to England in 1624.

[4] Originally numbered 145. The ship was the *Swan*.

error committed he had sufficiently smarted. This particular was passed by.

A second [charge] was, for an abuse done to his father, Sir Ferdinando Gorges, and to the State. The thing was this: he used him and others of the Council of New England, to procure him a license for the transporting of many pieces of great ordnance for New England, pretending great fortification here in the country, and I know not what shipping. The which when he had obtained, he went and sold them beyond seas for his private profit; for which (he said) the State was much offended, and his father suffered a shrewd check, and he had order to apprehend him for it.

Mr. Weston excused it as well as he could, but could not deny it, it being one main thing (as was said) for which he withdrew himself. But after many passages, by the mediation of the Governor and some other friends here, he was inclined to gentleness, though he apprehended the abuse of his father deeply. Which, when Mr. Weston saw, he grew more presumptuous and gave such provoking and cutting speeches as made him rise up in great indignation and distemper, and vowed that he would either curb him, or send him home for England. At which Mr. Weston was something daunted, and came privately to the Governor here to know whether they would suffer Captain Gorges to apprehend him. He was told they could not hinder him, but much blamed him, that after they had pacified things he should thus break out, by his own folly and rashness, to bring trouble upon himself, and them too. He confessed it was his passion, and prayed the Governor to entreat for him, and pacify him if he could. The which at last he did, with much ado; so he was called again, and the Governor was content to take his own bond to be ready to make further answer, when either he or the Lords should send for him. And at last he took only his word, and there was a friendly parting on all hands.[5]

But after he was gone, Mr. Weston in lieu of thanks to the

[5] Sir Ferdinando Gorges in *A Briefe Narration of the Originall Undertakings of the Advancement of Plantations into the Parts of America* (London 1658, reprinted in J. P. Baxter *Sir Ferdinando Gorges,* II) is even more severe than the Pilgrims on Thomas Weston and his beachcombers, for their abuse and deception of the Indians.

Governor[6] and his friends here, gave them this quib behind their backs for all their pains: That though they were but young justices, yet they were good beggars. Thus they parted at this time. And shortly after the Governor took his leave and went to the Massachusetts by land, being very thankful for his kind entertainment.

[*A Bad Fire*]

The ship stayed here and fitted herself to go for Virginia, having some passengers there to deliver. And with her returned sundry of those from hence which came over on their Particular, some out of discontent and dislike of the country, others by reason of a fire that broke out and burned the houses they lived in, and all their provisions |106| so as they were necessitated thereunto.[7]

This fire was occasioned by some of the seamen that were roistering in a house where it first began, making a great fire in very cold weather, which broke out of the chimney into the thatch and burned down three or four houses and consumed all the goods and provisions in them. The house in which it began was right against their storehouse, which they had much ado to save, in which were their common store and all their provisions, the which, if it had been lost, the plantation had been overthrown. But through God's mercy it was saved by the great diligence of the people and care of the Governor and some about him. Some would have had the goods thrown out; but if they had there would much have been stolen by the rude company that belonged to these two ships, which were almost all ashore. But a trusty company was placed within, as well as those that with wet cloths and other means kept off the fire without, that if necessity required they might have them out with all speed. For they suspected some malicious dealing, if not plain treachery, and whether it was only suspicion or not, God knows; but this is certain, that when the tumult was greatest, there was a voice heard (but from whom it was not known) that bid them look well about them, for all were not friends that were near them. And

[6] Robert Gorges.

[7] The date of this fire was 5 Nov. 1623.

shortly after, when the vehemency of the fire was over, smoke was seen to arise within a shed that was joined to the end of the storehouse, which was wattled up with boughs, in the withered leaves whereof the fire was kindled; which some running to quench, found a long firebrand of an ell long, lying under the wale [8] on the inside, which could not possibly come there by casualty but must be laid there by some hand, in the judgment of all that saw it. But God kept them from this danger, whatever was intended.

[*Weston Again in Trouble*]

Shortly after Captain Gorges, the general Governor, was come home to the Massachusetts, he sends a warrant to arrest Mr. Weston and his ship, and sends a master to bring her away thither, and one Captain Hanson (that belonged to him) to conduct him along. The Governor and others here were very sorry to see him take this course, and took exception at the warrant as not legal nor sufficient; and withal writ to him to dissuade him from this course, showing him that he would but entangle and burden himself in doing this. For he could not do Mr. Weston a better turn, as things stood with him. For he had a great many men that belonged to him in this bark, and was deeply engaged to them for wages, and was in a manner out of victuals (and now winter), all which would light upon him, if he did arrest his bark. In the meantime, Mr. Weston had notice to shift for himself; but it was conceived he either knew not whither to go or how to mend himself, but was rather glad of the occasion, and so stirred not.

But the Governor would not be persuaded, but |107| sent a very formal warrant under his hand and seal, with strict charge as they would answer it to the State; he also writ that he had better considered of things since he was here, and he could not answer it to let him go so, besides other things that were come to his knowledge since, which he must answer to. So he was suffered to proceed, but he found in the end that to be true that was

[8] Bradford may have meant *wall*, which he spells thus elsewhere; but he probably means what he writes, as *wale* is used for a horizontal member in the basket-like construction of sheds such as those that the Pilgrims erected.

told him; for when an inventory was taken of what was in the ship, there was not victuals found for above 14 days, at a poor allowance, and not much else of any great worth; and the men did so cry out of him for wages and diet in the meantime, as made him soon weary. So as in conclusion it turned to his loss and the expense of his own provisions. And towards the spring they came to agreement, after they had been to the eastward, and the Governor restored him his vessel again and made him satisfaction in biscuit, meal and such like provisions for what he had made use of that was his, or what his men had any way wasted or consumed. So Mr. Weston came hither again, and afterward shaped his course for Virginia, and so for present I shall leave him. He died afterwards at Bristol, in the time of the wars, of the sickness in that place.[9]

The Governor [1] and some that depended upon him returned for England, having scarcely saluted the country in his government, not finding the state of things here to answer his quality and condition. The people dispersed themselves; some went for England, others for Virginia; some few remained and were helped with supplies from hence. The Governor brought over a minister with him, one Mr. Morrell,[2] who about a year after the Governor returned, took shipping from hence. He had I know not what power and authority of superintendency over other churches granted him, and sundry instructions for that end, but he never showed it or made any use of it. (It should seem he saw it was in vain.) He only spoke of it to some here at his going away. This was in effect the end of a second plantation in that place.

There were also this year some scattering beginnings made in other places, as at Piscataqua, by Mr. David Thompson,[3] at Monhegan, and some other places by sundry others.

9 This sentence inserted later by Bradford.

1 Robert Gorges.

2 The Rev. William Morrell employed his leisure in Massachusetts in writing an ode to New England in Latin hexameters, which he published with his own English translation in 1625 as *New-England, or, A Briefe Ennaration of the Ayre, Earth, Water, Fish and Fowles of that Country*.

3 David Thompson, with a grant from the Council for New England, settled at Little Harbor, Portsmouth, N. H., but soon moved to the island still called Thompsons in Boston Harbor.

It rests now that I speak a word about the pinnace spoken of before,[4] which was sent by the Adventurers to be employed in the country. She was a fine vessel and with her flags and streamers, pendants and waistcloths, etc. bravely set out; and I fear the Adventurers did overpride themselves in her, for she had ill success. However, they erred grossly in two things about her. First, though she had a sufficient master, yet she was rudely manned, and all her men were upon shares, and none was to have any wages but the master. Secondly, whereas they mainly looked at trade, they had sent nothing of any value to trade with. When the men came here and met with ill counsel from Mr. Weston and his crew, with others of the same stamp, neither master nor Governor could scarce rule |108| them, for they exclaimed that they were abused and deceived. For they were told they should go for a man of war, and take I know not whom, French and Spaniards, etc. They would neither trade nor fish except they had wages; in fine, they would obey no command of the masters, so as it was apprehended they would either run away with the vessel or get away with the ships, and leave her. So as Mr. Peirce and others of their friends persuaded the Governor to change their condition and give them wages, which was accordingly done. And she was sent about the Cape to the Narragansetts to trade. But they made but a poor voyage of it; some corn and beaver they got, but the Dutch used to furnish them with cloth and better commodities, they having only a few beads and knives which were not there much esteemed. Also, in her return home, at the very entrance into their own harbor, she had like to have been cast away in a storm, and was forced to cut her mainmast by the board to save herself from driving on the flats that lie without, called Brown's Islands, the force of the wind being so great as made her anchors give way and she drove right upon them. But her mast and tackling being gone, they held her till the wind shifted.

[4] The *Little James*, 44 tons, John Bridge master. His own amusingly illiterate letter complaining of the men, "fowle weather" and ill fortune, is printed in Massachusetts Historical Society *Proceedings* XLIV 180.

CHAPTER XV

Anno Dom: 1624 [*Wreck of the* Little James]

The time of new election of their officers for this year being come, and the number of their people increased, and their troubles and occasions therewith, the Governor desired them to change the persons, as well as renew the election, and also to add more Assistants to the Governor for help and counsel and the better carrying on of affairs. Showing that it was necessary it should be so; if it was any honour or benefit, it was fit others should be made partakers of it; if it was a burthen (as doubtless it was) it was but equal others should help to bear it, and that this was the end [1] of annual elections. The issue was, that as before there was but one Assistant, they now chose five, giving the Governor a double voice; and afterwards they increased them to seven, which course hath continued to this day.

They having with some trouble and charge new-masted and rigged their pinnace, in the beginning of March they sent her well victualed to the eastward on fishing. She arrived safely at a place near Damariscove, and was there well harbored, in a place where ships used to ride, there being also some ships already arrived out of England. But shortly after there |109| arose such a violent and extraordinary storm, as the seas broke over such places in the harbor as was never seen before, and drove her against great rocks, which beat such a hole in her bilge as a horse and cart might have gone in, and after drove her into deep water, where she lay sunk.[2] The master was drowned, the rest of the men, all save one, saved their lives with much ado; all her provision, salt, and what else was in her was lost. And here I must leave her to lie till afterward.

Some of those that still remained here on their Particular be-

[1] I.e., purpose or object. The Pilgrims held annual elections because that was the custom in English corporations. New England became so accustomed to annual elections that Massachusetts did not have biennial state elections until 1917, and town officials are still elected annually. See W. H. Whitmore *The Massachusetts Civil List for the Colonial and Provincial Periods* (1870) for complete list of Plymouth Colony officials.

[2] The storm occurred 10 April 1624 according to the papers on litigation over the wreck of the *Little James,* which are printed in Massachusetts Historical Society *Proceedings* XLIV 178–89.

gan privately to nourish a faction; and being privy to a strong faction that was among the Adventurers in England, on whom sundry of them did depend. By their private whispering they drew some of the weaker sort of the company to their side, and so filled them with discontent as nothing would satisfy them except they might be suffered to be in their Particular also; and made great offers, so they might be freed from the General. The Governor, consulting with the ablest of the General Body what was best to be done herein, it was resolved to permit them so to do upon equal conditions. The conditions were the same in effect with the former before related, only some more added, as that they should be bound here to remain till the general partnership was ended. And also that they should pay into the store, the one half of all such goods and commodities as they should any wise raise above their food, in consideration of what charge had been laid out for them, with some such like things. This liberty granted, soon stopped this gap; for there was but a few that undertook this course when it came to, and they were as soon weary of it. For the other had persuaded them and Mr. Weston together, that there would never come more supply to the General Body, but the Particulars had such friends as would carry all, and do for them I know not what.

[*Winslow brings Cattle and Letters*]

Shortly after, Mr. Winslow came over and brought a pretty good supply, and the ship came on fishing—a thing fatal to this plantation.[3] He brought three heifers and a bull, the first beginning of any cattle of that kind in the land, with some clothing and other necessaries, as will further appear; but withal the report of a strong faction amongst the Adventurers against them, and especially against the coming of the rest from Leyden, and with what difficulty this supply was procured, and how, by their strong and long opposition, business was so retarded as not only they were now fallen too late for the fishing season, but the best men were taken up of the fishermen in the West Country; and he was forced to take such a master and company for that em-

[3] In the *Charity*, arriving in March 1624.

ployment as he could procure upon the present. Some letters from them shall better declare these things, being as followeth.[4] |111|

[*Objections of the "Particulars" Answered*]

With the former letter writ by Mr. Sherley, there were sent sundry objections concerning which he thus writeth: "These are the chief objections which they |112| that are now returned make against you and the country; I pray you consider them, and answer them by the first conveniency." These objections were made by some of those that came over on their Particular and were returned home, as is before mentioned, and were of the same suit with those that this other letter mentions. I shall here set them down, with the answers then made unto them, and sent over at the return of this ship. Which did so confound the objectors as some confessed their fault, and others denied what they had said and eat their words; and some others of them have since come over again, and here lived to convince themselves sufficiently, both in their own and other men's judgments.

1st objection was diversity about religion. *Answer:* We know no such matter, for here was never any controversy or opposition, either public or private (to our knowledge) since we came.

2nd obj.: Neglect of family duties on the Lord's Day. *Ans.:* We allow no such thing, but blame it in ourselves and others, and they that thus report it should have showed their Christian love the more if they had in love told the offenders of it, rather than thus to reproach them behind their backs. But (to say no more) we wish themselves had given better example.

3rd obj.: Want of both the sacraments. *Ans.:* The more is our grief, that our pastor is kept from us, by whom we might enjoy them; for we used to have the Lord's Supper every Sabbath, and baptism as often as there was occasion of children to baptize.[5]

[4] These will be found in Appendix V.

[5] English Puritans admitted only these two sacraments and only a regularly ordained minister could administer them; they did not consider a minister properly qualified unless ordained over a particular church by laying-on of hands. Elder Brewster, or any other layman, might conduct services and preach, but not baptize or administer the Lord's Supper. Compare the Rev. John Robinson's letter to Elder Brewster in Appendix V, which gives the basic texts. It is prob-

4th obj.: Children not catechized nor taught to read. *Ans.:* Neither is true, for divers take pains with their own as they can. Indeed, we have no common school for want of a fit person, or hitherto means to maintain one; though we desire now to begin.

5th obj.: Many of the Particular members of the plantation will not work for the General. *Ans.:* This also is not wholly true, for though some do it not willingly, and others not honestly, yet all do it; and he that doth worst gets his own food and something besides. But we will not excuse them, but labour to reform them the best we can; or else to quit the Plantation of them.

6th obj.: The water is not wholesome. *Ans.:* If they mean, not so wholesome as the good beer and wine in London (which they so dearly love), we will not dispute with them; but else for water it is as good as any in the world (for aught we know) and it is wholesome enough to us that can be content therewith.[6]

7th obj.: The ground is barren and doth bear no grass. |113| *Ans.:* It is here, as in all places, some better and some worse; and if they well consider their woods in England, they shall not find such grass in them as in their fields and meadows. The cattle find grass, for they are as fat as need be; we wish we had but one for every hundred, that here is grass to keep.[7] Indeed, this objection, as some other, are ridiculous to all here which see and know the contrary.

8th obj.: The fish will not take salt to keep sweet. *Ans.:* This is as true as that which was written, that there is scarce a fowl to be seen or a fish to be taken. Things likely to be true in a country where so many sail of ships come yearly a-fishing? They might as well say there can no ale or beer in London be kept from souring.

9th obj.: Many of them are thievish and steal one from another. *Ans.:* Would London had been free from that crime, then we should not have been troubled with these here. It is well

---

able that part of the trouble about Lyford arose from his administering sacraments privately to some of the "Particulars" without having been ordained, from the Puritan point of view.

[6] William Wood in *New Englands Prospect* (1634) pays another tribute to New England water: "Those that drink it be as healthful, fresh and lusty as they that drink beer."

[7] I.e., in the Colony there is grass enough to keep a hundredfold the cattle they now have.

known sundry have smarted well for it, and so are the rest like to do, if they be taken.

10th obj.: The country is annoyed with foxes and wolves. *Ans.:* So are many other good countries, too; but poison, traps and other such means will help to destroy them.

11th obj.: The Dutch are planted near Hudson's Bay [*sic*] and are likely to overthrow the trade. *Ans.:* They will come and plant in these parts, also, if we and others do not, but go home and leave it to them. We rather commend them than condemn them for it.

12th obj.: The people are much annoyed with mosquitoes. *Ans.:* They are too delicate and unfit to begin new plantations and colonies, that cannot endure the biting of a mosquito. We would wish such to keep at home till at least they be mosquito-proof. Yet this place is as free as any, and experience teacheth that the more the land is tilled, and the woods cut down, the fewer there will be, and in the end scarce any at all.

Having thus dispatched these things, that I may handle things together, I shall here insert two other letters from Mr. Robinson, their pastor, the one to the Governor, the other to Mr. Brewster their Elder. Which will give much light to the former things and express the tender love and care of a true pastor over them.[8]

[*Corn and Allotments of Land*]

|115| These things premised, I shall now prosecute the proceedings and affairs here. And before I come to other things, I must speak a word of their planting this year. They having found the benefit of their last year's harvest, and setting corn for their Particular, having thereby with a great deal of patience overcome hunger and famine. Which makes me remember a saying of Seneca's Epistle 123: "That a great part of liberty is a well governed belly, and to be patient in all wants." [9]

They began now highly to prize corn as more precious than silver, and those that had some to spare began to trade one with

[8] These will be found in Appendix V.

[9] *Magna pars libertatis est bene moratus venter et contumeliae patiens.* Seneca *ad Lucilium Epistulae Morales* cxxiii 3.

another for small things, by the quart, pottle[1] and peck, etc.; for money they had none, and if any had, corn was preferred before it. That they might therefore increase their tillage to better advantage, they made suit |116| to the Governor to have some portion of land given them for continuance, and not by yearly lot. For by that means, that which the more industrious had brought into good culture (by much pains) one year, came to leave it the next, and often another might enjoy it; so as the dressing of their lands were the more slighted over, and to less profit. Which being well considered, their request was granted. And to every person was given only one acre of land, to them and theirs, as near the town as might be; and they had no more till the seven years were expired. The reason was that they might be kept close together, both for more safety and defense, and the better improvement of the general employments.

Which condition of theirs did make me often think of what I had read in Pliny[2] of the Romans' first beginnings in Romulus's time. How every man contented himself with two acres of land, and had no more assigned them. And, Chapter 3, "It was thought a great reward, to receive at the hands of the people of Rome a pint of corn." And long after, the greatest present given to a Captain that had got a victory over their enemies, was as much ground as they could till in one day. And he was not counted a good, but a dangerous man, that would not content himself with seven acres of land. As also how they did pound their corn in mortars; as these people were forced to do many years before they could get a mill.[3]

[*Fishing, a Shipbuilder and a Salter*]

The ship which brought this supply was speedily discharged, and with her master and company sent to Cape Ann (of which

1 Two quarts.

2 Pliny *Naturalis Historiae* lib. 18, chap. 2 (Bradford). Translated from *Bina tunc iugera P. R. satis erant* (XVIII ii 9) and *dona amplissima imperatorum ac fortium civium quantum quis uno die plurimum circumaravisset, item quartarii farris aut heminae, conferente populo* (iii 9).

3 The first grist mill was established, on the Town Brook, in 1633. Why 13 years elapsed before this was done is not told; probably the Pilgrims could not get the machinery or the stones from England.

place they had got a patent, as before is showed)[4] on fishing; and because the season was so far spent some of the planters were sent to help to build their stage,[5] to their own hindrance. But partly by the lateness of the year, and more especially by the baseness of the master, one Baker, they made a poor voyage of it. He proved a very drunken beast, and did nothing (in a manner) but drink and guzzle and consume away the time and his victuals, and most of his company followed his example; and though Mr. William Peirce was to oversee the business and to be master of the ship home, yet he could do no good amongst them; so as the loss was great, and would have been more to them, but that they kept on a-trading there, which in those times got some store of skins, which was some help unto them.

The ship-carpenter that was sent them was an honest and very industrious man, and followed his labour very diligently, and made all that were employed with him do the like. He quickly built them two very good and strong shallops, which after did them great service, and a great and strong lighter, and had hewn timber for two ketches. But that was lost, for he fell into a fever in the hot season of the year, and though he had the best means the place could afford, yet he died; of whom they had a very |117| great loss, and were very sorry for his death. But he whom they sent to make salt was an ignorant, foolish, self-willed fellow. He bore them in hand, he could do great matters in making salt-works, so he was sent to seek out fit ground for his purpose; and after some search he told the Governor that he had found a sufficient place, with a good bottom to hold water, and otherwise very convenient, which he doubted not but in a short time to bring to good perfection, and to yield them great profit;

[4] On 1 Jan. 1624 Cushman and Winslow on behalf of "their Associates and Planters at Plymouth in New England" obtained a patent from the Earl of Sheffield of the Council for New England to "a certain tract of ground" in Cape Ann, together with islands, and fishing and hunting privileges, alleging that this had already been granted to Lord Sheffield by the Council for New England. It is described as 500 acres for public purposes, plus 30 acres for each planter, to "lie together upon the said Bay in one place, and not straggling." Text and facsimile of the original are in 1912 ed. Bradford I 407–10.

[5] A scaffold or light wharf for curing fish in the sun, as may be seen in many parts of the Maritime Provinces of Canada today; they are also used in Maine by lobstermen.

but he must have eight or ten men to be constantly employed. He was wished to be sure that the ground was good, and other things answerable, and that he could bring it to perfection; otherwise he would bring upon them a great charge by employing himself and so many men. But he was after some trial so confident as he caused them to send carpenters to rear a great frame for a large house to receive the salt, and such other uses. But in the end all proved vain; then he laid fault of the ground in which he was deceived; but if he might have the lighter to carry clay, he was sure then he could do it.

Now though the Governor and some other foresaw that this would come to little, yet they had so many malignant spirits amongst them, that would have laid it upon them in their letters of complaint to the Adventurers, as to be their fault that would not suffer him to go on, to bring his work to perfection. For as he by his bold confidence and large promises deceived them in England that sent him, so he had wound himself into these men's high esteem here, so as they were fain to let him go on till all men saw his vanity. For he could not do anything but boil salt in pans, and yet would make them that were joined with him believe there was so great a mystery in it as was not easy to be attained, and made them do many unnecessary things to blind their eyes, till they discerned his subtlety. The next year he was sent to Cape Ann, and the pans were set up there where the fishing was; but before summer was out he burnt the house and the fire was so vehement as it spoiled the pans, at least some of them, and this was the end of that chargeable business.

[*Rise and Fall of the Rev. John Lyford*]

The third eminent person (which the letters before mention) was the minister which they sent over, by name Mr. John Lyford. Of whom and whose doing I must be more large, though I shall abridge things as much as I can. When this man first came ashore, he saluted them with that reverence and humility as is seldom to be seen, and indeed made them ashamed, he so bowed and cringed unto them, and would have kissed their hands if they would have

|118| suffered him;[6] yea, he wept and shed many tears, blessing God that had brought him to see their faces, and admiring the things they had done in their wants, etc., as if he had been made all of love and the humblest person in the world. And all the while (if we may judge by his after carriages) he was but like him mentioned in Psalm x.10, "That croucheth and boweth, that heaps of poor may fall by his might." Or like to that dissembling Ishmael, who, when he had slain Gedaliah, went out weeping and met them that were coming to offer incense in the house of the Lord, saying "Come to Gedaliah" when he meant to slay them.[7]

They gave him the best entertainment they could, in all simplicity, and a larger allowance of food out of the store than any other had; and as the Governor had used, in all weighty affairs, to consult with their Elder, Mr. Brewster, together with his Assistants, so now he called Mr. Lyford also to counsel with them in their weightiest businesses. After some short time he desired to join himself a member to the church here, and was accordingly received. He made a large confession of his faith, and an acknowledgment of his former disorderly walking and his being entangled with many corruptions, which had been a burthen to his conscience, and blessed God for this opportunity of freedom and liberty to enjoy the ordinances of God in purity among His People; with many more such like expressions.

I must here speak a word also of Mr. John Oldham,[8] who was

[6] Of which were many witnesses (Bradford).

[7] Jeremiah xli.6 (Bradford). Although sundry writers eager to disparage the Pilgrims have searched assiduously, nothing has been found about Lyford before he arrived in Plymouth, except what Bradford relates in the following chapter. And although there has been a disposition in some quarters to make of him an Anglican martyr to Puritan bigotry (as Thomas Morton did in his *New English Canaan*) it is unlikely that he had ever taken holy orders. There is no record of him among the alumni of Oxford, Cambridge or Dublin, or on lists of ordinations; and although he did have a Protestant parish in Ireland, he may have obtained it under false pretenses. Having a large family he probably needed a job badly after having been expelled from his Irish parish, and he may well have ingratiated himself with the Adventurers, or have been a friend or relative to Richard Andrews, who later tried to recover Irish property for Lyford's son. C. K. Shipton well says, in his *Roger Conant* (1944) p. 35, that Lyford was "one of those individuals who so crave attention and importance that they take any path to gain them."

[8] Of Oldham, as of Lyford, there is no record before he came out in the *Anne* in 1623. He was a very different sort of person from the preacher; he

a copartner with him in his after courses. He had been a chief stickler in the former faction among the Particulars, and an intelligencer to those in England. But now, since the coming of this ship and he saw the supply that came, he took occasion to open his mind to some of the chief amongst them here, and confessed he had done them wrong both by word and deed, and writing into England. But he now saw the eminent hand of God to be with them, and His blessing upon them, which made his heart smite him; neither should those in England ever use him as an instrument any longer against them in anything. He also desired former things might be forgotten, and that they would look upon him as one that desired to close with them in all things, with such like expressions. Now whether this was in hypocrisy, or out of some sudden pang of conviction, which I rather think, God only knows. Upon it they show all readiness to embrace his love, and carry towards him in all friendliness, and called him to counsel with them in all chief affairs, as the other, without any distrust at all.

Thus all things seemed to go very comfortably and smoothly on amongst them, at which they did much rejoice. But this lasted not |119| long, for both Oldham and he[9] grew very perverse, and showed a spirit of great malignancy, drawing as many into faction as they could. Were they never so vile or profane, they did nourish and back them in all their doings, so they would but cleave to them and speak against the church here. So as there was nothing but private meetings and whisperings amongst them; they feeding themselves and others with what they should bring to pass in England by the faction of their friends there, which brought others as well as themselves into a fool's paradise. Yet they could not carry so closely but much of both their doings and sayings were discovered; yet outwardly they still set a fair face of things.

At length when the ship[1] was ready to go, it was observed Lyford was long in writing and sent many letters, and could not for-

quarreled with everyone, including Thomas Morton, who called him "Mad Jack." For his career see *Dictionary of American Biography* and C. F. Adams *Three Episodes*.

[9] Lyford.

[1] The *Charity*.

bear to communicate to his intimates such things as made them laugh in their sleeves, and thought he had done their errand sufficiently. The Governor and some other of his friends, knowing how things stood in England and what hurt these things might do, took a shallop and went out with the ship a league or two to sea, and called for all Lyford's and Oldham's letters. Mr. William Peirce being master of the ship (and knew well their evil dealing both in England and here) afforded him all the assistance he could. He found above twenty of Lyford's letters, many of them large and full of slanders and false accusations, tending not only to their prejudice, but to their ruin and utter subversion. Most of the letters they let pass, only took copies of them; but some of the most material they sent true copies of them and kept the originals lest he should deny them, and that they might produce his own hand against him. Amongst his letters they found the copies of two letters which he sent enclosed in a letter of his to Mr. John Pemberton, a minister and a great opposite[2] of theirs. These two letters, of which he took the copies, were one of them writ by a gentleman in England to Mr. Brewster here, the other by Mr. Winslow to Mr. Robinson in Holland, at his coming away, as the ship lay at Gravesend. They lying sealed in the great cabin, whilst Mr. Winslow was busy about the affairs of the ship, this sly merchant takes and opens them, takes these copies and seals them up again; and not only sends the copies of them thus to his friend and their adversary, but adds thereto in the margin many scurrilous and flouting annotations.

This ship went out towards evening, and in the night the Governor returned. They were somewhat blank at it, but after some weeks when they heard nothing, they then were as brisk as ever, thinking nothing had been known but all was gone current, and that the Governor went but to dispatch his own letters. The reason why the Governor and rest concealed these things the longer was to let things ripen that they |120| might better discover their intents and see who were their adherents. And the rather because amongst the rest they found a letter of one of their confederates, in which was written that Mr. Oldham and Mr. Lyford intended a reformation in church and commonwealth, and as soon as the

[2] Opponent.

ship was gone, they intended to join together and have the sacraments, etc.

For Oldham, few of his letters were found (for he was so bad a scribe as his hand was scarce legible) yet he was as deep in the mischief as the other. And thinking they were now strong enough, they began to pick quarrels at everything; Oldham being called to watch (according to order) refused to come, fell out with the Captain, called him rascal and beggarly rascal, and resisted him, drew his knife at him; though he offered him no wrong nor gave him no ill terms, but with all fairness required him to do his duty. The Governor, hearing the tumult, sent to quiet it, but he ramped more like a furious beast than a man, and called them all traitors and rebels and other such foul language as I am ashamed to remember. But after he was clapped up a while, he came to himself and with some slight punishment was let go upon his behaviour for further censure.

But to cut things short, at length it grew to this issue, that Lyford with his complices, without ever speaking one word either to the Governor, Church, or Elder, withdrew themselves and set up a public meeting apart on the Lord's Day; with sundry such insolent carriages, too long here to relate, beginning now publicly to act what privately they had been long plotting.

It was now thought high time, to prevent further mischief, to call them to account. So the Governor called a court and summoned the whole company to appear. And then charged Lyford and Oldham with such things as they were guilty of; but they were stiff, and stood resolutely upon the denial of most things, and required proof. They first alleged what was writ to them out of England, compared with their doings and practices here, that it was evident they joined in plotting against them, and disturbing their peace, both in respect of their civil and church state, which was most injurious. For both they and all the world knew they came hither to enjoy the liberty of their conscience and the free use of God's Ordinances, and for that end had ventured their lives and passed through so much hardship hitherto; and they and their friends had borne the charge of these beginnings, which was not small. And that Lyford for his part was sent over on this charge, and that both he and his great family was maintained on the same, and also was joined to the church and a member of them. And for him to plot against them, and seek their ruin, was most unjust and perfidious. And for |121| Oldham or any other that came over at their own charge, and were on their Particular: seeing they were received in courtesy by the Plantation, when they came only to seek shelter and protection under their wings, not being able to stand alone. That they (according to the fable) like the hedgehog whom the cony in a stormy day in pity received into her burrow, would not be content to take part with her, but in the end with her sharp pricks forced the poor cony to forsake her own burrow; so these men, with the like injustice, endeavoured to do the same to those that entertained them.

Lyford denied that he had anything to do with them in England, or knew of their courses, and made other things as strange, that he was charged with. Then his letters were produced and some of them read, at which he was struck mute. But Oldham began to rage furiously because they had intercepted and opened his letters, threatening them in very high language, and in a most audacious and mutinous manner stood up and called upon the people, saying, "My masters, where is your hearts? Now show your courage, you have oft complained to me so and so. Now is the time, if you will do anything, I will stand by you," etc. Thinking that everyone (knowing his humor) that had soothed and flattered him, or otherwise in their discontent uttered anything unto him, would now side with him in open rebellion. But he was deceived, for not a man opened his mouth, but all were silent, being strucken with the injustice of the thing.

Then the Governor turned his speech to Mr. Lyford and asked him if he thought they had done evil to open his letters; but he was silent, and would not say a word, well knowing what they might reply. Then the Governor showed the people he did it as a magistrate, and was bound to it by his place, to prevent the mischief and ruin that this conspiracy and plots of theirs, would bring on this poor Colony. But he, besides his evil dealing here, had dealt treacherously with his friends that trusted him, and stole their letters and opened them, and sent copies of them, with disgraceful annotations, to his friends in England. And then the

Governor produced them and his other letters under his own hand (which he could not deny) and caused them to be read before all the people, at which all his friends were blank, and had not a word to say.

It would be too long and tedious here to insert his letters, which would almost fill a volume, though I have them by me. I shall only note a few of the chief things collected out of them, with the answers to them as they were then given. And but a few of those many, only for instance, by which the rest may be judged of. |121 [8]|

First, he saith, the church would have none to live here but themselves; secondly, neither are any willing so to do if they had company to live elsewhere. Their answer was that this was false, in both the parts of it; for they were willing and desirous that any honest men may live with them, that will carry themselves peaceably and seek the common good, or at least do them no hurt. And again, there are many that will not live elsewhere so long as they may live with them.

2. That if there come over any honest men that are not of the Separation, they will quickly distaste them, etc. Their answer was as before, that it was a false calumniation; for they had many amongst them that they liked well of, and were glad of their company, and should be of any such like that should come amongst them.

3. That they excepted against him for these two doctrines raised from 2 Samuel xii.7. First that ministers must sometimes particularly apply their doctrine to special persons; secondly, that great men may be reproved as well as meaner. Their answer was that both these were without either truth or colour of the same, as was proved to his face, and that they had taught and believed these things long before they knew Mr. Lyford.

4. That they utterly sought the ruin of the Particulars; as appeareth by this, that they would not suffer any of the General either to buy or sell with them, or to exchange one commodity for another. Answer: This was a most malicious slander, and void of all truth, as was evidently proved to him before all men, for any of them did both buy, sell or exchange with them as of-

[8] The second folio so numbered.

ten as they had any occasion; yea, and also both lend and give to them when they wanted. And this the particular persons themselves could not deny, but freely confessed in open court. But the ground from whence this arose made it much worse. For he was in council with them, when one was called before them, and questioned, for receiving powder and biscuit from the gunner of the small ship which was the Company's, and had it put in at his window in the night; and also for buying salt of one that had no right to it, he not only stood to back him (being one of these Particulars) by excusing and extenuating his fault as long as he could, but upon this builds this mischievous and most false slander, that because they would not suffer them to buy stolen goods, *ergo* they sought their utter ruin. Bad logic for a divine!

5. Next he writes that he choked them with this: that they |122| turned men into their Particular and then sought to starve them and deprive them of all means of subsistence. To this was answered, he did them manifest wrong, for they turned none into their Particular; it was their own importunity and earnest desire that moved them, yea, constrained them to do it. And they appealed to the persons themselves for the truth hereof; and they testified the same against him before all present, as also that they had no cause to complain of any either hard or unkind usage.

6. He accuseth them with unjust distribution, and writeth that it was a strange difference, that some have been allowed 16 pounds of meal by the week, and others but four pounds; and then floutingly saith, "It seems some men's mouths and bellies are very little and slender over others." Answer: This might seem strange indeed to those to whom he writ his letters in England, which knew not the reason of it; but to him and others here it could not be strange, who knew how things stood. For the first comers had none at all, but lived on their corn. Those which came in the *Anne* the August before, and were to live 13 months of the provisions they brought, had as good allowance in meal and pease as it would extend to, the most part of the year. But a little before harvest, when they had not only fish but other fruits began to come in, they had but 4 pounds, having their liberty to make their own provisions. But some of these which came last,

as the ship carpenter, and sawyers, the salt men, and others that were to follow constant employments and had not an hour's time from their hard labours to look for anything above their allowance, they had at first 16 pounds allowed them; and afterwards, as fish and other food could be got, they had abatement, to 14 and 12; yea, some of them to 8 as the times and occasions did vary. And yet those which followed planting and their own occasions, and had but 4 pounds of meal a week, lived better than the other, as was well known to all. And yet it must be remembered that Lyford and his had always the highest allowance.

Many other things in his letters he accused them of, with many aggravations; as that he saw exceeding great waste of tools and vessels. And this, when it came to be examined, all the instance he could give was that he had seen an old hogshead or two fallen to pieces, and a broken hoe or two left carelessly in the fields by some; though he also knew that a godly, honest man was appointed to look to these things. But these things and such like was writ of by him, to cast disgrace and prejudice upon them, as thinking what came from a |123| minister would pass for current. Then he tells them that Winslow should say that there was not above seven of the Adventurers that sought the good of the Colony; that Mr. Oldham and himself had had much to do with them, and that the faction here might match the Jesuits for policy, with many the like grievous complaints and accusations. Then, in the next place, he comes to give his friends counsel and direction.

And first, that the Leyden company (Mr. Robinson and the rest) must still be kept back, or else all will be spoiled. And lest any of them should be taken in privately somewhere on the coast of England, as it was feared might be done, they must change the master of the ship (Mr. William Peirce) and put another also in Winslow's stead for merchant, or else it would not be prevented.

2. Then he would have such a number provided as might oversway them here. And that the Particulars should have voices in all courts and elections, and be free to bear any office. And that every Particular should come over as an Adventurer; if he be but

a servant; some other venturing £10, the bill may be taken out in the servant's name and then assigned to the party whose money it was, and good covenants drawn between them for the clearing of the matter; and this, saith he, would be a means to strengthen this side the more.

3. Then he tells them that if that Captain they spoke of should come over hither as a general,[4] he was persuaded he would be chosen Captain; for this Captain Standish looks like a silly boy and is in utter contempt.

4. Then he shows that if by the forementioned means they cannot be strengthened to carry and overbear things, it will be best for them to plant elsewhere by themselves; and would have it articled by them, that they might make choice of any place that they liked best within three or four miles' distance, showing there were far better places for plantation than this.

5. And lastly he concludes that if some number came not over to bear them up here, then there would be no abiding for them but by joining with these here. Then he adds, "Since I began to write, there are letters come from your company, wherein they would give sole authority in divers things unto the Governor here; which, if it take place, then *vae nobis*. But I hope you will be more vigilant hereafter, that nothing may pass in such a manner. I suppose" (saith he) "Mr. Oldham will write to you further of these things. I pray you conceal me in the discovery of these things," etc.

Thus I have briefly touched some chief things in his letters, and shall now return to their proceeding with him. After the reading of his letters before the whole company, he was demanded what he could say to these things. |124| But all the answer he made was, that Billington and some others had informed him of many things and made sundry complaints, which they now denied. He was again asked if that was a sufficient ground for him thus to accuse and traduce them by his letters and never say word to them, considering the many bonds between them.

And so they went on from point to point, and wished him or

[4] I.e., one of the Associates. The Captain was probably the famous John Smith, who states in his *General History* that he had applied for Standish's job, but the Pilgrims thought they could get his books "better cheap."

any of his friends and confederates not to spare them in anything. If he or they had any proof or witness of any corrupt or evil dealing of theirs, his or their evidence must needs be there present, for there was the whole company and sundry strangers. He said he had been abused by others in their informations (as he now well saw) and so had abused them. And this was all the answer they could have, for none would take his part in anything, but Billington and any whom he named denied the things and protested he wronged them and would have drawn them to such and such things which they could not consent to, though they were sometimes drawn to his meetings.

Then they dealt with him about his dissembling with them about the church, and that he professed to concur with them in all things, and what a large confession he made at his admittance, and that he held not himself a minister till he had a new calling, etc. And yet now he contested against them, and drew a company apart and sequestered himself, and would go minister the sacraments (by his Episcopal calling) without ever speaking a word unto them, either as magistrates or brethren.

In conclusion, he was fully convicted, and burst out into tears, and confessed he "feared he was a reprobate, his sins were so great that he doubted God would not pardon them, he was unsavory salt," etc. And that he had "so wronged them as he could never make them amends," confessing all he had writ against them was "false and nought, both for matter and manner." And all this he did with as much fullness as words and tears could express.

After their trial and conviction, the court censured them to be expelled the place; Oldham presently,[5] though his wife and family had liberty to stay all winter or longer till he could make provision to remove them comfortably. Lyford had liberty to stay six months. It was, indeed, with some eye to his release if he carried himself well in the meantime, and that his repentance proved sound. Lyford acknowledged his censure was far less than he deserved. Afterwards, he confessed his sin publicly in the church, with tears more largely than before. I shall here put it down as I find it recorded by some who took it from his own words, as him-

[5] I.e., immediately.

self uttered them. Acknowledging |125| "That he had done very evil, and slanderously abused them; and, thinking most of the people would take part with him, he thought to carry all by violence and strong hand against them. And that God might justly lay innocent blood to his charge, for he knew not what hurt might have come of these his writings, and blessed God they were stayed." And that he spared not to take knowledge from any, of any evil that was spoken, but shut his eyes and ears against all the good; and if God should make him a vagabond in the earth, as was Cain, it was but just for he had sinned in envy and malice against his brethren as he did. And he confessed three things to be the ground and causes of these his doings: pride, vain-glory, and self-love. Amplifying these heads with many other sad expressions, in the particulars of them. So as they began again to conceive good thoughts of him upon this his repentance, and admitted him to teach amongst them as before; and Samuel Fuller (a deacon amongst them) and some other tenderhearted men amongst them, were so taken with his signs of sorrow and repentance, as they professed they would fall upon their knees to have his censure released.

But that which made them all stand amazed in the end, and may do all others that shall come to hear the same (for a rarer precedent can scarce be shown) was, that after a month or two, notwithstanding all his former confessions, convictions, and public acknowledgments, both in the face of the church and whole company, with so many tears and sad censures of himself before God and men, he should go again to justify what he had done. For secretly he writ a second letter to the Adventurers in England, in which he justified all his former writings (save in some things which tended to their damage); the which, because it is briefer than the former, I shall here insert.

Worthy Sirs: Though the filth of mine own doings may justly be cast in my face, and with blushing cause my perpetual silence; yet that the truth may not hereby be injured, yourselves any longer deluded, nor injurious dealing carried out still, with bold out facings, I have adventured once more to write unto you.

First, I do freely confess I dealt very indiscreetly in some of my particular letters which I wrote to private friends, for the courses in coming hither and the like, which I do in no sort seek to justify, though stirred up thereunto in the beholding [of] the indirect courses held by others, both here and there with you, for effecting their designs. But am heartily sorry for it, and do to the glory of God and mine own shame acknowledge it. Which letters being intercepted by the Governor, I have for the same undergone the censure |126| of banishment. And had it not been for the respect I have unto you, and some other matters of private regard, I had returned again at this time by the pinnace for England; for here I purpose not to abide, unless I receive better encouragement from you than from the church (as they call themselves) here I do receive. I purposed before I came to undergo hardness; therefore I shall, I hope, cheerfully bear the conditions of the place, though very mean; and they have changed my wages ten times already.[6]

I suppose my letters, or at least copies of them, are come to your hands, for so they here report; which, if it be so, I pray you take notice of this, that I have written nothing but what is certainly true, and I could make so appear plainly to any indifferent[7] men, whatsoever colours be cast to darken the truth, and some there are very audacious this way; besides many other matters which are far out of order here. My mind was not to enlarge myself any further, but in respect of divers poor souls here, the care of whom in part belongs to you, being here destitute of the means of salvation. For howsoever the church are provided for to their content, who are the smallest number in the Colony, and do so appropriate the ministry to themselves, holding this principle, that the Lord hath not appointed any ordinary ministry for the conversion of those that are without. So that some of the poor souls have with tears complained of this to me, and I was taxed for preaching to all in general. Though in truth they have had no ministry here since they came, but such as may be performed by any of you by their own position, whatsoever great pretences they make. But herein they equivocate, as in many other things they do.

But I exceed the bounds I set myself; therefore resting thus, until I hear further from you, so it be within the time limited me. I rest, etc.

Remaining yours ever,
JOHN LYFORD, Exile

Dated August 22, Anno 1624

[6] Genesis xxxi.7.

[7] I.e., disinterested.

They made a brief answer to some things in this letter, but referred chiefly to their former. The effect was to this purpose: That if God in His providence had not brought these things to their hands (both the former and latter) they might have been thus abused, traduced and calumniated, overthrown and undone; and never have known by whom nor for what. They desired but this equal favour, that they would be pleased to hear their just defense, as well as his accusations, and weigh them in the balance of justice and reason, and then censure as they pleased. They had writ briefly to the heads of things before, and should be ready to give further |127| answer as any occasion should require; craving leave to add a word or two to this last.

And first, they desire to examine what filth that was, that he acknowledgeth might justly be thrown in his face, and might cause blushing and perpetual silence; some great matter sure? But if it be looked into, it amounts to no more than a point of indiscretion, and that's all. And yet he licks off that too, with this excuse, that he was stirred up thereunto by beholding the indirect course here. But this point never troubled him here; it was counted a light matter, both by him and his friends, and put off with this, that any man might do so, to advise his private friends to come over for their best advantage. All his sorrow and tears here was for the wrong and hurt he had done us, and not at all for this he pretends to be done to you: it was not counted so much as indiscretion.

2. Having thus paid you full satisfaction, he thinks he may lay load of [8] us here. And first complains that we have changed his wages ten times. We never agreed with him for any wages, nor made any bargain at all with him, neither know of any that you have made. You sent him over to teach amongst us,[9] and desired he might be kindly used; and more than this we know not. That he hath been kindly used, and far better than he deserves from us, he shall be judged first of his own mouth. If you please to look upon that writing of his, that was sent you amongst his letters, which he calls a general relation, in which though he doth otherwise traduce us, yet in this he himself clears us; in the latter

[8] I.e., to belabor with blows.
[9] I.e., to be a minister of the gospel.

end thereof he hath these words: "I speak not this," saith he, "out of any ill affection to the men, for I have found them very kind and loving to me." You may there see these to be his own words under his own hand.

Secondly, it will appear by this, that he hath ever had a larger allowance of food out of the store for him and his than any, and clothing as his need hath required; a dwelling in one of our best houses, and a man wholly at his own command to tend his private affairs. What cause he hath, therefore, to complain, judge ye; and what he means in his speech we know not, except he alludes to that of Jacob and Laban.[1] If you have promised him more or otherwise, you may do it when you please.

3. Then, with an impudent face he would have you take notice that in his letters he hath writ nothing but what is certainly true; yea, and he could make it so appear plainly to any indifferent men. This indeed doth astonish us and causeth us to tremble at the deceitfulness |128| and desperate wickedness of man's heart. This is to devour holy things, and after vows to inquire.[2] It is admirable that after such public confession, and acknowledgment in court, in church, before God and men, with such sad expressions as he used and with such melting into tears, that after all this he should now justify all again. If things had been done in a corner, it had been something to deny them; but being done in the open view of the country and before all men, it is more than strange now to avow to make them plainly appear to any indifferent men. And here where things were done, and all the evidence that could be were present, and yet could make nothing appear, but even his friends condemned him and gave their voice to his censure; so gross were they, we leave yourselves to judge herein. Yet lest this man should triumph in his wickedness, we shall be ready to answer him when or where you will, to anything he shall lay to our charge, though we have done it sufficiently already.

4. Then he saith he would not enlarge, but for some poor souls here who are destitute of the means of salvation, etc. But all his soothing is but that you would use means that his censure might be released, that he might here continue, and under you (at

[1] Genesis xxxi.7, 14. [2] Jeremiah xvii.9 and Proverbs xx.25.

least) be sheltered till he sees what his friends, on whom he depends, can bring about and effect. For such men pretend much for poor souls, but they will look to their wages and conditions; if that be not to their content, let poor souls do what they will, they will shift for themselves, and seek poor souls somewhere else among richer bodies.

5. Next he falls upon the church. That indeed is the burthensome stone that troubles him. First, he saith they hold this principle, that the Lord hath not appointed any ordinary ministry for the conversion of those without. The church needs not be ashamed of what she holds in this, having God's Word for her warrant; that ordinary officers are bound chiefly to their flocks, Acts xx.28, and are not to be extravagants, to go, come and leave them at their pleasures, to shift for themselves or to be devoured of wolves. But he perverts the truth in this as in other things, for the Lord hath as well appointed them to convert, as to feed in their several charges; and he wrongs the church to say otherwise. Again, he saith he was taxed for preaching to all in general. This is a mere untruth, for this dissembler knows that every Lord's Day some are appointed to visit suspected places, and if any be found idling and neglect the hearing of the Word (through idleness or profaneness), they are punished for the same. Now, to procure all to come to hear, and then to blame him for preaching to all, were to play the mad men. |129|

6. Next, he saith, they have had no ministry since they came, whatsoever pretenses they make, etc. We answer, the more is our wrong, that our Pastor is kept from us by these men's means, and then reproach us for it when they have done. Yet have we not been wholly destitute of the means of salvation as this man would make the world believe. For our reverend Elder hath laboured diligently in dispensing the Word of God to us, before he came; and since, hath taken equal pains with himself, in preaching the same. And, be it spoken without ostentation, he is not inferior to Mr. Lyford (and some of his betters) either in gifts or learning, though he would never be persuaded to take higher office upon him. Nor ever was more pretended in this matter. For equivocating, he may take it to himself; what the church holds

they have manifested to the world in all plainness, both in open confession, doctrine and writing.

This was the sum of their answer, and here I will let them rest for the present. I have been longer in these things than I desired, and yet not so long as the things might require; for I pass many things in silence, and many more deserve to have been more largely handled. But I will return to other things and leave the rest to its place.

[*Salvage of the Pinnace*]

The pinnace [3] that was left sunk and cast away near Damariscove as is before showed; some of the fishing masters said it was a pity so fine a vessel should be lost and sent them word that if they would be at the cost, they would both direct them how to weigh her and let them have their carpenters to mend her. They thanked them and sent men about it, and beaver to defray the charge, without which all had been in vain. So they got coopers to trim I know not how many tun of cask, and being made tight and fastened to her at low water, they buoyed her up; and then with many hands hauled her on shore in a convenient place where she might be wrought upon. And then hired sundry carpenters to work upon her, and other to saw plank, and at last fitted her and got her home. But she cost a great deal of money in thus recovering her, and buying rigging and sails for her, both now and when before she lost her mast; so as she proved a chargeable vessel to the poor Plantation. So they sent her home, and with her Lyford sent his last letter in great secrecy, but the party entrusted with it gave it the Governor.

The winter was passed over in their ordinary affairs, without any special matter worth noting; saving that many who before stood something off from the church, now seeing Lyford's unrighteous dealing and malignity against the church, now tendered themselves to the church and were joined to the same; professing that it was not out of the dislike of anything that they had

[3] The *Little James;* more details of her salvage are in Massachusetts Historical Society *Proceedings* XLIV 184–5. She sailed about 22 Aug. 1624.

stood off so long, but a desire to fit themselves better for such a state, and they saw now the Lord called for their help. |130|

And so these troubles produced a quite contrary effect, in sundry here, than these adversaries hoped for. Which was looked at as a great work of God, to draw on men by unlikely means, and that in reason which might rather have set them further off. And thus I shall end this year.

CHAPTER XVI

Anno Dom: 1625 [*Oldham and Lyford Disposed of*]

At the spring of the year, about the time of their Election Court, Oldham came again amongst them; and though it was a part of his censure for his former mutiny and miscarriage not to return without leave first obtained, yet in his daring spirit he presumed without any leave at all; being also set on and hardened by the ill counsel of others. And not only so, but suffered his unruly passion to run beyond the limits of all reason and modesty, insomuch that some strangers which came with him were ashamed of his outrage and rebuked him. But all reproofs were but as oil to the fire, and made the flame of his choler greater. He called them all to nought in this his mad fury, and a hundred rebels, and traitors and I know not what. But in conclusion they committed him till he was tamer, and then appointed a guard of musketeers which he was to pass through, and every one was ordered to give him a thump on the breech with the butt end of his musket, and then was conveyed to the waterside where a boat was ready to carry him away. Then they bid him go and mend his manners.

Whilst this was in doing, Mr. William Peirce and Mr. Winslow came up from the waterside, being come from England; but they were so busy with Oldham as they never saw them till they came thus upon them. They bid them not spare either him or Lyford, for they had played the villains with them.

But that I may here make an end with him, I shall here once for all relate what befell concerning him in the future, and that briefly. After the removal of his family from hence, he fell into some straits (as some others did) and about a year or more afterwards, towards winter, he intended a voyage for Virginia. But it so pleased God that the bark that carried him and many other passengers was in that danger as they despaired of life; so as many of them, as they fell to prayer, so also did they begin to examine their consciences |131| and confess such sins as did most burthen them. And Mr. Oldham did make a free and large confession of the wrongs and hurt he had done to the people and church here, in many particulars, that as he had sought their ruin, so God had now met with him and might destroy him; yea, he feared they all fared the worse for his sake. He prayed God to forgive him and made vows that if the Lord spared his life he would become otherwise, and the like. This I had from some of good credit, yet living in the Bay, and were themselves partners in the same dangers on the shoals of Cape Cod, and heard it from his own mouth.

It pleased God to spare their lives, though they lost their voyage; and in time afterwards, Oldham carried himself fairly towards them, and acknowledged the hand of God to be with them, and seemed to have an honourable respect of them; and so far made his peace with them as he in after time had liberty to go and come and converse with them at his pleasure. He went after this to Virginia and had there a great sickness, but recovered and came back again to his family in the Bay, and there lived till some store of people came over. At length, going a trading in a small vessel among the Indians, and being weakly manned, upon some quarrel they knocked him in the head with a hatchet, so as he fell down dead and never spake word more. Two little boys that were his kinsmen were saved, but had some hurt, and the vessel was strangely recovered from the Indians by another that belonged to the Bay of Massachusetts; and this his death was one ground of the Pequot War which followed.

I am now come to Mr. Lyford. His time being now expired, his censure was to take place. He was so far from answering their hopes by amendment in the time, as he had doubled his evil as is before noted. But first behold the hand of God concerning him, wherein that of the Psalmist is verified: Psalm vii.15: "He hath made a pit and digged it, and is fallen into the pit he made." He thought to bring shame and disgrace upon them, but instead thereof opens his own to all the world. For when he was dealt withal about his second letter, his wife was so affected with his doings as she could no longer conceal her grief and sorrow of mind, but opens the same to one of their deacons and some other of her friends, and after uttered the same to Mr. Peirce upon his arrival. Which was to this purpose, that she feared some great judgment of God would fall upon them and upon her, for her husband's cause, now that they were to remove. She feared to fall into the Indians' hands and to be defiled by them as he had defiled other women; or some such like |132| judgment, as God had threatened David, 2 Samuel xii.11: "I will raise up evil against thee and will take thy wives and give them," etc.

And upon it showed how he had wronged her, as first he had a bastard by another before they were married, and she having some inkling of some ill carriage that way, when he was a suitor to her, she told him what she heard, and denied him. But she not certainly knowing the thing, otherwise than by some dark and secret mutterings, he not only stiffly denied it, but to satisfy her took a solemn oath there was no such matter. Upon which she gave consent, and married with him; but afterwards it was found true, and the bastard brought home to them. She then charged him with his oath, but he prayed pardon and said he should else not have had her. And yet afterwards she could keep no maids but he would be meddling with them; and some time she hath taken him in the manner, as they lay at their beds' feet, with such other circumstances as I am ashamed to relate. The woman being a grave matron, and of good carriage all the while she was here, and spoke these things out of the sorrow of her heart sparingly and yet with some further intimations. And that which did most seem to affect her (as they conceived) was to see his former carriage in his repentance, not only here with the church but formerly about these things; shedding tears and using great and sad expressions, and yet eftsoon fall into the like things.

Another thing of the same nature did strangely concur herewith. When Mr. Winslow and Mr. Peirce were come over, Mr. Winslow informed them that they had had the like bickering with Lyford's friends in England, as they had with himself and his friends here, about his letters and accusations in them. And many meetings and much clamour was made by his friends thereabout, crying out, "A minister, a man so godly, to be so esteemed and taxed, they held a great scandal," and threatened to prosecute law against them for it. But things being referred to a further meeting of most of the Adventurers, to hear the case and decide the matters, they agreed to choose two eminent men for moderators in the business. Lyford's faction chose Mr. White, a counselor at law; the other part chose Reverend Mr. Hooker, the minister;[1] and many friends on both sides were brought in, so as there was a great assembly.

In the meantime, God in His providence had detected Lyford's evil carriage in Ireland to some friends amongst the company, who made it known to Mr. Winslow and directed him to two godly and grave witnesses who would testify the same, if called thereunto, upon their oath. The thing was this: he being got into Ireland had wound himself into the esteem of sundry godly and zealous professors[2] in those parts, who having been burthened with the ceremonies in England, found there some more liberty to their consciences; amongst whom were these two men which gave |133| this evidence.

Amongst the rest of his hearers there was a godly young man that intended to marry, and cast his affection on a maid which lived thereabout. But desiring to choose in the Lord, and preferred the fear of God before all other things, before he suffered his affection to run too far he resolved to take Mr. Lyford's advice and judgment of this maid (being the minister of the place) and so broke the matter unto him. And he promised faithfully to inform him, but would first take better knowledge of her and have private conference with her, and so had sundry times and in conclusion commended her highly to the young man as a very fit wife for him, so they were married together. But some time after marriage the woman was much troubled in mind and afflicted in conscience, and did nothing but weep and mourn, and long it was before her husband could get of her what was the cause. But at length she discovered the thing, and prayed him to forgive her; for Lyford had overcome her and defiled her body before marriage, after he had commended him unto her for a husband, and she resolved to have him, when he came to her in that private way. The circumstances I forbear, for they would offend chaste ears to hear them related (for though he satisfied his lust on her, yet he endeavoured to hinder conception.) These things being thus discovered, the woman's husband took some godly

1 The Rev. Thomas Hooker, later one of the founders of Connecticut, then rector of Esher, Surrey.

2 I.e., Puritans.

friends with him to deal with Lyford for this evil; at length he confessed it with a great deal of seeming sorrow and repentance, but was forced to leave Ireland upon it, partly for shame and partly for fear of further punishment, for the godly withdrew themselves from him upon it, and so coming into England, unhappily he was lit upon and sent hither.

But in this great assembly, and before the moderators, in handling the former matters about the letters, upon provocation in some heat of reply to some of Lyford's defenders, Mr. Winslow let fall these words, "That he had dealt knavishly." Upon which, one of his friends took hold and called for witnesses that he called a minister of the gospel "knave" and would prosecute law upon it, which made a great tumult. Upon which (to be short) this matter broke out, and the witnesses were produced, whose persons were so grave and evidence so plain and the fact so foul, yet delivered in such modest and chaste terms and with such circumstances as struck all his friends mute, and made them all ashamed. Insomuch as the moderators with great gravity declared that the former matters gave them cause enough to refuse him and to deal with him as they had done; but these made him unmeet forever to bear ministry any more, what repentance soever he should pretend; with much more to like effect, and so wished his friends to rest quiet. Thus was this matter ended.

From hence Lyford went to Nantasket in the Bay of the Massachusetts, with some other of his friends with him, where Oldham also lived. From thence he removed to Naumkeag, since called Salem. But after there came some people over, whether for hope of greater profit or what ends else I know not, he left his friends that followed him and went from thence to Virginia, where he shortly after died; and so I leave him to the Lord. His wife afterwards returned again to this country. And thus much of this matter.[3] |134|

[3] Lyford and Oldham spent about a year at Nantasket (not the present beach resort but the nearby village of Hull), where there were already a few settlers, and took with them Roger Conant, a discontented "Particular" at Plymouth. When Conant was made head of the Dorchester Adventurers' settlement on Gloucester Harbor, Lyford followed him thither; according to Thomas Morton, he preached at both places. Next, Lyford was called to be the Anglican minister for the parish of Martin's Hundred (*Virginia Magazine of History and*

[*The Company of Adventurers Breaks Up*]

This storm being thus blown over, yet sundry sad effects followed the same; for the Company of Adventurers broke in pieces hereupon, and the greatest part wholly deserted the Colony in regard of any further supply or care of their subsistence. And not only so, but some of Lyford's and Oldham's friends and their adherents set out a ship on fishing on their own account, and getting the start of the ships that came to the Plantation, they took away their stage and other necessary provisions that they had made for fishing at Cape Ann the year before, at their great charge, and would not restore the same, except they would fight for it. But the Governor sent some of the planters to help the fishermen to build a new one, and so let them keep it. This ship also brought them some small supply of little value; but they made so poor a business of their fishing (neither could these men make them any return for the supply sent) so as after this year they never looked more after them.

Also by this ship [4] they some of them sent, in the name of the rest, certain reasons of their breaking off from the Plantation, and some tenders upon certain conditions of reuniting again. The which because they are long and tedious, and most of them about the former things already touched, I shall omit them; only giving an instance in one, or two.

First reason, they charged them for dissembling with His Majesty in their petition and with the Adventurers about the French discipline, etc. Secondly, for receiving a man [5] into their church that in his confession renounced all universal, national and diocesan churches, etc.; by which (say they) it appears that though they deny the name of Brownists, yet they practice the same, etc.

Biography XXXI 214), where he died; the only record of him there is of difficulty collecting his salary. His widow, Sarah, returned to Massachusetts with three of their children, married in 1634 Edmund Hobart of Hingham and died there in 1649. An estuary of Weir River is, or until recently was, known as Lyford's Liking. Lyford's son Mordecai claimed lands or leases in County Tyrone and County Armagh, Ireland, as formerly his father's property; and Richard Andrews, one of the Adventurers, handled the matter in England. See 1912 ed. Bradford I 358 note.

[4] The *Charity*.

[5] This was Lyford himself (Bradford).

And therefore they should sin against God in building up such a people.

Then, they add, "Our dislikes thus laid down, that we may go on in trade with better content and credit, our desires are as followeth":

1. That as we are partners in trade, so we may be in government there, as the Patent doth give us power, etc.

2. That the French discipline [6] may be practiced in the Plantation, as well in the circumstances thereof as in the substance, whereby the scandalous name of the Brownists [7] and other church differences may be taken away.

3. Lastly, that Mr. Robinson and his company may not go over to our Plantation unless he and they will reconcile themselves to our church by a recantation under their hands, etc.

Their answer in part to these things was then as followeth:

Whereas you tax us for dissembling with His Majesty and the Adventurers about the French discipline, you do us wrong; for we both hold and practice the discipline of the French and other reformed churches, as they have published the same in the Harmony of Confessions,[8] according to our means in effect and substance. But whereas you would tie us to the French discipline in every circumstance, you derogate from the liberty we have in Christ Jesus. The Apostle Paul would have none to follow him in anything but wherein he follows Christ; [9] much less ought any Christian or church in the world to do it. The French may err, we may err, and other churches may err,

[6] The French Discipline, which was also brought up when the Pilgrims were dickering with the Virginia Company (see "First Brief Note" in Appendix II), meant the forms of worship, government and ceremonies of the French Calvinists or Huguenots with whom some of the English exiles in Queen Mary's reign had worshipped. This discipline became a standard of excellence to which English Puritan divines constantly referred; but it was a Presbyterian, not a Congregational form of polity, and on that point most of the English and practically all the New English Puritans begged to differ.

[7] Robert Browne wrote *Reformation without Tarrying for Any* (1582). Hence Separatist Puritans, such as the Leyden Pilgrims originally had been (but were not at the time of their emigration), often were called Brownists, a nickname they disliked rather more than that of Puritan.

[8] *An Harmony of the Confessions of the Faith of the Christian and Reformed Churches Which Purelie Professe the Holy Doctrine of the Gospell*, London 1586 and many later editions.

[9] 1 Corinthians xi.1.

and doubtless do in many circumstances. That honour, therefore, belongs only to the infallible Word of God, and pure Testament of Christ, to be propounded and followed as the only rule and pattern for direction herein to all churches and Christians. And it is too great arrogancy for any man or church |135| to think that he or they have so sounded the Word of God to the bottom, as precisely to set down the church's discipline without errour in substance or circumstance, as that no other without blame may digress or differ in anything from the same.[1] And it is not difficult to show that the reformed churches differ in many circumstances amongst themselves.

The rest I omit for brevity's sake and so leave to prosecute these men or their doings any further; but shall return to the rest of their friends of the company which stuck to them. And I shall first insert some part of their letters as followeth; for I think it best to render their minds in their own words.

[*James Sherley* et al. *to Bradford* et al.] [2]

To Our Loving Friends, etc.

Though the thing we feared be come upon us,[3] and the evil we strove against has overtaken us, yet we cannot forget you, nor our friendship and fellowship which together we have had some years. Wherein though our expressions have been small, yet our hearty affections towards you, unknown by face, have been no less than to our nearest friends, yea, to our own selves. And though this your friend Mr. Winslow can tell you the state of things here, yet lest we should seem to neglect you, to whom by a wonderful providence of God, we are so nearly united, we have thought good once more to write unto you, to let you know what is here befallen, and the reasons of it; as also our purposes and desires toward you for hereafter.

The former course, for the generality here, is wholly dissolved from what it was, and whereas you and we were formerly sharers and partners in all voyages and dealings, this way is now no more;

[1] This sentence is often quoted to show the fundamental humility and tolerance of the Pilgrim Fathers; it is almost a direct quotation from one of the writings of the Rev. John Robinson.

[2] This letter is copied in greater fullness in the Governor's *Letter Book* (Massachusetts Historical Society *Collections* III p. 29).

[3] Job iii.25

but you and we are left to bethink ourselves what course to take in the future that your lives and our moneys be not lost.

The reasons and causes of this alteration have been these. First and mainly, the many losses and crosses at sea, and abuses of seamen, which have caused us to run into so much charge, debts and engagements as our estates and means were not able to go on without impoverishing ourselves; except our estates had been greater and our associates cloven better unto us. Secondly, as here hath been a faction and siding amongst us now more than two years, so now there is an utter breach and sequestration amongst us; and in two parts of us a full desertion and forsaking of you, without any intent or purpose of meddling more with you. And though we are persuaded, the main cause of this their doing is want of money, for need whereof men use to make many excuses, yet other things are pretended; as that you are Brownists, etc. Now what use you or we ought to make of these things it remaineth to be considered; for we know the hand of God to be in all these things, and no doubt He would admonish something thereby and to look what is amiss. And although it be now too late for us or you to prevent and stay these things, yet is it not too late to exercise patience, wisdom, and conscience in bearing them, and in carrying ourselves in and under them for the time to come. |136|

And as we ourselves stand ready to embrace all occasions that may tend to the furtherance of so hopeful a work, rather admiring of what is than grudging for what is not, so it must rest in you to make all good again. And if in nothing else you can be approved, yet let your honesty and conscience be still approved, and lose not one jot of your innocency amidst your crosses and afflictions. And surely if you upon this alteration behave yourselves wisely and go on fairly, as men whose hope is not in this life, you shall need no other weapon to wound your adversaries; for when your righteousness is revealed as the light, they shall cover their faces with shame that causelessly have sought your overthrow.

Now we think it but reason that all such things as there appertain to the General, be kept and preserved together, and rather increased daily, than any way be dispersed or embezzled away for any private ends or intents whatsoever.[4] And after your necessities are served,

[4] In the letter as copied in the *Letter Book*, there are a couple of pages of pious exhortations about keeping the community going, which Bradford omits here. It is clear that the writers of this letter, representing those of the original Adventurers who still had confidence in the Pilgrims and who shared their religious ideas, were very keen to keep the business part of the enterprise going, as it was just beginning to pay dividends. Bradford and the other leaders at Plym-

you gather together such commodities as the country yields and send them over to pay debts and clear engagements here, which are not less than £1400.[5] And we hope you will do your best to free our engagements, etc. Let us all endeavour to keep a fair and honest course, and see what time will bring forth, and how God in His providence will work for us. We still are persuaded you are the people that must make a plantation in those remote places when all others fail and return. And your experience of God's providence and preservation of you is such as we hope your hearts will not fail you, though your friends should forsake you (which we ourselves shall not do whilst we live, so long as your honesty so well appeareth). Yet surely help would arise from some other place whilst you wait on God, with uprightness, though we should leave you also.

And lastly, be you all entreated to walk circumspectly and carry yourselves so uprightly in all your ways, as that no man may make just exceptions against you. And more especially that the favour and countenance of God may be so toward you as that you may find abundant joy and peace even amidst tribulations, that you may say with David, "Though my father and mother should forsake me, yet the Lord would take me up." [6]

We have sent you here some cattle,[7] cloth, hose, shoes, leather, etc.; but in another nature than formerly, as it stood us in hand to do. We have committed them to the charge and custody of Mr. Allerton and Mr. Winslow as our factors; at whose discretion they are to be sold, and commodities to be taken for them, as is fitting. And by how much the more they will be chargeable unto you, the better they had need to be husbanded, etc. Go on, good friends, comfortably; pluck up your spirits, and quit yourselves like men [8] in all your difficulties; that notwithstanding all displeasure and threats of men, yet the work may go on you are about, and not be neglected. Which is so much

---

outh would probably have liked to split up at this time and abolish the General; but they were helpless, in view of the debt that their friends in England had contracted in their name, and their constant need for clothing, trading goods and other supplies from home.

[5] A large part of the remainder of this *History* relates to the Pilgrims' pathetic attempts to discharge this debt, which seemed to grow rather than decrease with every payment on account.

[6] Psalm xxvii.10.

[7] Including a heifer, a gift of Sherley "to begin a stock for the poor," a bull and "three or four jades"—the first horses to arrive in New England. Bradford *I etter Book*, p. 35.

[8] 1 Corinthians xvi.13.

for the glory of God and the furtherance of our countrymen, as that a man may with more comfort |137| spend his life in it, than live the life of Methuselah in wasting the plenty of a tilled land or eating the fruit of a grown tree.

Thus with hearty salutations to you all, and hearty prayers for you all, we lovingly take our leaves, this 18th of December 1624.

Your assured friends to our powers,
JAMES SHERLEY
WILLIAM COLLIER
THOMAS FLETCHER
ROBERT HOLLAND
etc.[9]

By this letter it appears in what state the affairs of the Plantation stood at this time. These goods they bought, but they were at dear rates, for they put £40 in the hundred upon them for profit and adventure, outward bound. And because of the venture of the payment homeward, they would have £30 [1] in the 100 more, which was in all 70 per cent; a thing thought unreasonable by some, and too great an oppression upon the poor people, as their case stood. The cattle were the best goods, for the other being ventured ware were, neither of the best (some of them) nor at the best prices. Sundry of their friends disliked these high rates, but coming from many hands, they could not help it.

[*More Losses and Crosses at Sea*]

They sent over also two ships [2] on fishing on their own account. The one was the pinnace that was cast away the last year here in the country and recovered by the Planters (as was before related); who, after she came home, was attached by one of the Company for his particular debt, and now sent again on this account. The other was a great ship, who was well fitted with an experienced master and company of fishermen, to make a voyage,

[9] These were evidently not the only signers, but those whom Bradford regarded as particular friends of the Colony. Collier later emigrated to Plymouth.

[1] If I mistake not, it was not much less (Bradford).

[2] The *Little James* and the *White Angel*.

and to go to Bilbao or Sebastians with her fish. The lesser, her order was to load with cor-fish [3] and to bring the beaver home for England that should be received for the goods sold to the Plantation. This bigger ship made a great voyage of good dry fish, the which if they had gone to a market with, would have yielded them (as such fish was sold that season) £1800, which would have enriched them. But because there was a bruit of war with France, the master neglected (through timorousness) his order, and put first into Plymouth and after into Portsmouth, and so lost their opportunity and came by the loss. The lesser ship had as ill success, though she was as hopeful as the other for the merchants' profit; for they had filled her with goodly cor-fish taken upon the bank, as full as she could swim, and besides she had some 800 pounds' weight of beaver, besides other furs to a good value from the Plantation.

The master seeing so much goods come, put it aboard the bigger ship for more safety. But Mr. Winslow, their factor in this business, was bound in a bond of £500 to send it to London in the small ship; there was some contending between the master and him about it. But he told the master he would follow his order about it; if he would take it out afterward, it should be at his peril; so it went in the small ship and he sent bills of lading in both. The master was so careful, being both so well laden, as they went joyfully home together, for he towed the lesser ship at his stern all the way over bound, and they had such fair weather as he never cast her off till they were shot deep into the English Channel, almost within the sight of Plymouth. And yet there she was unhaply taken by a Turks' man of war and carried into Sallee,[4] where the master and men were made slaves and many of the beaver skins were sold for 4*d* apiece. |138|

[3] Cod or other fish that was cured on shore a few days after being caught; better esteemed than the hard-dried kind caught on remote banks, which was called poor-john.

[4] Salé on the coast of French Morocco, near which American troops landed in November 1942, was formerly a notorious pirate stronghold. One English punitive expedition of 1621 under Sir Robert Mansell had failed, which emboldened the corsairs to sail right into the English Channel in search of prizes. A second expedition in 1637 under Capt. William Rainsborough (an early settler of New England) and Sir George Carteret of Jersey fame, suppressed the nuisance for the time being. *Mariner's Mirror* XXXI 178.

Thus was all their hopes dashed and the joyful news they meant to carry home turned to heavy tidings. Some thought this a hand of God for their too great exaction of the poor Plantation, but God's judgments are unsearchable,[5] neither dare I be bold therewith. But, however, it shows us the uncertainty of all human things and what little cause there is of joying in them or trusting to them.

In the bigger of these ships was sent over Captain Standish from the Plantation, with letters and instructions both to their friends of the Company which still clave to them, and also to the Honourable Council of New England. To the Company to desire that, seeing that they meant only to let them have goods upon sale, that they might have them upon easier terms, for they should never be able to bear such high interest or to allow so much per cent. Also, that what they would do in that way that it might be disbursed in money, or such goods as were fit and needful for them, and bought at best hand. And to acquaint them with the contents of his letters to the Council abovesaid, which was to this purpose, to desire their favour and help; that such of the Adventurers as had thus forsaken and deserted them, might be brought to some order and not to keep them bound and themselves be free. But that they might either stand to their former covenants, or else come to some fair end by dividend or composition.

But he came in a very bad time, for the State was full of trouble and the plague very hot in London, so as no business could be done.[6] Yet he spake with some of the Honoured Council, who promised all helpfulness to the Plantation which lay in them. And sundry of their friends the Adventurers were so weakened with their losses the last year, by the loss of the ship taken by the Turks, and the loss of their fish which by reason of the wars they were forced to land at Portsmouth, and so came to little. So as, though their wills were good, yet their power was little. And there died such multitudes weekly of the plague as all trade was dead, and little money stirring. Yet with much ado he took up

[5] Romans xi.33.

[6] It was this plague which carried off so many members of the Harvard family of Southwark that John's mother inherited enough money to send him to Emmanuel College, Cambridge.

£150 (and spent a good deal of it in expenses) at 50 per cent, which he bestowed in trading goods and such other most needful commodities as he knew requisite for their use. And so returned passenger in a fishing ship, having prepared a good way for the composition that was afterward made.

In the meantime it pleased the Lord to give the Plantation peace and health and contented minds,[7] and so to bless their labours as they had corn sufficient, and some to spare to others, with other food; neither ever had they any supply of food but what they first brought with them. After harvest this year, they send out a boat's load of corn 40 or 50 leagues to the eastward, up a river called Kennebec, it being one of those two shallops which their carpenter had built them the year before, for bigger vessel had they none. They had laid a little deck over her midships to keep the corn dry, but the men were fain to stand it out all weathers without shelter, and that time |139| of the year begins to grow tempestuous. But God preserved them and gave them good success, for they brought home 700 pounds of beaver, besides some other furs, having little or nothing else but this corn which themselves had raised out of the earth. This voyage was made by Mr. Winslow and some of the old standers,[8] for seamen they had none.

[7] Bradford wrote to Cushman 9 June 1625 that the Pilgrims "never felt the sweetness of the country till this year; and not only we but all planters in the land begin to do it." *Letter Book* pp. 36–7.

[8] The *Mayflower* passengers; Bradford generally calls them the Old Comers.

CHAPTER XVII

Anno Dom: 1626

[*Death of the Rev. John Robinson and Robert Cushman*]

About the beginning of April they heard of Captain Standish his arrival, and sent a boat to fetch him home, and the things he had brought. Welcome he was, but the news he brought was sad in many regards; not only in regard of the former losses before related, which their friends had suffered, by which some in a manner were undone, others much disabled from doing any further help, and some dead of the plague. But also that Mr. Robinson their pastor was dead, which struck them with much sorrow and sadness, as they had cause. His and their adversaries had been long and continually plotting how they might hinder his coming hither, but the Lord had appointed him a better place; concerning whose death and the manner thereof, it will appear by these few lines writ to the Governor and Mr. Brewster:

Loving and Kind Friends, etc. I know not whether this will ever come to your hands or miscarry, as other my letters have done. Yet in regard of the Lord's dealing with us here, I have had a great desire to write unto you. Knowing your desire to bear a part with us, both in our joys and sorrows, as we do with you. These are therefore to give you to understand that it hath pleased the Lord to take out of this vale of tears, your and our loving and faithful pastor and my dear and Reverend brother, Mr. John Robinson, who was sick some eight days. He began to be sick on Saturday in the morning, yet the next day, being the Lord's Day, he taught us twice. And so the week after grew weaker, every day more than other; yet he felt no pain, but weakness all the time of his sickness. The physic he took wrought kindly in man's judgment, but he grew weaker every day, feeling little or no pain, and sensible to the very last. He fell sick the 22 of February and departed this life the 1 of March. He had a continual inward ague, but free from infection, so that all his friends came freely to him. And if either prayers, tears or means would have saved his life, he had not gone hence. But he having faithfully finished his course and performed his work which the Lord had appointed him here to do, he now resteth with the Lord in eternal happiness.

We wanting him and all church governors, yet we still by the mercy of God continue and hold close together in peace and quietness; and so hope we shall do, though we be very weak. Wishing (if such were the will of God) that you and we were again united together in one, either there or here. But seeing it is the will of the Lord thus to dispose of things, we must labour with patience to rest contented till it please the Lord otherwise to dispose.

For news |140| here is not much, only as in England we have lost our old King James, who departed this life about a month ago; so here they have lost the old prince, Grave Maurice. Who both departed this life since my brother Robinson, and as in England we have a new King, Charles, of whom there is great hope; so here they have made Prince Hendrick general in his brother's place, etc. Thus with my love remembered, I take leave and rest

Leyden, April 28 Your assured loving friend,
Anno 1625 ROGER WHITE

Thus these two great princes, and their pastor, left this world near about one time. Death makes no difference.

He further brought them notice of the death of their ancient friend Mr. Cushman, whom the Lord took away also this year, and about this time; who was as their right hand with their friends the Adventurers, and for divers years had done and agitated all their business with them, to their great advantage. He had writ to the Governor but some few months before of the sore sickness of Mr. James Sherley (who was a chief friend to the Plantation) and lay at the point of death, declaring his love and helpfulness in all things; and much bemoaned the loss they should have of him, if God should now take him away, as being the stay and life of the whole business. As also his own purpose this year to come over and spend his days with them. But he that thus writ of another's sickness knew not that his own death was so near. It shows also that a man's ways are not in his own power, but in His hands who hath the issues of life and death. Man may purpose, but God doth dispose.

Their other friends from Leyden writ many letters to them, full of sad laments for their heavy loss; and though their wills were good to come to them, yet they saw no probability of means how it might be effected, but concluded as it were that all their hopes were cut off. And many, being aged, began to drop away by death.

All which things before related, being well weighed and laid together, it could not but strike them with great perplexity, and to look humanly on the state of things as they presented themselves at this time. It is a marvel it did not wholly discourage them and sink them. But they gathered up their spirits, and the Lord so helped them, whose work they had in hand, as now when they were at lowest [1] they began to rise again, and being stripped in a manner of all human helps and hopes, He brought things about otherwise, in His divine providence as they were not only upheld and sustained, but their proceedings both honoured and imitated by others. As by the sequel will more appear, if the Lord spare me life and time to declare the same.

[*Corn-Growing and Down-East Trucking*]

Having now no fishing business or other things to intend, but only their trading and planting, they set themselves to follow the same with the best industry they could. The Planters finding their corn (what they could spare from their necessities) to be a commodity (for they sold it at *6s* a bushel) used great diligence in planting the same. And the Governor and such as were designed to manage the trade (for it was retained for the general good |141| and none were to trade in particular) they followed it to the best advantage they could. And wanting trading goods, they understood that a plantation which was at Monhegan and belonged to some merchants of Plymouth, was to break up and divers useful goods was there to be sold. The Governor and Mr. Winslow took a boat and some hands and went thither.[2] But Mr. David Thompson, who lived at Piscataqua, understanding their

[1] Note (writes Bradford in the margin).

[2] Abraham Jenness, merchant of Plymouth in Devon, a shareholder in the Council for New England, started a fishing settlement on the island of Monhegan in 1625, but it did not prosper. He was bought out by Robert Aldworth and Giles Elbridge of Bristol, who sent Abraham Shurt to take possession. Apparently the word got around that there was to be a bargain day at Monhegan, but Shurt was intent on starting a settlement, and also took over Samoset's deed to John Brown at New Harbor. In 1632 Aldworth and Elbridge obtained the Pemaquid Patent from the Council for New England to a section of the mainland over against Monhegan. Ida S. Proper *Monhegan the Cradle of New England* (1930) chap. xiv.

purpose, took opportunity to go with them, which was some hindrance to them both. For they, perceiving their joint desires to buy, held their goods at higher rates, and not only so, but would not sell a parcel of their trading goods except they sold all. So lest they should further prejudice one another, they agreed to buy all and divide them equally between them. They bought also a parcel of goats which they distributed at home as they saw need and occasion, and took corn for them of the people, which gave them good content; their moiety of the goods came to above £400 sterling.

There was also that spring a French ship cast away at Sagadahoc,[3] in which were many Biscay rugs and other commodities, which were fallen into these men's hands, and some other fishermen at Damariscove; which were also bought in partnership and made their part arise to above £500. This they made shift to pay for, for the most part, with the beaver and commodities they had got the winter before, and what they had gathered up that summer. Mr. Thompson having something overcharged himself, desired they would take some of his, but they refused except he would let them have his French goods only, and the merchant (who was one of Bristol) would take their bill for to be paid the next year. They were both willing, so they became engaged for them and took them. By which means, they became very well furnished for trade, and took off thereby some other engagements which lay upon them, as the money taken up by Captain Standish and the remains of former debts.

With these goods and their corn after harvest, they got good store of trade, so as they were enabled to pay their engagements against the time, and to get some clothing for the people, and had some commodities beforehand. But now they began to be envied, and others went and filled the Indians with corn and beat down the price, giving them twice as much as they had done, and undertraded them in other commodities also.[4]

This year they sent Mr. Allerton into England, and gave him order to make a composition with the Adventurers upon as good

[3] The lower reach of the Kennebec River.

[4] Bradford complained about this irregular, unlicensed trading to the Council for New England in a letter of 15 June 1627 (*Letter Book* p. 56).

terms as he could, unto which some way had been made the year before by Captain Standish. But yet enjoined him not to conclude absolutely till they knew the terms and had well considered of them, but to drive it to as good an issue as he could, and refer the conclusion to them. Also, they gave him a commission under their hands and seals to take up some money, provided it exceeded not such a sum specified, for which they engaged themselves and gave him order how to lay out the same for the use of the Plantation.

And finding they ran a great hazard to go so long voyages in a small open boat, especially the winter season, they began to think how they might get a small pinnace,[5] as for the reason aforesaid; so also because others had raised the price with the Indians above the half of what they had formerly given, so as in such a boat they could not |143| [6] carry a quantity sufficient to answer their ends. They had no ship carpenter amongst them, neither knew how to get one at present; but they having an ingenious man that was a house carpenter, who also had wrought with the ship carpenter that was dead when he built their boats; at their request he put forth himself to make a trial that way of his skill. And took one of the biggest of their shallops and sawed her in the middle, and so lengthened her some five or six foot, and strengthened her with timbers, and so built her up and laid a deck on her. And so made her a convenient and wholesome vessel, very fit and comfortable for their use, which did them service seven years after. And they got her finished and fitted with sails and anchors the ensuing year.

And thus passed the affairs of this year.

[5] The dimensions of a small pinnace built at Duxbury in 1640 are given in *Note-Book kept by Thomas Lechford, Esq. in Boston* (*Archaeologia Americana* VII) pp. 418–19, as 32-foot keel, 5½-foot depth of hold and full deck; it cost £40.

[6] There is no folio 142.

CHAPTER XVIII

Anno Dom: 1627

[*New Deal with the Adventurers and within the Colony*]

At the usual season of the coming of ships, Mr. Allerton [1] returned and brought some useful goods with him, according to the order given him. For upon his commission he took up £200 which he now got at 30 per cent. The which goods they got safely home and well conditioned, which was much to the comfort and content of the Plantation. He declared unto them also how with much ado and no small trouble he had made a composition with the Adventurers, by the help of sundry of their faithful friends there, who had also took much pains thereabout. The agreement or bargain he had brought a draft of, with a list of their names thereto annexed, drawn by the best counsel of law they could get, to make it firm. The heads whereof I shall here insert:

To ALL CHRISTIAN PEOPLE, GREETING, etc. Whereas at a meeting the 26th of October last past, divers and sundry persons, whose names to the one part of these presents are subscribed in a schedule hereunto annexed, Adventurers to New Plymouth in New England in America, were contented and agreed, in consideration of the sum of one thousand and eight hundred pounds sterling to be paid (in manner and form following) to sell and make sale of all and every the stocks, shares, lands, merchandise and chattels whatsoever to the said Adventurers, and other their fellow Adventurers, to New Plymouth aforesaid, any way accruing or belonging to the generality of the said Adventurers aforesaid; as well by reason of any sum or sums of money or merchandise at any time heretofore adventured or disbursed by them, or otherwise howsoever.

For the better expression and setting forth of which said agree-

[1] Of Isaac Allerton, the Pilgrim Father who used his fellows even worse than did the merchants adventurers, there is a good account by R. G. Usher in the *Dictionary of American Biography*. Born about 1586, trained to the tailor's trade in London, he joined the Leyden congregation at an early age, sailed in the *Mayflower* and became Governor Bradford's first Assistant. About this time he married Elder Brewster's daughter Fear. Eventually, after the various speculations recorded in this *History*, he removed to New Haven, engaged in trading ventures and died in 1659.

ment, the parties to these presents subscribing, do for |144| themselves severally, and as much as in them is, grant, bargain, alien, sell, and transfer all and every the said shares, goods, lands, merchandise and chattels to them belonging as aforesaid, unto Isaac Allerton, one of the Planters resident at Plymouth aforesaid, assigned, and sent over as agent for the rest of the Planters there. And to such other Planters at Plymouth aforesaid as the said Isaac, his heirs or assigns, at his or their arrival, shall by writing or otherwise think fit to join or partake in the premises, their heirs, and assigns, in as large, ample, and beneficial manner and form to all intents and purposes, as the said subscribing Adventurers here could or may do, or perform. All which stocks, shares, lands, etc. to the said Adventurers in severality allotted, apportioned or any way belonging, the said Adventurers do warrant and defend unto the said Isaac Allerton, his heirs and assigns, against them, their heirs and assigns, by these presents. And therefore the said Isaac Allerton doth, for him, his heirs and assigns, covenant, promise and grant to and with the Adventurers whose names are hereunto subscribed, their heirs, etc. well and truly to pay, or cause to be paid unto the said Adventurers, or five of them which were at that meeting aforesaid nominated and deputed; viz. JOHN POCOCK, JOHN BEAUCHAMP, ROBERT KEANE, EDWARD BASS, and JAMES SHERLEY,[2] merchants, their heirs, etc. to and for the use of the generality of them, the sum of £1800 of lawful money of England, at the place appointed for the receipts of money, on the west side of the Royal Exchange in London; by £200 yearly, and every year on the feast of St. Michael, the first payment to be made Anno 1628, etc.

Also, the said Isaac is to endeavour to procure and obtain from the Planters of New Plymouth aforesaid, security, by several obligations or writings obligatory, to make payment of the said sum of £1800 in form aforesaid, according to the true meaning of these presents. In testimony whereof to this part of these presents, remaining with the said Isaac Allerton, the said subscribing Adventurers have set to their names, etc. And to the other part remaining with the said Adventurers, the said Isaac Allerton hath subscribed his

[2] Pocock and Keane were members of the Massachusetts Bay Company in 1629; the latter became a leading merchant in Boston, often in trouble with the authorities for profiteering. Of the other three nothing is known except what is contained in this *History*. Bradford's *Letter Book* p. 48 gives the names of 42 signers to this agreement, including the five above mentioned and one woman, Eliza Knight. Four others, Thomas Goffe, Samuel Sharpe, John Revell and Thomas Andrews, became members of the Massachusetts Bay Company.

name, the 15 November, Anno 1626, in the second year of His Majesty's reign.

This agreement was very well liked of and approved by all the Plantation, and consented unto, though they knew not well how to raise the payment and discharge their other engagements and supply the yearly wants of the Plantation, seeing they were forced for their necessities to take up money or goods at so high interests. Yet they undertook it, and seven or eight of the chief of the place became jointly bound for the payment of this £1800 in the behalf of the rest, at the several days. In which they ran a great adventure, as their present state stood, having many other heavy burthens already upon them, and all things in an uncertain condition amongst them. So the next return it was absolutely confirmed on both sides, and the bargain fairly engrossed in parchment and in many things put into better form, by the advice of the learnedest counsel they could get. And lest any forfeiture should fall on the whole for none payment at any of the days, it ran thus: To forfeit 30*s* a week if they missed the time, and was concluded under their hands and seals, as may be seen at large by the deed itself.[3] |145|

Now though they had some untoward persons mixed amongst them from the first, which came out of England, and more afterwards by some of the Adventurers, as friendship or other affections led them—though sundry were gone, some for Virginia and some to other places—yet divers were still mingled amongst them, about whom the Governor and Council with other of their chief friends had serious consideration how to settle things in regard of this new bargain or purchase made, in respect of the distribution of things both for the present and future. For the present, except peace and union were preserved, they should be able to do nothing, but endanger to overthrow all, now that other ties and bonds were taken away. Therefore they resolved, for sundry reasons, to take in all amongst them that were either heads of families, or single young men, that were of ability and free (and able to govern themselves with meet discretion, and their

[3] This deed has not been preserved.

affairs, so as to be helpful in the commonwealth) into this partnership or purchase.

First, they considered that they had need of men and strength both for defense and carrying on of businesses. Secondly, most of them had borne their parts in former miseries and wants with them, and therefore in some sort but equal to partake in a better condition if the Lord be pleased to give it. But chiefly they saw not how peace would be preserved without so doing, but danger and great disturbance might grow to their great hurt and prejudice otherwise. Yet they resolved to keep such a mean in distribution of lands, and other courses, as should not hinder their growth in others coming to them.

So they called the company together and conferred with them, and came to this conclusion, that the trade should be managed as before to help to pay the debts, and all such persons as were above named should be reputed and enrolled for purchasers; single free men to have a single share, and every father of a family to be allowed to purchase so many shares as he had persons in his family, that is to say, one for himself and one for his wife; and for every child that he had living with him, one. As for servants, they had none but what either their masters should give them out of theirs or their deservings should obtain from the company afterwards.

Thus all were to be cast into single shares according to the order abovesaid; and so every one was to pay his part according to his proportion towards the purchase and all other debts, what the profit of the trade would not reach to: viz. a single man for a single share, a master of a family for so many as he had. This gave all good content.

And first accordingly the few cattle which they had were divided, which arose to this proportion: a cow to six persons or shares, and two goats to the same; which were first equalized for age and goodness and then lotted for; single persons consorting with others as they thought good and smaller families likewise; and swine though more |146| in number, yet by the same rule. Then they agreed that every person or share should have 20 acres of land divided unto them, besides the single acres they had already. And they appointed were to begin first, on the one side of the town, and how far to go, and then on the other side in like manner, and so to divide it by lot, and appointed sundry by name to do it, and tied them to certain rules to proceed by; as, that they should only lay out settable or tillable land, at least such of it as should butt on the waterside (as the most they were to lay out did) and pass by the rest as refuse and common; and what they judged fit should be so taken. And they were first to agree of the goodness and fitness of it before the lot was drawn, and so it might as well prove some of their own as another man's; and this course they were to hold throughout.

But yet seeking to keep the people together as much as might be,[4] they also agreed upon this order, by mutual consent before any lots were cast, that whose lots soever should fall next the town, or most convenient for nearness, they should take to them a neighbour or two whom they best liked, and should suffer them to plant corn with them for four years; and afterwards they might use as much of theirs for as long time, if they would. Also every share or 20 acres was to be laid out five acres in breadth by the waterside, and four acres in length, excepting nooks and corners which were to be measured as they would bear to best advantage. But no meadows were to be laid out at all, nor were not of many years after, because they were but strait of meadow grounds; and if they had been now given out it would have hindered all addition to them afterwards. But every season all were appointed where they should mow, according to the proportion of cattle they had.

This distribution gave generally good content, and settled men's minds. Also they gave the Governor and four or five of the special men amongst them the houses they lived in; the rest were valued and equalized at an indifferent rate, and so every man kept his own and he that had a better allowed something to him that had a worse, as the valuation went.

[4] This endeavor to keep the Colony one compact settlement is discernible throughout the *History*. Bradford's object was not merely defense against the Indians, but to enable everyone to attend divine service, to maintain a vigorous community life, and to keep a strict watch over sinners. The *Plymouth Colony Records* for 3 June 1656 record an order to Joseph Ramsden who "hath lived long in the woods, in an uncivil way" to shift "to some neighbourhood" by October "or that then his house be pulled down."

[*Wreck of the* Sparrowhawk *and Rescue of the Virginians*]

There is one thing that fell out in the beginning of the winter before, which I have referred to this place, that I may handle the whole matter together. There was a ship,[5] with many passengers in her and sundry goods bound for Virginia. They had lost themselves at sea, either by the insufficiency of the master, or his illness, for he was sick and lame of the scurvy, so that he could but lie in the cabin door and give direction, and it should seem was badly assisted either with mate or mariners. Or else, the fear and unruliness of the passengers were such as they made them steer a course between the southwest and the northwest, that they might fall with some land, whatsoever it was they cared not. For they had been six weeks at sea and had no water nor beer nor any wood left, but had burnt up all their empty cask; only one of the company had a hogshead of wine or two which was also almost spent, so as they feared they should be starved at sea or consumed with diseases, which made them run this desperate course.

But it pleased God that though they came so near the shoals of Cape Cod |147| or else ran stumbling over them in the night, they knew not how, they came right before a small blind harbor that lies about the middle of Manamoyick Bay to the southward of Cape Cod, with a small gale of wind, and about high water touched upon a bar of sand that lies before it, but had no hurt,

[5] The *Sparrowhawk* entered Manamoyick Bay (now Pleasant Bay, Cape Cod) by the same inlet that Bradford used on the corn voyage of 1622 (see chap. xiii above). This section of Nauset Beach had some valuable meadow land on the harbor side. One of the meadow lots became known as the Old Ship, and the adjoining part of the Bay, Old Ship Harbor, everyone had forgotten why, until a storm of May 1863, shifting sand, uncovered the bones of an ancient vessel. The bones were exhumed, put together, and now rest in Pilgrim Hall, Plymouth. I have no doubt from the place where this wreck was found, and the form and size of it, that these are the actual timbers of the *Sparrowhawk*. An estimation of her by a marine architect indicates that she must have been ketch-rigged and that she measured about 40 feet over all, very beamy and deep for her length. The place where she was wrecked, directly opposite Sipsons Island, may be seen from the high ground crossed by Route 28 just before it descends to the shores of Pleasant Bay, from the north. C. W. Livermore and Leander Crosby *The Ancient Wreck: Loss of the Sparrow-Hawk* (Boston 1865).

the sea being smooth; so they laid out an anchor. But towards the evening the wind sprung up at sea, and was so rough as broke their cable and beat them over the bar into the harbor, where they saved their lives and goods, though much were hurt with salt water. For with beating they had sprung the butt end of a plank or two, and beat out their oakum; but they were soon over and ran on a dry flat within the harbor close by a beach. So at low water they gat out their goods on dry shore and dried those that were wet and saved most of their things without any great loss; neither was the ship much hurt but she might be mended, and made serviceable again.

But though they were not a little glad that they had thus saved their lives, yet when they had a little refreshed themselves and began to think on their condition, not knowing where they were nor what they should do, they began to be strucken with sadness. But shortly after they saw some Indians come to them in canoes, which made them stand upon their guard; but when they heard some of the Indians speak English unto them, they were not a little revived, especially when they heard them demand if they were the Governor of Plymouth's men or friends; and that they would bring them to the English houses or carry their letters.

They feasted these Indians and gave them many gifts. And sent two men and a letter with them to the Governor and did intreat him to send a boat unto them, with some pitch and oakum and spikes, with divers other necessaries for the mending of their ship, which was recoverable. Also, they besought him to help them with some corn and sundry other things they wanted, to enable them to make their voyage to Virginia. And they should be much bound to him and would make satisfaction for anything they had, in any commodities they had aboard. After the Governor was well informed by the messengers of their condition, he caused a boat to be made ready, and such things to be provided as they writ for; and because others were abroad upon trading and such other affairs, as had been fit to send unto them, he went himself, and also carried some trading commodities to buy them corn of the Indians. It was no season of the year to go without the Cape, but understanding where the ship lay, he went into the bottom of the bay on the inside, and put into a creek called

Namskaket [6] where it is not much above two mile over |148| land to the bay where they were, where he had the Indians ready to carry over anything to them. Of his arrival they were very glad, and received the things to mend their ship, and other necessaries. Also he bought them as much corn as they would have; and whereas some of their seamen were run away among the Indians, he procured their return to the ship, and so left them well furnished and contented, being very thankful for the courtesies they received. But after the Governor thus left them, he went into some other harbors thereabout and loaded his boat with corn which he traded and so went home.

But he had not been at home many days but he had notice from them that by the violence of a great storm and the bad mooring of their ship after she was mended, she was put ashore, and so beaten and shaken as she was now wholly unfit to go to sea. And so their request was that they might have leave to repair to them and sojourn with them till they could have means to convey themselves to Virginia, and that they might have means to transport their goods, and they would pay for the same, or anything else wherewith the Plantation should relieve them. Considering their distress, their requests were granted and all helpfulness done unto them; their goods transported, and themselves and goods sheltered in their houses as well as they could.

The chief amongst these people was one Mr. Fells and Mr. Sibsey,[7] which had many servants belonging unto them, many of them being Irish. Some others there were that had a servant or two apiece, but the most were servants, and such as were engaged to the former persons who also had the most goods. After they were hither come and something settled, the masters desired some ground to employ their servants upon. Seeing it was like to be the latter end of the year, before they could have passage for Virginia. And they had now the winter before them, they might clear some ground and plant a crop, seeing they had tools and necessaries for the same, to help to bear their charge and keep their servants in employment; and if they had opportunity to de-

[6] Still so called, on the Bay side of the Cape in the town of Orleans.

[7] Capt. John Sibsey settled in Norfolk County, Virginia and became a burgess and councilor of the Colony.

part before the same was ripe, they would sell it on the ground. So they had ground appointed them in convenient places and Fells and some other of them raised a great deal of corn, which they sold at their departure. This Fells, amongst his other servants, had a maidservant which kept his house and did his household affairs, and by the intimation of some that belonged unto him he was suspected to keep her as his concubine.[8] And both of them were examined thereupon but nothing could be proved, and they stood upon their justification. So with admonition they were dismissed, but afterward it appeared she was with child, so he got a small boat and ran away with her for fear of punishment. First he went to Cape Ann, and after into the Bay of the Massachusetts, but could get no passage, and had like to have been cast away; and was forced to come again and submit himself. But they packed him away and those that belonged unto him by the first opportunity, and dismissed all the rest as soon as could, being many untoward people amongst them; though there were also some that carried themselves very orderly all the time they stayed. |149|

And the Plantation had some benefit by them in selling them corn and other provisions of food, for clothing; for they had of divers kinds, as cloth, perpetuanes and other stuffs, besides hose and shoes and such like commodities as the Planters stood in need of. So they both did good, and received good one from another. And a couple of barks carried them away at the latter end of summer. And sundry of them have acknowledged their thankfulness since from Virginia.

[*Trading with the Dutch at Buzzards Bay*]

That they might better take all convenient opportunity to follow their trade, both to maintain themselves and to disengage them of those great sums which they stood charged with and bound for, they resolved to build a small pinnace at Manomet, a

[8] This damsel possibly is the one referred to in Thomas Morton *New English Canaan* (C. F. Adams ed. pp. 264, 273) as the "Barren doe of Virginia grown fruitful in New Canaan." On Nauset Beach, just south of the site of the old inlet, is a piece of land traditionally known as Slut's Bush, which may have been where she and Mr. Fells camped.

place 20 miles from the Plantation, standing on the sea to the southward of them, unto which by another creek on this side they carry their goods within four or five miles, and then transport them overland to their vessel.[9] And so avoid the compassing of Cape Cod and those dangerous shoals, and so make any voyage to the southward in much shorter time and with far less danger. Also for the safety of their vessel and goods they built a house there and kept some servants, who also planted corn and reared some swine and were always ready to go out with the bark when there was occasion. All which took good effect and turned to their profit.

They now sent with the return of the ships Mr. Allerton again into England, giving him full power under their hands and seal to conclude the former bargain with the Adventurers, and sent their bonds for the payment of the money.[1] Also they sent what beaver they could spare to pay some of their engagements and to defray his charges, for those deep interests still kept them low. Also he had order to procure a patent for a fit trading place in the river of Kennebec. For being emulated both by the planters at Piscataqua and other places to the eastward of them, and also by the fishing ships which used to draw much profit from the Indians of those parts, they threatened to procure a grant and shut them out from thence, especially after they saw them so well furnished with commodities as to carry the trade from them. They thought it but needful to prevent such a thing, at least that they might not be excluded from free trade there, where themselves had first begun and discovered the same and brought it to so good effect.

[9] Manomet, not to be confused with the high promontory south of Plymouth, was a Wampanoag Indian village on a river of the same name that flows into Buzzards Bay. It is in the present town of Bourne, where Manomet has been corrupted to "Monument." Across this narrow neck of Cape Cod the Cape Cod Canal was dug early in the present century. The Indians had used the carrying place between the Manomet River and the Scusset (Bradford's "other creek on this side") since time immemorial; and both Dutch and French had come there to trade. The site of the trading house that the Pilgrims built near Manomet, at a place called by the Indians Aptucxet, has been excavated, and the house faithfully restored. Percival Hall Lombard *The Aptucxet Trading Post* (Bourne Historical Society, 1934); first published in two parts in *Old Time New England* Oct. 1927 and April 1933.

[1] Allerton sailed at the end of May in the *Marmaduke,* John Gibbs master.

This year also they had letters and messengers from the Dutch plantation sent unto them from the Governor there written both in Dutch and French. The Dutch had traded in these southern parts divers years before they came, but they began no plantation here till four or five years after their coming and here beginning.[2] Their letters were as followeth—it being their manner to be full of complimental titles.[3]

After this there was many passages between them both by letters and other intercourse, and they had some profitable commerce together for divers years, till other occasions interrupted the same, as may happily appear afterwards, more at large.[4]

[*The Undertakers Organized*]

Before they sent Mr. Allerton away for England this year, the Governor and some of their chief friends had serious consideration, not only how they might discharge those great engagements which lay so heavily upon them, as is afore mentioned; but also how they might (if possibly they could) devise means to help some of their friends and brethren of Leyden over unto them, who desired so much to come to them and they desired as much their company. To effect which they resolved to run a high course and of great adventure, not knowing otherwise how to bring it about. Which was to hire the trade of the company for certain years, and in that time to undertake to pay that £1800 and all the rest of the debts that then lay upon the Plantation, which was about some £600 more; and so to set them free and return the trade to the generality again at the end of the term. Upon which resolution they called the company together and made it clearly appear unto all what their debts were and upon what terms they would undertake to pay them all in such a time, and set them clear. But their other ends they were fain to keep secret, having only privately acquainted some of their trusty friends therewith, which were glad of the same, but doubted

[2] New Amsterdam on Manhattan, founded 1626.

[3] See Appendix VI.

[4] A full account of the earliest exchanges is given in notes to 1912 ed. Bradford II 25–8.

how they would be able to perform it. So after some agitation of the thing with the company, it was yielded unto and the agreement made upon the conditions following.

Articles of agreement between the Colony of New Plymouth of the one party, and William Bradford, Captain Myles Standish, Isaac Allerton, etc. on the other party, and such others as they shall think good to take as partners and Undertakers with them,[5] concerning the trade for beaver and other furs and commodities, etc. Made July, 1627.

First it is agreed and covenanted betwixt the said parties, that the aforesaid William Bradford, Captain Myles Standish and Isaac Allerton, etc. have undertaken and do by these presents covenant and agree to pay, discharge and acquit the said Colony of all the debts both due for the purchase, or any other belonging to them, at the day of the date of these presents. |153|

Secondly, the abovesaid parties are to have and freely enjoy the pinnace lately built, the boat at Manomet, and the shallop called the bass boat, with all other implements to them belonging, that is in the store of the said Company. With all the whole stock of furs, fells, beads, corn, wampumpeag, hatchets, knives, etc. that is now in the store, or any way due unto the same upon account.

Thirdly, that the above said parties have the whole trade to themselves, their heirs and assigns, with all the privileges thereof, as the said Colony doth now or may use the same, for six full years, to begin in the last of September next ensuing.

Fourthly, in further consideration of the discharge of the said debts, every several purchaser doth promise and covenant yearly to pay or cause to be paid to the abovesaid parties, during the full term of the said six years, three bushels of corn or six pounds of tobacco, at the Undertakers' choice.

Fifthly, the said Undertakers shall during the aforesaid term bestow £50 per annum in hose and shoes, to be brought over for the Colony's use, to be sold unto them for corn at 6*s* per bushel.

Sixthly, that at the end of the said term of six years, the whole trade shall return to the use and benefit of the said Colony, as before.

[5] These were Edward Winslow, William Brewster, John Howland, John Alden and Thomas Prence. The London Associates were James Sherley, John Beauchamp, Richard Andrews and Timothy Hatherley. These names and those of the signers of the agreement, representing the Freemen of the Colony, are in Bradford's *Letter Book* p. 61.

Lastly, if the aforesaid Undertakers, after they have acquainted their friends in England with these covenants, do upon the first return resolve to perform them and undertake to discharge the debts of the said Colony, according to the true meaning and intent of these presents; then they are (upon such notice given) to stand in full force. Otherwise all things to remain as formerly they were, and a true account to be given to the said Colony of the disposing of all things according to the former order.

Mr. Allerton carried a copy of this agreement with him into England; and amongst other his instructions, had order given him to deal with some of their special friends to join with them in this trade upon the above recited conditions; as also to impart their further ends that moved them to take this course, namely the helping over of some of their friends from Leyden as they should be able, in which, if any of them would join with them, they should thankfully accept of their love and partnership herein. And withal by their letters gave them some grounds of their hopes of the accomplishment of these things with some advantage.

CHAPTER XIX

Anno Dom: 1628 [*Correspondence about the Undertakers*]

After Mr. Allerton's arrival in England he acquainted them with his commission and full power to conclude the forementioned bargain and purchase. Upon |154| the view whereof, and the delivery of the bonds for the payment of the money yearly (as is before mentioned) it was fully concluded, and a deed [1] fairly engrossed in parchment was delivered him, under their hands and seals confirming the same. Moreover he dealt with them about other things according to his instructions, as to admit some of these their good friends into this purchase if they pleased, and to deal with them for moneys at better rates, etc. Touching which I shall here insert a letter of Mr. Sherley's, giving light to what followed thereof, writ to the Governor as followeth.

SIR: I have received yours of the 26th of May by Mr. Gibbs, and Mr. Goffe,[2] with the barrel of otter skins according to the contents, for which I got a bill of store, and so took them up and sold them together at £78 12*s* sterling; [3] and since, Mr. Allerton hath received the money, as will appear by the account.

It is true (as you writ) that your engagements are great, not only the purchase, but you are yet necessitated to take up the stock you work upon, and that not at 6 or 8 per cent as it is here let out, but at 30, 40, yea and some at 50 per cent. Which, were not your gains great, and God's blessing on your honest endeavours more than ordinary, it could not be that you should long subsist in the maintaining

[1] Nov. 6, 1627, page 238 (Bradford). His page reference, however, is to the Articles of Agreement of 15 Oct. 1641, printed in Appendix IX.

[2] John Gibbs was master of the *Marmaduke,* in which Allerton sailed, arriving in late summer of 1627. Thomas Goffe, one of the Adventurers, later became freeman and deputy governor of the Massachusetts Bay Company. Plymouth Colony delivered to the Salem settlement "six sowes with pigg" in 1629 to discharge a debt of £9 they owed Goffe.

[3] Sherley's account of 1631, printed in Massachusetts Historical Society *Collections* 3rd ser. I 201, indicates that this sum was for 220 otter skins with a few mink and musquash thrown in, and that the 494¾ lb. beaver sent later in the *White Angel* brought 15*s* 6*d* a pound. The same account shows that Sherley, who was a goldsmith—what we should call a private banker—was charging the Pilgrims 30 per cent interest. 1912 ed. Bradford II 334.

of and upholding of your worldly affairs. And this your honest and discreet agent Mr. Allerton hath seriously considered and deeply laid to mind, how to ease you of it. He told me you were contented to accept of me and some few others, to join with you in the purchase as partners, for which I kindly thank you and all the rest, and do willingly accept of it. And though absent, shall willingly be at such charge as you and the rest shall think meet, and this year am contented to forbear my former £50 and two years' increase for the venture, both which now makes it £80, without any bargain or condition for the profit [that] you, I mean the generality, stand to the adventure, outward and homeward. I have persuaded Mr. Andrews and Mr. Beauchamp to do the like, so as you are eased of the high rate you were at the other two years. I say we leave it freely to yourselves to allow us what you please, and as God shall bless. What course I run Mr. Beauchamp desireth to do the same, and though he have been or seemed somewhat harsh heretofore, yet now you shall find he is new moulded.

I also see by your letter, you desire I should be your agent or factor here. I have ever found you so faithful, honest and upright men, as I have even resolved with myself (God assisting me) to do you all the good lieth in my power. And therefore if you please to make choice of so weak a man, both for abilities and body, to perform your business, I promise (the Lord enabling me) to do the best I can according to those abilities he hath given me; and wherein I fail, blame yourselves that you made no better choice. Now, because I am sickly, and we are all mortal, I have advised Mr. Allerton to join Mr. Beauchamp with me in your deputation, which I conceive to be very necessary and good for you. Your charge shall be no more, for it is not your salary makes me undertake your |156| business. Thus commending you and yours, and all God's people, unto the guidance and protection of the Almighty, I ever rest,

Your faithful loving friend,

London, November 17, 1628 JAMES SHERLEY[4]

With this letter they sent a draught of a formal deputation to be here sealed and sent back unto them, to authorize them as their agents, according to what is mentioned in the abovesaid letter, and because some inconvenience grew thereby afterward, I shall here insert it.

[4] For an earlier letter, see Appendix VII.

To ALL TO WHOM THESE PRESENTS SHALL COME, GREETING. Know ye that we, William Bradford, Governor of Plymouth in New England in America, Isaac Allerton, Myles Standish, William Brewster and Edward Winslow of Plymouth aforesaid, merchants, do by these presents for us and in our names make, substitute, and appoint James Sherley, goldsmith, and John Beauchamp, salter, citizens of London, our true and lawful agents, factors, substitutes and assigns. As well to take and receive all such goods, wares and merchandise whatsoever as to our said substitutes, or either of them, or to the City of London, or other place of the Realm of England shall be sent, transported, or come from us or any of us, as also to vend, sell, barter, or exchange the said goods, wares, and merchandise so from time to time to be sent, to such person or persons upon credit, or otherwise in such manner as to our said agents and factors jointly, or to either of them severally, shall seem meet. And further we do make and ordain our said substitutes and assigns jointly and severally for us, and to our uses and accounts, to buy and consign for and to us into New England, aforesaid, such goods and merchandise to be provided here, and to be returned hence, as by our said assigns, or either of them, shall be thought fit. And to recover, receive, and demand for us and in our names all such debts and sums of money as now are or hereafter shall be due incident accruing or belonging to us, or any of us, by any ways or means; and to acquit, discharge or compound for any debt or sum of money which now or hereafter shall be due or owing by any persons or persons to us, or any of us. And generally for us and in our names to do, perform and execute every act and thing which to our said assigns, or either of them shall seem meet to be done in or about the premises, as fully and effectually to all intents and purposes as if we, or any of us, were in person present. And whatsoever our said agents and factors jointly or severally shall do, or cause to be done, in or about the premises, we will and do and every of us doth ratify, allow and confirm by these presents. In witness whereof we have hereunto put our hands and seals. Dated 18 November 1628.

This was accordingly confirmed, by the above named, and four more of the chief of them under their hands and seals, and delivered unto them. Also Mr. Allerton formerly had authority under their hands and seals for the transacting of the former business and taking up of moneys, etc., which still he retained whilst he was employed in these affairs; they mistrusting neither him nor any of their friends' faithfulness, which made them more remiss in looking to such acts as had passed under their hands, as necessary for the time. But letting them run on too long unminded or recalled, it turned to their harm afterwards as will appear in its place. |157|

Mr. Allerton having settled all things thus in a good and hopeful way, he made haste to return in the first of the spring to be here, with their supply for trade, for the fishermen with whom he came used to set forth in winter and be here betimes. He brought a reasonable supply of goods for the Plantation,[5] and without those great interests as before is noted; and brought an account of the beaver sold and how the money was disposed for goods, and the payment of other debts, having paid all debts abroad to others, save to Mr. Sherley, Mr. Beauchamp and Mr. Andrews, from whom likewise he brought an account which to them all amounted not to above £400, for which he had passed bonds. Also he had paid the first payment for the purchase, being due for this year, viz. £200, and brought them the bond for the same, canceled. So as they now had no more foreign debts but the abovesaid £400 and odd pounds, and the rest of the yearly purchase money. Some other debts they had in the country, but they were without any interest and they had wherewith to discharge them when they were due. To this pass the Lord had brought things for them. Also he brought them further notice that their friends, the above named, and some others that would join with them in the trade and purchase, did intend for to send over to Leyden for a competent number of them to be here the next year without fail, if the Lord pleased to bless their journey.

He also brought them a patent for Kennebec,[6] but it was so strait and ill bounded as they were fain to renew and enlarge it

[5] Sherley's invoice is of interest as showing the kind of supplies for which the Colony depended on England: shoes, leather, cloth and Irish stockings; pitch, tar, ropes and twine; knives, scissors and rowel (*sic*); rudge (rugs, coarse thick woolen cloth); lead, shot and powder; hatchets, hoes, axes, scythes, reaphooks, shovels, spades, saws, files, nails and iron pots; drugs and spices; total value, £232.

[6] This patent for land on the Kennebec for a trading post, later superseded by the one of 13 Jan. 1630, has not been preserved. It was from the Council for New England and cost Sherley about £40.

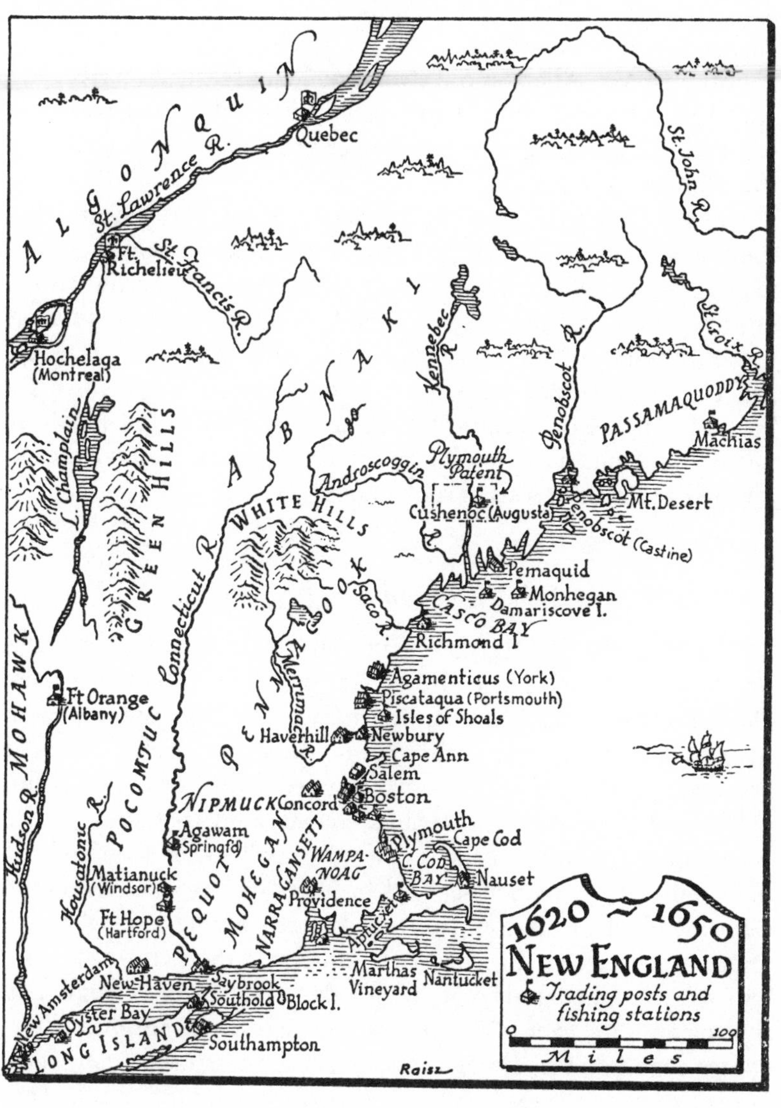

1620 ~ 1650
NEW ENGLAND
Trading posts and fishing stations
0
100
Miles
ALGONQUIN
St. Lawrence R.
Quebec
St. John R.
Ft. Richelieu
St. Francis R.
ABNAKI
Kennebec R.
Penobscot R.
St. Croix R.
PASSAMAQUODDY
Machias
Hochelaga (Montreal)
L. Champlain
GREEN HILLS
WHITE HILLS
Androscoggin
Plymouth Patent
Cushenoc (Augusta)
Mt. Desert
Penobscot (Castine)
Pemaquid
Monhegan
Damariscove I.
CASCO BAY
Richmond I.
Saco R.
PENNACOOK
Merrimac R.
Connecticut R.
MOHAWK
Ft Orange (Albany)
Agamenticus (York)
Piscataqua (Portsmouth)
Isles of Shoals
Haverhill
Newbury
Cape Ann
Salem
Boston
Concord
NIPMUCK
POCOMTUC
Hudson R.
Housatonic R.
Agawam (Springfd)
Plymouth
Cape Cod
C. COD BAY
Nauset
WAMPANOAG
NARRAGANSETT
MOHEGAN
PEQUOT
Matianuck (Windsor)
Ft Hope (Hartford)
Providence
Apuxet
Marthas Vineyard
Nantucket
New Amsterdam
New Haven
Saybrook
Southold
Block I.
Oyster Bay
LONG ISLAND
Southampton
Raisz

the next year, as also that which they had at home, to their great charge as will after appear.

Hitherto Mr. Allerton did them good and faithful service, and well had it been if he had so continued, or else they had now ceased for employing him any longer thus into England. But of this more afterwards.

Having procured a patent (as is above said) for Kennebec, they now erected a house up above in the river in the most convenientest place for trade (as they conceived) and furnished the same with commodities for that end, both winter and summer; not only with corn but also with such other commodities as the fishermen had traded with them, as coats, shirts, rugs and blankets, biscuit, pease, prunes, etc. And what they could not have out of England, they bought of the fishing ships, and so carried on their business as well as they could.[7]

[*A Visit from the Dutch*]

This year the Dutch sent again unto them from their Plantation both kind letters, and also divers commodities, as sugar, linen cloth, holland, finer and coarser stuffs, etc. They came up with their bark to Manomet, to their house there, in which came their Secretary, Rasier, who was accompanied with a noise of trumpeters and some other attendants, and desired that they would send a boat for him, for he could not travel so far overland. So they sent a boat to Scusset and brought him to the Plantation with the chief of his company. And after some few days' entertainment he returned to his bark, and some of them went with him and bought sundry of his goods.[8] After which beginning thus made, they sent oftentimes to the same place and had intercourse together for divers years. And amongst other commodities they vended |158| much tobacco for linen cloth, stuffs, etc.,

[7] The trading house was erected at the site of Augusta, Maine.

[8] Isaack de Rasieres's description of Plymouth (written after this visit in October 1627) is translated in J. F. Jameson ed. *Narratives of New Netherland* (1909) 109–13. Scusset, which Bradford spells Manoanscusset, is a little creek that flows into Cape Cod Bay near the present eastern entrance to the Canal. It was part of the natural canoe route between Buzzards and Cape Cod bays.

which was a good benefit to the people, till the Virginians found out their Plantation.[9]

But that which turned most to their profit, in time, was an entrance into the trade of wampumpeag. For they now bought about £50 worth of it of them, and they told them how vendible it was at their fort Orania,[1] and did persuade them they would find it so at Kennebec. And so it came to pass in time, though at first it stuck, and it was two years before they could put off this small quantity, till the inland people knew of it; and afterwards they could scarce ever get enough for them, for many years together. And so this with their other provisions cut off their trade quite from the fishermen, and in great part from other of the straggling planters. And strange it was to see the great alteration it made in a few years among the Indians themselves; for all the Indians of these parts and the Massachusetts had none or very little of it,[2] but the sachems and some special persons that wore a little of it for ornament. Only it was made and kept among the Narragansetts and Pequots, which grew rich and potent by it, and these people were poor and beggarly and had no use of it. Neither did the English of this Plantation or any other in the land, till now that they had knowledge of it from the Dutch, so much as know what it was, much less that it was a commodity of that worth and value. But after it grew thus to be a commodity in these parts, these Indians fell into it also, and to learn how to make it; for the Narragansetts do gather the shells of which they make it from their shores. And it hath now continued a current commodity about this 20 years, and it may prove a drug in time.

[9] I.e., the Dutch Plantation at Manhattan. Plymouth had been getting tobacco from Virginia for some time, probably from the Virginia fishing fleet that frequented the New England coast.

[1] Fort Orange, now Albany.

[2] Peag (Bradford). Wampumpeag, now called wampum but more commonly abbreviated *peag* in the colonial period, was shell money. Parts of the quahaug or hard-shell clam, the whelk and the native periwinkle were drilled and polished into little hollow cylinders which could be strung together, while several strings parallel made a "belt," and by the use of different-colored shell very beautiful and striking designs could be made. Wampum was not only used in trade among the Indians, it was legal tender in the New England colonies for small sums in the 17th century. See article "Wampum" in F. H. Hodge *Handbook of American Indians.*

In the meantime, it makes the Indians of these parts rich and powerful and also proud thereby, and fills them with pieces, powder and shot, which no laws can restrain, by reason of the baseness of sundry unworthy persons, both English, Dutch and French, which may turn to the ruin of many. Hitherto the Indians of these parts had no pieces nor other arms but their bows and arrows, nor of many years after; neither durst they scarce handle a gun, so much were they afraid of them. And the very sight of one (though out of kilter) was a terror unto them. But those Indians to the east parts, which had commerce with the French, got pieces of them, and they in the end made a common trade of it. And in time our English fishermen, led with the like covetousness, followed their example for their own gain. But upon complaint against them, it pleased the King's Majesty to prohibit the same by a strict proclamation, commanding that no sort of arms or munition should by any of his subjects be traded with them.

[*Thomas Morton of Merrymount*]

About some three or four years before this time, there came over one Captain Wollaston (a man of pretty parts) and with him three or four more of some eminency, who brought with them a great many servants, with provisions and other implements for to begin a plantation. And pitched themselves in a place within the Massachusetts which they called after their Captain's name, Mount Wollaston. Amongst whom was one Mr. Morton, who it should seem had some small adventure of his own or other men's amongst them, but had little respect |159| amongst them, and was slighted by the meanest servants.[3] Having continued there some time, and not finding things to answer

[3] Nothing certain is known about Capt. Wollaston's antecedents; for various guesses see 1912 ed. Bradford II 45–6. Of Thomas Morton "of Merrymount" there is an extensive literature, the best being Charles Francis Adams *Three Episodes of Massachusetts History* and introduction to the Prince Society edition of Morton's *New English Canaan*; Charles E. Banks brought out more facts about him in Massachusetts Historical Society *Proceedings* LVIII 147–86. It is clear that he was a well-educated gentleman with a tendency to get into fights and lawsuits, a lawyer of Clifford's (not Furnival's) Inn, who had "left his country for his country's good."

their expectations nor profit to arise as they looked for, Captain Wollaston takes a great part of the servants and transports them to Virginia, where he puts them off at good rates, selling their time to other men; and writes back to one Mr. Rasdall (one of his chief partners and accounted their merchant) to bring another part of them to Virginia likewise, intending to put them off there as he had done the rest. And he, with the consent of the said Rasdall, appointed one Fitcher to be his Lieutenant and govern the remains of the Plantation till he or Rasdall returned to take further order thereabout. But this Morton abovesaid, having more craft than honesty (who had been a kind of pettifogger of Furnival's Inn) in the others' absence watches an opportunity (commons being but hard amongst them) and got some strong drink and other junkets and made them a feast; and after they were merry, he began to tell them he would give them good counsel. "You see," saith he, "that many of your fellows are carried to Virginia, and if you stay till this Rasdall return, you will also be carried away and sold for slaves with the rest. Therefore I would advise you to thrust out this Lieutenant Fitcher, and I, having a part in the Plantation, will receive you as my partners and consociates; so may you be free from service, and we will converse, plant, trade, and live together as equals and support and protect one another," or to like effect. This counsel was easily received, so they took opportunity and thrust Lieutenant Fitcher out o' doors, and would suffer him to come no more amongst them, but forced him to seek bread to eat and other relief from his neighbours till he could get passage for England.

After this they fell to great licentiousness and led a dissolute life, pouring out themselves into all profaneness. And Morton became Lord of Misrule, and maintained (as it were) a School of Atheism. And after they had got some goods into their hands, and got much by trading with the Indians, they spent it as vainly in quaffing and drinking, both wine and strong waters in great excess (and, as some reported) £10 worth in a morning. They also set up a maypole, drinking and dancing about it many days together, inviting the Indian women for their consorts, dancing and frisking together like so many fairies, or furies, rather; and worse practices. As if they had anew revived and celebrated the feasts of the Roman goddess Flora, or the beastly practices of the mad Bacchanalians. Morton likewise, to show his poetry composed sundry rhymes and verses, some tending to lasciviousness, and others to the detraction and scandal of some persons, which he affixed to this idle or idol maypole.[4] They changed also the name of their place, and instead of calling it Mount Wollaston they call it Merry-mount, |160| as if this jollity would have lasted ever. But this continued not long, for after Morton was sent for England (as follows to be declared) shortly after came over that worthy gentleman Mr. John Endecott, who brought over a patent under the broad seal for the government of the Massachusetts. Who, visiting those parts, caused that maypole to be cut down and rebuked them for their profaneness and admonished them to look there should be better walking. So they or others now changed the name of their place again and called it Mount Dagon.[5]

Now to maintain this riotous prodigality and profuse excess, Morton, thinking himself lawless, and hearing what gain the French and fishermen made by trading of pieces, powder and shot to the Indians, he as the head of this consortship began the practice of the same in these parts. And first he taught them how to use them, to charge and discharge, and what proportion of powder to give the piece, according to the size or bigness of the same; and what shot to use for fowl and what for deer. And

[4] Morton gives some of the verses, which he says "puzzled the Separatists most pitifully to expound," in his *New English Canaan* (the book which he wrote to get even with the Pilgrims), pp. 277–81. The best is a drinking song, of which one verse goes:

> Give to the Nymph that's free from scorn
> No Irish stuff nor Scotch over-worn.
> Lasses in beaver coats, come away,
> Ye shall be welcome to us night and day.
>   Then drink and be merry, merry, merry boys,
>   Let all your delight be in Hymen's joys;
>   Io! to Hymen, now the day is come,
>   About the merry Maypole take a room.

It perhaps should be explained that the "Irish stuff" and "Scotch" were not whisky but woolens. Neither whisky nor rum had as yet appeared in New England; the only strong liquors known were aqua vitae and brandy.

[5] After the god of the Philistines—Judges xvi.23. The site of Merrymount or Mount Wollaston is marked on Route 3, in Quincy.

having thus instructed them, he employed some of them to hunt and fowl for him, so as they became far more active in that employment than any of the English, by reason of their swiftness of foot and nimbleness of body, being also quick-sighted and by continual exercise well knowing the haunts of all sorts of game. So as when they saw the execution that a piece would do, and the benefit that might come by the same, they became mad (as it were) after them and would not stick to give any price they could attain to for them; accounting their bows and arrows but baubles in comparison of them.

And here I may take occasion to bewail the mischief that this wicked man began in these parts, and which since, base covetousness prevailing in men that should know better, has now at length got the upper hand and made this thing common, notwithstanding any laws to the contrary. So as the Indians are full of pieces all over, both fowling pieces, muskets, pistols, etc. They have also their moulds to make shot of all sorts, as musket bullets, pistol bullets, swan and goose shot, and of smaller sorts. Yea some have seen them have their screw-plates to make screw-pins themselves when they want them, with sundry other implements, wherewith they are ordinarily better fitted and furnished than the English themselves. Yea, it is well known that they will have powder and shot when the English want it nor cannot get it; and that in a time of war or danger, as experience hath manifested, that when lead hath been scarce and men for their own defense would gladly have given a groat a pound, which is dear enough, yet hath it been bought up and sent to other places and sold to such as trade it with the Indians at 12*d* the pound. And it is like they give 3*s* or 4*s* the pound, for they will have it at any rate. And these things have been done in the same times when some of their neighbours and friends are daily killed by the Indians, or are in danger thereof and live but at the Indians' mercy. |161| Yea some, as they have acquainted them with all other things, have told them how gunpowder is made, and all the materials in it, and that they are to be had in their own land; and I am confident, could they attain to make saltpeter, they would teach them to make powder.

O, the horribleness of this villainy! How many both Dutch

and English have been lately slain by those Indians thus furnished, and no remedy provided; nay, the evil more increased, and the blood of their brethren sold for gain (as is to be feared) and in what danger all these colonies are in is too well known. O that princes and parliaments would take some timely order to prevent this mischief and at length to suppress it by some exemplary punishment upon some of these gain-thirsty murderers, for they deserve no better title, before their colonies in these parts be overthrown by these barbarous savages thus armed with their own weapons, by these evil instruments and traitors to their neighbours and country! But I have forgot myself and have been too long in this digression; but now to return.

This Morton having thus taught them the use of pieces, he sold them all he could spare, and he and his consorts determined to send for many out of England and had by some of the ships sent for above a score. The which being known, and his neighbours meeting the Indians in the woods armed with guns in this sort, it was a terror unto them who lived stragglingly and were of no strength in any place. And other places (though more remote) saw this mischief would quickly spread over all, if not prevented. Besides, they saw they should keep no servants, for Morton would entertain any, how vile soever, and all the scum of the country or any discontents would flock to him from all places, if this nest was not broken. And they should stand in more fear of their lives and goods in short time from this wicked and debased crew than from the savages themselves.

So sundry of the chief of the straggling plantations, meeting together, agreed by mutual consent to solicit those of Plymouth (who were then of more strength than them all) to join with them to prevent the further growth of this mischief, and suppress Morton and his consorts before they grew to further head and strength. Those that joined in this action, and after contributed to the charge of sending him for England, were from Piscataqua, Naumkeag, Winnisimmet, Wessagusset, Nantasket and other places where any English were seated.[6] Those of Plymouth being

[6] In Bradford's *Letter Book* there is a list of the plantations that contributed, and the amount. Roger Conant and the remnants of the Cape Ann fishing colony, then at Naumkeag (Salem), contributed £1 10*s*; planters at the Piscata-

thus sought to by their messengers and letters, and weighing both their reasons and the common danger, were willing to afford them their help though themselves had least cause of fear or hurt. So, to be short, they first resolved jointly to write to him, and in a friendly and neighbourly way to admonish him to forbear those courses, and sent a messenger with their letters to bring his answer.

But he was so high as he scorned all advice, and asked who had to do with him, he had and would trade pieces with the Indians, in despite of all, with many other scurrilous terms full of disdain. They sent to him a second time and bade him be better advised and more temperate in his terms, for the country could not bear the injury he did. It was against their common safety and against the King's proclamation. He answered in high terms as before; and that the King's proclamation was no law, demanding what penalty was upon it. It was answered, more than he could |162| bear—His Majesty's displeasure. But insolently he persisted and said the King was dead and his displeasure with him, and many the like things. And threatened withal that if any came to molest him, let them look to themselves for he would prepare for them.

Upon which they saw there was no way but to take him by force; and having so far proceeded, now to give over would make him far more haughty and insolent. So they mutually resolved to proceed, and obtained of the Governor of Plymouth to send Captain Standish and some other aid with him, to take Morton by force. The which accordingly was done. But they found him to stand stiffly in his defense, having made fast his doors, armed his consorts, set divers dishes of powder and bullets ready on the table; and if they had not been over-armed with drink, more hurt might have been done. They summoned him to yield, but he kept his house and they could get nothing but scoffs and

---

qua, £2 10*s;* Jeffrey and Burslem at Wessagusset (Weymouth), £2; the widow Thompson on Thompson's Island, Boston Harbor, 15*s;* William Blackstone at Shawmut (Boston), 12*s;* Edward Hilton at Cocheco (Dover, N. H.), £1; and Plymouth itself, £2 10*s*. John Oldham and his friends at Nantasket (Hull) and Maverick at Winnisimmet (Chelsea) apparently gave nothing, but it is clear that Plymouth was acting for the "United Nations" of New England, and that Myles Standish was a U. N. commander.

scorns from him. But at length, fearing they would do some violence to the house, he and some of his crew came out, but not to yield but to shoot; but they were so steeled with drink as their pieces were too heavy for them. Himself with a carbine, overcharged and almost half filled with powder and shot, as was after found, had thought to have shot Captain Standish; but he stepped to him and put by his piece and took him. Neither was there any hurt done to any of either side, save that one was so drunk that he ran his own nose upon the point of a sword that one held before him, as he entered the house; but he lost but a little of his hot blood.[7]

Morton they brought away to Plymouth, where he was kept till a ship went from the Isle of Shoals for England, with which he was sent to the Council of New England, and letters written to give them information of his course and carriage. And also one was sent at their common charge to inform their Honours more particularly and to prosecute against him. But he fooled of the messenger, after he was gone from hence, and though he went for England yet nothing was done to him, not so much as rebuked, for aught was heard, but returned the next year. Some of the worst of the company were dispersed and some of the more modest kept the house till he should be heard from. But I have been too long about so unworthy a person, and bad a cause.

[*Allerton Brings Over a Minister*]

This year Mr. Allerton brought over a young man for a minister to the people here, whether upon his own head or at the motion of some friends there I well know not. But it was without the church's sending, for they had been so bitten by Mr. Lyford as they desired to know the person well whom they should invite amongst them. His name was Mr. Rogers; [8] but they perceived

7 Morton's account naturally differs. According to his *New English Canaan* pp. 285–7, "Captain Shrimpe," as he calls Standish, and his army of eight "came within danger like a flock of wild geese, as if they had been tailed one to another, as colts to be sold at a fair," but "Mine Host" generously yielded to avoid bloodshed.

8 The antiquarians have been unable to identify Mr. Rogers, the second of the Pilgrims' four bad choices of a minister. By some he is supposed to be the mysterious "Mr. Bubble" of Morton's narrative.

upon some trial that he was crazed in his brain, so they were fain to be at further charge to send him back again the next year, and lose all the charge that was expended in his hither bringing, which was not small by Mr. Allerton's account in provisions, apparel, bedding, etc. After his return he grew quite distracted, and Mr. Allerton was much blamed that he would bring such a man over, they having charge enough otherwise.

Mr. Allerton in the years before had brought over some small quantity of goods upon his own particular, and sold them for his own private benefit, which was more than any man had yet hitherto attempted. But because he had otherwise done them good service, and also he sold them among the people at the Plantation, by which their wants were supplied, and he alleged it was the |163| love of Mr. Sherley and some other friends that would needs trust him with some goods, conceiving it might do him some good and none hurt, it was not much looked at but passed over. But this year he brought over a greater quantity, and they were so intermixed with the goods of the General as they knew not which were theirs and which was his, being packed up together. So as they well saw that if any casualty had befallen at sea, he might have laid the whole on them if he would, for there was no distinction. Also what was most vendible and would yield present pay, usually that was his; and he now began also to sell abroad to others of foreign places. Which, considering their common course, they began to dislike.

Yet, because love thinks no evil nor is suspicious, they took his fair words for excuse and resolved to send him again this year for England, considering how well he had done the former business and what good acceptation he had with their friends there; as also seeing sundry of their friends from Leyden were sent for, which would or might be much furthered by his means. Again, seeing the Patent for Kennebec must be enlarged, by reason of the former mistakes in the bounding of it, and it was conceived (in a manner) the same charge would serve to enlarge this at home with it; and he that had begun the former the last year would be the fittest to effect this. So they gave him instructions and sent him for England this year again.

And in his instructions bound him to bring over no goods on

their account, but £50 in hose and shoes and some linen cloth, as they were bound by covenant when they took the trade; also some trading goods to such a value, and in no case to exceed his instructions nor run them into any further charge, he well knowing how their state stood. Also that he should so provide that their trading goods came over betimes; and whatsoever was sent on their account should be packed up by itself, marked with their mark, and no other goods to be mixed with theirs. For so he prayed them to give him such instructions as they saw good, and he would follow them, to prevent any jealousy or further offense, upon the former forementioned dislikes. And thus they conceived they had well provided for all things.

CHAPTER XX

Anno Dom: 1629

[*Arrivals from Leyden and Heavy Expenses*]

Mr. Allerton safely arriving in England and delivering his letters to their friends there and acquainting them with his instructions, found good acceptation with them, and they were very forward and willing to join with them in the partnership of trade and in the charge to send over the Leyden people; a company whereof were already come out of Holland, and prepared to come over, and so were sent away before Mr. Allerton could be ready to come. They had passage with the ships that came to Salem that brought over many godly persons to begin the plantations and churches of Christ there and in the Bay of the Massachusetts.[1] So their long stay and keeping back |164| was recompensed by the Lord to their friends here with a double blessing; in that they not only enjoyed them now beyond their late expectation (when all their hopes seemed to be cut off) but with them, many more godly friends and Christian brethren as the beginning of a larger harvest unto the Lord. In the increase of His churches and people in these parts, to the admiration of many, and almost wonder of the world, that of so small beginnings so great things should ensue, as time after manifested. And that here should be a resting place for so many of the Lord's people, when so sharp a scourge came upon their own nation. But it was the Lord's doing, and it ought to be marvelous in our eyes.[2]

But I shall here insert some of their friends' letters, which do best express their own minds in these their proceedings.[3]

|165| That I may handle things together, I have put these two companies that came from Leyden in this place. Though they came at two several times, yet they both came out of England this year. The former company, being 35 persons, were shipped in May and arrived here about August. The latter were shipped

[1] This was the beginning of the great Puritan migration to Massachusetts Bay and other New England colonies; five or six ships brought about 350 settlers to Salem that spring and summer, and within a year Massachusetts Bay had fivefold the population of New Plymouth.

[2] Psalm cxviii.23.

[3] These will be found in Appendix VII.

in the beginning of March and arrived here the latter end of May, 1630.[4] Mr. Sherley's two letters, the effect whereof I have before related, as much of them as is pertinent, mentions both.

Their charge as Mr. Allerton brought it in afterwards on account, came to above £500 besides their fetching hither from Salem and the Bay where they and their goods were landed; viz., their transportation from Holland to England and their charges lying there and passages hither, with clothing provided for them.[5] For I find by account for the one company, 125 yards of kersey, 127 ellons [6] of linen cloth, shoes 66 pair, with many other particulars. The charge of the other company is reckoned on the several families; some £50, some £40, and some £30, and so more or less as their number and expenses were. And besides all this charge their friends and brethren here were to provide corn and other provisions for them till they could reap a crop, which was long before; those that came in May were thus maintained upward of 16 or 18 months before they had any harvest of their own, and the other by proportion. And all they could do in the meantime was to get them some housing and prepare them grounds to plant on, against the season. And this charge of maintaining them all this while was little less than the former sum. These things I note more particularly, for sundry regards.

First, to show a rare example herein of brotherly love and Christian care in performing their promises and covenants to their brethren, to, and in a sort beyond their power; that they should venture so desperately to engage themselves to accomplish this thing and bear it so cheerfully. For they never demanded, much less had any repayment of all these great sums thus disbursed.

Secondly, it must needs be that there was more than of man in these achievements that should thus readily stir up the hearts of

[4] In the *Lyon*, William Peirce master, Bristol to Salem. Isaac Allerton, who came in her, borrowed her shallop to sail down east, speaking the *Arbella*, Governor Winthrop's flagship, off Cape Ann on 12 June 1630.

[5] The cost of transatlantic passage in 1629–30, complained the Rev. Francis Higginson of Salem, was "wondrous dear, as £5 a man and £10 a horse and commonly of £3 for every tun of goods." (1912 ed. Bradford II 67.)

[6] An old form of *ell*, a measure equal to 45 inches.

such able friends to join in partnership with them in such a case, and cleave so faithfully to them as these did, in so great adventures. And the more because the most of them never saw their faces to this day, there being neither kindred, alliance or other acquaintance or relations between any of them than hath been before mentioned. It must needs be therefore the special work and hand of God.

Thirdly, that these poor people here in a wilderness should notwithstanding be enabled in time to repay all these engagements, and many more unjustly brought upon them through the unfaithfulness of some and many other great losses which they sustained. Which will be made manifest, if the Lord be pleased to give life and time. In the meantime I cannot but admire His ways and works towards His servants, and humbly desire to bless His holy name for His great mercies hitherto. |166|

The Leyden people being thus come over, and sundry of the generality seeing and hearing how great the charge was like to be that was that way to be expended, they began to murmur and repine at it, notwithstanding the burthen lay on other men's shoulders. Especially at the paying of the three bushels of corn a year, according to the former agreement, when the trade was let for the six years aforesaid. But to give them content herein also it was promised them that if they could do it in the time without it, they would never demand it of them, which gave them good content. And indeed it never was paid, as will appear by the sequel.

[*Strange Proceedings of Mr. Allerton*]

Concerning Mr. Allerton's proceedings about the enlarging and confirming of their Patent, both that at home and Kennebec, will best appear by another letter of Mr. Sherley's, for though much time and money was expended about it, yet he left it unaccomplished this year and came without it. See Mr. Sherley's letter.[7]

By which it appears what progress was made herein, and in part what charge it was, and how left unfinished, and some rea-

[7] Printed in Appendix VII.

son of the same.[8] But in truth, as was afterwards apprehended, the main reason was Mr. Allerton's policy to have an opportunity to be sent over again for other regards, and for that end procured them thus to write. For it might then well enough have been finished, if not with that clause about the customs, which was Mr. Allerton's and Mr. Sherley's device and not at all thought on by the Colony here, nor much regarded, yet it might have been done without it, without all question, having passed the King's hand; nay it was conceived it might then have been done with it, if he had pleased. But covetousness never brings aught home, as the proverb is, for this opportunity being lost, it was never accomplished but a great deal of money vainly and lavishly cast away about it, as doth appear upon their accounts. But of this, more in its place. |167 v.|

Mr. Allerton gave them great and just offense in this, which I had omitted and almost forgotten, in bringing over this year for base gain that unworthy man and instrument of mischief Morton, who was sent home but the year before for his misdemeanors. He not only brought him over, but to the town (as it were to nose them) and lodged him at his own house; and for a while used him as a scribe to do his business, till he was caused to pack him away.[9] So he went to his old nest in the Massachusetts, where it was not long but by his miscarriage he gave them just occasion to lay hands on him, and he was by them again sent prisoner into England, where he lay a good while in Exeter gaol. For besides his miscarriage here, he was vehemently suspected for the murder of a man that had adventured moneys with him when he came first into New England. And a warrant was sent from the Lord Chief Justice to apprehend him, by virtue whereof he was by the Governor of the Massachusetts sent into England; and for other his misdemeanors amongst them they demolished his house, that it might be no longer a roost for such unclean birds to nestle

[8] About obtaining the Patent of 1630 and the failure to obtain a royal charter. In defense of Allerton it should be said that Massachusetts Bay had a 21 years' exemption from custom duties by charter, so he tried to obtain the same for Plymouth.

[9] Morton refused to recognize the authority of the Massachusetts Bay Company, especially its law against selling arms to the Indians, and so was transported to England in 1630.

in. Yet he got free again, and writ an infamous and scurrilous book [1] against many godly and chief men of the country, full of lies and slanders and fraught with profane calumnies against their names and persons and the ways of God. After sundry years when the wars were hot in England, he came again into the country and was imprisoned at Boston for this book, and other things, being grown old in wickedness.

Concerning the rest of Mr. Allerton's instructions, in which they strictly enjoined him not to exceed above that £50 in the goods before mentioned, not to bring any but trading commodities, he followed them not at all but did the quite contrary, bringing over many other sorts of retail goods, selling what he could by the way on his own account, and delivering the rest, which he said to be theirs, into the store. And for trading goods, brought but little in comparison; excusing the matter–they had laid out much about the Leyden people and Patent, etc.; and for other goods they had much of them of their own dealings, without present disbursement, and to like effect. And as for passing his bounds and instructions, he laid it on Mr. Sherley, etc., who he said, they might see his mind in his letters. Also that they had set out Ashley at great charge, but next year they should have what trading goods they would send for, if things were now settled, etc. And thus were they put off. Indeed, Mr. Sherley writ things tending this way, but it is like he was overruled by Mr. Allerton and hearkened more to him than to their letters from hence. Thus he further writes in the former letter: [2]

By this it appears that there was a kind of concurrence between Mr. Allerton and them in these things, and that they gave

[1] *New English Canaan* (Amsterdam 1637). This is the most amusing of all books about early New England, full of malicious humor, good animal spirits, and appreciation of the country and the Indians. After doing his utmost to prejudice the English authorities against the Puritan colonies, Morton found himself on the losing side of the English Civil War in the fall of 1643 and turned up again at Plymouth, where Bradford allowed him to board with one of the settlers at 4*s* per week, "but begone as soon as winter breaks up." Winslow, writing of this to Winthrop, observed with astonishment that Morton had fallen so low that he was "content to drink water." From Plymouth he went to Maine, where he resumed his old practices, for which he spent a winter in jail in Boston. That really broke the old rascal's spirit, and he died in 1647.

[2] The letter of 19 March 1629/30; see Appendix VII.

more regard to his way and course in these things than to the advice from hence, which made him bold to presume above his instructions and to run on in the course he did, to their greater hurt afterwards as will appear. These things did much trouble them here, but they well knew not how to help it, being loath to make any breach or contention hereabout, being so premonished as before in the letter above recited. Another more secret cause was herewith concurrent. Mr. Allerton had married the daughter of their Reverend Elder, Mr. Brewster, a man beloved and honoured amongst them and who took great pains in teaching and dispensing the Word of God unto them, whom they were loath to grieve or any way offend, so as they bore with much in that respect. And withal Mr. Allerton carried so fair with him, and procured such letters from Mr. Sherley to him, with such applause of Mr. Allerton's wisdom, care and faithfulness in the business. And as things stood, none were so fit to send about them as he, and if any should suggest otherwise it was rather out of envy or some other sinister respect than otherwise. Besides, though private gain I do persuade myself was some cause to lead Mr. Allerton aside in these beginnings; yet I think or at least charity carries me to hope, that he intended to deal faithfully with them in the main. And had such an opinion of his own ability, and some experience of the benefit that he had made in this singular way, as he conceived he might both raise himself an estate and also be a means to bring in such profit to Mr. Sherley (and it may be the rest) as might be as likely to bring in their moneys again with advantage, and, it may be, sooner than from the general way; or at least it was looked upon by some of them to be a good help thereunto. And that neither he nor any other did intend to charge the general account with anything that ran in particular, or that Mr. Sherley or any other did purpose but that the general should be first and fully supplied. I say charity makes me thus conceive, though things fell out otherwise, and they missed of their aims, and the general suffered abundantly hereby, as will afterwards appear. |169|

[*The Penobscot Venture*]

Together herewith sorted another business contrived by Mr. Allerton and them there, without any knowledge of the partners, and so far proceeded in as they were constrained to allow thereof and join in the same, though they had no great liking of it, but feared what might be the event of the same. I shall relate it in a further part of Mr. Sherley's letter, as followeth: [3]

This matter of the buying the debts of the purchase was part of Mr. Allerton's instructions, and in many of them it might have been done to good profit for ready pay (as some were), but Mr. Sherley had no mind to it. But this business about Ashley did not a little trouble them. For though he had wit and ability enough to manage the business, yet some of them knew him to be a very profane young man, and he had for some time lived among the Indians as a savage and went naked amongst them and used their manners, in which time he got their language. So they feared he might still run into evil courses (though he promised better) and God would not prosper his ways.

As soon as he was landed at the place intended, called Penobscot,[4] some fourscore leagues from this place, he writ and afterwards came for to desire to be supplied with wampumpeag, corn against winter and other things. They considered these were of their chief commodities and would be continually needed by him, and it would much prejudice their own trade at Kennebec if they did not join with him in the ordering of things if thus they should supply him. And on the other hand, if they refused to join with him and also to afford any supply unto him, they should greatly offend their above-named friends and might haply lose them hereby, and he and Mr. Allerton, laying their crafty wits together might get supplies of these things elsewhere. Be-

[3] This third part of the Sherley-Hatherley letter of 19 March 1629/30 will be found in Appendix VII. Bradford and the leading men of the Colony must have emitted loud groans in reading that letter, for it informed them that Allerton and Sherley had committed them to a new fur-trading venture on the Maine coast and had sent out a "profane young man," Edward Ashley, to manage it. Ashley came out in the *Lyon* with Allerton and a good supply of truck.

[4] The exact site is not known, but it was at or very near the present town of Castine; see G. A. Wheeler *Castine Past and Present* (1896) p. 5.

sides they considered that if they joined not in the business, they knew Mr. Allerton would be with them in it, and so would swim as it were between both to the prejudice of both, but of themselves especially. For they had reason to think this business was chiefly of his contriving, and Ashley was a man fit for his turn and dealings.

So they, to prevent a worse mischief, resolved to join in the business, and gave him supplies in what they could, and overlooked his proceedings as well as they could; the which they did the better by joining an honest young man that came from Leyden, with him as his fellow (in some sort) and not merely as a servant. Which young man [5] being discreet, and one whom they could trust, they so instructed as kept Ashley in some good measure within bounds. And so they returned their answer to their friends in England that they accepted of their motion and joined with them in Ashley's business, and yet withal told them what their fears were concerning him.

But when they came to have full notice of all the goods brought them that year, they saw they fell very short of trading goods, and Ashley far better supplied than |171| themselves, so as they were forced to buy of the fishermen to furnish themselves; yea, and cottons and kerseys and other such like cloth (for want of trading cloth) of Mr. Allerton himself, and so to put away a great part of their beaver at under rate in the country. Which they should have sent home to help to discharge their great engagements, which was to their great vexation, but Mr. Allerton prayed them to be content, and the next year they might have what they would write for. And their engagements of this year were great indeed when they came to know them, which was not wholly till two years after; and that which made them the more, Mr. Allerton had taken up some large sums at Bristol at £50 per cent again, which he excused, that he was forced to it because otherwise he could at the spring of year get no goods transported, such were

[5] Thomas Willet, son of an English clergyman. A youthful member of the Leyden congregation, he came over in 1629 at the age of 24, prospered and became a leading citizen of Plymouth; accompanied the English expeditionary force that wrested New Amsterdam from the Dutch in 1664, and was appointed by Gov. Nicolls the first English Mayor of New York. Returning to Plymouth Colony, he settled at Rehoboth and died, greatly respected, in 1674.

their envy against their trade. But whether this was any more than an excuse, some of them doubted, but however, the burden did lie on their backs, and they must bear it as they did many heavy loads more in the end.

This paying of £50 per cent and difficulty of having their goods transported by the fishing ships at the first of the year (as was believed) which was the chief season for trade, put them upon another project. Mr. Allerton after the fishing season was over, light of a bargain of salt at a good fishing place, and bought it, which came to about £113. And shortly after he might have had £30 clear profit for it, without any more trouble about it. But Mr. Winslow coming that way from Kennebec, and some of their partners with him in the bark, they met with Mr. Allerton and falling into discourse with him, they stayed him from selling the salt. And resolved if it might please the rest, to keep it for themselves and to hire a ship in the west country to come on fishing for them on shares according to the custom. And seeing she might have her salt here ready, and a stage ready built and fitted where the salt lay safely landed and housed, instead of bringing salt they might stow her full of trading goods as bread, pease, cloth, etc. And so they might have a full supply of goods without paying freight, and in due season, which might turn greatly to their advantage. Coming home, this was propounded and considered on and approved by all but the Governor, who had no mind to it, seeing they had always lost by fishing. But the rest were so earnest, as thinking that they might gain well by the fishing in this way, and if they should but save, yea or lose something by it, the other benefit would be advantage enough. So, seeing their earnestness, he gave way, and it was referred to their friends in England to allow or disallow it. Of which more in its place.

Upon the consideration of the business about the Patent, and in what state it was left (as is before remembered), and Mr. Sherley's earnest pressing to have Mr. Allerton to come over again to finish it and perfect the accounts, etc., it was concluded to send him over this year again [6] though it was with some fear and jeal-

[6] This happened in the fall of 1630. Allerton's movements, carefully worked out by Prince, were: departed Bristol 1 Dec. 1630, arrived Nantasket Roads,

ousy. Yet he gave them fair words and promises of well performing all their businesses according to their directions, and to mend his former errours. So he was accordingly sent with full instructions for all things, with large letters to Mr. Sherley and the rest, both about Ashley's business and their own supply with trading commodities, and how much it did concern them to be furnished therewith, and what they had suffered for want thereof, and of what little use other goods were |172| in comparison thereof. And so likewise about this fishing ship to be thus hired and fraught with trading goods, which might both supply them and Ashley and the benefit thereof. Which was left to their consideration to hire and set her out or not, but in no case not to send any except she was thus freighted with trading goods. But what these things came to will appear in the next year's passages.

[*Plymouth Gets a Pastor and Salem Forms a Church*]

I had like to have omitted another passage that fell out the beginning of this year. There was one Mr. Ralph Smith and his wife and family that came over into the Bay of the Massachusetts, and sojourned at present with some straggling people that lived at Nantasket. Here being a boat of this place, putting in there on some occasion, he earnestly desired that they would give him and his passage for Plymouth, and some such things as they could well carry, having before heard that there was likelihood he might procure house room for some time till he should resolve to settle there if he might, or elsewhere as God should dispose, for he was weary of being in that uncouth place and in a poor house that would neither keep him nor his goods dry. So, seeing him to be a grave man and understood he had been a minister, though they had no order for any such thing, yet they presumed and brought him. He was here accordingly kindly entertained and housed, and had the rest of his goods and servants sent for, and exercised

Boston Harbor, 5 Feb. 1630/31, departed Salem 1 April 1631, arrived London 29 April (a fast passage), sailed some time that fall, arrived Nantasket Roads 2 Nov. 1631.

his gifts amongst them and afterwards was chosen into the ministry and so remained for sundry years.[7]

It was before noted that sundry of those that came from Leyden came over in the ships that came to Salem, where Mr. Endecott had chief command; and by infection that grew among the passengers at sea, it spread also among them ashore, of which many died, some of the scurvy, other of an infectious fever which continued some time amongst them, though our people through God's goodness escaped it. Upon which occasion he writ hither for some help, understanding here was one that had some skill that way and had cured divers of the scurvy, and others of other diseases by letting blood and other means. Upon which his request, the Governor here sent him unto them and also writ to him from whom he received an answer, the which, because it is brief and shows the beginning of their acquaintance and closing in the truth and ways of God, I thought it not unmeet nor without use here to insert it, and another showing the beginning of their fellowship and church estate there. Being as followeth:

Right Worthy Sir: It is a thing not usual that servants to one master and of the same household should be strangers; I assure you I desire it not, nay to speak more plainly I cannot be so to you. God's People are all marked with one and the same mark and sealed with one and the same seal, and have for the main, one and the same heart guided by one and same spirit of truth. And where this is there can be no discord, nay here must needs be sweet harmony. And the same request (with you) I make unto the Lord that we may, as Christian brethren be united by a heavenly and unfeigned love, bending all our hearts and forces in furthering a work beyond our strength, with reverence and fear, fastening our eyes always on Him that only is able to direct and prosper all our ways.

I acknowledge myself much bound to you for your kind love and care in sending Mr. Fuller among us, and rejoice much that I am by him satisfied touching your judgments of the outward form of God's

[7] Ralph Smith, a scholar of Christ's College, Cambridge, did not stay at Salem, because he was a Separatist. He was ordained the first pastor of the Plymouth Church before the end of 1629, "Yet he proved but a poor help to them in that, being of very weak parts." (Plymouth Church Records in Colonial Society of Massachusetts *Publications* XXII 64.)

worship. It is, as far as |173| I can gather, no other than is warranted by the evidence of truth. And the same which I have professed and maintained ever since the Lord in mercy revealed Himself unto me. Being far from the common report that hath been spread of you touching that particular.[8] But God's children must not look for less here below, and it is the great mercy of God that He strengthens them to go through with it. I shall not need at this time to be tedious unto you, for God willing I purpose to see your face shortly. In the meantime, I humbly take my leave of you, committing you to the Lord's blessed protection, and rest

Your assured loving friend,

Naumkeag, May 11, Anno 1629 JOHN ENDECOTT

This second letter showeth their proceedings in their church affairs at Salem, which was the second church erected in these parts; and afterwards the Lord established many more in sundry places.

SIR: I make bold to trouble you with a few lines, for to certify you how it hath pleased God to deal with us since you heard from us. How, notwithstanding all opposition that hath been here and elsewhere, it hath pleased God to lay a foundation, the which I hope is agreeable to His Word in everything.

The 20th of July it pleased the Lord to move the heart of our Governor [9] to set it apart for a solemn day of humiliation for the choice of a pastor and teacher. The former part of the day being spent in prayer and teaching, the latter part about the election, which was after this manner. The persons thought on (who had been ministers in England) were demanded concerning their callings. They acknowledged there was a twofold calling, the one an inward calling when the Lord moved the heart of a man to take that calling upon

[8] Endecott means that he had heard rumors of the Pilgrims being rigid Separatists and was glad to find that they were not; for although he and his friends inclined to the Congregational form of church government, they did not wish to separate from the Church of England. The influence of Fuller's visit on church polity in the Bay Colony is discussed in Williston Walker *History of the Congregational Churches in the United States* (1894) p. 85; Perry Miller *Orthodoxy in Massachusetts* (1933), and notes to 1912 ed. Bradford II 90–5.

[9] John Endecott. This letter, describing the forming of the first Congregational church in Massachusetts Bay if not in New England (since the Plymouth church had so far been but a section of the Leyden one), is considered a classic by all Congregationalists.

him and fitted him with gifts for the same; the second was an outward calling which was from the people, when a company of believers are joined together in covenant to walk together in all the ways of God. And every member (being men) are to have a free voice in the choice of their officers, etc. Now, we being persuaded that these two men were so qualified as the Apostle speaks to Timothy, where he says, "A bishop must be blameless, sober, apt to teach," etc.,[1] I think I may say, as the eunuch said unto Philip, "What should let from being baptized, seeing there was water?" and he believed.[2] So these two servants of God, clearing all things by their answers, and being thus fitted, we saw no reason but we might freely give our voices for their election after this trial. So Mr. Skelton was chosen pastor and Mr. Higginson to be teacher. And they accepting the choice, Mr. Higginson with three or four of the gravest members of the church laid their hands on Mr. Skelton, using prayer therewith. This being done, there was imposition of hands on Mr. Higginson also. And since that time, Thursday (being as I take it the 6th of August) is appointed for another day of humiliation for the choice of elders and deacons and ordaining of them.[3]

And now, good Sir, I hope that you and the rest of God's people (who are acquainted with the ways of God) with you, will say that here was a right foundation laid and that these two blessed servants of the Lord came in at the door and not at the window.[4] Thus I have made bold to trouble you with these few lines, desiring you to remember us, etc. And so rest

At your service in what I may,

Salem, July 30, 1629 CHARLES GOTT[5]

[1] 1 Timothy iii.1–3.

[2] Acts viii.36–7.

[3] Bradford and others, on receiving this interesting news, tried to get there but were prevented by head winds from arriving until after the ceremony was over—in time, no doubt, for the feast that followed.

[4] An allusion to John x.1.

[5] One of the prominent early settlers of Salem who came out with Endecott.

CHAPTER XXI

Anno Dom: 1630 [*Allerton's New Venture*] |174|

Ashley, being well supplied, had quickly gathered a good parcel of beaver, and like a crafty pate, he sent it all home and would not pay for the goods he had had of the Plantation here, but let them stand still on the score and took up still more. Now, though they well enough knew his aim, yet they let him go on and writ of it into England; but partly the beaver they received and sold (of which they were sensible) and partly by Mr. Allerton's extolling of him, they cast more how to supply him than the Plantation, and something to upbraid them with it. They were forced to buy him a bark also, and to furnish her with a master and men to transport his corn and provisions (of which he had put off much, for the Indians of those parts have no corn growing); and at harvest after corn is ready the weather grows foul and the seas dangerous, so as he could do little good with his shallop for that purpose.

They looked earnestly for a timely supply this spring,[1] by the fishing ship which they expected, and had been at charge to keep a stage for her; but none came nor any supply heard of for them. At length they heard some supply was sent to Ashley by a fishing ship, at which they something marveled, and the more that they had no letters either from Mr. Allerton or Mr. Sherley. So they went on in their business as well as they could.

At last they heard of Mr. Peirce his arrival in the Bay of the Massachusetts, who brought passengers and goods thither.[2] They presently sent a shallop, conceiving they should have something by him. But he told them he had none. And a ship was set out on fishing, but after 11 weeks' beating at sea she met with such foul weather as she was forced back again for England, and the sea-

[1] Of 1631; most of the events related in this chapter occurred in that year.

[2] This was the *White Angel,* whose arrival at Saco, Maine, with Allerton on board and supplies for Plymouth Colony, is noted by Governor Winthrop in his *Journal* for 27 June 1631. Peirce was master of the *Lyon,* not this ship. John Oldham (our old friend) and Richard Vines had obtained a patent from the Council for New England, 12 Feb. 1630, for the west side of Saco River, including Wood Island and Cape Porpoise Harbors.

son being over gave off the voyage.[3] Neither did he hear of much goods in her for the Plantation, or that she did belong to them, for he had heard something from Mr. Allerton tending that way. But Mr. Allerton had bought another ship and was to come in her and was to fish for bass to the eastward, and to bring goods, etc. These things did much trouble them, and half astonish them. Mr. Winslow having been to the eastward brought news of the like things with some more particulars, and that it was like Mr. Allerton would be late before he came.

At length, they having an opportunity, resolved to send Mr. Winslow with what beaver they had ready into England to see how the squares[4] went, being very jealous of these things and Mr. Allerton's courses. And writ such letters and gave him such instructions as they thought meet; and if he found things not well, to discharge Mr. Allerton for being any longer agent for them, or to deal any more in the business, and to see how the accounts stood, etc.

About the middle of summer arrives Mr. Hatherley in the Bay of the Massachusetts, being one of the partners, and came over in the same ship that was set out on fishing (called the *Friendship*.) They presently sent to him, making no question but now they had goods come and should know how all things stood. But they found |175| the former news true, how this ship had been so long at sea, and spent and spoiled her provisions and overthrown the voyage. And he being sent over by the rest of the partners to see how things went here, being at Bristol with Mr. Allerton in the ship bought (called the *White Angel*) ready to set sail, overnight came a messenger from Barnstaple to Mr. Allerton and told him of the return of the ship and what had befallen. And he not knowing what to do, having a great charge under hand, the ship lying at his rates and now ready to set sail, got him to go and discharge the ship[5] and take order for the goods.

To be short, they found Mr. Hatherley something reserved and troubled in himself (Mr. Allerton not being there) not know-

[3] This, we gather from the same source, was the *Friendship*. She made a fresh start from Barnstaple, Devon, in mid-May and arrived Boston 14 July 1631.

[4] I.e., quarrels, disputes.

[5] I.e., of her fishermen crew.

ing how to dispose of the goods till he came. But he heard he was arrived with the other ship to the eastward [6] and expected his coming. But he told them there was not much for them in this ship, only two packs of Barnstaple rugs and two hogsheads of metheglin, drawn out in wooden flackets.[7] But when these flackets came to be received, there was left but six gallons of the two hogsheads, it being drunk up under the name leakage and so lost. But the ship was filled with goods for sundry gentlemen and others that were come to plant in the Massachusetts, for which they paid freight by the tun. And this was all the satisfaction they could have at present. So they brought this small parcel of goods and returned with this news, and a letter as obscure, which made them much to marvel thereat. The letter was as followeth:

GENTLEMEN, PARTNERS, AND LOVING FRIENDS, etc.

Briefly thus: we have this year set forth a fishing ship and a trading ship, which latter we have bought; and so have disbursed a great deal of money, as may and will appear by the accounts. And because this ship (called the *White Angel*) is to act two parts (as I may say), fishing for bass and trading; and that while Mr. Allerton was employed about the trading, the fishing might suffer by carelessness or neglect of the sailors, we have entreated your and our loving friend Mr. Hatherley to go over with him, knowing he will be a comfort to Mr. Allerton, a joy to you to see a careful and loving friend, and a great stay to the business. And so great content to us. That if it should please God the one should fail (as God forbid) yet the other would keep both reckonings and things upright. For we are now out great sums of money, as they will acquaint you withal, etc. When we were out but four or five hundred pounds apiece, we looked not much after it but left it to you and your agent (who without flattery deserveth infinite thanks and commendations both of you and us for his pains, etc.). But now we are out double, nay, treble apiece, some of us, etc. Which makes us both write and send over our friend Mr. Hatherley, whom we pray you to entertain kindly, of which we doubt not of.

The main end of sending him is to see the state and account of all the business, of all which we pray you inform him fully, though the

[6] The *White Angel,* then at Biddeford Pool or Saco, Maine.

[7] There is more on these "ruggs" in the next chapter. Metheglin, made of sage, thyme, rosemary and other herbs boiled in honey and fermented, was a favorite country beverage in England; a flacket is a small keg.

ship and business wait for it and him. For we should take it very unkindly that we should entreat him to take such a journey, and that when it pleaseth God he returns he could not give us content and satisfaction in this particular through default of any of you. |176| But we hope you will so order business, as neither he nor we shall have cause to complain, but to do as we have ever done, think well of you all, etc.

I will not promise, but shall endeavour and hope to effect the full desire and grant of your Patent, and that ere it be long. I would not have you take anything unkindly. I have not writ out of jealousy of any unjust dealing.

Be you all kindly saluted in the Lord, so I rest,

Yours in what I may,

March 25, 1631. JAMES SHERLEY

It needs not be thought strange that these things should amaze and trouble them; first that this fishing ship should be set out and fraught with other men's goods, and scarce any of theirs, seeing their main end was (as is before remembered) to bring them a full supply, and their special order not to set out any except this was done. And now a ship to come on their account, clean contrary to their both end and order, was a mystery they could not understand. And so much the worse, seeing she had such ill success as to lose both her voyage and provisions. The second thing, that another ship should be bought and sent out on new designs, a thing not so much as once thought on by any here, much less not a word intimated or spoken of by any either by word or letter. Neither could they imagine why this should be. Bass fishing was never looked at by them, but as soon as ever they heard on it, they looked at it as a vain thing, that would certainly turn to loss.[8] And for Mr. Allerton to follow any trade for them, it was never in their thoughts. And thirdly, that their friends should complain of disbursements and yet run into such great things, and charge of shipping and new projects of their own heads, not only without but against all order and advice, was to them very

[8] Striped bass (see footnote 3 page 122 above) were very well for local consumption, and could be cured like mackerel, herring or any other fat fish by leaving in a pickle for a few days, drying in the sun and packing in barrels (Capt. Enos Verge). But there was no market for bass in Europe, which wanted salt codfish and no other kind.

strange. And fourthly, that all these matters of so great charge and employments should be thus wrapped up in a brief and obscure letter; they knew not what to make of it.

But amidst all their doubts they must have patience till Mr. Allerton and Mr. Hatherley should come. In the meantime, Mr. Winslow was gone for England; and others of them were forced to follow their employments with the best means they had, till they could hear of better.

At length Mr. Hatherley and Mr. Allerton came unto them (after they had delivered their goods) [9] and finding them strucken with some sadness about these things, Mr. Allerton told them that the ship *White Angel* did not belong to them nor their account, neither need they have anything to do with her, except they would. And Mr. Hatherley confirmed the same, and said that they would have had him to have had a part, but he refused. But he made question whether they would not turn her upon the general account if there came loss (as he now saw was like) seeing Mr. Allerton laid down this course and put them on this project. But for the fishing ship, he told them they need not be so much troubled for he had her accounts here, and showed them that her first setting out came not much to exceed £600, as they might see by the account which he showed them; and for this later voyage, it would arise to profit by the freight of the goods and the sale of some cattle which he shipped and had already sold, and was to be paid for partly here and partly by bills into England. So as they should not have this put on their account at all, except they would. |178| [1] And for the former, he had sold so much goods out of her in England and employed the money in this second voyage, as it together with such goods and implements as Mr. Allerton must need about his fishing, would rise to a good part of the money; for he must have the salt and nets, also spikes, nails, etc. All which would rise to near £400. So, with the bearing of their parts of the rest of the losses (which would not be much above £200) they would clear them of this whole account.

[9] At Saco and Boston, where the *Friendship* arrived 14 July 1631. She sailed for St. Kitts the 29th. The *White Angel* arrived Salem or Boston 22 July, sailed for Plymouth the 30th but ran aground on the Gurnet. (Thomas Prince's ms. note on p. 175 v.)

[1] There is no folio 177 in the ms.

Of which motion they were glad, not being willing to have any accounts lie upon them but about their trade; which made them willing to hearken thereunto; and demand of Mr. Hatherley how he could make this good if they should agree thereunto. He told them he was sent over as their agent and had this order from them, that whatsoever he and Mr. Allerton did together, they would stand to it, but they would not allow of what Mr. Allerton did alone, except they liked it; but if he did it alone they would not gainsay it. Upon which they sold to him and Mr. Allerton all the rest of the goods, and gave them present possession of them. And a writing was made and confirmed under both Mr. Hatherley's and Mr. Allerton's hands, to the effect aforesaid. And Mr. Allerton being best acquainted with the people, sold away presently all such goods as he had no need of for the fishing, as nine shallop sails made of good new canvas, and the rodes for them being all new, with sundry such useful goods, for ready beaver, by Mr. Hatherley's allowance. And thus they thought they had well provided for themselves. Yet they rebuked Mr. Allerton very much for running into these courses, fearing the success of them.

Mr. Allerton and Mr. Hatherley brought to the town with them, after he had sold what he could abroad, a great quantity of other goods besides trading commodities, as linen cloth, bedticks, stockings, tape, pins, rugs, etc. And told them they were to have them, if they would. But they told Mr. Allerton that they had forbid him before, for bringing any such on their account; it would hinder their trade and returns. But he and Mr. Hatherley said, if they would not have them, they would sell them themselves, and take corn for what they could not otherwise sell. They told them they might if they had order for it. The goods of one sort and other came to upward of £500.

[*Hatherley's Cruise Down East*]

After these things Mr. Allerton went to the ship about his bass fishing, and Mr. Hatherley (according to his order) after he took knowledge how things stood at the Plantation, of all which they informed him fully. He then desired a boat of them to go and visit the trading houses, both Kennebec and Ashley at Penobscot; for so they in England had enjoined him. They accordingly furnished him with a boat and men for the voyage, and acquainted him plainly and thoroughly with all things, by which he had good content and satisfaction. And saw plainly that Mr. Allerton played his own game and ran a course not only to the great wrong and detriment of the Plantation who employed and trusted him, but abused them in England also in possessing them with prejudice against the Plantation: as that they would never be able to repay their moneys, in regard of their great charge. But if |179| they would follow his advice and projects, he and Ashley (being well supplied) would quickly bring in their moneys with good advantage.

Mr. Hatherley disclosed also a further project about the setting out of this ship, the *White Angel;* how she being well fitted with good ordnance and known to have made a great fight at sea (when she belonged to Bristol) and carried away the victory, they had agreed (by Mr. Allerton's means) that after she had brought a freight of goods here into the country, and fraught herself with fish, she should go from hence to Port of Porte,[2] and there be sold, both ship, goods and ordnance. And had for this end had speech with a factor of those parts beforehand, to whom she should have been consigned. But this was prevented at this time (after it was known) partly by the contrary advice given by their friends here to Mr. Allerton and Mr. Hatherley, showing how it might ensnare their friends in England (being men of estate) if it should come to be known; and for the Plantation, they did and would disallow it and protest against it. And partly by their bad voyage, for they both came too late to do any good for fishing, and also had such a wicked and drunken company as neither Mr. Allerton nor any else could rule, as Mr. Hatherley to his great grief and shame saw and beheld, and all others that came near them.

Ashley likewise was taken in a trap, before Mr. Hatherley returned,[3] for trading powder and shot with the Indians; and was

[2] Oporto, Portugal.

[3] From his trip in the Plymouth boat to Penobscot, in the summer of 1631. The Proclamation of 24 Nov. 1630 by Charles I "Forbidding the disorderly

seized upon by some in authority, who also would have confiscated above a thousand weight of beaver. But the goods were freed, for the Governor here made it appear by a bond under Ashley's hand wherein he was bound to them in £500 not to trade any munition with the Indians or otherwise to abuse himself. It was also manifest against him that he had committed uncleanness with Indian women, things that they feared at his first employment which made them take this strict course with him in the beginning. So, to be short, they got their goods freed, but he was sent home prisoner. And that I may make an end concerning him, after some time of imprisonment in the Fleet, by the means of friends he was set at liberty and intended to come over again. But the Lord prevented it. For he had a motion made to him by some merchants, to go into Russia because he had such good skill in the beaver trade; the which he accepted of and in his return home was cast away at sea. This was his end.

Mr. Hatherley fully understanding the state of all things, had good satisfaction and could well inform them how all things stood between Mr. Allerton and the Plantation. Yea, he found that Mr. Allerton had got within him, and |180| got all the goods into his own hands, for which Mr. Hatherley stood jointly engaged to them here, about the ship *Friendship*, as also most of the freight money, besides some of his own particular estate; about which more will appear hereafter. So he returned to England,[4] and they sent a good quantity of beaver with him to the rest of the partners; so both he and it was very welcome unto them.

Mr. Allerton followed his affairs and returned with his *White Angel*, being no more employed by the Plantation. But these businesses were not ended till many years after, nor well understood of a long time, but folded up in obscurity and kept in the clouds, to the great loss and vexation of the Plantation, who in the end were (for peace sake) forced to bear the unjust burthen

---

Trading with the Saluages in New England in America, especially the furnishing of the Natiues . . . with Weapons, and Habiliments of Warre" is reproduced in 1912 ed. Bradford II 106–9, along with some testimony by witnesses such as Thomas Willett as to Ashley's guilt.

[4] In the *White Angel*; she departed Boston 6 Sept. 1631 according to a ms. note by Prince, and arrived England in November.

of them, to their almost undoing. As will appear if God give life to finish this history.

They sent their letters also by Mr. Hatherley to the partners there, to show them how Mr. Hatherley and Mr. Allerton had discharged them of the *Friendship's* account, and that they both affirmed that the *White Angel* did not at all belong to them, and therefore desired that their account might not be charged therewith. Also they writ to Mr. Winslow, their agent, that he in like manner should in their names protest against it, if any such thing should be intended; for they would never yield to the same. As also to signify to them that they renounced Mr. Allerton wholly for being their agent, or to have anything to do in any of their business.

[*Billington Hanged*]

This year John Billington the elder, one that came over with the first, was arraigned, and both by grand and petty jury found guilty of wilful murder, by plain and notorious evidence. And was for the same accordingly executed. This, as it was the first execution amongst them, so was it a matter of great sadness unto them. They used all due means about his trial and took the advice of Mr. Winthrop and other the ablest gentlemen in Bay of the Massachusetts, that were then newly come over, who concurred with them that he ought to die, and the land to be purged from blood. He and some of his had been often punished for miscarriages before, being one of the profanest families amongst them; they came from London, and I know not by what friends shuffled into their company. His fact was that he waylaid a young man, one John Newcomen, about a former quarrel and shot him with a gun, whereof he died.[5]

[*News from the Bay Colony*]

Having by a providence a letter or two that came to my hands concerning the proceedings of their reverend friends in the Bay of the Massachusetts who were lately come over, I thought it not

[5] The above paragraph is written on fol. 179 v. We are now back in 1630; the execution took place in September.

amiss here to insert them, so far as is pertinent and may be useful for after times, before I conclude this year.

SIR: Being at Salem the 25th of July, being the Sabbath; after the evening exercise Mr. Johnson received a letter from the Governor Mr. John Winthrop, manifesting the hand of God to be upon them and against them at Charlestown, in visiting them with sickness and taking divers from amongst them; not sparing the righteous but partaking with the wicked in these bodily judgments. It was therefore by his desire taken into the godly consideration of the best here, what was to be done to pacify the Lord's wrath, etc. Where it was concluded that the Lord was to be sought in righteousness; and to that end the 6th day (being Friday) of this present week, is set apart that they may humble themselves before God and seek Him in His ordinances. And that then also such godly persons that are amongst them, and known each to other, may publicly at the end of their exercise make known their godly desire and practice the same; viz. solemnly to enter into |181| covenant with the Lord to walk in His ways.

And since they are so disposed of in their outward estates as to live in three distinct places, each having men of ability amongst them, there to observe the day and become three distinct bodies. Not then intending rashly to proceed to the choice of officers or the admitting of any other to their society than a few, to wit, such as are well known unto them; promising after to receive in such by confession of faith, as shall appear to be fitly qualified for that estate. They do earnestly entreat that the Church of Plymouth would set apart the same day for the same ends, beseeching the Lord as to withdraw His hand of correction from them, so as also to establish and direct them in His ways. And though the time be short, we pray you be provoked to this godly work, seeing the causes are so urgent; wherein God will be honoured and they and we undoubtedly have sweet comfort.

Be you all kindly saluted, etc.

Your brethren in Christ, etc.
EDWARD WINSLOW
SAMUEL FULLER [6]

Salem, July 26, 1630

SIR, etc. The sad news here is that many are sick and many are dead, the Lord in mercy look upon them. Some are here entered into

[6] Names of signers from Bradford's *Letter Book*.

church covenant.[7] The first were four, namely the Governor Mr. John Winthrop, Mr. Johnson, Mr. Dudley, and Mr. Wilson. Since that five more are joined unto them, and others it is like will add themselves to them daily. The Lord increase them, both in number and in holiness, for His mercy's sake. Here is a gentleman, one Mr. Coddington (a Boston man) who told me that Mr. Cotton's [8] charge at Hampton was that, they should take advice of them at Plymouth, and should do nothing to offend them. Here are divers honest Christians that are desirous to see us, some out of love which they bear to us, and the good persuasion they have of us; others to see whether we be so ill as they have heard of us. We have a name of holiness, and love to God and His saints; the Lord make us more and more answerable and that it may be more than a name, or else it will do us no good.

Be you lovingly saluted, and all the rest of our friends. The Lord Jesus bless us and the whole Israel of God.[9] Amen.

Your loving brother, etc.
Charlestown, August 2, 1630 SAMUEL FULLER

Thus out of small beginnings greater things have been produced by His hand that made all things of nothing, and gives being to all things that are; and, as one small candle may light a thousand, so the light here kindled hath shone unto many, yea in some sort to our whole nation; let the glorious name of Jehovah have all the praise.

[7] This was the First Church of Boston, although formed at Charlestown. The text of the covenant is in *Memorial History of Boston* I 114.

[8] The Rev. John Cotton of Boston, Lincs., who did not emigrate until 1631, delivered a sermon before the sailing of the Winthrop fleet from Southampton, published as *God's Promise to His Plantation.* Bradford's gratitude over this extension into the new Bay Colony of his own (and the Rev. John Robinson's) Congregational principles, prompted his oft-quoted conclusion to this chapter.

[9] Galatians vi.16.

CHAPTER XXII

Anno Dom: 1631 [*Allerton's Rash Enterprises*] |182|

Ashley being thus by the hand of God taken away, and Mr. Allerton discharged of his employment for them, their business began again to run in one channel and themselves better able to guide the same, Penobscot being wholly now at their disposing. And though Mr. William Peirce had a part there as is before noted, yet now, as things stood, he was glad to have his money repaid him and stand out. Mr. Winslow, whom they had sent over, sent them over some supply as soon as he could; and afterwards when he came, (which was somewhat long by reason of business) he brought a large supply of suitable goods with him, by which their trading was well carried on.[1] But by no means either he or the letters they writ, could take off Mr. Sherley and the rest from putting both the *Friendship* and *White Angel* on the general account; which caused continual contention between them, as will more appear.

I shall insert a letter of Mr. Winslow's about these things, being as followeth:

SIR: It fell out by God's providence that I received and brought your letters per Mr. Allerton from Bristol, to London, and do much fear what will be the event of things. Mr. Allerton intended to prepare the ship again, to set forth upon fishing. Mr. Sherley, Mr. Beauchamp, and Mr. Andrews, they renounce all particulars, protesting but for us they would never have adventured one penny into those parts; Mr. Hatherley stands inclinable to either. And whereas you write that he and Mr. Allerton have taken the *White Angel* upon them, for their partners here, they profess they neither gave any such order, nor will make it good. If themselves will clear the account and do it, all shall be well; what the event of these things will be, I know not. The Lord so direct and assist us, as He may not be dishonoured by our divisions.

I hear (per a friend) that I was much blamed for speaking what I heard in the spring of the year, concerning the buying and setting forth of the ship.[2] Sure, if I should not have told you what I heard so peremptorily reported (which report I offered now to prove at Bris-

[1] He arrived Boston in the *William and Francis* 5 June 1632.

[2] This was about the selling the ship in Spain (Bradford).

tol) I should have been unworthy my employment. And concerning the commission so long since given to Mr. Allerton, the truth is the thing we feared is come upon us, for Mr. Sherley and the rest have it, and will not deliver it, that being the ground of our agents' credit to procure such great sums. But I look for bitter words, hard thoughts and sour looks from sundry, as well for writing this as reporting the former. I would I had a more thankful employment, but I hope a good conscience shall make it comfortable, etc.

Thus far he. Dated November 16, 1631.

The commission abovesaid was given by them under their hand and seal, when Mr. Allerton was first employed by them; and re-demanded of him in the year '29 when they began to suspect his course. He told them it was amongst his papers, but he would seek it out and give it them before he went; but he being ready to go, it was demanded again. He said he could not find it, but it was amongst his papers, which he must take with him, |183| and he would send it by the boat from the eastward; but there it could not be had neither, but he would seek it up at sea. But whether Mr. Sherley had it before or after it is not certain; but having it, he would not let it go but keeps it to this day. Wherefore, even amongst friends, men had need be careful whom they trust, and not let things of this nature lie long unrecalled.[3]

|185| A few observations from the former letters, and then I shall set down the simple truth of the things thus in controversy between them, at least as far as by any good evidence it could be made to appear. And so labour to be brief in so tedious and intricate a business, which hung in expostulation between them many years before the same was ended. That though there will be often occasion to touch these things about other passages, yet I shall not need to be large therein, doing it here once for all.

1. It seems to appear clearly that Ashley's business and the buying of this ship, and the courses framed thereupon, were first contrived and proposed by Mr. Allerton. As also that the pleas and pretences which he made of the inability of the Plantation to repay their moneys, etc., and the hopes he gave them of doing it

[3] The letters from Sherley that follow are in Appendix VII.

with profit, was more believed and rested on by them (at least some of them) than anything the Plantation did or said.

2. It is like, though Mr. Allerton might think not to wrong the Plantation in the main, yet his own gain and private ends led him aside in these things. For it came to be known (and I have it in a letter under Mr. Sherley's hand) that in the first two or three years of his employment he had cleaned up £400 and put it into a brewhouse of Mr. Collier's in London, at first under Mr. Sherley's name, etc. besides what he might have otherwise. Again, Mr. Sherley and he had particular dealings in some things, for he bought up the beaver that seamen and other passengers brought over to Bristol, and at other places, and charged the bills to London, which Mr. Sherley paid. And they got sometimes £50 apiece in a bargain, as was made known by Mr. Hatherley and others, besides what might be otherwise. Which might make Mr. Sherley hearken unto him in many things, and yet I believe as he in his forementioned letter writ, he never would side in any particular trade which he conceived would wrong the Plantation and eat up and destroy the General.

3. It may be perceived that, seeing they had done so much for the Plantation both in former adventures and late disbursements, and also that Mr. Allerton was the first occasioner of bringing them upon these new designs (which at first seemed fair and profitable unto them) and unto which they agreed; but now seeing them to turn to loss and decline to greater entanglements, they thought it more meet for the Plantation to bear them than themselves, who had borne much in other things already. And so took advantage of such commission and power as Mr. Allerton had formerly had as their agent, to devolve these things upon them.

4. With pity and compassion touching Mr. Allerton, I may say with the Apostle to Timothy (1 Timothy vi.9) "They that will be rich fall into many temptations and snares," etc., "and pierce themselves through with many sorrows," etc.; "for the love of money is the root of all evil," verse 10. God give him to see the evil in his failings, that he may find mercy by repentance, for the wrongs he hath done to any and this poor Plantation in special. They that do such things do not only bring themselves into snares and sorrows, but many with them, though in another

kind, as lamentable experience shows, and is too manifest in this business. |186|

[*The* Friendship *and* White Angel]

Now about these ships and their setting forth, the truth, as far as could be learned is this. The motion about setting forth the fishing ship called the *Friendship* came first from the Plantation, and the reasons of it (as is before remembered); but wholly left to themselves [4] to do or not to do, as they saw cause. But when it fell into consideration, and the design was held to be profitable and hopeful, it was propounded by some of them, why might not they do it of themselves, seeing they must disburse all the money; and what need they have any reference to the Plantation in it? They might take the profit themselves, towards other losses, and need not let the Plantation share therein. And if their ends were otherwise answered, for their supplies to come to them in time, it would be well enough. So they hired her and set her out and freighted her as full as she could carry with passengers' goods that belonged to the Massachusetts, which rose to a good sum of money; intending to send the Plantation's supply in the other ship. The effect of this Mr. Hatherley not only declared afterward upon occasion, but affirmed upon oath taken before the Governor and Deputy Governor of the Massachusetts, Mr. Winthrop and Mr. Dudley: That this ship *Friendship* was not set out nor intended for the joint partnership of the Plantation, but for the particular account of Mr. James Sherley, Mr. Beauchamp, Mr. Andrews, Mr. Allerton and himself. This deposition was taken at Boston the 29th of August 1639, as is to be seen under their hands; besides some other concurrent testimonies declared at several times to sundry of them.

About the *White Angel*, though she was first bought, or at least the price beaten [down] by Mr. Allerton at Bristol, yet that had been nothing if Mr. Sherley had not liked it and disbursed the money. And that she was not intended for the Plantation appears by sundry evidences, as first, the bills of sale or charterparties were taken in their own names, without any mention or

[4] I.e., the English partners.

reference to the Plantation at all; viz. Mr. Sherley, Mr. Beauchamp, Mr. Andrews, Mr. Denison, and Mr. Allerton, for Mr. Hatherley fell off and would not join with them in this. That she was not bought for their account, Mr. Hatherley took his oath before the parties aforesaid, the day and year above written.[5]

Mr. Allerton took his oath to like effect concerning this ship, the *White Angel*, before the Governor and Deputy the 7th of September 1639, and likewise deposed the same time that Mr. Hatherley and himself did, in the behalf of themselves and the said Mr. Sherley, Mr. Andrews, and Mr. Beauchamp, agree and undertake to discharge and save harmless all the rest of the partners and purchasers of and from the said losses of *Friendship* for £200, which was to be discounted thereupon. As by their depositions (which are in writing) may appear more at large, and some other depositions and other testimonies by Mr. Winslow, etc.[6]

But I suppose these may be sufficient to evince the truth in these things against all pretences to the contrary. And yet the burthen lay still upon the Plantation; or to speak more truly and rightly, upon those few that were engaged for all, for they were fain to wade through these things without any help from any. |187|

Concerning Mr. Allerton's accounts. They were so large and intricate as they could not well understand them, much less examine and correct them without a great deal of time and help and

5 About the *White Angel* they all met at a certain tavern in London, where they had a dinner prepared, and had conference with a factor about selling of her in Spain, or at Port a Porte, as hath been before mentioned, as Mr. Hatherley manifested and Mr. Allerton could not deny. (Bradford's note, on fol. 185 v.)

6 Mr. Winslow deposed the same time before the Governor aforesaid, etc. that when he came into England, and the partners inquired of the success of the *White Angel* which should have been laden with bass and so sent for Port of Portingall, and their ship and goods to be sold; having informed them that they were like to fail in their lading of bass, that then Mr. James Sherley used these terms: "Feck, we must make one account of all," and thereupon pressed him, as agent for the partners in New England, to accept the said ship *White Angel* and her account into the joint partnership, which he refused for many reasons; and after received instructions from New England to refuse her if she should be offered, which instructions he showed them. And whereas he was often pressed to accept her, he ever refused her, etc. (Second note by Bradford on fol. 185 v.)

his own presence, which was now hard to get amongst them. And it was two or three years before they could bring them to any good pass, but never make them perfect. I know not how it came to pass, or what mystery was in it, for he took upon him to make up all accounts till this time, though Mr. Sherley was their agent to buy and sell their goods, and did more than he therein. Yet he passed in accounts in a manner for all disbursements, both concerning goods bought which he never saw, but were done when he was here in the country or at sea, and all the expenses of the Leyden people done by others in his absence, the charges about the Patent, etc. In all which he made them debtor to him above £300, and demanded payment of it. But when things came to scanning, he was found above £2000 debtor to them—this wherein Mr. Hatherley and he being jointly engaged (which he only had), being included. Besides I know not how much that could never be cleared; and interest moneys which ate them up, which he never accounted. Also they were fain to allow such large bills of charges as were intolerable; the charges of the Patent came to above £500, and yet nothing done in it but what was done at first without any confirmation; £30 given at a clap, and £50 spent in a journey. No marvel, therefore, if Mr. Sherley said in his letter, if their business had been better managed they might have been the richest plantation of any English at that time.

Yea, he screwed up his poor old father-in-law's [7] account to above £200 and brought it on the general account, and to befriend him made most of it to arise out of those goods taken up by him at Bristol, at £50 per cent, because he knew they would never let it lie on the old man; when, alas! he, poor man, never dreamt of any such thing, nor that what he had could arise near that value, but thought that many of them had been freely bestowed on him and his children by Mr. Allerton. Neither in truth did they come near that value in worth, but that sum was blown up by interest and high prices, which the company did for the most part bear (he deserving far more), being most sorry that he should have a name to have much, when he had in effect little.

This year also Mr. Sherley sent over an account which was in

[7] William Brewster, whose daughter Fear married Allerton in 1626.

a manner but a cash account, what Mr. Allerton had had of them, and disbursed, for which he referred to his accounts. Besides an account of beaver sold, which Mr. Winslow and some others had carried over, and a large supply of goods which Mr. Winslow had sent and brought over. All which was comprised in that account, and all the disbursements about the *Friendship* and *White Angel*, and what concerned their accounts from first to last, or anything else he could charge the partners with. So they were made debtor in the foot of that account £4,770 19*s* 2*d*, besides £1000 still due for the purchase yet unpaid. Notwithstanding all the beaver and returns that both Ashley and they had made, which were not small.[8] |188|

In these accounts of Mr. Sherley's some things were obscure and some things twice charged, as a hundred of Barnstaple rugs which came in the *Friendship*, and cost £75, charged before by Mr. Allerton, and now by him again, with other particulars of like nature doubtful, to be twice or thrice charged. As also a sum of £600 which Mr. Allerton denied and they could never understand for what it was. They sent a note of these and such-like things afterward to Mr. Sherley by Mr. Winslow, but I know not how it came to pass could never have them explained.

Into these deep sums had Mr. Allerton run them in two years. For in the latter end of the year 1628 all their debts did not amount to much above £400, as was then noted, and now come to so many thousands. And whereas in the year 1629 Mr. Sherley and Mr. Hatherley being at Bristol, and writ a large letter from thence in which they had given an account of the debts and what sums were then disbursed, Mr. Allerton never left begging and entreating of them till they had put it out. So they blotted out two lines in that letter in which the sums were contained, and writ upon it so as not a word could be perceived, as since by them

[8] So as a while before, whereas their great care was how to pay the purchase and those other few debts which were upon them, now it was with them as it was some times with Saul's father, who left caring for the asses and sorrowed for his son. 1 Samuel x.2. So that which before they looked at as a heavy burden, they now esteem but a small thing and a light matter, in comparison of what was now upon them. And thus the Lord oftentimes deals with His people to teach them and humble them, that He may do them good in the latter end. (Bradford's note, on fol. 186 v.)

was confessed, and by the letters may be seen. And thus were they kept hoodwinked till now they were so deeply engaged. And whereas Mr. Sherley did so earnestly press that Mr. Allerton might be sent over to finish the great business about the Patent, as may be seen in his letter writ 1629, as is before recorded, and that they should be earnest with his wife to suffer him to go, etc., he hath since confessed by a letter under my hands, that it was Mr. Allerton's own doings and not his, and he made him write his words and not his own. The Patent was but a pretence and not the thing. Thus were they abused in their simplicity, and no better than bought and sold, as it may seem.

And to mend the matter, Mr. Allerton doth in a sort wholly now desert them; having brought them into the briars, he leaves them to get out as they can. But God crossed him mightily, for he having hired the ship of Mr. Sherley at £30 a month, he set forth again with a most wicked and drunken crew, and for covetousness' sake did so overlade her, not only filling her hold but so stuffed her between decks as she was walte,[9] and could not bear sail. And they had like to have been cast away at sea, and were forced to put for Milford Haven and new stow her, and put some of their ordnance and more heavy goods in the bottom. Which lost them time and made them come late into the country, lose their season, and made a worse voyage than the year before.

But being come into the country, he sells trading commodities to any that will buy, to the great prejudice of the Plantation here. But that which is worse, what he could not sell he trusts, and sets up a company of base fellows and makes them traders, to run into every hole and into the river of Kennebec to glean away the trade from the house there, about the Patent and privilege whereof he had dashed away so much money of theirs here. |189| And now what in him lay went about to take away the benefit thereof, and to overthrow them. Yea, not only this, but he furnishes a company and joins with some consorts, being now deprived of Ashley at Penobscot, and sets up a trading house beyond Penobscot,[1] to cut off the trade from thence also.

[9] "We say a ship is walt when she is not stiffe"—Capt. John Smith *A Sea Grammar* (1627) p. 54.

[1] At Machias, Maine.

[*Frenchmen Rifle the Trading Posts at Machias and Castine*]

But the French, perceiving that that would be greatly to their damage also, they came in their beginning before they were well settled and displanted them, slew two of their men and took all their goods to a good value; [2] the loss being most if not all Mr. Allerton's. For, though some of them should have been his partners, yet he trusted them for their parts. The rest of the men were sent into France, and this was the end of that project.

The rest of those he trusted, being loose and drunken fellows, did for the most part but cozen and cheat him of all they got into their hands. [So] that howsoever he did his friends some hurt hereby for the present, yet he gat little good, but went by the loss by God's just hand.

After in time, when he came to Plymouth, the church called him to account for these and other his gross miscarriages. He confessed his fault and promised better walking, and that he would wind himself out of these courses so soon as he could, etc.

This year also Mr. Sherley would needs send them over a new accountant. He had made mention of such a thing the year before, but they writ him word that their charge was great already and they need not increase it, as this would; but if they were well dealt with and had their goods well sent over, they could keep their accounts here themselves. Yet he now sent one, which they did not refuse, being a younger brother of Mr. Winslow's whom they had been at charge to instruct at London before he came. He came over in the *White Angel* with Mr. Allerton, and there began his first employment; for though Mr. Sherley had so far befriended Mr. Allerton as to cause Mr. Winslow to ship the supply sent to the partners here in his ship, and give him £4 per tun, whereas others carried for £3, and he made them pay their freight ready down before the ship went out of the harbor, whereas others paid upon certificate of the goods being delivered, and their freight came to upward of six score pounds; yet

[2] This occurred in 1633; the French were sent by Claude de la Tour, one of the rival French proprietors of L'Acadie, of whom there is an entertaining account in Francis Parkman *The Old Régime in Canada.*

they had much ado to have their goods delivered, for some of them were changed, as bread and pease; they were forced to take worse for better, neither could they ever get all. And if Josias Winslow had not been there it had been worse, for he had the invoice and order to send them to the trading houses[3] |187 v.|

This year their house at Penobscot was robbed by the French, and all their goods of any worth they carried away to the value of £400 or £500 worth as they cost first penny; in beaver 300 pounds' weight, and the rest in trading goods, as coats, rugs, blanket, biscuit, etc. It was in this manner. The master of the house and part of the company with him were come with their vessel to the westward to fetch a supply of goods which was brought over for them. In the meantime comes a small French ship into the harbor, and amongst the company was a false Scot. They pretended they were newly come from the sea and knew not where they were, and that their vessel was very leaky, and desired they might haul her ashore and stop their leaks. And many French compliments they used, and congees they made; and in the end, seeing but three or four simple men that were servants, and by this Scotchman understanding that the master and the rest of the company were gone from home, they fell of commending their guns and muskets that lay upon racks by the wall side, and took them down to look on them, asking if they were charged. And when they were possessed of them, one presents a piece ready charged against the servants, and another a pistol, and bid them not stir but quietly deliver them their goods, and carries some of the men aboard and made the other help to carry away the goods. And when they had took what they pleased, they set them at liberty and went their way with this mock, bidding them tell their master when he came that some of the Ile of Rey gentlemen had been there.[4]

[3] The rest of this chapter is written on the verso of fols. 187 and 188, indicating that Bradford inserted it later.

[4] The allusion is to the Duke of Buckingham's abortive expedition to the Ile de Rhé, 1627.

[*Sir Christopher Gardiner, Knight*]

This year, one Sir Christopher Gardiner, being as himself said, descended of that house that the Bishop of Winchester came of, who was so great a persecutor of God's saints in Queen Mary's days; and, being a great traveler, received his first honour of knighthood at Jerusalem, being made Knight of the Sepulchre there.[5] He came into these parts under pretence of forsaking the world and to live a private life in a godly course, not unwilling to put himself upon any mean employments and take any pains for his living; and some time offered himself to join the churches in sundry places. He brought over with him a servant or two and a comely young woman whom he called his cousin; but it was suspected she, after the Italian manner, was his concubine. Living at the Massachusetts, for some miscarriages which he should have answered he fled away from authority and got among the Indians of these parts. They sent after him but could not get him, and promised some reward to those that should find him.

The Indians came to the Governor here and told where he was, and asked if they might kill him. He told them no, by no means, but if they could take him and bring him hither, they should be paid for their pains. They said he had a gun and a rapier and he would kill them if they went about it; and the Massachusetts Indians said they might kill him. But the Governor told them no, they should not kill him, but watch their opportunity and take him. And so they did, for when they light of him by a river side, he got into a canoe to get from them, and when they came near him, whilst he presented his piece at them to keep them off, the stream carried the canoe against a rock and tumbled both him and his piece and rapier into the water. Yet he got out, and having a little dagger by his side they durst not close with him but getting long poles they soon beat his dagger out of his hand, so he was glad to yield, and they brought him to the Governor. But his hands and arms were swollen and very sore with

[5] All that is known of this character is told by C. F. Adams in *Three Episodes of Massachusetts History*. His knighthood was in an obscure Papal order, the *Milizia Aureata* or Golden Melice. He was probably an agent of Sir Ferdinando Gorges.

the blows they had given him. So he used him kindly and sent him to a lodging where his arms were bathed and anointed, and he was quickly well again and blamed the Indians for beating him so much. They said that they did but a little whip him with sticks. In his lodging house those that made his bed found a little notebook that by accident had slipped out of his pocket or some private place, in which was a memorial what day he was reconciled to the Pope and Church of Rome, and in what university he took his scapula, and such and such degrees. It being brought to the Governor he kept it, and sent the Governor of the Massachusetts word of his taking; who sent for him. So the Governor sent him and these notes to the Governor there who took it very thankfully. But after he got for England, he showed his malice but God prevented him.

See the Governor's letter on the other side. |189 v.|

Sir: It hath pleased God to bring Sir Christopher Gardiner safe to us, with those that came with him. And howsoever I never intended any hard measure to him, but to respect and use him according to his quality, yet I let him know your care of him, and that he shall speed the better for your mediation. It was a special providence of God to bring those notes of his to our hands. I desire that you will please to speak to all that are privy to them, not to discover them to anyone, for that may frustrate the means of any further use to be made of them. The good Lord our God who hath always ordered things for the good of His poor churches here, direct us in this aright, and dispose it to a good issue. I am sorry we put you to so much trouble about this gentleman, especially at this time of great employment, but I knew not how to avoid it. I must again entreat you to let me know what charge and trouble any of your people have been at about him, that it may be recompensed.

So with the true affection of a friend, desiring all happiness to yourself and yours, and to all my worthy friends with you (whom I love in the Lord) I commend you to His grace and good providence, and rest

Your most assured friend,

Boston, May 5, 1631. John Winthrop

By occasion hereof I will take a little liberty to declare what fell out by this man's means and malice, complying with others.

And though I doubt not but it will be more fully done by my honoured friends whom it did more directly concern, and have more particular knowledge of the matter, yet I will here give a hint of the same, and God's providence in preventing the hurt that might have come by the same.

The intelligence I had by a letter from my much honoured and beloved friend, Mr. John Winthrop, Governor of the Massachusetts.[6]

Sir: Upon a petition exhibited by Sir Christopher Gardiner, Sir Ferdinando Gorges, Captain Mason, etc., against you and us, the cause was heard before the Lords of the Privy Council and after reported to the King, the success whereof makes it evident to all that the Lord hath care of His people here. The passages are admirable, and too long to write. I heartily wish an opportunity to impart them to you, being many sheets of paper. But conclusion was, against all men's expectation, an order for our encouragement, and much blame and disgrace upon the adversaries, which calls for much thankfulness from us all. Which we purpose (the Lord willing) to express in a day of thanksgiving to our merciful God (I doubt not but you will consider, if it be not fit for you to join in it) who, as He hath humbled us by His late correction, so He hath lifted us up by an abundant rejoicing, in our deliverance out of so desperate a danger; so as that which our enemies built their hopes upon to ruin us by, He hath |190 v.| mercifully disposed to our great advantage. As I shall further acquaint you, when occasion shall serve.

The copy of the order follows.[7]

[6] Ford shows in 1912 ed. Bradford II 141, that the date of this letter was May 1633. Ample details from other sources in Ford's notes indicate that Bradford's and Winthrop's accounts of the machinations of "Sir" Christopher were correct. His "cousin" did not return to England but married and settled down in Maine.

[7] See Appendix XII, Official Documents, No. 1.

CHAPTER XXIII

Anno Dom: 1632 [*More Allerton Doings*] |189|

Mr. Allerton, returning for England, little regarded his bond of a £1000 to perform covenants. For whereas he was bound by the same to bring the ship to |190| London and to pay £30 per month for her hire, he did neither of both, for he carried her to Bristol again, from whence he intended to set her out again, and so did the third time into these parts, as after will appear. And though she had been ten months upon the former voyage, at £30 per month, yet he never paid penny for hire. It should seem he knew well enough how to deal with Mr. Sherley. And Mr. Sherley, though he would needs tie her and her account upon the General, yet he would dispose of her as himself pleased; for though Mr. Winslow had in their names protested against the receiving her on that account, or if ever they should hope to prevail in such a thing, yet never to suffer Mr. Allerton to have any more to do in her, yet he the last year let her wholly unto him, and enjoined them to send all their supply in her to their prejudice, as is before noted.

And now, though he broke his bonds, kept no covenant, paid no hire, nor was ever like to keep covenants, yet now he goes and sells him all, both ship and all her accounts from first to last—and in effect he might as well have given him the same. And not only this, but he doth as good as provide a sanctuary for him, for he gives him one year's time to prepare his account and then to give up the same to them here; and then another year for him to make payment of what should be due upon that account. And in the meantime writes earnestly to them not to interrupt or hinder him from his business, or stay him about clearing accounts, etc. So as he in the meantime gathers up all moneys due for freight and any other debts belonging either to her or the *Friendship's* accounts, as his own particular; and after, sells ship and ordnance, fish and what he had raised, in Spain according to the first design in effect; and who had or what became of the money, he best knows.

In the meantime their hands were bound, and could do nothing but look on, till he had made all away into other men's hands, save a few cattle and a little land and some small matters he had here at Plymouth. And so in the end removed as he had already his person so all his from hence. This will better appear by Mr. Sherley's letter.

Sir: These few lines are further to give you to understand, that seeing you and we, that never differed yet but about the *White Angel*, which somewhat troubleth us as I perceive it doth you. And now Mr. Allerton being here, we have had some conference with him about her, and find him very willing to give you and us all content that possibly he can, though he burthen himself. He is content to take the *White Angel* wholly on himself, notwithstanding he met with pirates near the coast of Ireland, which took away his best sails and other provisions from her, so as verily if we should now sell her, she would yield but a small price besides her ordnance. And to set her forth again with fresh money we would not, she being now at Bristol. Wherefore we thought it best, both for you and us, Mr. Allerton being willing to take her, to accept of his bond of two thousand pounds to give |191| you a true and perfect account, and take the whole charge of the *White Angel* wholly to himself from the first to the last. The account he is to make and perfect within twelve months from the date of this letter; and then to pay you at six and six months after whatsoever shall be due unto you and us, upon the foot of that account. And verily, notwithstanding all the disasters he hath had, I am persuaded he hath enough to pay all men here and there. Only they must have patience till he can gather in what is due to him there. I do not write this slightly, but upon some ground of what I have seen, and perhaps you know not of, under the hands and seals of some, etc. I rest

Your assured friend,

December 6, 1632. James Sherley

But here's not a word of the breach of former bonds and covenants, or payment of the ship's hire. This is passed by as if no such thing had been. Besides, what bonds or obligements soever they had of him, there never came any to the hands or sight of the partners here. And for this that Mr. Sherley seems to intimate (as a secret) of his ability under the hands and seals of some, it was but a trick. Having gathered up an account of what was owing from such base fellows as he had made traders for him, and other debts, and then got Mr. Mayhew and some others to affirm under their hand and seal that they had seen such accounts that were due to him.

Mr. Hatherley came over again this year,[1] but upon his own occasions, and began to make preparation to plant and dwell in the country. He with his former dealings had wound in what money he had in the partnership into his own hands, and so gave off all partnership (except in name) as was found in the issue of things; neither did he meddle or take any care about the same. Only he was troubled about his engagement about the *Friendship*, as will after appear. And now partly about that account in some reckonings between Mr. Allerton and him, and some debts that Mr. Allerton otherwise owed him upon dealing between them in particular, he drew up an account of above £2000 and would fain have engaged the partners here with it, because Mr. Allerton had been their agent. But they told him they had been fooled long enough with such things, and showed him that it no way belonged to them, but told him he must look to make good his engagement for the *Friendship*, which caused some trouble between Mr. Allerton and him.

Mr. William Peirce did the like, Mr. Allerton being wound into his debt also upon particular dealings, as if they had been bound to make good all men's debts; but they easily shook off these things. But Mr. Allerton hereby ran into much trouble and vexation, as well as he had troubled others, for Mr. Denison sued him for the money he had disbursed for the sixth part of the *White Angel*, and recovered the same with damages.

Though the partners were thus plunged into great engagements and oppressed with unjust debts, yet the Lord prospered their trading, that they made yearly large returns and had soon wound themselves out of all if yet they had otherwise been well dealt withal as will more appear hereafter. |192|

[*Prosperity Brings Dispersal of Population*]

Also the people of the Plantation began to grow in their outward estates, by reason of the flowing of many people into the

[1] Arriving Boston June 5, 1632 (Prince). Hatherley became a leading citizen of Scituate.

country, especially into the Bay of the Massachusetts. By which means corn and cattle rose to a great price, by which many were much enriched and commodities grew plentiful. And yet in other regards this benefit turned to their hurt, and this accession of strength to their weakness. For now as their stocks increased and the increase vendible, there was no longer any holding them together, but now they must of necessity go to their great lots. They could not otherwise keep their cattle, and having oxen grown they must have land for plowing and tillage. And no man now thought he could live except he had cattle and a great deal of ground to keep them, all striving to increase their stocks. By which means they were scattered all over the Bay quickly and the town in which they lived compactly till now was left very thin and in a short time almost desolate.

And if this had been all, it had been less, though too much; but the church must also be divided, and those that had lived so long together in Christian and comfortable fellowship must now part and suffer many divisions. First, those that lived on their lots on the other side of the Bay, called Duxbury, they could not long bring their wives and children to the public worship and church meetings here, but with such burthen as, growing to some competent number, they sued to be dismissed and become a body of themselves. And so they were dismissed about this time, though very unwillingly.[2] But to touch this sad matter, and handle things together that fell out afterward; to prevent any further scattering from this place and weakening of the same, it was thought best to give out some good farms to special persons that would promise to live at Plymouth, and likely to be helpful to the church or commonwealth, and so tie the lands to Plymouth as farms for the same; and there they might keep their cattle and tillage by some servants and retain their dwellings here. And so some special lands were granted at a place general called Green's Harbor,[3] where no allotments had been in the former division, a place very

[2] John Alden, Myles Standish, Jonathan Brewster and Thomas Prence were the first prominent settlers of Duxbury. Bradford's efforts to stop what would now be called "progress" are amusing and pathetic. The great Puritan emigration to the Bay created such a market for corn and cattle that the compact settlement at Plymouth no longer sufficed for the increased production.

[3] The present Marshfield.

well meadowed and fit to keep and rear cattle good store. But alas, this remedy proved worse than the disease; for within a few years those that had thus got footing there rent themselves away, partly by force and partly wearing the rest with importunity and pleas of necessity, so as they must either suffer them to go or live in continual opposition and contention. And other still, as they conceived themselves straitened or to want accommodation, broke away under one pretence or other, thinking their own conceived necessity and the example of others a warrant sufficient for them. And this I fear will be the ruin of New England, at least of the churches of God there, and will provoke the Lord's displeasure against them. |193|

[*The Wreck of the* Lyon]

This year Mr. William Peirce came into the country and brought goods and passengers in a ship called the *Lyon,* which belonged chiefly to Mr. Sherley and the rest of the London partners, but these here had nothing to do with her.[4] In this ship, besides beaver which they had sent home before, they sent upward of 800 pounds in her and some otter skins. And also the copies of Mr. Allerton's accounts, desiring that they would also peruse and examine them and rectify such things as they should find amiss in them. And the rather because they were better acquainted with the goods bought there and the disbursements made, than they could be here; yea a great part were done by themselves, though Mr. Allerton brought in the account and sundry things seemed to them obscure and had need of clearing. Also they sent a book of exceptions against his accounts in such things as they could manifest, and doubted not but they might add more thereunto. And also showed them how much Mr. Allerton was debtor to the account, and desired seeing they had now put the ship *White Angel* and all wholly into his power and tied their hands here, that they could not call him to account for anything till the time was expired which they had given him. And by that time other men would get their debts of him, as some had done already by

[4] She arrived Boston 16 Sept. 1632 with 123 passengers, 50 of them children, after an ocean passage of eight weeks. Winthrop's *Journal.*

suing him, and he would make all away here quickly out of their reach. And therefore prayed them to look to things and get payment of him there, as it was all the reason they should, seeing they kept all the bonds and covenants they made with him in their own hands; and here they could do nothing by the course they had taken, nor had anything to show if they should go about it. But it pleased God this ship, being first to go to Virginia before she went home, was cast away on that coast, not far from Virginia, and their beaver was all lost, which was the first loss they sustained in that kind. But Mr. Peirce and the men saved their lives and also their letters, and got into Virginia and so safely home, and the accounts were now sent from hence again to them. And thus much of the passages of this year.[5]

[5] Mr. Peirce's Letter appears as a note on fol. 192 v. as follows: "A Part of Mr. Peirce his Letter from Virginia. It was dated in December 25, 1632 and came to their hand the 7th of April before they heard anything from England." DEAR FRIENDS, etc. The bruit of this fatal stroke that the Lord hath brought both on me and you all, will come to your ears before this cometh to your hands, it is like, and therefore I shall not need to enlarge in particulars, etc. My whole estate for the most part is taken away, and so yours in a great measure by this and your former losses. It is time to look about us, before the wrath of the Lord break forth to utter destruction. The good Lord give us all grace to search our hearts and try our ways and turn unto the Lord and humble ourselves under His mighty hand, and seek atonement, etc.

Dear friends, you may know that all your beaver and the books of your accounts are swallowed up in the sea. Your letters remain with me and shall be delivered if God bring me home. But what should I more say; have we lost our outward estates? Yet a happy loss if our souls may gain. There is yet more in the Lord Jehovah than ever we had yet in the world. Oh that our foolish hearts could yet be weaned from the things here below, which are vanity and vexation of spirit; and yet we fools catch after shadows that fly away and are gone in a moment, etc.

Thus with my continual remembrance of you in my poor desires to the throne of grace, beseeching God to renew His love and favour towards you all, in and through the Lord Jesus Christ, both in spiritual and temporal good things as may be most to the glory and praise of His name and your everlasting good. So I rest,

Your afflicted brother in Christ,

Virginia, December 25, 1632. WILLIAM PEIRCE

CHAPTER XXIV

Anno Dom: 1633 [*More on Allerton*] |193|

This year Mr. Edward Winslow was chosen Governor.

By the first return this year they had letters from Mr. Sherley of Mr. Allerton's further ill success and the loss by Mr. Peirce, with many sad complaints; but little hope of anything to be got of Mr. Allerton, or how their accounts might be either eased or any way rectified by them there. But now saw plainly that the burthen of all would be cast on their backs. The special passages of his letters I shall here insert as shall be pertinent to these things; for though I am weary of this tedious and uncomfortable subject, yet for the clearing of the truth I am compelled to be more large in the opening of these matters, upon which |194| so much trouble hath ensued, and so many hard censures have passed on both sides. I would not be partial to either, but deliver the truth in all, and as near as I can in their own words and passages. And so leave it to the impartial judgment of any that shall come to read or view these things. His letters are as follows, dated June 24, 1633.[1]

By this it appears when Mr. Sherley sold him the ship and all her accounts, it was more for Mr. Allerton's advantage than theirs; and if they could get any there, well and good, for they were like to have nothing here. And what course was held to hinder them there hath already been manifested. And though Mr. Sherley became more sensible of his own condition by these losses, and thereby more sadly and plainly to complain of Mr. Allerton, yet no course was taken to help them here, but all left unto themselves; not so much as to examine and rectify the accounts by which (it is like) some hundreds of pounds might have been taken off. But very probable it is the more they saw was taken off, the less might come unto themselves. But I leave these matters and come to other things.

[1] Printed in Appendix VII.

[*Mr. Roger Williams*]

Mr. Roger Williams,[2] a man godly and zealous, having many precious parts but very unsettled in judgment, came over first to the Massachusetts; but upon some discontent left that place and came hither, where he was friendly entertained according to their poor ability, and exercised his gifts amongst them and after some time was admitted a member of the church. And his teaching well approved, for the benefit whereof I still bless God and am thankful to him even for his sharpest admonitions and reproofs so far as they agreed with truth. He this year began to fall into some strange opinions, and from opinion to practice, which caused some controversy between the church and him. And in the end some discontent on his part, by occasion whereof he left them something abruptly. Yet afterwards sued for his dismission to the church of Salem, which was granted, with some caution to them concerning him and what care they ought to have of him. But he soon fell into more things there, both to their and the government's trouble and |196| disturbance. I shall not need to name particulars; they are too well known now to all, though for a time the church here went under some hard censure by his occasion from some that afterwards smarted themselves. But he is to be pitied and prayed for; and so I shall leave the matter and desire the Lord to show him his errors and reduce him into the way of truth and give him a settled judgment and constancy in the same, for I hope he belongs to the Lord, and that He will show him mercy.

[*The Trading Post on the Connecticut*]

Having had formerly converse and familiarity with the Dutch (as is before remembered) they seeing them seated here in a barren quarter, told them of a river called by them the Fresh River, but now is known by the name of Connecticut River, which they often commended unto them for a fine place both for plantation and trade, and wished them to make use of it. But their hands be-

[2] The famous founder of Rhode Island. He arrived at Boston with his family in the *Lyon* in Feb. 1631. He had already preached at Salem and got into trouble with the Bay authorities before coming to Plymouth.

ing full otherwise, they let it pass. But afterwards there coming a company of banished Indians into these parts, that were driven out from thence by the potency of the Pequots, which usurped upon them and drove them from thence; they often solicited them to go thither and they should have much trade, especially if they would keep a house there.[3] And having now good store of commodities, and also need to look out where they could advantage themselves to help them out of their great engagements, they now began to send that way to discover the same and trade with the natives. They found it to be a fine place but had no great store of trade. But the Indians excused the same in regard of the season, and fear the Indians were in of their enemies. So they tried divers times, not without profit, but saw the most certainty would be by keeping a house there to receive the trade when it came down out of the inland.

These Indians, not seeing them[4] very forward to build there, solicited them of the Massachusetts in like sort (for their end was to be restored to their country again); but they in the Bay being but lately come, were not fit for the same. But some of their chief made a motion to join with the partners here, to trade jointly with them in that river. The which they willing to embrace, and so they should have built and put in equal stock together. A time of meeting was appointed at the Massachusetts, and some of the chief here were appointed to treat with them and went accordingly. But they cast many fears of danger and loss and the like, which was perceived to be the main obstacles, though they alleged they were not provided of trading goods. But those here offered at present to put in sufficient for both, provided they would become engaged for the half and prepare against the next year. They confessed more could not be offered, but thanked them and told them they had no mind to it. They then answered, they hoped it would be no offense unto |197| them, if themselves went on without them, if they saw it meet. They said there was no reason they should; and thus this treaty broke off, and those

[3] I.e., the Indians solicited the Dutch. The "banished Indians" were the Mohegan or Mohican, who had been driven from the Hudson River by the Mohawk tribe of the Iroquois Confederacy.

[4] I.e., the Dutch.

here took convenient time to make a beginning there, and were the first English that both discovered that place and built in the same. Though they were little better than thrust out of it afterward, as may appear.

But the Dutch began now to repent, and hearing of their purpose and preparation endeavoured to prevent them, and got in a little before them and made a slight fort [5] and planted two pieces of ordnance, threatening to stop their passage. But they having made a small frame of a house ready and having a great new bark, they stowed their frame in her hold and boards to cover and finish it, having nails and all other provisions fitting for their use. This they did the rather that they might have a present defense against the Indians, who were much offended that they brought home and restored the right sachem of the place, called Natawanute; so as they were to encounter with a double danger in this attempt, both the Dutch and the Indians.

When they came up the river, the Dutch demanded what they intended and whither they would go. They answered, up the river to trade, now their order was to go and seat above them. They bid them strike and stay, or else they would shoot them, and stood by their ordnance ready fitted. They answered they had commission from the Governor of Plymouth to go up the river to such a place, and if they did shoot, they must obey their order and proceed; they would not molest them, but would go on. So they passed along, and though the Dutch threatened them hard, yet they shot not. Coming to their place, they clapped up their house quickly and landed their provisions and left the company appointed, and sent the bark home, and afterwards palisadoed their house about and fortified themselves better.

The Dutch sent word home to the Manhattan what was done, and in process of time they sent a band of about seventy men in warlike manner, with colours displayed, to assault them, but seeing them strengthened and that it would cost blood, they came to parley and returned in peace.[6] And this was their entrance

[5] Fort Good Hope, near the site of Hartford. The Pilgrims' trading post was on the site of Windsor; the Indians called the place Matianuck.

[6] A hilarious if fictitious account of this episode is in Washington Irving *Knickerbocker's History of New York*.

there, who deserved to have held it, and not by friends to have been thrust out as in a sort they were as will after appear. They did the Dutch no wrong, for they took not a foot of any land they bought, but went to the place above them and bought that tract of land which belonged to these Indians which they carried with them, and their friends, with whom the Dutch had nothing to do. But of these matters more in another place.

[*Pestilence and Locusts*]

It pleased the Lord to visit them this year with an infectious fever of which many fell very sick and upward of 20 persons died, men and women, besides children, and sundry of them of their ancient friends which had lived in Holland, as Thomas Blossom, Richard Masterson, with sundry |198| others; and in the end, after he had much helped others, Samuel Fuller who was their surgeon and physician and had been a great help and comfort unto them. As in his faculty, so otherwise being a deacon of the church, a man godly and forward to do good, being much missed after his death. And he and the rest of their brethren much lamented by them and caused much sadness and mourning amongst them, which caused them to humble themselves and seek the Lord; and towards winter it pleased the Lord the sickness ceased.

This disease also swept away many of the Indians from all the places near adjoining. And the spring before, especially all the month of May, there was such a quantity of a great sort of flies like for bigness to wasps or bumblebees, which came out of holes in the ground and replenished all the woods, and ate the green things, and made such a constant yelling noise as made all the woods ring of them, and ready to deaf the hearers.[7] They have not by the English been heard or seen before, or since. But the Indians told them that sickness would follow, and so it did in June, July, August and the chief heat of summer.

It pleased the Lord to enable them this year to send home a great quantity of beaver besides paying all their charges and

[7] The seventeen-year locust, *Cicada septendecim*. They of course had nothing to do with the disease, which was the smallpox.

debts at home, which good return did much encourage their friends in England. They sent in beaver 3,366 pounds weight, and much of it coat beaver which yielded 20*s* per pound and some of it above, and of otter skins 346 sold also at a good price.

And thus much of the affairs of this year.

[8] The skin was sold at 14*s* and 15*s* the pound (Bradford).

CHAPTER XXV

Anno Dom: 1634 |198|

This year Mr. Thomas Prence was chosen Governor.

Mr. Sherley's letters were very brief in answer of theirs this year. I will forbear to copy any part thereof, only name a head or two therein. First, he desires they will take nothing ill in what he formerly writ, professing his good affection towards them as before, etc. Secondly, for Mr. Allerton's accounts he is persuaded they must suffer and that in no small sums; and that they have cause enough to complain, but it was now too late. And that he had failed them there, those here and himself, in his own aims. And that now having thus left them here, he feared God had or would leave him, and it would not be strange but a wonder if he fell not into worse things, etc. Thirdly, he blesseth God and is thankful to them for the good return made this year. This is the effect of his letters; other things being of more private nature.

[*Murder on the Kennebec*]

I am now to enter upon one of the saddest things that befell them since they came; but before I begin, it will be needful to premise such part of their Patent [1] as gives them right and privilege at Kennebec, as followeth: |199|

The said Council hath further given, granted, bargained, sold, enfeoffed, allotted, assigned, and set over, and by these presents do clearly and absolutely give, grant, bargain, sell, alien, enfeoff, allot, assign and confirm unto the said William Bradford, his heirs, associates and assigns, all that tract of land or part of New England in America aforesaid, which lieth within or between and extendeth itself from the utmost limits of Cobbosseecontee, which adjoineth to the river of Kennebec, towards the western ocean, and a place called the Falls of Nequamkick in America, aforesaid; and the space of 15 English miles on each side of the said river, commonly called Kennebec River, and all the said river called Kennebec that lieth within the said limits and bounds, eastward, westward, northward, and southward, last above mentioned, and all lands, grounds, soils, rivers, wa-

[1] The Patent of 13 Jan. 1630, referred to above.

ters, fishing, etc. And by virtue of the authority to us derived by his said late Majesty's Letters patents, to take, apprehend, seize and make prize of all such persons, their ships and goods as shall attempt to inhabit or trade with the savage people of that country within the several precincts and limits of his and their several plantations, etc.

Now it so fell out that one Hocking, belonging to the Plantation of Piscataqua, went with a bark and commodities to trade in that river, and would needs press into their limits. And not only so, but would needs go up the river above their house, towards the falls of the river, and intercept the trade that should come to them. He that was chief of the place [2] forbade them, and prayed him that he would not offer them that injury nor go about to infringe their liberties which had cost them so dear. But he answered he would go up and trade there in despite of them and lie there as long as he pleased. The other told him he must then be forced to remove him from thence or make seizure of him if he could. He bid him do his worst, and so went up and anchored there. The other took a boat and some men and went up to him, when he saw his time, and again entreated him to depart by what persuasion he could. But all in vain; he could get nothing of him but ill words. So he considered that now was the season for trade to come down, and if he should suffer him to lie and take it from them, all their former charge would be lost and they had better throw up all. So consulting with his men, who were willing thereto, he resolved to put him from his anchors and let him drive down the river with the stream, but commanded the men that none should shoot a shot upon any occasion except he commanded them. He spoke to him again, but all in vain. Then he sent a couple in a canoe to cut his cable, the which one of them performs, but Hocking takes up a piece which he had laid ready, and as the bark sheered by the canoe he shot |200| him close under her side, in the head (as I take it) so he fell down dead instantly.[3] One of his fellows which loved him well could not hold, but with a musket shot Hocking, who fell down dead and never spake word. This was the truth of the thing. The rest of the men carried home the vessel and the sad tidings of these things.

[2] John Howland.

[3] This was Moses Talbot.

Now the Lord Saye and the Lord Brooke with some other great persons had a hand in this Plantation.[4] They writ home to them as much as they could to exasperate them in the matter, leaving out all the circumstances as if he had been killed without any offense of his part, concealing that he had killed another first and the just occasion that he had given in offering such wrong. At which their Lordships were much offended till they were truly informed of the matter.

The bruit of this was quickly carried all about, and that in the worst manner, and came into the Bay to their neighbours there. Their own bark coming home and bringing a true relation of the matter, sundry were sadly affected with the thing, as they had cause. It was not long before they had occasion to send their vessel into the Bay of the Massachusetts. But they were so prepossessed with this matter and affected with the same as they committed Mr. Alden to prison, who was in the bark, and had been at Kennebec, but was no actor in the business but went to carry them supply. They dismissed the bark about her business, but kept him for some time. This was thought strange here, and they sent Captain Standish to give them true information, together with their letters, and the best satisfaction they could, and to procure Mr. Alden's release. I shall recite a letter or two which will show the passages of these things, as followeth.

[*Governors Dudley and Prence Settle the Dispute*]

Good Sir: I have received your letter by Captain Standish, and am unfeignedly glad of God's mercy towards you in the recovery of your health, or some way thereto. For the business you write of, I thought meet to answer a word or two to yourself, leaving the answer of your Governor's letter to our Court, to whom the same, together with myself, is directed. I conceive, till I hear new matter to the contrary, that your Patent may warrant your resistance of any English from trading at Kennebec; and that blood of Hocking and the party he slew will be required at his hands—yet do I with yourself and oth-

[4] I.e., Hilton's former plantation on the Piscataqua River, New Hampshire. Lord Saye, Lord Brooke, Sir Richard Saltonstall and Sir Arthur Heselrige had bought out Hilton's associates. As these were important people, all New England was concerned to see that justice was done. The correspondence and depositions are printed by Ford in 1912 ed. Bradford II 178–80.

ers sorrow for their deaths. I think likewise that your general letters will satisfy our Court and make them cease from any further intermeddling in the matter. I have upon the same letter set Mr. Alden at liberty and his sureties, and yet lest I should seem to neglect the opinion of our Court and the frequent speeches of others with us, I have bound Captain Standish to appear the 3rd of June at our next Court to make affidavit for the copy of the Patent, and to manifest the circumstances of Hocking's provocations; both which will tend to the clearing of your innocency.

If any unkindness hath been taken from what we have done, let it be further and better considered of, I pray you; and I hope the more you think of it, the less blame you will impute to us. At least you ought to be just in differencing them whose opinions concur with your own, from |201| others who were opposites; and yet I may truly say I have spoken with no man in the business who taxed you most, but they are such as have many ways heretofore declared their good affections towards your Plantation. I further refer myself to the report of Captain Standish and Mr. Alden, leaving you for this present to God's blessing, wishing unto you perfect recovery of health and the long continuance of it.

I desire to be lovingly remembered to Mr. Prence your Governor, Mr. Winslow, Mr. Brewster, whom I would see if I knew how. The Lord keep you all. Amen.

Your very loving friend in our Lord Jesus,
Newtown, the 22 of May, 1634 THOMAS DUDLEY

Another of his about these things as followeth.

SIR: I am right sorry for the news that Captain Standish and other of your neighbours and my beloved friends will bring now to Plymouth, wherein I suffer with you by reason of my opinion which differeth from others who are godly and wise amongst us here, the reverence of whose judgments causeth me to suspect mine own ignorance. Yet must I remain in it until I be convinced thereof. I thought not to have showed your letter written to me, but to have done my best to have reconciled differences in the best season and manner I could; but Captain Standish requiring an answer thereof publicly in the Court, I was forced to produce it, and that made the breach so wide as he can tell you. I propounded to the Court to answer Mr. Prence's letter (your Governor) but our Court said it required no answer, itself being an answer to a former letter of ours. I pray you certify Mr. Prence so much, and others whom it concerneth, that no neglect or ill manners be imputed to me thereabout.

The late letters I received from England wrought in me divers fears [5] of some trials which are shortly like to fall upon us; and this unhappy contention between you and us, and between you and Piscataqua, will hasten them, if God with an extraordinary hand do not help us. To reconcile this for the present will be very difficult, but time cooleth distempers and a common danger to us both approaching, will necessitate our uniting again. I pray you therefore, Sir, set your wisdom and patience a work and exhort others to the same, that things may not proceed from bad to worse. So making our contentions like the bars of a palace,[6] but that a way of peace may be kept open, whereat the God of peace may have entrance in His own time. If you suffer wrong, it shall be your honour to bear it patiently; but I go far in needless putting you in mind of these things. God hath done great things for you, and I desire His blessings may be multiplied upon you more and more. I will commit no more to writing, but commending myself to your prayers, do rest,

Your truly loving friend in our Lord Jesus,
June 4, 1634 THOMAS DUDLEY

By these things it appears what troubles rose hereupon, and how hard they were to be reconciled; for though they here were heartily sorry for what was fallen out, yet they conceived they were unjustly injured and provoked to what was done. And that their neighbours, having no jurisdiction over them, did more than was meet thus to imprison one of theirs and bind them to |202| their Court.[7] But yet being assured of their Christian love, and persuaded what was done was out of godly zeal that religion might not suffer nor sin any way covered or borne with, especially the guilt of blood, of which all should be very conscientious in any whomsoever, they did endeavour to appease and sat-

[5] There was cause enough of these fears, which arise by the underworking of some enemies to the churches here, by which this Commission following was procured from His Majesty (Bradford). The Commission is printed in Appendix XII, Official Documents, No. 2.

[6] Proverbs xviii.19 (Geneva version).

[7] This was a typical case of Massachusetts Bay arrogance, for which Governor Dudley, to do him credit, was evidently ashamed. Both the scene of the crime and the Piscataqua Plantation were outside Bay jurisdiction.

isfy them the best they could. First, by informing them the truth in all circumstances about the matter; secondly, in being willing to refer the case to any indifferent and equal hearing and judgment of the thing here, and to answer it elsewhere when they should be duly called thereunto. And further they craved Mr. Winthrop's and other of the reverend magistrates there, their advice and direction herein. This did mollify their minds and bring things to a good and comfortable issue in the end.

For they had this advice given them by Mr. Winthrop and others concurring with him, that from their Court they should write to the neighbour plantations, and especially that of the Lords at Piscataqua, and theirs of the Massachusetts, to appoint some to give them meeting at some fit place to consult and determine in this matter, so as the parties meeting might have full power to order and bind, etc. And that nothing be done to the infringing or prejudice of the liberties of any place. And for the clearing of conscience, the law of God is that the priest's lips must be consulted with.[8] And therefore it was desired that the ministers of every plantation might be present to give their advice in point of conscience. Though this course seemed dangerous to some, yet they were so well assured of the justice of their cause and the equity of their friends, as they put themselves upon it and appointed a time of which they gave notice to the several places, a month beforehand; viz. Massachusetts, Salem and Piscataqua or any other that they would give notice to, and desired them to produce any evidence they could in the case. The place for meeting was at Boston. But when the day and time came, none appeared but some of the magistrates and ministers of the Massachusetts, and their own. Seeing none of Piscataqua or other places came, having been thus desired and convenient time given them for that end, Mr. Winthrop and the rest said they could do no more than they had done thus to request them; the blame must rest on them. So they fell into a fair debating of things themselves; and after all things had been fully opened and discussed and the opinion of each one demanded, both magistrates and ministers, though they all could have wished these things had never been, yet they could not but lay the blame and guilt on Hock-

[8] Malachi ii.7.

ing's own head. And withal gave them such grave and godly exhortations and advice as they thought meet both for the present and future; which they also embraced with love and thankfulness, promising to endeavour to follow the same.

And thus was this matter ended, and their love and concord renewed. And also Mr. Winthrop and Mr. Dudley writ in their behalves to the Lord Saye and other gentlemen that were interested in that Plantation, very effectually. With which, together with their own letters and Mr. Winslow's further declaration of things unto them, they rested well satisfied. |203|

Mr. Winslow was sent by them this year into England, partly to inform and satisfy the Lord Saye and others in the former matter. As also to make answer and their just defense for the same, if anything should by any be prosecuted against them at Council table or elsewhere. But this matter took end without any further trouble, as is before noted. And partly to signify unto the partners in England that the term of their trade with the Company here was out, and therefore he was sent to finish the accounts with them and to bring them notice how much debtor they should remain on that account, and that they might know what further course would be best to hold. But the issue of these things will appear in the next year's passages. They now sent over by him a great return, which was very acceptable unto them; which was in beaver 3738 pounds' weight (a great part of it, being coat-beaver, sold at 20*s* per pound) and 234 otter skins;[9] which altogether rose to a great sum of money. |202 *v.*|

[*Captain Stone, the Dutch, and the Connecticut Indians*]

This year in the forepart of the same they sent forth a bark to trade at the Dutch plantation, and they met there with one Captain Stone that had lived in Christopher's, one of the West India Islands, and now had been some time in Virginia and came from thence into these parts.[1] He kept company with the Dutch Governor and I know not in what drunken fit he got leave of the

[9] And the skin at 14*s* (Bradford).

[1] Capt. John Stone, an English trader. He was carrying cattle from Virginia to Boston and put in at New Amsterdam for water.

Governor to seize on their [2] bark when they were ready to come away and had done their market, having to the value of £500 worth of goods aboard her. Having no occasion at all, or any colour of ground for such a thing, but having made the Governor drunk so as he could scarce speak a right word, and when he urged him hereabout, he answered him, *Als't u beleeft.*[3] So he gat aboard, the chief of their men and merchant being ashore, and with some of his own men made the rest of theirs weigh anchor, set sail and carry her away towards Virginia. But divers of the Dutch seamen which had been often at Plymouth and kindly entertained there, said one to another, "Shall we suffer our friends to be thus abused and have their goods carried away before our faces, whilst our Governor is drunk?" They vowed they would never suffer it and so got a vessel or two and pursued him and brought him in again and delivered them their bark and goods again.

Afterwards Stone came into the Massachusetts and they sent and commenced suit against him for this fact; but by mediation of friends it was taken up and the suit let fall. And in the company of some other gentlemen Stone came afterwards to Plymouth and had friendly and civil entertainment amongst them with the rest. But revenge boiled within his breast (though concealed) for some conceived he had a purpose at one time to have stabbed the Governor, and put his hand to his dagger for that end; but by God's providence and the vigilance of some, was prevented.

He afterward returned to Virginia in a pinnace with one Captain Norton and some others, and, I know not for what occasion, they would needs go up Connecticut River. And how they carried themselves I know not, but the Indians knocked him [4] in the head as he lay in his cabin, and had thrown the covering over his face, whether out of fear or desperation is uncertain. This was his end; they likewise killed all the rest, but Captain Norton defended himself a long time against them all in the cook room, till by accident the gunpowder took fire which for readiness he had set in an open thing before him, which did so burn and scald him and

[2] I.e., the Plymouth Plantation's.

[3] "As you please."

[4] Capt. Stone. This murder, and the clumsy attempts of the English to punish the Indian culprits, eventually led to the Pequot War.

blind his eyes as he could make no longer resistance but was slain also by them, though they much commended his valour. And having killed the men, they made a prey of what they had, and chaffered away some of their things to the Dutch that lived there. But it was not long before a quarrel fell between the Dutch and them, and they would have cut off their bark, but they slew the chief sachem with the shot of a murderer.[5] |203|

I am now to relate some strange and remarkable passages. There was a company of people lived in the country up above in the River of Connecticut a great way from their trading house there, and were enemies to those Indians which lived about them, and of whom they stood in some fear, being a stout people. About a thousand of them had enclosed themselves in a fort which they had strongly palisadoed about. Three or four Dutchmen went up in the beginning of winter to live with them, to get their trade and prevent them for bringing it to the English or to fall into amity with them; but at spring to bring all down to their place. But their enterprise failed. For it pleased God to visit these Indians with a great sickness and such a mortality that of a thousand, above nine and a half hundred of them died, and many of them did rot above ground for want of burial. And the Dutchmen almost starved before they could get away, for ice and snow; but about February they got with much difficulty to their trading house; whom they kindly relieved, being almost spent with hunger and cold. Being thus refreshed by them divers days, they got to their own place and the Dutch were very thankful for this kindness.

This spring also, those Indians that lived about their trading house there,[6] fell sick of the small pox and died most miserably; for a sorer disease cannot befall them, they fear it more than the plague. For usually they that have this disease have them in abundance, and for want of bedding and linen and other helps they fall into a lamentable condition as they lie on their hard mats, the pox breaking and mattering and running one into another, their skin cleaving by reason thereof to the mats they lie on. When they turn them, a whole side will flay off at once |204| as it were, and

[5] A small cannon, charged with grapeshot.

[6] The Plymouth trading house at the site of Windsor.

they will be all of a gore blood, most fearful to behold. And then being very sore, what with cold and other distempers, they die like rotten sheep. The condition of this people was so lamentable and they fell down so generally of this disease as they were in the end not able to help one another, no not to make a fire nor to fetch a little water to drink, nor any to bury the dead. But would strive as long as they could, and when they could procure no other means to make fire, they would burn the wooden trays and dishes they ate their meat in, and their very bows and arrows. And some would crawl out on all fours to get a little water, and sometimes die by the way and not be able to get in again. But of those of the English house, though at first they were afraid of the infection, yet seeing their woeful and sad condition and hearing their pitiful cries and lamentations, they had compassion of them, and daily fetched them wood and water and made them fires, got them victuals whilst they lived; and buried them when they died. For very few of them escaped, notwithstanding they did what they could for them to the hazard of themselves. The chief sachem himself now died and almost all his friends and kindred. But by the marvelous goodness and providence of God, not one of the English was so much as sick or in the least measure tainted with this disease, though they daily did these offices for them for many weeks together. And this mercy which they showed them was kindly taken and thankfully acknowledged of all the Indians that knew or heard of the same. And their masters here did much commend and reward them for the same.

CHAPTER XXVI

Anno Dom: 1635 [*Winslow Talks Back to the Archbishop*]

Mr. Winslow was very welcome to them in England, and the more in regard of the large return he brought with him which came all safe to their hands and was well sold. And he was borne in hand (at least he so apprehended) that all accounts should be cleared before his return and all former differences thereabout well settled. And so he writ over to them here that he hoped to clear the accounts and bring them over with him, and that the account of the *White Angel* would be taken off and all things fairly ended. But it came to pass |205| that, being occasioned to answer some complaints made against the country at Council Board, more chiefly concerning their neighbours in the Bay than themselves here, the which he did to good effect. And further prosecuting such things as might tend to the good of the whole, as well themselves as others, about the wrongs and encroachments that the French and other strangers both had and were like further to do unto them if not prevented; he preferred this petition following to their Honours that were deputed Commissioners for the Plantations:

To the Right Honourable the Lords Commissioners
for the Plantations in America.

The Humble Petition of Edward Winslow, on the behalf of the Plantations in New England,

Humbly sheweth unto your Lordships that whereas your Petitioners have planted themselves in New England under His Majesty's most gracious protection, now so it is, right Honourables, that the French and Dutch do endeavour to divide the land between them; for which purpose the French have on the east side entered and seized upon one of our houses and have carried away the goods, slew two of the men in another place and took the rest prisoners with their goods. And the Dutch on the west have also made entry upon Connecticut River within the limits of His Majesty's letters patent, where they have raised a fort and threaten to expel your Petitioners thence who are also planted upon the same river, maintaining possession for His Majesty to their great charge and hazard both of lives and goods.

In tender consideration hereof, your Petitioners humbly pray that your Lordships will either procure their peace with those foreign states, or else to give special warrant unto your Petitioners and the English Colonies to right and defend themselves against all foreign enemies. And your Petitioners shall pray, etc.

This petition found good acceptation with most of them and Mr. Winslow was heard sundry times by them and appointed further to attend for an answer from their Lordships. Especially [because he] having upon conference with them laid down a way how this might be done without any either charge or trouble to the State: only by furnishing some of the chief of the country here with authority, who would undertake it at their own charge and in such a way as should be without any public disturbance.

But this crossed both Sir Ferdinando Gorges's and Captain Mason's design, and the Archbishop of Canterbury's by them. For Sir Ferdinando Gorges, by the Archbishop's favour, was to have been sent over General Governor into the country and to have had means from the State for that end, and was now upon dispatch and conclude of the business. And the Archbishop's purpose and intent was, by his means and some he should send with him (to be furnished with episcopal power) |206| to disturb the peace of the churches here and to overthrow their proceedings and further growth, which was the thing he aimed at. But it so fell out (by God's providence) that though he in the end crossed this petition from taking any further effect in this kind, yet by this as a chief means, the plot and whole business of his and Sir Ferdinando's fell to the ground and came to nothing. When Mr. Winslow should have had his suit granted (as indeed upon the point it was) and should have been confirmed, the Archbishop put a stop upon it, and Mr. Winslow, thinking to get it freed, went to the Board again. But the Bishop, Sir Ferdinando and Captain Mason had, as it seems, procured Morton (of whom mention is made before and his base carriage) to complain; to whose complaints Mr. Winslow made answer to the good satisfaction of the Board, who checked Morton and rebuked him sharply, and also blamed Sir Ferdinando Gorges and Mason for countenancing him.

But the Bishop had a further end and use of his presence, for he now began to question Mr. Winslow of many things, as of teaching in the church publicly of which Morton accused him, and gave evidence that he had seen and heard him do it. To which Mr. Winslow answered that some time (wanting a minister) he did exercise his gift to help the edification of his brethren when they wanted better means, which was not often.[1] Then about marriage, the which he also confessed that having been called to place of magistracy, he had sometimes married some. And further told their Lordships that marriage was a civil thing and he found nowhere in the Word of God that it was tied to ministry. Again, they were necessitated so to do, having for a long time together at first no minister; besides, it was no new thing for he had been so married himself in Holland by the magistrates in their Statt-house.

But in the end (to be short) for these things the Bishop by vehement importunity got the Board at last to consent to his commitment. So he was committed to the Fleet and lay there seventeen weeks or thereabout, before he could get to be released. And this was the end of this petition and this business; only the others' design was also frustrated hereby, with other things concurring, which was no small blessing to the people here.

But the charge fell heavy on them here, not only in Mr. Winslow's expenses (which could not be small) but by the hindrance of their business both there and here by his personal employment. For though this was as much or more for others than for them here, and by them [2] chiefly he was put on this business (for the Plantation knew nothing of it till they heard of his imprisonment) yet the whole charge lay on them.[3]

1 Morton's charge, as he gives it in *New English Canaan* pp. 172–3, was "The Church of the Separatists is governed by Pastors, Elders and Deacons, and there is not any of these, though he be but a cow keeper, but is allowed to exercise his gifts in the public assembly on the Lord's day, so as he do not make use of any notes for the help of his memory." True enough! Winslow's defense is in 1912 ed. Bradford II 202 note.

2 Massachusetts Bay.

3 Plymouth.

Now for their own business. Whatsoever Mr. Sherley's mind was before, or Mr. Winslow's apprehension of the same, he now declared himself plainly, that he would neither take off the *White Angel* from the account, nor |207| give any further account till he had received more into his hands. Only a pretty good supply of goods were sent over, but of the most no note of their prices or so orderly an invoice as formerly, which Mr. Winslow said he could not help because of his restraint. Only now Mr. Sherley and Mr. Beauchamp and Mr. Andrews sent over a letter of attorney under their hands and seals to recover what they could of Mr. Allerton for the *Angel's* account, but sent them neither the bonds nor covenants or such other evidence or accounts as they had about these matters. I shall here insert a few passages out of Mr. Sherley's letters about these things.[4]

[*D'Aunay Seizes Penobscot Trading Post*]

This year they sustained another great loss from the French. Monsieur d'Aunay coming into the harbor of Penobscot, and having before got some of the chief that belonged to the house aboard his vessel, by subtlety coming upon them in their shallop he got them to pilot him in; and after getting the rest into his power he took possession of the house in the name of the King of France.[5] And partly by threatening and otherwise, made Mr. Willett, their agent there, to approve of the sale of the goods there unto him, of which he set the price himself |208| in effect, and made an inventory thereof, yet leaving out sundry things. But made no payment for them, but told them in convenient time he would do it if they came for it. For the house and fortification etc. he would not allow nor account anything, saying that they which build on another man's ground do forfeit the same. So thus turning them out of all, with a great deal of compliment

[4] Printed in Appendix VII.

[5] This was the Pilgrims' trading post at Pentagoët, on the site of Castine; the captor was Charles de Menou d'Aunay Charnisay, the Acadian rival of La Tour. Many documents on this affair are in 1912 ed. Bradford II 206–10; the best account of the rivalry, and of Governor Winthrop's inept attempt to settle it, is in Parkman *Old Régime in Canada.*

and many fine words, he let them have their shallop and some victuals to bring them home.

Coming home and relating all the passages, they here were much troubled at it, and having had this house robbed by the French once before and lost then above £500 (as is before remembered) and now to lose house and all, did much move them. So as they resolved to consult with their friends in the Bay, and if they approved of it (there being now many ships there) they intended to hire a ship of force and seek to beat out the French and recover it again. Their course was well approved on—if themselves could bear the charge. So they hired a fair ship of above 300 tun [6] well fitted with ordnance, and agreed with the master (one Girling) to this effect, that he and his company should deliver them the house after they had driven out or surprised the French, and give them peaceable possession thereof and of all such trading commodities as should there be found; and give the French fair quarter and usage if they would yield. In consideration whereof, he was to have 700 pounds of beaver, to be delivered him there when he had done the thing; but if he did not accomplish it he was to lose his labour and have nothing. With him they also sent their own bark and about 20 men with Captain Standish to aid him (if need were) and to order things if the house was regained; and then to pay him the beaver which they kept aboard their own bark. So they with their bark piloted him thither and brought him safe into the harbor. But he was so rash and heady as he would take no advice, nor would suffer Captain Standish to have time to summon them (who had commission and order so to do), neither would do it himself. The which, it was like if it had been done and they come to a fair parley (seeing their force) they would have yielded. Neither would he have patience to bring his ship where she might do execution, but began to shoot at distance like a madman, and did them no hurt at all. The which when those of the Plantation saw, they were much grieved and went to him and told him he would do no good if he did not lay his ship better to pass for she might lie within pistol shot of the house. At last when he saw his own folly he was persuaded and layed her well, and bestowed a few shot to good pur-

[6] The *Great Hope.*

pose. But now when he was in a way to do some good, his powder was gone; for though he had [7] pieces of ordnance, it did now |209| appear he had but a barrel of powder and a piece. So he could do no good but was fain to draw off again, by which means the enterprise was made frustrate and the French encouraged. For all the while that he shot so unadvisedly, they lay close under a work of earth and let him consume himself. He advised with the Captain how he might be supplied with powder, for he had not [enough] to carry him home; so he told him he would go to the next Plantation and do his endeavour to procure him some, and so did. But understanding by intelligence that he intended to seize on the bark and surprise the beaver, he sent him the powder and brought the bark and beaver home. But Girling never assaulted the place more, seeing himself disappointed, but went his way. And this was the end of this business.

Upon the ill success of this business, the Governor and Assistants here by their letters certified their friends in the Bay how by this ship they had been abused and disappointed, and that the French partly had, and were now likely to fortify themselves more strongly, and likely to become ill neighbours to the English. Upon this they thus writ to them as followeth:

Worthy Sirs: Upon the reading of your letters and consideration of the weightiness of the cause therein mentioned, the Court hath jointly expressed their willingness to assist you with men and munition for the accomplishing of your desires upon the French. But because here are none of yours that have authority to conclude of anything herein, nothing can be done by us for the present. We desire, therefore, that you would with all convenient speed send some man of trust, furnished with instructions from yourselves, to make such agreement with us about this business as may be useful for you and equal for us. So in haste we commit you to God, and remain

Your assured loving friends,
John Haynes, Governor
Richard Bellingham, Deputy
John Winthrop
Thomas Dudley
John Humfry

[7] Blank in the original.

William Coddington
William Pynchon
Atherton Hough
Increase Nowell
Richard Dummer
Simon Bradstreet

Newtown, October 9, 1635

Upon the receipt of the above mentioned, they presently deputed two of theirs to treat with them, giving them full power to conclude, according to the instructions they gave them. Being to this purpose, that if they would afford such assistance, as together with their own was like to effect the thing, and also bear a considerable part of the charge, they would go on; if not, |210| they having lost so much already should not be able but must desist and wait further opportunity, as God should give, to help themselves. But this came to nothing, for when it came to the issue they would be at no charge. But sent them this letter and referred them more at large to their own messengers.

Sir: Having, upon the consideration of your letter, with the message you sent, had some serious consultations about the great importance of your business with the French, we gave our answer to those whom you deputed to confer with us about the voyage to Penobscot. We showed our willingness to help, but withal we declared our present condition, and in what state we were, for our ability to help; which we for our parts shall be willing to improve, to procure you sufficient supply of men and munition. But for matter of moneys we have no authority at all to promise, and if we should, we should rather disappoint you than encourage you by that help which we are not able to perform. We likewise thought it fit to take the help of other Eastern plantations; but those things we leave to your own wisdoms.

And for other things we refer you to your own committees, who are able to relate all the passages more at large. We salute you, and wish you all good success in the Lord.

Your faithful and loving friend,
Richard Bellingham, Dep.
In the name of the rest of the Committees

Boston, October 16, 1635

This thing did not only thus break off, but some of their merchants shortly after sent to trade with them and furnished them both with provisions and powder and shot; and so have continued to do till this day, as they have seen opportunity for their profit. So as in truth the English themselves have been the chiefest supporters of these French; for besides these, the Plantation at Pemaquid (which lies near unto them) doth not only supply them with what they want, but gives them continual intelligence of all things that pass among the English, especially some of them. So as it is no marvel though they still grow and encroach more and more upon the English, and fill the Indians with guns and munition. To the great danger of the English, who lie open and unfortified, living upon husbandry, and the other closed up in their forts, well fortified, and live upon trade in good security. If these things be not looked to and remedy provided in time, it may easily be conjectured what they may come to. But I leave them.

[*The Great Hurricane*]

This year, the 14th or 15th of August (being Saturday) was such a mighty storm of wind and rain as none living in these parts, either English or Indians, ever saw. Being like, for the time it continued, to those hurricanes and typhoons that writers make mention of in the Indies. It began in the morning a little before day, and grew not by degrees but came with violence in the beginning, to the great amazement of many. It blew down sundry |211| houses and uncovered others. Divers vessels were lost at sea and many more in extreme danger. It caused the sea to swell to the southward of this place above 20 foot right up and down, and made many of the Indians to climb into trees for their safety. It took off the boarded roof of a house which belonged to this Plantation at Manomet, and floated it to another place, the posts still standing in the ground. And if it had continued long without the shifting of the wind, it is like it would have drowned some part of the country. It blew down many hundred thousands of trees, turning up the stronger by the roots and breaking the higher pine trees off in the middle. And the tall young oaks and walnut trees of good bigness were wound like a withe, very strange and fearful to behold. It began in the southeast and parted toward the south and east, and veered sundry ways, but the greatest force of it here was from the former quarters. It continued not (in the extremity) above five or six hours but the violence began to abate. The signs and marks of it will remain this hundred years in these parts where it was sorest. The moon suffered a great eclipse the second night after it.[8]

[*Settlement on the Connecticut River*]

Some of their neighbours in the Bay, hearing of the fame of Connecticut River, had a hankering mind after it (as was before noted) and now understanding that the Indians were swept away with the late great mortality, the fear of whom was an obstacle unto them before, which being now taken away, they began now to prosecute it with great eagerness. The greatest differences fell between those of Dorchester Plantation and them here; for they set their mind on that place, which they had not only purchased of the Indians, but where they had built; intending only (if they could not remove them) that they should have but a small moiety left to the house as to a single family. Whose doings and proceedings were conceived to be very injurious, to attempt not only to intrude themselves into the rights and possessions of others, but in effect to thrust them out of all. Many were the letters and passages that went between them hereabout, which would be too long here to relate.

I shall here first insert a few lines that was writ by their own agent from thence.

SIR, etc.: The Massachusetts men are coming almost daily, some by water and some by land, who are not yet determined where to settle, though some have a great mind to the place we are upon, and which

[8] Bradford's description of this hurricane tallies remarkably with that of September 1938, in which hundreds of people in southern New England were drowned. It was in the 1635 hurricane that a pinnace belonging to Allerton, sailing from Ipswich to Marblehead with Anthony Thacher, the Rev. Joseph Avery and their families on board, struck on a rock off Cape Ann, and many were drowned. Cotton Mather's account of this wreck inspired Whittier's "Swan Song of Parson Avery," and Thacher's Island and Avery's Rock are permanent memorials.

was last bought. Many of them look at that which this river will not afford, except it be at this place which we have; namely, to be a great town and have commodious dwellings for many together. So as what they will do I cannot yet resolve you. For [in] this place there is none of them [that] say anything to me, but what I hear from their servants, by whom I perceive their minds. I shall do what I can to withstand them. I hope they will hear reason, as that we were here first and entered with much difficulty and danger |212| both in regard of the Dutch and Indians, and bought the land, to your great charge already disbursed, and have since held here a chargeable possession and kept the Dutch from further encroaching, which would else long before this day have possessed all, and kept out all others, etc. I hope these and such-like arguments will stop them.

It was your will we should use their persons and messengers kindly, and so we have done and do daily, to your great charge; for the first company had well nigh starved, had it not been for this house, for want of victuals; I being forced to supply twelve men for nine days together. And those which came last, I entertained the best we could, helping both them and the other with canoes and guides. They got me to go with them to the Dutch, to see if I could procure some of them to have quiet settling near them, but they did peremptorily withstand them. But this later company did not once speak thereof, etc. Also I gave their goods house room according to their earnest request, and Mr. Pynchon's letter in their behalf, which I thought good to send you, here enclosed. And what trouble and charge I shall be further at I know not, for they are coming daily, and I expect these back again from below, whither they are gone to view the country. All which trouble and charge we undergo for their occasion, may give us just cause in the judgment of all wise and understanding men, to hold and keep that [which] we are settled upon.

Thus with my duty remembered, etc. I rest

Yours to be commanded,

Matianuck, July 6, 1635 JONATHAN BREWSTER [9]

Amongst the many agitations that passed between them, I shall note a few out of their last letters, and for the present omit the

[9] Eldest son of William Brewster. The encroachment he writes of was the well-known Hooker-Haynes-Warham emigration to the Connecticut, which founded Hartford, Windsor and Wethersfield, nuclei of the Connecticut Colony. William Pynchon started the trading post up-river at Springfield, which remained in the Massachusetts jurisdiction.

rest, except upon other occasion I may have fitter opportunity. After their[1] thorough view of the place they began to pitch themselves upon their land and near their house, which occasioned much expostulation between them, some of which are such as follow:

Brethren, having lately sent two of our body unto you, to agitate and bring to an issue some matters in difference between us about some lands at Connecticut, unto which you lay challenge, upon which God by His providence cast us, and as we conceive in a fair way of providence tendered it to us, as a meet place to receive our body, now upon removal.

We shall not need to answer all the passages of your large letter, etc. But whereas you say God in His providence cast you, etc., we told you before, and upon this occasion must now tell you still, that our mind is otherwise. And that you cast a rather partial if not a covetous eye, upon that which is your neighbours' and not yours; and in so doing, your way could not be fair unto it. Look that you abuse not God's providence in such allegations.

Theirs:

Now, albeit we at first judged the place so free that we might with God's good leave take and use it, without just offense to any man. It being the Lord's |213| waste, and for the present altogether void of inhabitants, that indeed minded the employment thereof to the right ends for which land was created (Gen. i.28). And for future intentions of any, and uncertain possibilities of this or that to be done by any, we judging them (in such a case as ours especially) not meet to be equalled with present actions (such as ours was) much less worthy to be preferred before them. And therefore did we make some weak beginnings in that good work, in the place aforesaid.

Answer: Their answer was to this effect. That if it was the Lord's waste, it was themselves that found it so and not they; and have since bought it of the right owners, and maintained a chargeable possession upon it all this while, as themselves could not but know. And because they could not presently remove themselves

[1] The emigrants from Massachusetts Bay.

to it, because of present engagements and other hindrances which lay at present upon them; must it therefore be lawful for them to go and take it from them? It was well known that they are upon a barren place, where they were by necessity cast; and neither they nor theirs could long continue upon the same. And why should they, because they were more ready and more able at present, go and deprive them of that which they had with charge and hazard provided and intended to remove to, as soon as they could and were able?

They had another passage in their letter: They had rather have to do with the Lords in England,[2] to whom, as they heard it reported, some of them should say that they had rather give up their right to them (if they must part with it) than to the church of Dorchester, etc. And that they should be less fearful to offend the Lords than they were them.

Answer: Their answer was, that whatsoever they had heard, more than was true, yet the case was not so with them that they had need to give away their rights and adventures, either to the Lords or them. Yet, if they might measure their fear of offense by their practice, they had rather (in that point) they should deal with the Lords, who were better able to bear it or help themselves, than they were.

But lest I should be tedious, I will forbear other things and come to the conclusion that was made in the end. To make any forcible resistance was far from their thoughts—they had enough of that about Kennebec—and to live in continual contention with their friends and brethren would be uncomfortable and too heavy a burthen to bear. Therefore, for peace sake, though they conceived they suffered much in this thing, they thought it better to let them have it upon as good terms as they could get. And so they fell to treaty.

The first thing that (because they had made so many and long disputes about it) they would have them to grant, was that they had right to it, or else they would never treat about it. The which

[2] Lords Saye and Sele and Lord Brooke, who had a patent of vague bounds from the Council for New England, which the Connecticut settlers purchased to legitimatize their occupancy. Sundry documents on this dispute are printed in 1912 ed. Bradford II 219–22.

being acknowledged and yielded unto by them, this was the conclusion they came unto in the end, after much ado. That they should retain their house and have the sixteenth part of all they had bought of the Indians, and the other should have all the rest of the land, leaving such a moiety to those |214| of Newtown[3] as they reserved for them. This sixteenth part was to be taken in two places, one towards the house, the other towards Newtown's proportion. Also they were to pay according to proportion what had been disbursed to the Indians for the purchase.

Thus was the controversy ended but the unkindness not so soon forgotten. They of Newtown dealt more fairly, desiring only what they could conveniently spare from a competency reserved for a plantation for themselves. Which made them the more careful to procure a moiety for them in this agreement and distribution.

[*Another Failure to Procure a Minister*]

Amongst the other businesses that Mr. Winslow had to do in England, he had order from the church to provide and bring over some able and fit man for to be their minister. And accordingly he had procured a godly and worthy man, one Mr. Glover. But it pleased God when he was prepared for the voyage, he fell sick of a fever and died. Afterwards when he[4] was ready to come away, he became acquainted with Mr. Norton, who was willing to come over but would not engage himself to this place, otherwise than he should see occasion when he came here, and if he liked better elsewhere, to repay the charge laid out for him (which came to about £70) and to be at his liberty. He stayed about a year with them after he came over, and was well liked of

[3] Shortly to be renamed Cambridge. The inhabitants of Newtown removed almost as a body to the Connecticut under their pastor, the Rev. Thomas Hooker, and sold their homesteads to a new company from England, under the Rev. Thomas Shepard.

[4] Winslow; the next candidate was the Rev. John Norton. Glover may have been the Rev. Jose Glover, whose widow established the first printing press in the English Colonies, at Cambridge, in 1639. S. E. Morison *Founding of Harvard College* p. 255.

them and much desired by them; but he was invited to Ipswich, where were many rich and able men and sundry of his acquaintance. So he went to them and is their minister. About half of the charge was repaid, and the rest he had for the pains he took amongst them.

CHAPTER XXVII

Anno Dom: 1636

[*Differences with the English Partners about Beaver*]

Mr. Edward Winslow was chosen Governor this year.

In the former year, because they perceived by Mr. Winslow's later letters that no accounts would be sent, they resolved to keep the beaver and send no more till they had them or came to some further agreement. At least they would forbear till Mr. Winslow came over, that by more full conference with him they might better understand what was meet to be done. But when he came, though he brought no accounts, yet he persuaded them to send the beaver and was confident upon the receipt of the beaver and his letters they should have accounts the next year. And though they thought his grounds but weak that gave him this hope and made him so confident, yet by his importunity they yielded and sent the same. There being a ship at the latter end of the year by whom they sent 1,150 pounds' weight of beaver and 200 otter skins, besides sundry small furs, as 55 minks, two black fox skins, etc.

And this year in the spring came in a Dutchman who thought to have traded at the Dutch fort, |215| but they [1] would not suffer him. He having good store of trading goods came to this place and tendered them to sell, of whom they bought a good quantity, they being very good and fit for their turn, as Dutch roll,[2] kettles, etc., which goods amounted to the value of £500, for the payment of which they passed bills to Mr. Sherley in England, having before sent the forementioned parcel of beaver.

And now this year, by another ship, sent another good round parcel that might come to his hands and be sold before any of these bills should be due. The quantity of beaver now sent was 1,809 pounds' weight, and of otters 10 skins; and shortly after the same year was sent by another ship (Mr. Langrume master) in beaver 719 pounds' weight and of otter skins 199, concerning which Mr. Sherley thus writes:

[1] The Dutch West Indies Company, which had the monopoly of the fur trade in New Netherland.

[2] Virginia tobacco made up in a tight roll, as the Dutch and other European merchants liked to buy it.

Your letters I have received, with 8 hogsheads of beaver by Ed. Wilkinson, master of the *Falcon;* blessed be God for the safe coming of it. I have also seen and accepted three bills of exchange, etc.

But I must now acquaint you, how the Lord's heavy hand is upon this kingdom in many places, but chiefly in this city, with His judgment of the plague. The last week's bill was 1200 and odd. I fear this will be more, and it is much feared it will be a winter sickness. By reason whereof it is incredible the number of people that are gone into the country and left the city; I am persuaded many more than went out the last great sickness. So as here is no trading, carriers from most places put down, nor no receiving of any money though long due. Mr. Hall owes us more than would pay these bills, but he, his wife and all are in the country sixty miles from London. I writ to him, he came up, but could not pay us. I am persuaded if I should offer to sell the beaver at 8*s* per pound, it would not yield money; but when the Lord shall please to cease His hand I hope we shall have better and quicker markets, so it shall lie by.

Before I accepted the bills, I acquainted Mr. Beauchamp and Mr. Andrews with them, and how there could be no money made nor received; and that it would be a great discredit to you, which never yet had any turned back, and a shame to us, having 1800 pounds of beaver lying by us, and more owing than the bills come to, etc. But all was nothing, neither of them both will put to their finger to help. I offered to supply my third part, but they gave me their answer they neither would nor could, etc. However, your bills shall be satisfied to the parties' good content; but I would not have thought they would have left either you or me at this time, etc. You will and may expect I should write more and answer your letters, but I am not a day in the week at home at town, but carry my books and all to Clapham. For here is the miserablest time that I think hath been known in many ages. I have known three great sicknesses, but none like this. And that which should be a means to pacify the Lord and help us, that is taken away, preaching put down in many places, not a sermon in Westminster on the Sabbath, nor in many towns about us; the Lord in mercy look upon us!

In the beginning of the year was a great |216| drought, and no rain for many weeks together, so as all was burnt up, hay at £5 a load; and now, all rain, so as much summer corn and later hay is spoiled. Thus the Lord sends judgment after judgment, and yet we cannot see nor humble ourselves, and therefore may justly fear heavier judgments unless we speedily repent and return unto Him, which the Lord give us grace to do, if it be His blessed will.

Thus desiring you to remember us in your prayers, I ever rest

Your loving friend,

Sept. 14, 1636 JAMES SHERLEY

This was all the answer they had from Mr. Sherley, by which Mr. Winslow saw his hopes failed him. So they now resolved to send no more beaver in that way which they had done, till they came to some issue or other about these things.

But now came over letters from Mr. Andrews and Mr. Beauchamp, full of complaints that they marveled that nothing was sent over, by which any of their moneys should be paid in; for it did appear by the account sent in anno 1631 that they were each of them out about £1100 apiece, and all this while had not received one penny towards the same. But now Mr. Sherley sought to draw more money from them, and was offended because they denied him. And blamed them here very much that all was sent to Mr. Sherley, and nothing to them. They marveled much at this, for they conceived that much of their moneys had been paid in, and that yearly each of them had received a proportionable quantity out of the large returns sent home. For they had sent home since that account was received in anno 1631, in which all and more than all their debts, with that year's supply, was charged upon them, these sums following:

Date	*Sent by Ship, of which Master was*	*Pounds of Beaver*	*Number of Otter Skins*
Nov. 18, 1631	Mr. Peirce	400	20
July 13, 1632	Mr. Griffin	1,348	147
Anno 1633	Mr. Graves	3,366	346
Anno 1634	Mr. Andrews	3,738	234
Anno 1635	Mr. Babb	1,150	200
June 24, 1636	Mr. Wilkinson	1,809	10
1636	Mr. Langrume	719	199
		12,150[8]	1,156

[8] Bradford's addition; 12,530 is correct.

All these sums were safely received and well sold, as appears by letters. The coat beaver usually at 20*s* per pound, and some at 24*s*, the skin at 15*s* and sometimes 16*s*; I do not remember any under 14*s*. It may be last year might be something lower, so also there were some small furs that are not reckoned in this account, and some black beaver at higher rates to make up the defects. |217| It was conceived that the former parcels of beaver came to little less than £10,000 sterling, and the otter skins would pay all the charge, and they with other furs make up besides if anything wanted of the former sum. When the former account was passed, all their debts, those of *White Angel* and *Friendship* included, came but to £4,770. And they could not estimate that all the supplies since sent them, and bills paid for them, could come to above £2000. So as they conceived their debts had been paid, with advantage or interest. But it may be objected, how comes it that they could not as well exactly set down their receipts as their returns, but thus estimate it? I answer, two things were the cause of it. The first and principal was that the new accountant,[4] which they in England would needs press upon them, did wholly fail them and could never give them any account; but trusting to his memory and loose papers, let things run into such confusion that neither he nor any with him could bring things to rights. But being often called upon to perfect his accounts, he desired to have such a time and such a time of leisure, and he would do it. In the interim he fell into a great sickness, and in conclusion it fell out he could make no account at all. His books were, after a little good beginning, left altogether unperfect; and his papers, some were lost and others so confused as he knew not what to make of them himself when they came to be searched and examined. This was not unknown to Mr. Sherley; and they came to smart for it to purpose (though it was not their fault) both thus in England and also here. For they conceived they lost some hundreds of pounds for goods trusted out in the place, which were lost for want of clear accounts to call them in. Another reason of this mischief was, that after Mr. Winslow was sent into England to demand accounts, and to except against the *White Angel*, they never had any price sent with their goods, nor any certain invoice of them;

[4] Josias Winslow.

but all things stood in confusion, and they were fain to guess at the prices of them.

They writ back to Mr. Andrews and Mr. Beauchamp and told them they marveled they should write they had sent nothing home since the last accounts, for they had sent a great deal, and it might rather be marveled how they could be able to send so much, besides defraying all charge at home and what they had lost by the French, and so much cast away at sea when Mr. Peirce lost his ship on the coast of Virginia. What they had sent was to them all and to themselves, as well as Mr. Sherley; and if they did not look after it, it was their own faults. They must refer them to Mr. Sherley, who had received |218| it, to demand it of him. They also writ to Mr. Sherley to the same purpose, and what the others' complaints were.

This year two shallops going to Connecticut with goods from the Massachusetts of such as removed thither to plant, were in an easternly storm cast away in coming into this harbor, in the night.[5] The boats' men were lost and the goods were driven all along the shore, and strewed up and down at high water mark. But the Governor caused them to be gathered up and drawn together, and appointed some to take an inventory of them, and others to wash and dry such things as had need thereof, by which means most of the goods were saved and restored to the owners. Afterwards another boat of theirs, going thither likewise, was cast away near unto Scusset, and such goods as came ashore were preserved for them. Such crosses they met with in their beginnings, which some imputed as a correction from God for their intrusion, to the wrong of others, into that place. But I dare not be bold with God's judgments in this kind.

[*War Threatened with the Pequots*]

In the year 1634 the Pequots (a stout and warlike people) who had made wars with sundry of their neighbours and, puffed up with many victories, grew now at variance with the Narragansetts, a great people bordering upon them there. These Narra-

[5] Governor Winthrop says this wreck occurred 6 Oct. 1635 on Brown's Bank.

gansetts held correspondence and terms of friendship with the English of the Massachusetts. Now the Pequots, being conscious of the guilt of Captain Stone's death, whom they knew to be an Englishman, as also those that were with him, and being fallen out with the Dutch, lest they should have overmany enemies at once, sought to make friendship with the English of the Massachusetts. And for that end sent both mesengers and gifts unto them, as appears by some letters sent from the Governor hither.

Dear and Worthy Sir, etc. To let you know somewhat of our affairs, you may understand that the Pequots have sent some of theirs to us, to desire our friendship, and offered much wampum and beaver, etc. The first messengers were dismissed without answer. With the next we had divers days' conference; and taking the advice of some of our ministers and seeking the Lord in it, we concluded a peace and friendship with them, upon these conditions: That they should deliver up to us those men who were guilty of Stone's death, etc. And if we desired to plant in Connecticut, they should give up their right to us, and so we would send to trade with them as our friends—which was the chief thing we aimed at, [they] being now in war with the Dutch and the rest of their neighbours.

To this they readily agreed, and that we should mediate a peace between them and the Narragansetts, for which end they were content we should give the Narragansetts part of that present they would bestow on us. For they stood |219| so much on their honour as they would not be seen to give anything of themselves. As for Captain Stone, they told us there were but two left of those who had any hand in his death, and that they killed him in a just quarrel. For, say they, he surprised two of our men and bound them to make them by force to show him the way up the river;[6] and he with two other coming on shore, nine Indians watched him, and when they were asleep in the night, they killed them to deliver their own men. And some of them going afterwards to the pinnace, it was suddenly blown up. We are now preparing to send a pinnace unto them, etc.

In another of his, dated the 12th of the first month, he hath this:

Our pinnace is lately returned from the Pequots; they put off but little commodity, and found them a very false people, so as they mean

[6] There is little trust to be given to their relations in these things (Bradford).

to have no more to do with them. I have divers other things to write unto you, etc.

Yours ever assured,
Boston, 12 of the 1st month, 1634[7] JOHN WINTHROP

After these things, and as I take this year, John Oldham (of whom much is spoken before) being now an inhabitant of the Massachusetts, went with a small vessel and slenderly manned a-trading into these south parts, and upon a quarrel between him and the Indians, was cut off by them (as hath been before noted) at an island called by the Indians Munisses, but since by the English, Block Island. This, with the former about the death of Stone, and the baffling[8] of the Pequots with the English of the Massachusetts, moved them to set out some to take revenge and require satisfaction for these wrongs. But it was done so superficially, and without their acquainting those of Connecticut and other neighbours with the same, as they did little good, but their neighbours had more hurt done. For some of the murderers of Oldham fled to the Pequots, and though the English went to the Pequots and had some parley with them, yet they did but delude them, and the English returned without doing anything to purpose, being frustrate of their opportunity by the others' deceit.[9]

After the English were returned, the Pequots took their time and opportunity to cut off some of the English as they passed in boats and went on fowling, and assaulted them the next spring at their habitations, as will appear in its place. I do but touch these things, because I make no question they will be more fully and distinctly handled by themselves who had more exact knowledge of them and whom they did more properly concern.

[*The Coming of Rev. John Rayner*]

This year Mr. Smith laid down his place of ministry, partly by his own willingness as thinking it too heavy a burthen, and partly

[7] I.e., 12 March 1634/35. The Bay people adopted the stricter Puritan usage of numbering the months.

[8] In the old sense of disgracing, losing face. Bradford spells it "baffoyling."

[9] This was the expedition under John Endecott, which accomplished nothing except to stir up the Pequots. The correspondence about it is in 1912 ed. Bradford II 235–6.

at the desire and by the persuasion of others. And the church sought out |220| for some other, having often been disappointed in their hopes and desires heretofore. And it pleased the Lord to send them an able and a godly man, Mr. John Rayner,[1] and or a meek and humble spirit, sound in the truth and every way unreproveable in his life and conversation. Whom after some time of trial they chose for their teacher, the fruits of whose labours they enjoyed many years with much comfort, in peace and good agreement.

1 At last the Pilgrim church had found a satisfactory minister! John Rayner was a well-to-do graduate of Magdalene College, Cambridge, who emigrated in 1635. Yet even he, in consequence of some unrecorded but "unhappy" difference with his congregation, resigned in 1654 and migrated to Dover, N. H.

CHAPTER XXVIII

Anno Dom: 1637 [*The Pequot War*]

In the fore part of this year, the Pequots fell openly upon the English at Connecticut, in the lower parts of the river, and slew sundry of them as they were at work in the fields, both men and women, to the great terrour of the rest, and went away in great pride and triumph, with many high threats. They also assaulted a fort at the river's mouth, though strong and well defended; and though they did not there prevail, yet it struck them with much fear and astonishment to see their bold attempts in the face of danger. Which made them in all places to stand upon their guard and to prepare for resistance, and earnestly to solicit their friends and confederates in the Bay of Massachusetts to send them speedy aid, for they looked for more forcible assaults. Mr. Vane, being then Governor, writ from their General Court to them here to join with them in this war. To which they were cordially willing, but took opportunity to write to them about some former things, as well as present, considerable hereabout. The which will best appear in the Governor's answer, which he returned to the same, which I shall here insert.[1] |222|

In the meantime, the Pequots, especially in the winter before, sought to make peace with the Narragansetts, and used very pernicious arguments to move them thereunto: as that the English were strangers and began to overspread their country, and would deprive them thereof in time, if they were suffered to grow and increase. And if the Narragansetts did assist the English to subdue them, they did but make way for their own overthrow, for if they were rooted out, the English would soon take occasion to subjugate them. And if they would hearken to them they should not need to fear the strength of the English, for they would not come to open battle with them but fire their houses, kill their cattle, and lie in ambush for them as they went abroad upon their occasions; and all this they might easily do without any or little danger to themselves. The which course being held, they well saw the English could not long subsist but they would either be starved with hunger or be forced to forsake the country. With

[1] See Appendix VIII.

many the like things; insomuch that the Narragansetts were once wavering and were half minded to have made peace with them, and joined against the English. But again, when they considered how much wrong they had received from the Pequots, and what an opportunity they now had by the help of the English to right themselves; revenge was so sweet unto them as it prevailed above all the rest, so as they resolved to join with the English against them, and did. |223|

The Court here agreed forthwith to send fifty men at their own charge; and with as much speed as possibly they could, got them armed and had made them ready under sufficient leaders,[2] and provided a bark to carry them provisions and tend upon them for all occasions. But when they were ready to march, with a supply from the Bay, they had word to stay; for the enemy was as good as vanquished and there would be no need.

I shall not take upon me exactly to describe their proceedings in these things, because I expect it will be fully done by themselves who best know the carriage and circumstances of things. I shall therefore but touch them in general. From Connecticut, who were most sensible of the hurt sustained and the present danger, they set out a party of men, and another party met them from the Bay, at Narragansetts', who were to join with them.[3] The Narragansetts were earnest to be gone before the English were well rested and refreshed, especially some of them which came last. It should seem their desire was to come upon the enemy suddenly and undiscovered. There was a bark of this place, newly put in there, which was come from Connecticut, who did encourage them to lay hold of the Indians' forwardness, and to show as great forwardness as they, for it would encourage them, and expedition might prove to their great advantage. So they went on, and so ordered their march as the Indians brought them to a fort of the enemy's (in which most of their chief men were) before day.[4] They approached the same with great silence and surrounded it both with English and Indians, that they might not

[2] Lieut. William Holmes, Thomas Prence and 42 men.

[3] Capt. John Mason commanded the Connecticut contingent of 90 men; Capt. John Underhill the Bay contingent of 40; 100 more were to follow. There is a good account of the Pequot War in J. G. Palfrey *History of New England*.

[4] Mystic Fort, on the west bank of the Mystic River near its mouth.

break out; and so assaulted them with great courage, shooting amongst them, and entered the fort with all speed. And those that first entered found sharp resistance from the enemy who both shot at and grappled with them; others ran into their houses and brought out fire and set them on fire, which soon took in their mat; and standing close together, with the wind all was quickly on a flame, and thereby more were burnt to death than was otherwise slain; It burnt their bowstrings and made them unserviceable; those that scaped the fire were slain with the sword, some hewed to pieces, others run through with their rapiers, so as they were quickly dispatched and very few escaped. It was conceived they thus destroyed about 400 at this time. It was a fearful sight to see them thus frying in the fire and the streams of blood quenching the same, and horrible was the stink and scent thereof; but the victory seemed a sweet sacrifice,[5] and they gave the praise thereof to God, who had wrought so wonderfully for them, thus to enclose their enemies in their hands and give them so speedy a victory over so proud and insulting an enemy.

The Narragansett Indians all this while stood round about, but aloof from all danger and left the whole |224| execution to the English, except it were the stopping of any that broke away. Insulting over their enemies in this their ruin and misery, when they saw them dancing in the flames, calling them by a word in their own language, signifying "O brave Pequots!" which they used familiarly among themselves in their own praise in songs of triumph after their victories. After this service was thus happily accomplished, they marched to the waterside where they met with some of their vessels, by which they had refreshing with victuals and other necessaries. But in their march the rest of the Pequots drew into a body and accosted them, thinking to have some advantage against them by reason of a neck of land. But when they saw the English prepare for them they kept aloof, so as they neither did hurt nor could receive any.

After their refreshing, and repair together for further counsel and directions, they resolved to pursue their victory and follow the war against the rest. But the Narragansett Indians, most of them, forsook them, and such of them as they had with them for

[5] Leviticus ii.1–2.

guides or otherwise, they found them very cold and backward in the business, either out of envy, or that they saw the English would make more profit of the victory than they were willing they should; or else deprive them of such advantage as themselves desired, by having them become tributaries unto them, or the like.

For the rest of this business, I shall only relate the same as it is in a letter which came from Mr. Winthrop to the Governor here, as followeth.[6]

That I may make an end of this matter, this Sassacus (the Pequots' chief sachem) being fled to the Mohawks, they cut off his head, with some other of the chief of them, whether to satisfy the English or rather the Narragansetts (who, as I have since heard, hired them to do it) or for their own advantage, I well know not; but thus this war took end.[7] The rest of the Pequots were wholly driven from their place, and some of them submitted themselves to the Narragansetts and lived under them. Others of them betook themselves to the Mohegans under Uncas, their sachem, with the approbation of the English of Connecticut, under whose protection Uncas lived; and he and his men had been faithful to them in this war and done them very good service. But this did so vex the Narragansetts, that they had not the whole sway over them, as they have never ceased plotting and contriving how to bring them under; and because they cannot attain their ends, because of the English who have protected them, they have sought to raise a general conspiracy against the English, as will appear in another place.

[*Mr. Sherley Discharged*]

They had now letters again out of England from Mr. Andrews and Mr. Beauchamp, that Mr. Sherley neither had nor would pay them any money or give them any account; and so with much

[6] See Appendix VIII.

[7] Sassacus, said to have been 77 years old at the time of this war, was the most powerful sachem in southern New England. At the height of his power he ruled from Narragansett Bay to the Hudson, and a great part of Long Island too. It is believed that the Mohawks slew him in order to get possession of a treasure of wampum which he carried in his escape.

discontent desired them here to send them some, much blaming them still that they had sent all to Mr. Sherley and none to themselves. Now, though they might have justly referred them to their former answer and insisted thereupon (and some wise men counseled them so to do) yet because they believed that |227| they were really out round sums of money (especially Mr. Andrews) and they had some in their hands, they resolved to send them what beaver they had, but stayed it till the next year.

Mr. Sherley's letters were to this purpose, that, as they had left him in the payment of the former bills, so he had told them he would leave them in this; and believe it they should find it true? And he was as good as his word, for they could never get penny from him, nor bring him to any account, though Mr. Beauchamp sued him in the Chancery.[8]

But they all of them turned their complaints against them here, where there was least cause, and who had suffered most unjustly; first, from Mr. Allerton and them, in being charged with so much of that which they never had nor drunk for, and now in paying all, and more than all, as they conceived. And yet still thus more demanded, and that with many heavy charges. They now discharged Mr. Sherley from his agency and forbade him to buy or send over any more goods for them, and pressed him to come to some end about these things.

[8] Documents on this case are printed in Massachusetts Historical Society *Proceedings* XLV 611–23.

CHAPTER XXIX

Anno Dom: 1638

[*Englishmen Executed for Murdering an Indian*]

This year Mr. Thomas Prence was chosen Governor.

Amongst other enormities that fell out amongst them; this year three men were after due trial executed for robbery and murder which they had committed. Their names were these: Arthur Peach, Thomas Jackson and Richard Stinnings. There was a fourth, Daniel Cross, who was also guilty, but he escaped away and could not be found.

This Arthur Peach was the chief of them, and the ringleader of all the rest. He was a lusty and a desperate young man, and had been one of the soldiers in the Pequot War and had done as good service as the most there, and one of the forwardest in any attempt. And being now out of means and loath to work, and falling to idle courses and company, he intended to go to the Dutch plantation; and had allured these three, being other men's servants and apprentices, to go with him. But another cause there was also of his secret going away in this manner. He was not only run into debt, but he had got a maid with child (which was not known till after his death), a man's servant in the town, and fear of punishment made him get away. The other three complotting with him ran away from their masters in the night, and could not be heard of; for they went not the ordinary way, but shaped such a course as they thought to avoid the pursuit of any. |228| But falling into the way that lieth between the Bay of Massachusetts and the Narragansetts, and being disposed to rest themselves, struck fire and took tobacco, a little out of the way by the wayside.

At length there came a Narragansett Indian by, who had been in the Bay a-trading, and had both cloth and beads about him—they had met him the day before, and he was now returning. Peach called him to drink tobacco with them, and he came and sat down with them. Peach told the other he would kill him and take what he had from him, but they were something afraid. But he said, "Hang him, rogue, he had killed many of them." So they let him alone to do as he would. And when he saw his time, he took a rapier and ran him through the body once or twice and took from him five fathom of wampum and three coats of cloth and went their way, leaving him for dead. But he scrambled away when they were gone, and made shift to get home, but died within a few days after. By which means they were discovered. And by subtlety the Indians took them; for they, desiring a canoe to set them over a water, not thinking their fact had been known, by the sachem's command they were carried to Aquidneck Island and there accused of the murder, and were examined and committed upon it by the English there.

The Indians sent for Mr. Williams and made a grievous complaint; his friends and kindred were ready to rise in arms and provoke the rest thereunto, some conceiving they should now find the Pequots' words true, that the English would fall upon them. But Mr. Williams pacified them and told them they should see justice done upon the offenders, and went to the man and took Mr. James, a physician, with him. The man told him who did it, and in what manner it was done; but the physician found his wounds mortal and that he could not live, as he after testified upon oath before the jury in open court. And so he died shortly after, as both Mr. Williams, Mr. James and some Indians testified in court.

The Government in the Bay were acquainted with it but referred it hither because it was done in this jurisdiction;[1] but pressed by all means that justice might be done in it, or else the country must rise and see justice done; otherwise it would raise a war. Yet some of the rude and ignorant sort murmured that any English should be put to death for the Indians. So at last they of the Island[2] brought them hither, and being often examined and the evidence produced, they all in the end freely confessed in effect all that the Indian accused them of, and that they

[1] And yet afterwards they laid claim to those parts in the controversy about Seekonk (Bradford.)

[2] Rhode Island. This is believed to have been the first case of Englishmen being tried, found guilty and executed for the murder of an Indian. The reaction of the "rude and ignorant" is as significant as the action of the jury. More on this case in *Plymouth Colony Records* I 96, and 1912 ed. Bradford II 265–8. Crose or Cross, the murderer who escaped, was given sanctuary at the plantation he belonged to, Piscataqua, where (says Governor Winthrop) "all such lewd persons as fled from us" were given "countenance."

had done it in the manner aforesaid. And so, upon the forementioned evidence, were cast by the jury and condemned, and executed for the same, September 4. And some of the Narragansett Indians and of the party's friends were present when it was done, which gave them and all the country good satisfaction. But it was a matter of much sadness to them here, and was the second execution which they had since they came; being both for wilful murder, as hath been before related. Thus much of this matter. |229|

[*Beaver, Beef and Corn*]

They received this year more letters from England full of renewed complaints: on the one side, that they could get no money nor account from Mr. Sherley; and he again, that he was pressed thereto, saying he was to account with those here and not with them, etc. So, as was before resolved if nothing came of their last letters, they would now send them what they could, as supposing, when some good part was paid them, that Mr. Sherley and they would more easily agree about the remainder.

So they sent to Mr. Andrews and Mr. Beauchamp by Mr. Joseph Young in the *Mary and Anne* 1,325 pounds' weight of beaver, divided between them. Mr. Beauchamp returned an account of his moiety, that he made £400 sterling of it, freight and all charges paid. But Mr. Andrews, though he had the more and better part, yet he made not so much of his, through his own indiscretion; and yet turned the loss, being about £40, upon them here, but without cause.

They sent them more by bills and other payment, which was received and acknowledged by them, in money, and the like, and divided between them, which was for cattle sold of Mr. Allerton's, and the price of a bark sold which belonged to the stock, and made over to them in money £434 sterling. The whole sum was £1,234 sterling, save what Mr. Andrews lost in the beaver, which was otherwise made good. But yet this did not stay their clamours, as will appear hereafter more at large.

It pleased God in these times so to bless the country with such access and confluence of people into it, as it was thereby much enriched, and cattle of all kinds stood at a high rate for divers years together. Kine were sold at £20 and some at £25 apiece; yea, sometimes at £28; a cow calf usually at £10. A milch goat at £3 and some at £4, and female kids at 30*s* and often at 40*s* apiece. By which means the ancient planters which had any stock, began to grow in their estates. Corn also went at a round rate; viz. 6*s* a bushel, so as other trading began to be neglected, and the old partners (having now forbidden Mr. Sherley to send them any more goods) broke off their trade at Kennebec and, as things stood, would follow it no longer. But some of them, with other they joined with, being loath it should be lost by discontinuance, agreed with the company for it and gave them about the sixth part of their gains for it, |230| with the first fruits of which they built a house for a prison. And the trade there hath been since continued to the great benefit of the place. For some well foresaw that these high prices of corn and cattle would not long continue, and that then the commodities there raised would be much missed.

[*Great and Fearful Earthquake*]

This year, about the first or second of June, was a great and fearful earthquake. It was in this place heard before it was felt. It came with a rumbling noise or low murmur, like unto remote thunder. It came from the northward and passed southward; as the noise approached nearer, the earth began to shake and came at length with that violence as caused platters, dishes and suchlike things as stood upon shelves, to clatter and fall down. Yea, persons were afraid of the houses themselves. It so fell out that at the same time divers of the chief of this town were met together at one house, conferring with some of their friends that were upon their removal from the place, as if the Lord would hereby show the signs of His displeasure, in their shaking a-pieces and removals one from another. However, it was very terrible for the time, and as the men were set talking in the house, some women and others were without the doors, and the earth shook with that violence as they could not stand without catching hold of the posts and pales that stood next them. But the violence lasted not long. And about half an hour, or less came another noise and shaking, but neither so loud nor strong as the former, but quickly passed over and so it ceased. It was not only on the seacoast, but the Indians felt it within land, and some ships that were upon the coast were shaken by it. So powerful is the mighty hand of the Lord, as to make both the earth and sea to shake, and the mountains to tremble before Him, when He pleases. And who can stay His hand? [8]

It was observed that the summers for divers years together after this earthquake were not so hot and seasonable for the ripening of corn and other fruits as formerly, but more cold and moist, and subject to early and untimely frosts by which, many times, much Indian corn came not to maturity. But whether this was any cause I leave it to naturalists to judge.

[8] Haggai ii.6 and Daniel iv.35.

CHAPTER XXX

Anno Dom: 1639, *Anno Dom:* 1640

[*Border Dispute with the Bay Colony*]

These two years I join together, because in them fell not out many things more than the ordinary passages of their common affairs, which are not needful to be touched. |231|

Those of this Plantation having at sundry times granted lands for several townships, and amongst the rest to the inhabitants of Scituate,[1] some whereof issued from themselves. And also a large tract of land was given to their four London partners in that place, viz. Mr. Sherley, Mr. Beauchamp, Mr. Andrews and Mr. Hatherley. At Mr. Hatherley's request and choice it was by him taken for himself and them in that place, for the other three had invested him with power and trust to choose for them. And this tract of land extended to their utmost limits that way and bordered on their neighbours of the Massachusetts, who had some years after seated a town called Hingham on their lands next to these parts. So as now there grew great difference between these two townships about their bounds and some meadow grounds that lay between them.[2] They of Hingham presumed to allot part of them to their people, and measure and stake them out; the other pulled up their stakes and threw them. So it grew to a controversy between the two governments, and many letters and passages were between them about it. And it hung some two years in suspense. The Court of Massachusetts appointed some to range their line, according to the bounds of their Patent, and as they went to work, they made it to take in all Scituate, and I know not how much more. Again on the other hand, according to the line of the Patent of this place, it would take in Hingham, and much more within their bounds.

[1] In 1639 Plymouth Colony established representative government to replace the general assembly of all freemen. The towns represented besides Plymouth were Duxbury adjoining it on the north, Barnstable, Sandwich and Yarmouth on Cape Cod, Taunton on the Narragansett Bay watershed, and Scituate. This last town, northernmost of the Colony, became a flourishing farming and fishing community at an early date; a church was gathered there in 1635.

[2] The "Threescore Acres" of meadows lying in Cohasset, which was part of Hingham until 1775. In the absence of good native upland grass, the salt and fresh meadows were very highly valued in colonial New England.

In the end both Courts agreed to choose two commissioners of each side, and to give them full and absolute power to agree and settle the bounds between them; and what they should do in the case should stand irrevocably. One meeting they had at Hingham, but could not conclude; for their commissioners stood stiffly on a clause in their grant, that, from Charles River, or any branch or part thereof, they were to extend their limits and three miles further to the southward; or from the most southward part of the Massachusetts Bay, and three mile further. But they chose to stand on the former terms, for they had found a small river, or brook rather, that a great way within land trended southward, and issued into some part of that river taken to be Charles River; and from the most southerly part of this, and three mile more southward of the same, they would run a line east to the sea about 20 mile, which will (say they) take in a part of Plymouth itself. Now it is to be known that though this Patent and Plantation were much the ancienter, yet this enlargement of the same, in which Scituate stood, was granted after theirs; and so theirs were first to take place, before this enlargement.

Now their answer was, first, that however according to their own plan, they could no way come upon any part of their ancient grant. |232| Secondly, they could never prove that to be a part of Charles River, for they knew not which was Charles River, but as the people of this place, which came first, imposed such a name upon that river upon which, since, Charlestown is built—supposing that was it which Captain Smith in his map so named. Now they that first named it, have best reason to know it and to explain which is it. But they only took it to be Charles River as far as it was by them navigated, and that was as far as a boat could go. But that every runlet or small brook that should far within land come into it or mix their streams with it, and were by the natives called by other and different names from it, should now by them be made Charles River or parts of it, they saw no reason for it. And gave instance in Humber, in Old England, which had the Trent, Ouse, and many others of lesser note fell into it, and yet were not counted parts of it; and many smaller rivers and brooks fell into the Trent and Ouse, and no parts of them, but had names apart, and divisions and nominations of

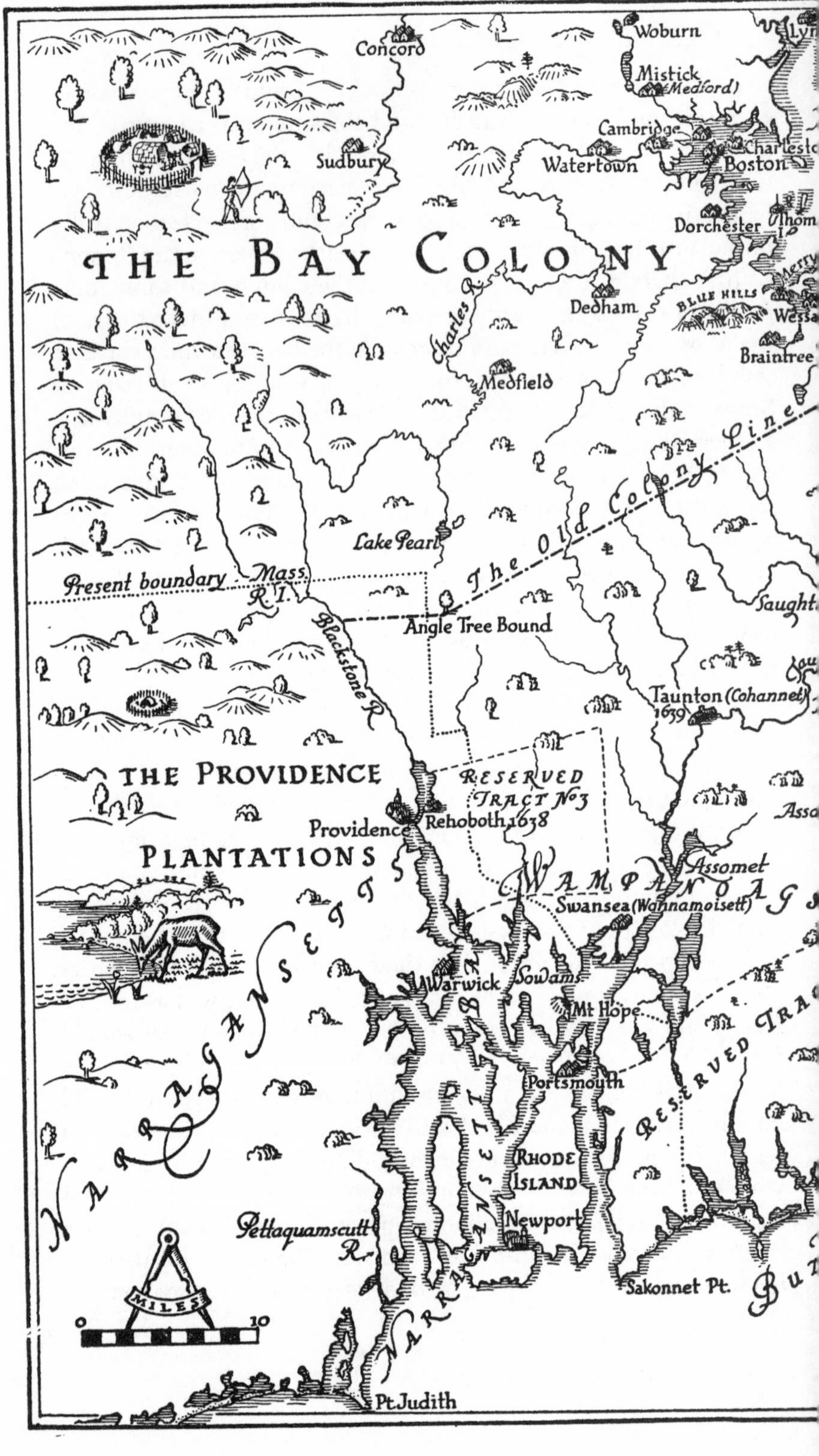

Concord
Woburn
Mistick
(Medford)
Cambridge
Charlestown
Sudbury
Watertown
Boston
Dorchester
THE BAY COLONY
Charles R.
Dedham
BLUE HILLS
Braintree
Medfield
The Old Colony Line
Lake Pearl
Present boundary
Mass.
R.I.
Angle Tree Bound
Blackstone R.
Taunton (Cohannet)
1639
THE PROVIDENCE
PLANTATIONS
RESERVED TRACT No 3
Providence
Rehoboth 1638
Assomet
WAMPANOAGS
Swansea (Wannamoisett)
NARRAGANSETTS
Warwick
Sowams
Mt Hope
Portsmouth
RESERVED TRACT
RHODE ISLAND
NARRAGANSETT BAY
Newport
Pettaquamscutt R.
MILES
0
10
Sakonnet Pt.
Pt Judith

The Colony of
NEW PLYMOUTH
Commonly known as "The Plymouth Plantation"
1620 ~ 1650
with Adjacent Settlements
SIGILLVM SOCIETATIS PLIMOTH NOVA ANGLIA
1620
Cohasset
Scituate, 1636
1640
Rexham
Greene Harbor
Duxbury 1637
Gurnet Pt.
Plymouth, 1620 (Patuxet)
Manomet Pt
Eel R.
Kittaumut
Manomet
Aptucxet Trading Post
Sandwich, 1639
Pocasset Hb.
Cataumet Hb.
MASHPEE
Cotuit
Woods Hole
CAPAWACK
Marthas Vineyard
Cape Cod
HIGHLANDS
Cape Cod Hb.
CAPE COD BAY
Nauset, 1643 (Eastham)
Nauset Hb.
Namskaket Cr.
RESERVED TRACT No 1
Yarmouth, 1638 (Mattakeeset)
Barnstable 1639
Shoals
NANTUCKET SOUND
Great Pt.
NANTUCKET I.
E. Raisz

themselves. Again, it was pleaded that they had no east line in their Patent but were to begin at the sea and go west by a line, etc.

At this meeting no conclusion was made, but things discussed and well prepared for an issue. The next year the same commissioners had their power continued or renewed, and met at Scituate and concluded the matter as followeth.[3] |233|

Whereas the Patent was taken in the name of William Bradford (as in trust) and ran in these terms: To him, his heirs, and associates and assigns. And now the number of freemen being much increased, and divers townships established and settled in several quarters of the government, as Plymouth, Duxbury, Scituate, Taunton, Sandwich, Yarmouth, Barnstable, Marshfield, and not long after Seekonk (called afterward at the desire of the inhabitants Rehoboth) and Nauset; it was by the Court desired that William Bradford should make a surrender of the same into their hands. The which he willingly did, in this manner following.[4] |235|

[*Sharp Business Deals*]

In these two years they had sundry letters out of England to send one over to end the business and account with Mr. Sherley, who now professed he could not make up his accounts without the help of some from hence, especially Mr. Winslow's. They had serious thoughts of it, and the most part of the partners here thought it best to send. But they had formerly written such bitter and threatening letters, as Mr. Winslow was neither willing to go, nor that any other of the partners should; for he was persuaded, if any of them went they should be arrested and an action of such a sum laid upon them as they should not procure bail but must lie in prison, and then they would bring them to what

[3] See Appendix XII, Official Documents, No. 3. A detailed history of this controversy is given in notes to 1912 ed. Bradford II 275–8. The boundary here described is still, for the most part, the present boundary between Norfolk and Plymouth Counties. Bound Brook, which flows into Cohasset Harbor, is marked where the main motor road from Boston to Plymouth crosses it; Accord Pond, still so called, is near Queen Anne's Corner in the south part of Hingham.

[4] See Appendix XII, Official Documents, No. 4.

they list; or otherwise they might be brought into trouble by the Archbishop's means, as the times then stood.[5] But, notwithstanding, they were much inclined to send, and Captain Standish was willing to go; but they resolved, seeing they could not all agree in this thing and that it was weighty and the consequence might prove dangerous, to take Mr. Winthrop's advice in the thing, and the rather because Mr. Andrews had by many letters acquainted him with the differences between them, and appointed him for his assign to receive his part of the debt.[6] And though they denied to pay him any as a debt till the controversy was ended, yet they had deposited £110 in money in his hands for Mr. Andrews, to pay to him in part as soon as he would come to any agreement with the rest.

But Mr. Winthrop was of Mr. Winslow's mind and dissuaded them from sending; so they broke off their resolution from sending, and returned this answer, that the times were dangerous as things stood with them, for they knew how Mr. Winslow had suffered formerly, and for a small matter was clapped up in the Fleet, and it was long before he could get out, to both his and their great loss and damage, and times were not better, but worse, in that respect. Yet that their equal and honest minds might appear to all men, they made them this tender; to refer the case to some gentlemen and merchants in the Bay of the Massachusetts, such as they should choose and were well known unto themselves—as they perceived there were many of their acquaintance and friends there, better known to them than the partners here. And let them be informed in the case by both sides, and have all the evidence that could be produced in writing or otherwise; and they would be bound to stand to their determination, and make good their award though it should cost them all they had in the world.

[5] Winslow wrote to Winthrop that with the death of the Lord Keeper Coventry and the retirement of Mr. Secretary Coke from the Privy Council, New England had lost her two best friends at court.

[6] The Andrews-Winthrop correspondence will be found in the Massachusetts Historical Society edition of *Winthrop Papers* IV and V. Andrews, by bringing forward his alleged munificence in a gift of cattle for the poor of Plymouth, managed to persuade Winthrop to act as his collection agency.

But this did not please them, but they were offended at it, without any great reason for aught I know, seeing neither side could give in clear accounts. The partners here could not, by reason they (to their smart) were failed by the accountant they sent them, and Mr. Sherley pretended he could not also; save, as they conceived it, a disparagement to yield to their inferiors in respect of the place, and other concurring circumstances. So this came to nothing; and afterward Mr. Sherley writ that if Mr. Winslow would meet him in France, the Low Countries or Scotland, let the place be known, and he come to him there. |236| But in regard of the troubles that now began to arise in our own nation, and other reasons, this did not come to any effect.

That which made them so desirous to bring things to an end, was partly to stop the clamours and aspersions raised and cast upon them hereabout, though they conceived themselves to sustain the greatest wrong, and had most cause of complaint. And partly because they feared the fall of cattle, in which most part of their estates lay. And this was not a vain fear, for they fell indeed before they came to a conclusion, and that so suddenly, as a cow that but a month before was worth £20 and would so have passed in any payment, fell now to £5 and would yield no more. And a goat that went at £3 or 50*s*, would now yield but 8*s* or 10*s* at most. All men feared a fall of cattle, but it was thought it would be by degrees, and not be from the highest pitch at once to the lowest as it did, which was greatly to the damage of many and the undoing of some.[7]

Another reason was, they many of them grew aged; and indeed a rare thing it was that so many partners should all live together so many years as these did; and saw many changes were like to befall, so as they were loath to leave these entanglements

[7] The same literal fall in the stock market is noted in Governor Winthrop's *Journal*. Hitherto the influx of people, bringing money and consumers' goods, had brought an abnormally high market for cattle. The sudden stoppage of emigration from England, due to the "troubles" that preceded the Civil War, was responsible for the decline. As Samuel Danforth jingled in his Almanac:

"That since the mighty *Cow* her crown hath lost,
In every place she's made to rule the roast."

—K. B. Murdock *Handkerchiefs from Paul* p. 106.

upon their children and posterity, who might be driven to remove places as they had done. Yea, themselves might do it yet before they died. But this business must yet rest, the next year gave it more ripeness, though it rendered them less able to pay, for the reasons aforesaid.

CHAPTER XXXI

Anno Dom: 1641 [*Agreement with the English Partners*]

Mr. Sherley being weary of this controversy and desirous of an end, as well as themselves, writ to Mr. John Atwood and Mr. William Collier, two of the inhabitants of this place, and of his special acquaintance, and desired them to be a means to bring this business to an end by advising and counseling the partners here by some way to bring it to a composition by mutual agreement. And he writ to themselves also to that end, as by his letter may appear, so much thereof as concerns the same I shall here relate.[1] |237|

Being thus by this letter, and also by Mr. Atwood's and Mr. Collier's mediation urged to bring things to an end; and the continual clamours from the rest, and by none more urged than by their own desires; they took this course because many scandals had been raised upon them. They appointed these two men before mentioned to meet on a certain day, and called some other friends on both sides, and Mr. Freeman, brother-in-law to Mr. Beauchamp, and having drawn up a collection of all the remains of the stock, in whatsoever it was, as housing, boats, bark and all implements belonging to the same, as they were used in the time of trade were they better or worse, with the remains of all commodities as beads, knives, hatchets, cloth or anything else, as well the refuse as the more vendible, with all debts, as well those that were desperate as others more hopeful. And having spent divers days to bring this to pass, having the help of all books and papers which either any of themselves had, or Josias Winslow who was their accountant. And they found the sum in all to arise (as the things were valued) to about £1400. And they all of them took a voluntary but a solemn oath in the presence one of another and of all their friends, the persons abovesaid that were now present, that this was all that any of them knew of or could remember; and Josias Winslow did the like for his part.

But the truth is, they wronged themselves much in the valuation, for they reckoned some cattle as they were taken of Mr.

[1] See Appendix IX.

Allerton, for instance, a cow in the hands of one cost £25 and so she was valued in this account; but when she came to be passed away in part of payment, after the agreement, she would be accepted but at £4 15*s*. |238| Also, being tender of their oaths, they brought in all they knew owing to the stock, but they had not made the like diligent search what the stock might owe to any; so as many scattering debts fell upon afterwards more than now they knew of. Upon this they drew certain articles of agreement between Mr. Atwood, on Mr. Sherley's behalf, and themselves. The effect is as followeth.[2]

The next year, this long and tedious business came to some issue, as will then appear, though not to a final end with all the parties, but thus much for the present.

[*Another Troublesome Minister*]

I had forgotten to insert in its place how the church here had invited and sent for Mr. Charles Chauncy,[3] a reverend, godly and very learned man, intending upon trial to choose him pastor of the church here, for the more comfortable performance of the ministry with Mr. John Rayner, the teacher of the same. Mr. Chauncy came to them in the year 1638 and stayed till the latter part of this year 1641. But there fell out some difference about baptizing, he holding it ought only to be by dipping, and putting the whole body under water, and that sprinkling was unlawful. The church yielded that immersion or dipping was lawful but in this cold country not so convenient. But they could not, nor durst not yield to him in this, that sprinkling (which all the churches of Christ do for the most part use at this day) was unlawful and an human invention, as the same was pressed. But they were willing

[2] See Appendix IX.

[3] The Rev. Charles Chauncy B.D., sometime fellow and Greek lecturer at Trinity College, Cambridge, and subsequently a minister of the Church of England, was probably the most learned man of the Puritan migration; but he was handicapped by an over-tender conscience and a tendency to adopt odd conceits. During his English career he was thrice brought up sharp by the University or by the Archbishop, thrice recanted and thrice retracted his recantation.

to yield to him as far as they could, and to the utmost, and were contented to suffer him to practice as he was persuaded. And when he came to minister that ordinance he might so do it to any that did desire it in that way, provided he could peaceably suffer Mr. Rayner and such as desired to have theirs otherwise baptized by him by sprinkling or pouring on of water upon them, so as there might be no disturbance in the church hereabout. But he said he could not yield hereunto. Upon which the church procured some other ministers to dispute the point with him publicly, as Mr. Ralph Partridge of Duxbury, who did it sundry times, very ably and sufficiently; as also some other ministers within this government. But he was not satisfied. So the church sent to many other churches to crave their help and advice in |241| this matter, and with his will and consent sent them his arguments written under his own hand. They sent them to the church at Boston in the Bay of Massachusetts, to be communicated with other churches there. Also they sent the same to the churches of Connecticut and New Haven, with sundry others. And received very able and sufficient answers, as they conceived, from them and their learned ministers who all concluded against him. But himself was not satisfied therewith. Their answers are too large here to relate.

They conceived the church had done what was meet in the thing, so Mr. Chauncy, having been the most part of three years here removed himself to Scituate, where he now remains a minister to the church there.[4]

Also about these times, now that cattle and other things began greatly to fall from their former rates and persons began to fall into more straits, and many being already gone from them, as is noted before, both to Duxbury, Marshfield and other places, and those of the chief sort, as Mr. Winslow, Captain Standish, Mr.

[4] Chauncy was not long getting in trouble there; Governor Winthrop in his *Journal* for 1642 tells of his baptizing his own twins by total immersion, which caused one of them to swoon, after which an irate mother whose child's turn came next, caught hold of the pastor and "near pulled him into the water." Chauncy also insisted on celebrating the Lord's Supper in the evening. In 1654 he was about to return to England when he was elected President of Harvard College, and accepted after promising to keep his views on baptism to himself.

Alden and many other, and still some dropping away daily, and some at this time and many more unsettled, it did greatly weaken the place. And by reason of the straitness and barrenness of the place, it set the thoughts of many upon removal, as will appear more hereafter.

CHAPTER XXXII

Anno Dom: 1642 [*Wickedness Breaks Forth*]

Marvelous it may be to see and consider how some kind of wickedness did grow and break forth here, in a land where the same was so much witnessed against and so narrowly looked unto, and severely punished when it was known, as in no place more, or so much, that I have known or heard of; insomuch that they have been somewhat censured even by moderate and good men for their severity in punishments. And yet all this could not suppress the breaking out of sundry notorious sins (as this year, besides other, gives us too many sad precedents and instances), especially drunkenness and uncleanness. Not only incontinency between persons unmarried, for which many both men and women have been punished sharply enough, but some married persons also. But that which is worse, even sodomy and buggery (things fearful to name) have broke forth in this land oftener than once.

I say it may justly be marveled at and cause us to fear and tremble at the consideration of our corrupt natures, which are so hardly bridled, subdued and mortified; nay, cannot by any other means but the powerful work and grace of God's Spirit. But (besides this) one reason may be that the Devil may carry a greater spite against the churches of Christ and the gospel here, by how much the more they endeavour to preserve holiness and purity amongst them and strictly punisheth the contrary when it ariseth either in church or commonwealth; that he might cast a |242| blemish and stain upon them in the eyes of [the] world, who use to be rash in judgment. I would rather think thus, than that Satan hath more power in these heathen lands, as some have thought, than in more Christian nations, especially over God's servants in them.

2. Another reason may be, that it may be in this case as it is with waters when their streams are stopped or dammed up. When they get passage they flow with more violence and make more noise and disturbance than when they are suffered to run quietly in their own channels; so wickedness being here more stopped by strict laws, and the same more nearly looked unto so as it cannot run in a common road of liberty as it would and is

inclined, it searches everywhere and at last breaks out where it gets vent.

3. A third reason may be, here (as I am verily persuaded) is not more evils in this kind, nor nothing near so many by proportion as in other places; but they are here more discovered and seen and made public by due search, inquisition and due punishment; for the churches look narrowly to their members, and the magistrates over all, more strictly than in other places. Besides, here the people are but few in comparison of other places which are full and populous and lie hid, as it were, in a wood or thicket and many horrible evils by that means are never seen nor known; whereas here they are, as it were, brought into the light and set in the plain field, or rather on a hill, made conspicuous to the view of all.

But to proceed. There came a letter from the Governor in the Bay to them here, touching matters of the forementioned nature which, because it may be useful, I shall here relate it and the passages thereabout.

SIR: Having an opportunity to signify the desires of our General Court in two things of special importance, I willingly take this occasion to impart them to you, that you may impart them to the rest of your magistrates and also to your Elders for counsel, and give us your advice in them. The first is concerning heinous offenses in point of uncleanness; the particular cases with the circumstances and the questions thereupon, you have here enclosed.

The second thing is concerning the Islanders at Aquidneck.[1] That seeing the chiefest of them are gone from us in offenses either to churches or commonwealth or both, others are dependents on them, and the best sort are such as close with them in all their rejections of us. Neither is it only in faction that they are divided from us, but in very deed they rend themselves from all the true churches of Christ

[1] I.e., Rhode Island. Roger Williams was already settled at Providence, Anne Hutchinson at Portsmouth and William Coddington at Newport; Samuel Gorton was about to found a fourth settlement of sectaries at Warwick. The Bay authorities were in a great stew about the "Islanders," whom they viewed in much the same light as Catholics now regard Communists, and debated whether to annex their territory and try to suppress dissent by force, or to persuade Plymouth to do it, or to let them alone. Before they could reach a decision, Roger Williams obtained the Providence Plantations Patent from Parliament in 1644, which gave Rhode Island an unassailable legal standing.

and, many of them, from all the powers of magistracy. We have had some experience hereof by some of their underworkers or emissaries who have lately come amongst us and have made public defiance against magistracy, ministry, churches and church covenants, etc. as antichristian. Secretly, also, sowing the seeds of Familism and Anabaptistry, to the infection of some and danger of others; so that we are not willing to join with them in any league or confederacy at all, but rather that you would consider and advise with us how we may avoid them and keep ours from being infected by them.

Another thing I should mention to you, for the maintenance of the trade of beaver. If there be not a company to order it in every jurisdiction among the English, which companies should agree in general of their way in trade, I suppose that the trade will be overthrown and the Indians will abuse us. For this cause we have lately put it into order amongst us, hoping of encouragement from you (as we have had) that we may continue the same.

Thus not further to trouble you, I rest, with my loving remembrance to yourself, etc.

Your loving friend,
Boston, 28. 1. [March] 1642 RICHARD BELLINGHAM

The note enclosed follows on the other side.[2] |244|

WORTHY AND BELOVED SIR: Your letter (with the questions enclosed) I have communicated with our Assistants, and we have referred the answer of them to such Reverend Elders as are amongst us, some of whose answers thereto we have here sent you enclosed under their own hands; from the rest we have not yet received any. Our far distance hath been the reason of this long delay, as also that they could not confer their counsels together.

For ourselves (you know our breedings and abilities), we rather

[2] The verso of fol. 242, which Bradford usually means by "the other side," is not written on, and the next folio is numbered 244. Prince noted at the beginning of the ms. that there was no fol. 243 when the book came into his possession in 1728. There is, however, no evidence, such as a stub, of a leaf having been cut out at that place. I think that Bradford merely skipped a number inadvertently or that he intended to copy Governor Bellingham's "note enclosed" on 242 v. and number it 243, but either forgot to do so or decided that it was unnecessary because the substance of the Governor's enclosure is contained in the questions answered by Mr. Rayner (Appendix X). The New England colonies had not yet got around to passing laws against unnatural vice, so they had to fall back on Biblical law; hence this reference to the theologians.

desire light from yourselves and others, whom God hath better enabled, than to presume to give our judgments in cases so difficult and of so high a nature. Yet under correction, and submission to better judgments, we propose this one thing to your prudent considerations. As it seems to us, in the case even of wilful murder, that though a man did smite or wound another with a full purpose or desire to kill him (which is murder in a high degree before God), yet if he did not die, the magistrate was not to take away the other's life.[3] So by proportion in other gross and foul sins, though high attempts and near approaches to the same be made, and such as in the sight and account of God may be as ill as the accomplishment of the foulest acts of that sin, yet we doubt whether it may be safe for the magistrate to proceed to death; we think, upon the former grounds, rather he may not. As, for instance, in the case of adultery. If it be admitted that it is to be punished with death, which to some of us is not clear; if the body be not actually defiled, then death is not to be inflicted. So in sodomy and bestiality, if there be not penetration. Yet we confess foulness of circumstances, and frequency in the same, doth make us remain in the dark and desire further light from you, or any as God shall give.

As for the second thing, concerning the Islanders? We have no conversing with them, nor desire to have, further than necessity or humanity may require.

As for trade? We have as far as we could, ever therein held an orderly course, and have been sorry to see the spoil thereof by others, and fear it will hardly be recovered.[4] But in these, or any other things which may concern the common good, we shall be willing to advise and concur with you in what we may. Thus with my love remembered to yourself, and the rest of our worthy friends your Assistants, I take leave, and rest

Your loving friend,
Plymouth: 17, 3 month [May] 1642 — William Bradford

Now follows the ministers' answer. And first, Mr. Rayner's.[5] Besides the occasion before mentioned in these writings con-

[3] Exodus xxi.22, Deuteronomy xix.11, Numbers xxxv.16–18 (Bradford).

[4] The local fur trade was evidently running out, since the General Court of Plymouth in 1640–1 offered to grant the monopoly to anyone for £20. *Plymouth Colony Records* II 4, 10.

[5] See Appendix X.

cerning the abuse of those two children,[6] they had about the same time a case of buggery fell out amongst them, which occasioned these questions, to which these answers have been made.

[*A Horrible Case of Bestiality*]

And after the time of the writing of these things befell a very sad accident of the like foul nature in this government, this very year, which I shall now relate. There was a youth whose name was Thomas Granger. He was servant to an honest man of Duxbury, being about 16 or 17 years of age. (His father and mother lived at the same time at Scituate.) He was this year detected of buggery, and indicted for the same, with a mare, a cow, two goats, five sheep, two calves and a turkey. Horrible |249| it is to mention, but the truth of the history requires it. He was first discovered by one that accidentally saw his lewd practice towards the mare. (I forbear particulars.) Being upon it examined and committed, in the end he not only confessed the fact with that beast at that time, but sundry times before and at several times with all the rest of the forenamed in his indictment. And this his free confession was not only in private to the magistrates (though at first he strived to deny it) but to sundry, both ministers and others; and afterwards, upon his indictment, to the whole Court and jury; and confirmed it at his execution. And whereas some of the sheep could not so well be known by his description of them, others with them were brought before him and he declared which were they and which were not. And accordingly he was cast by the jury and condemned, and after executed about the 8th of September, 1642. A very sad spectacle it was. For first the mare and then the cow and the rest of the lesser cattle were killed before his face, according to the law, Leviticus xx.15; and then he himself was executed. The cattle were all cast into a great and

[6] John Humfry, one of the Assistants of the Bay Colony, went back to England, leaving his 8- and 9-year-old daughters in charge of a former servant at Lynn, a married man "member of the church there, and in good esteem for piety and sobriety." This man and a hired man raped the girls. Despite the opinions of the reverend elders, both men got off with a fine and whipping, since the offense was not capital by any law of Massachusetts. Governor Winthrop gives the lurid details in his *Journal* for 1641.

large pit that was digged of purpose for them, and no use made of any part of them.

Upon the examination of this person and also of a former that had made some sodomitical attempts upon another, it being demanded of them how they came first to the knowledge and practice of such wickedness, the one confessed he had long used it in old England; and this youth last spoken of said he was taught it by another that had heard of such things from some in England when he was there, and they kept cattle together. By which it appears how one wicked person may infect many, and what care all ought to have what servants they bring into their families.

But it may be demanded how came it to pass that so many wicked persons and profane people should so quickly come over into this land and mix themselves amongst them? Seeing it was religious men that began the work and they came for religion's sake? I confess this may be marveled at, at least in time to come, when the reasons thereof should not be known; and the more because here was so many hardships and wants met withal. I shall therefore endeavour to give some answer hereunto.

1. And first, according to that in the gospel, it is ever to be remembered that where the Lord begins to sow good seed, there the envious man will endeavour to sow tares.

2. Men being to come over into a wilderness, in which much labour and service was to be done about building and planting, etc., such as wanted help in that respect, when they could not have such as they would, were glad to take such as they could; and so, many untoward servants, sundry of them proved, that were thus brought over, both men and womenkind who, when their times were expired, became families of themselves, which gave increase hereunto.

3. Another and a main reason hereof was that men, finding so many godly disposed persons willing to come into these parts, some began to make a trade of it, to transport passengers and their goods, and hired ships for that end. And then, to make up their freight and advance their profit, cared not who the persons were, so they had money to pay them. And by this means the country became pestered with many unworthy persons who, being come over, crept into one place or other.

4. Again, the Lord's blessing usually following His people as well in outward as spiritual things (though afflictions be mixed withal) do make many to adhere to the People of God, as many followed Christ for the loaves' sake (John vi.26) and a "mixed multitude" came into the wilderness with the People of God out of Egypt of old (Exodus xii.38). So also there were sent by their friends, some under hope that they would be made better; others that they might be eased of such burthens, and they kept from shame at home, that would necessarily follow their dissolute courses. And thus, by one means or other, in 20 years' time it is a question whether the greater part be not grown the worser? [7] |250|

[*Conclusion of a Long and Tedious Business*]

I am now come to the conclusion of that long and tedious business between the partners here and them in England, the which I shall manifest by their own letters as followeth, in such parts of them as are pertinent to the same.[8]

Mr. Andrews his discharge was to the same effect.[9] He was by agreement to have £500 of the money, the which he gave to them in the Bay, who brought his discharge and demanded the money. And they took in his release and paid the money according to agreement; viz. one third of the £500 they paid down in hand, and the rest in four equal payments, to be paid yearly, for which they gave their bonds. And whereas £44 was more demanded, they conceived they could take it off with Mr. Andrews, and therefore it was not in the bond. |252| But Mr. Beauchamp would not part with any of his, but demanded £400 of the partners here, and sent a release to a friend to deliver it to them upon the receipt of the money. But his release was not perfect, for he

7 Captain John Smith in his *Generall Historie of Virginia, New England, and the Summer Isles* (1624) tells of a very similar outbreak of bestiality at Bermuda in 1622. "Such a multitude of wild people were sent to this Plantation," he says, that Governor Butler "thought himself happy his time was so near expired."

8 See Appendix XI.

9 As Sherley's release, for which see Appendix XI; Sherley discharged the Undertakers for a payment of £1200, £900 of which was transferred to the Bay Colony to collect.

had left out some of the partners' names, with some other defects, and besides the other gave them to understand he had not near so much due. So no end was made with him till four years after, of which in its place. And in that regard, that themselves did not agree, I shall insert some part of Mr. Andrews' letter, by which he conceives the partners here were wronged, as followeth. This letter of his was writ to Mr. Edmund Freeman, brother-in-law to Mr. Beauchamp.

This letter was writ the year after the agreement, as doth appear; and what his judgment was herein the contents doth manifest; and so I leave it to the equal judgment of any to consider as they see cause, only I shall add what Mr. Sherley further writ in a letter of his, about the same time, and so leave this business. His is as followeth on the other side.[1]

[1] Both letters are in Appendix XI.

CHAPTER XXXIII

Anno Dom: 1643 [*The Life and Death of Elder Brewster*]

I am to begin this year with that which was a matter of great sadness and mourning unto them all. About the 18th of April died their Reverend Elder and my dear and loving friend Mr. William Brewster, a man that had done and suffered much for the Lord Jesus and the gospel's sake, and had borne his part in weal and woe with this poor persecuted church above 36 years |254| in England, Holland and in this wilderness, and done the Lord and them faithful service in his place and calling. And notwithstanding the many troubles and sorrows he passed through, the Lord upheld him to a great age. He was near fourscore years of age (if not all out) when he died. He had this blessing added by the Lord to all the rest; to die in his bed, in peace, amongst the midst of his friends, who mourned and wept over him and ministered what help and comfort they could unto him, and he again recomforted them whilst he could. His sickness was not long, and till the last day thereof he did not wholly keep his bed. His speech continued till somewhat more than half a day, and then failed him, and about nine or ten a clock that evening he died without any pangs at all. A few hours before, he drew his breath short, and some few minutes before his last, he drew his breath long as a man fallen into a sound sleep without any pangs or gaspings, and so sweetly departed this life unto a better.

I would now demand of any, what he was the worse for any former sufferings? What do I say, worse? Nay, sure he was the better, and they now added to his honour. "It is a manifest token," saith the Apostle, 2 Thessalonians i.5, 6, 7, "of the righteous judgment of God that ye may be counted worthy of the kingdom of God, for which ye also suffer; seeing it is a righteous thing with God to recompense tribulation to them that trouble you; and to you who are troubled, rest with us, when the Lord Jesus shall be revealed from heaven, with his mighty angels." 1 Peter iv.14: "If you be reproached for the name of Christ, happy are ye, for the spirit of glory and a God resteth upon you."

What though he wanted [1] the riches and pleasure of the world in his life, and pompous monuments at his funeral? Yet "the memorial of the just shall be blessed, when the name of the wicked shall rot" (with their marble monuments). Proverbs x.7.[2]

I should say something of his life, if to say a little were not worse than to be silent. But I cannot wholly forbear, though happily more may be done hereafter. After he had attained some learning, viz. the knowledge of the Latin tongue and some insight in the Greek, and spent some small time at Cambridge, and then being first seasoned with the seeds of grace and virtue, he went to the Court and served that religious and godly gentleman Mr. Davison, divers years when he was Secretary of State. Who found him so discreet and faithful as he trusted him above all other that were about him, and only employed him in all matters of greatest trust and secrecy; he esteemed him rather as a son than a servant, and for his wisdom and godliness, in private he would converse with him more like a friend and familiar than a master. He attended his master when he was sent in ambassage by the Queen into the Low Countries, in the Earl of Leicester's time, as for other weighty affairs of state; so to receive possession of the cautionary towns, and in token and sign thereof the keys of Flushing being delivered to him in Her Majesty's name, he kept them some time and committed them to this his servant who kept them under his pillow, on which he slept the first night. And at his return the States honoured him with a gold chain and his master committed it to him and commanded him to wear it when they arrived in England, as they rid through the country, till they came to the Court. He afterwards remained with him till his troubles, that he was put from his place about the death of the Queen of Scots; and some good time after doing him many faithful offices of service in the time of his troubles. Afterwards he went and lived in the country, in good esteem amongst his friends and the gentlemen of those parts, especially the godly and religious.

He did much good in the country where he lived in promoting and furthering religion, not only by his practice and example, and provoking and encouraging of others, but by procuring of

[1] I.e., lacked.

[2] This quotation is from the Geneva Bible; the others from the King James.

good preachers to the places thereabout and drawing on of others to assist and help forward in such a work. He himself most commonly deepest in the charge, and sometimes above his ability. And in this state he continued many years, doing the best good he could and walking according to the light he saw, till the Lord revealed further unto him. And in the end, by the tyranny of the bishops against godly preachers and people in silencing the one and persecuting the other, he and many more of those times began to look further into things and to see into the unlawfulness of their callings, and the burthen of many antichristian corruptions, which both he and they endeavoured to cast off; as they also did as in the beginning of this treatise is to be seen. |255|

After they were joined together in communion, he was a special stay and help unto them. They ordinarily met at his house on the Lord's Day (which was a manor of the bishop's) and with great love he entertained them when they came, making provision for them to his great charge, and continued so to do whilst they could stay in England. And when they were to remove out of the country he was one of the first in all adventures, and forwardest in any charge. He was the chief of those that were taken at Boston, and suffered the greatest loss, and of the seven that were kept longest in prison and after bound over to the assizes. After he came into Holland he suffered much hardship after he had spent the most of his means, having a great charge and many children; and in regard of his former breeding and course of life, not so fit for many employments as others were, especially such as were toilsome and laborious. But yet he ever bore his condition with much cheerfulness and contentation.

Towards the latter part of those twelve years spent in Holland, his outward condition was mended, and he lived well and plentifully; for he fell into a way (by reason he had the Latin tongue) to teach many students who had a desire to learn the English tongue, to teach them English; and by his method they quickly attained it with great facility, for he drew rules to learn it by after the Latin manner. And many gentlemen, both Danes and Germans, resorted to him as they had time from other studies, some of them being great men's sons. He also had means to set up printing by the help of some friends, and so had employment enough, and by reason of many books which would not be allowed to be printed in England, they might have had more than they could do.

But now removing into this country all these things were laid aside again, and a new course of living must be framed unto, in which he was no way unwilling to take his part, and to bear his burthen with the rest, living many times without bread or corn many months together, having many times nothing but fish and often wanting that also; and drunk nothing but water for many years together, yea till within five or six years of his death. And yet he lived by the blessing of God in health till very old age. And besides that, he would labour with his hands in the fields as long as he was able. Yet when the church had no other minister, he taught twice every Sabbath, and that both powerfully and profitably, to the great contentment of the hearers and their comfortable edification; yea, many were brought to God by his ministry. He did more in this behalf in a year than many that have their hundreds a year do in all their lives.

For his personal abilities, he was qualified above many. He was wise and discreet and well spoken, having a grave and deliberate utterance, of a very cheerful spirit, very sociable and pleasant amongst his friends, of an humble and modest mind, of a peaceable disposition, undervaluing himself and his own abilities and sometime overvaluing others. Inoffensive and innocent in his life and conversation, which gained him the love of those without as well as those within; yet he would tell them plainly of their faults and evils, both publicly and privately, but in such a manner as usually was well taken from him. He was tenderhearted and compassionate of such as were in misery, but especially of such as had been of good estate and rank and were fallen unto want and poverty either for goodness and religion's sake or by the injury and oppression of others; he would say of all men these deserved to be pitied most. And none did more offend and displease him than such as would haughtily and proudly carry and lift up themselves, being risen from nothing and having little else in them to commend them but a few fine clothes or a little riches more than others.

In teaching, he was very moving and stirring of affections, also very plain and distinct in what he taught; by which means he became the more profitable to the hearers. He had a singular good gift in prayer, both public and private, in ripping up the heart and conscience before God in the humble confession of sin, and begging the mercies of God in Christ for the pardon of the same. He always thought it were better for ministers to pray oftener and divide their prayers, than be long and tedious in the same, except upon solemn and special occasions as in days of humiliation and the like. His reason was that the heart and spirits of all, especially the weak, could hardly continue and stand bent as it were so long towards God as they ought to do in that duty, without flagging and falling off.

For the government of the church, which was most |256| proper to his office, he was careful to preserve good order in the same, and to preserve purity both in the doctrine and communion of the same, and to suppress any errour or contention that might begin to rise up amongst them. And accordingly God gave good success to his endeavours herein all his days, and he saw the fruit of his labours in that behalf. But I must break off, having only thus touched a few, as it were, heads of things.

[*Longevity of the Pilgrim Fathers*]

I cannot but here take occasion not only to mention but greatly to admire the marvelous providence of God! That notwithstanding the many changes and hardships that these people went through, and the many enemies they had and difficulties they met withal, that so many of them should live to very old age! It was not only this reverend man's condition (for one swallow makes no summer as they say) but many more of them did the like, some dying about and before this time and many still living, who attained to sixty years of age, and to sixty-five, divers to seventy and above, and some near eighty as he did. It must needs be more than ordinary and above natural reason, that so it should be. For it is found in experience that change of air, famine or unwholesome food, much drinking of water, sorrows and troubles, etc., all of them are enemies to health, causes of many diseases, consumers of natural vigour and the bodies of men, and shorteners of life. And yet of all these things they had a large part and suffered deeply in the same. They went from England to Holland, where they found both worse air and diet than that they came from; from thence, enduring a long imprisonment as it were in the ships at sea, into New England; and how it hath been with them here hath already been shown, and what crosses, troubles, fears, wants and sorrows they had been liable unto is easy to conjecture. So as in some sort they may say with the Apostle, 2 Corinthians xi.26, 27, they were "in journeyings often, in perils of waters, in perils of robbers, in perils of their own nation, in perils among the heathen, in perils in the wilderness, in perils in the sea, in perils among false brethren; in weariness and painfulness, in watching often, in hunger and thirst, in fasting often, in cold and nakedness."

What was it then that upheld them? It was God's visitation that preserved their spirits. Job x.12: "Thou hast given me life and grace, and thy visitation hath preserved my spirit." He that upheld the Apostle upheld them. "They were persecuted, but not forsaken, cast down, but perished not." "As unknown, and yet known; as dying, and behold we live; as chastened, and yet not killed"; 2 Corinthians vi.9.

God, it seems, would have all men to behold and observe such mercies and works of His providence as these are towards His people, that they in like cases might be encouraged to depend upon God in their trials, and also to bless His name when they see His goodness towards others. Man lives not by bread only, Deuteronomy viii.3. It is not by good and dainty fare, by peace and rest and heart's ease in enjoying the contentments and good things of this world only that preserves health and prolongs life; God in such examples would have the world see and behold that He can do it without them; and if the world will shut their eyes and take no notice thereof, yet He would have His people to see and consider it. Daniel could be better liking with pulse than others were with the king's dainties. Jacob, though he went from one nation to another people and passed through famine, fears and many afflictions, yet he lived till old age and died sweetly and rested in the Lord, as infinite others of God's servants have done and still shall do, through God's goodness, notwithstanding all the malice of their enemies, "when the branch of the wicked shall be cut off before his day" (Job xv.32) "and the bloody and deceitful men shall not live [out] half their days"; Psalm lv.23.

[*The New England Confederation and the Narragansetts*]

By reason of the plottings of the Narragansetts ever since the Pequots' War the Indians were drawn into a general conspiracy against the English in all parts, as was in part discovered the year before; and now made more plain and evident by many discoveries and free confessions of sundry Indians upon several occasions from divers places, concurring in one. With such other concurring circumstances as gave them sufficiently to understand the truth thereof. And to think of means how to prevent the same and secure themselves. Which made them enter into this more near union and confederation following.[3] |260|

These were the articles of agreement in the union and confederation which they now first entered into. And in this their first meeting held at Boston the day and year abovesaid, amongst other things they had this matter of great consequence to consider on:

The Narragansetts, after the subduing of the Pequots, thought to have ruled over all the Indians about them. But the English, especially those of Connecticut, holding correspondency and friendship with Uncas, sachem of the Mohegan Indians which lived near them (as the Massachusetts had done with the Narragansetts) and he had been faithful to them in the Pequot War, they were engaged to support him in his just liberties and were contented that such of the surviving Pequots as had submitted to him should remain with him and quietly under his protection. This did much increase his power and augment his greatness, which the Narragansetts could not endure to see. But Miantonomo,[4] their chief sachem, an ambitious and politic man, sought

[3] See Appendix XII, Official Documents, No. 5.

[4] Miantonomo, a nephew of Canonicus, was apparently jealous of the favor shown by the English to their faithful ally, Uncas.

privately and by treachery, according to the Indian manner, to make him away by hiring some to kill him. Sometime they assayed to poison him; that not taking, then in the night time to knock him on the head in his house or secretly to shoot him, and suchlike attempts. But none of these taking effect, he made open war upon him (though it was against the covenants both between the English and them, as also between themselves and a plain breach of the same). He came suddenly upon him with 900 or 1000 men, never denouncing any war before. The other's power at that present was not above half so many, but it pleased God to give Uncas the victory and he slew many of his men and wounded many more; but the chief of all was, he took Miantonomo prisoner.

And seeing he was a great man, and the Narragansetts a potent people and would seek revenge, he would do nothing in the case without the advice of the English, so he, by the help and direction of those of Connecticut, kept him prisoner till this meeting of the Commissioners. The Commissioners weighed the cause and passages as they were clearly represented and sufficiently evidenced betwixt Uncas and Miantonomo; and the things being duly considered, the Commissioners apparently saw that Uncas could not be safe whilst Miantonomo lived; but either by secret treachery or open force, his life would be still in danger. Wherefore they thought he might justly put such a false and bloodthirsty enemy to death; but in his own jurisdiction, not in the English plantations. And they advised in the manner of his death all mercy and moderation should be showed, contrary to the practice of the Indians, who exercise tortures and cruelty. And |261| Uncas having hitherto showed himself a friend to the English, and in this craving their advice, if the Narragansett Indians or others shall unjustly assault Uncas for this execution, upon notice and request the English promise to assist and protect him as far as they may against such violence.

This was the issue of this business. The reasons and passages hereof are more at large to be seen in the acts and records of this meeting of the Commissioners. And Uncas followed this advice and accordingly executed him in a very fair manner according as they advised, with due respect to his honour and greatness.[5] But what followed on the Narragansetts' part will appear hereafter.

[5] The alleged "fair manner" was being bound and slain by a hatchet wielded by Uncas's brother. "This disgraceful proceeding," as Hodge's *Handbook* terms it, has lain heavily on the New England conscience ever since; and it is strongly suspected that the Confederation wished to make an example of Miantonomo because he had sold land to Roger Williams and Samuel Gorton. A monument was erected to Miantonomo in 1841 at the scene of his murder in Norwich, Conn., and several vessels of the United States Navy have been named after him; a better tribute to his "honour and greatness" than being dispatched with a hatchet.

CHAPTER XXXIV

Anno Dom: 1644 [*Proposal to Remove to Nauset*]

Mr. Edward Winslow was chosen Governor this year.

Many having left this place (as is before noted) by reason of the straitness and barrenness of the same and their finding of better accommodations elsewhere more suitable to their ends and minds; and sundry others still upon every occasion desiring their dismissions, the church began seriously to think whether it were not better jointly to remove to some other place than to be thus weakened and as it were insensibly dissolved.[1] Many meetings and much consultation was held hereabout, and divers were men's minds and opinions. Some were still for staying together in this place, alleging men might here live if they would be content with their condition, and that it was not for want or necessity so much that they removed as for the enriching of themselves. Others were resolute upon removal and so signified that here they could not stay; but if the church did not remove, they must. Insomuch as many were swayed rather than there should be a dissolution, to condescend to a removal if a fit place could be found that might more conveniently and comfortably receive the whole, with such accession of others as might come to them for their better strength and subsistence; and some such-like cautions and limitations.

So as, with the aforesaid provisos, the greater part consented to a removal to a place called Nauset, which had been superficially viewed and the good will of the purchasers to whom it belonged obtained, with some addition thereto from the Court. But now they began to see their errour, that they had given away already the best and most commodious places to others, and now

[1] Bradford and likeminded Pilgrims welcomed the establishment of new towns and churches in the Colony by newcomers, as at Scituate and Taunton, but they wanted the original Plymouth church, including members of the second generation, to stick together. There was, however, a very narrow strip of arable land on Plymouth Bay; the back country was too rugged and rocky for profitable agriculture; and after the founding of Boston, ships from England found it more convenient to put in there. Boston gave them more business than Plymouth, which lay dead to windward of Cape Cod in the prevailing breezes, and where goods had to be lightered ashore instead of being landed on a wharf.

wanted themselves. For this place was about 50 miles from hence, and at an outside of the country remote from all society; also that it would prove so strait as it would not be competent to receive the whole body, much less be capable of any addition or increase; so as, at least in a short time, they should be worse there than they are now here. The which with sundry other like considerations and inconveniences made them change their resolutions. But such as were before resolved upon removal took advantage of this agreement and went on, notwithstanding; neither could the rest hinder them, they having made some beginning.[2]

And thus was this poor church left, like an ancient mother grown old and forsaken of her children, though not in their affections yet in regard of their bodily presence and personal helpfulness; her ancient members being most of them worn away by death, and these of later time being like children translated into other families, and she like a widow left only to trust in God.[3] Thus, she that had made many rich became herself poor.[4] |262|

Some Things Handled and Pacified by the Commissioners,[5] this Year.

Whereas, by a wise providence of God, two of the jurisdictions in the western parts, viz. Connecticut and New Haven, have been lately exercised by sundry insolencies and outrages from the Indians; as, first, an Englishman running from his master out of the Massachusetts was murdered in the woods in or near the limits of Connecticut jurisdiction, and about six weeks after, upon discovery by an Indian, the Indian sagamore in these parts promised to deliver the murderer to the English, bound, and having accordingly brought him within the sight of Uncaway,[6]

[2] Nauset was in the first of the Old Comers' or Purchasers' reserved tracts of 1640. After looking it over twice, a committee of the Plymouth church reported that there was not enough room for all. Thomas Prence Jr., John Doane, Edward Bangs and other leading Plymotheans did remove, purchased lands of the sachem of Manamoyick, and eventually became the town and church of Eastham, the third that came "out of the bowels" of the Plymouth church; the first two being Duxbury and Marshfield.

[3] 1 Timothy v.5.

[4] 2 Corinthians vi.10.

[5] I.e., of the United Colonies of New England.

[6] Fairfield, Conn.

by their joint consent as it is informed, he was there unbound and left to shift for himself. Whereupon ten Englishmen forthwith coming to the place, being sent by Mr. Ludlow at the Indians' desire, to receive the murderer, who seeing him escaped, laid hold of eight of the Indians there present, amongst whom there was a sagamore or two and kept them in hold two days till four sagamores engaged themselves within one month to deliver the prisoner. And about a week after this agreement, an Indian came presumptuously and with guile, in the daytime, and murtherously assaulted an English woman in her house at Stamford, and by three wounds supposed mortal left her for dead after he had robbed the house.[7]

By which passages the English were provoked, and called to a due consideration of their own safety. And the Indians generally in those parts arose in an hostile manner, refused to come to the English to carry on treaties of peace, departed from their wigwams, left their corn unweeded,[8] and showed themselves tumultuously about some of the English plantations, and shot off pieces within hearing of the town, and some Indians came to the English and told them the Indians would fall upon them. So that most of the English thought it unsafe to travel in those parts by land, and some of the plantations were put upon strong watch and ward night and day, and could not attend their private occasions, and yet distrusted their own strength for their defense. Whereupon Hartford and New Haven were sent unto for aid, and saw cause both to send into the weaker parts of their own jurisdiction thus in danger and New Haven for conveniency of situation sent aid to Uncaway, though belonging to Connecticut.[9] Of all which passages they presently acquainted the Commissioners in the Bay, and had the allowance and approbation from the General Court there, with directions neither to hasten war nor to bear such insolencies too long. Which courses, though chargeable to themselves, yet through God's blessing they hope fruit is

[7] The woman recovered and the Indian was executed. Stamford demanded a declaration of war forthwith.

[8] As the Indians thereabouts were supposed to pay an annual tribute in corn, this was a gesture of defiance.

[9] New Haven and Connecticut (or the River) were separate jurisdictions until 1662.

and will be sweet and wholesome to all the colonies. The murderers are since delivered to justice, the public peace preserved for the present and probability it may be better secured for the future.

Thus this mischief was prevented and the fear of a war hereby diverted. But now another broil was begun by the Narragansetts. Though they unjustly had made war upon Uncas, as is before declared, and had, the winter before this, earnestly pressed the Governor of the Massachusetts that they might still make war upon them to revenge the death of their sagamore which being taken prisoner was by them put to death (as before was noted) pretending that they had first received and accepted his ransom and then put him to death. But the Governor refused their presents and told them that it was themselves had done the wrong and broken the conditions of peace, and he nor the English neither could nor would allow them to make any further war upon him, but if they did, must assist him and oppose them. But if it did appear upon good proof that he had received a ransom for his life before he put him to death; when the Commissioners met they should have a fair hearing, and they would cause Uncas to return the same. But notwithstanding, at the spring of the year, they gathered a great power and fell upon Uncas and slew sundry of his men and wounded more and also had some loss themselves. Uncas called for aid from the English. They told him what the Narragansetts objected, he deny the same. They told him it must come to trial and if he was innocent, if the Narragansetts would not desist they would aid and assist him. So at this meeting they |263| sent both to Uncas and the Narragansetts and required their sagamores to come or send to the Commissioners now met at Hartford and they should have a fair and impartial hearing in all their grievances and would endeavour that all wrongs should be rectified where they should be found. And they promised that they should safely come and return without any danger or molestation. And sundry the like things, as appears more at large in the messenger's instructions. Upon which the Narragansetts sent one sagamore and some other deputies with full power to do in the case as should be meet. Uncas came in person, accompanied with some chief about him. After the agitation of the business, the issue was this. The Commissioners declared to the Narragansett deputies as followeth:

1. That they did not find any proof of any ransom agreed on.

2. It appeared not that any wampum had been paid as a ransom, or any part of a ransom, for Miantonomo's life.

3. That if they had in any measure proved their charge against Uncas, the Commissioners would have required him to have made answerable satisfaction.

4. That if hereafter they can make satisfying proof, the English will consider the same and proceed accordingly.

5. The Commissioners did require that neither themselves nor the Niantics make any war or injurious assault upon Uncas or any of his company until they make proof of the ransom charged, and that due satisfaction be denied, unless he first assault them.

6. That if they assault Uncas the English are engaged to assist him.

Hereupon the Narragansett sachem, advising with the other deputies, engaged himself in the behalf of the Narragansetts and Niantics that no hostile acts should be committed upon Uncas or any of his, until after the next planting of corn. And that after that, before they begin any war, they will give thirty days' warning to the Governor of the Massachusetts or Connecticut.

The Commissioners approving of this offer, and taking their engagement under their hands, required Uncas, as he expected the continuance of the favour of the English, to observe the same terms of peace with the Narragansetts and theirs.

These foregoing conclusions were subscribed by the Commissioners, for the several jurisdictions, the 19th of September, 1644.

Edward Hopkins, President
Simon Bradstreet
William Hathorne
Edward Winslow
John Browne
George Fenwick
Theophilus Eaton
Thomas Gregson

The forenamed Narragansetts' deputies did further promise that, if contrary to this agreement any of the Niantic Pequots should make any assault upon Uncas or any of his, they would deliver them up to the English to be punished according to their demerits; and that they would not use any means to procure the Mohawks to come against Uncas during this truce.

These were their names subscribed with their marks:

WEETOWISH CHINNOUGH
PAMPIAMETT PUMMUNISH

CHAPTER XXXV |264|

Anno Dom: 1645 [*War with the Narragansetts Averted*]

The Commissioners this year were called to meet together at Boston before their ordinary time, partly in regard of some differences fallen between the French and the Government of the Massachusetts about their aiding of Monsieur La Tour against Monsieur d'Aunay, and partly about the Indians who had broken the former agreements about the peace concluded the last year. This meeting was held at Boston the 28th of July.

Besides some underhand assaults made on both sides, the Narragansetts gathered a great power and fell upon Uncas and slew many of his men and wounded more, by reason that they far exceeded him in number and had got store of pieces with which they did him most hurt. And as they did this without the knowledge and consent of the English, contrary to former agreement so they were resolved to prosecute the same notwithstanding anything the English said or should do against them. So, being encouraged by their late victory and promise of assistance from the Mohawks (being a strong, warlike and desperate people) they had already devoured Uncas and his in their hopes; and surely they had done it indeed if the English had not timely set in for his aid. For those of Connecticut sent him forty men who were a garrison to him till the Commissioners could meet and take further order.

Being thus met, they forthwith sent three messengers; viz. Sergeant John Davis, Benedict Arnold and Francis Smith, with full and ample instructions both to the Narragansetts and Uncas, to require them that they should either come in person or send sufficient men fully instructed to deal in the business. And if they refused or delayed, to let them know (according to former agreements) that the English are engaged to assist against these hostile invasions and that they have sent their men to defend Uncas and to know of the Narragansetts whether they will stand to the former peace, or they will assault the English also, that they may provide accordingly.

But the messengers returned, not only with a slighting but a threatening answer from the Narragansetts as will more appear hereafter. Also, they brought a letter from Mr. Roger Williams wherein he assures them that the war would presently break forth and the whole country would be all of a flame. And that the sachems of the Narragansetts had concluded a neutrality with the English of Providence and those of Aquidneck Island. Whereupon the Commissioners considering the great danger and provocations offered and the necessity we should be put unto of making war with the Narragansetts, and being also careful in a matter of so great weight and general concernment to see the way cleared and to give satisfaction to all the Colonies, did think fit to advise with such of the magistrates and elders of the Massachusetts as were then at hand, and also with some of the chief military commanders there. Who, being assembled, it was then agreed:

First, that our engagement bound us to aid and defend Uncas.

2. That this aid could not be intended only to defend him and his fort or habitation, but according to the common acceptation of such covenants or engagements, considered with the grounds or occasion thereof, so to aid him as he might be preserved in his liberty and estate. |265|

3. That this aid must be speedy, lest he might be swallowed up in the meantime, and so come too late.

4. The justice of this war being cleared to ourselves and the rest then present, it was thought meet that the case should be stated, and the reasons and grounds of the war declared and published.

5. That a day of humiliation should be appointed, which was the fifth day of the week following.

6. It was then also agreed by the Commissioners that the whole number of men to be raised in all the Colonies should be 300, whereof from Massachusetts a 190, Plymouth 40, Connecticut 40, New Haven 30. And considering that Uncas was in present danger, 40 men of this number were forthwith sent from the Massachusetts for his succour. And it was but need, for the other 40 from Connecticut had order to stay but a month, and their time being out they returned, and the Narragansetts, hearing thereof, took the advantage and came suddenly upon him and gave him another blow, to his further loss, and were ready to do

the like again; but these 40 men being arrived, they returned and did nothing.

The declaration which they set forth I shall not transcribe, it being very large and put forth in print,[1] to which I refer those that would see the same, in which all passages are laid open from the first. I shall only note their proud carriage and answers to the three messengers sent from the Commissioners. They received them with scorn and contempt, and told them they resolvėd to have no peace without Uncas his head. Also they gave this further answer, that it mattered not who began the war, they were resolved to follow it and that the English should withdraw their garrison from Uncas, or they would procure the Mohawks against them. And withal gave them this threatening answer: that they would lay the English cattle on heaps as high as their houses, and that no Englishman should stir out of his door to piss, but he should be killed. And whereas they required guides to pass through their country to deliver their message to Uncas from the Commissioners, they denied them; but at length (in way of scorn) offered them an old Pequot woman. Besides also they conceived themselves in danger, for whilst the interpreter was speaking with them about the answer he should return, three men came and stood behind him with their hatchets according to their murderous manner; but one of his fellows gave him notice of it, so they broke off and came away, with sundry such-like affronts, which made those Indians they carried with them to run away for fear and leave them to go home as they could.

Thus whilst the Commissioners in care of the public peace sought to quench the fire kindled amongst the Indians, these children of strife breathe out threatenings, provocations and war against the English themselves. So that, unless they should dishonour and provoke God by violating a just engagement, and expose the Colonies to contempt and danger from the barbarians, they cannot but exercise force when no other means will prevail to reduce the Narragansetts and their confederates to a more just and sober temper. So as hereupon they went on to hasten the preparations according to the former agreement, and sent to

[1] *A Declaration of Former Passages and Proceedings betwixt the English and the Narrowgansetts, with their Confederates* (Cambridge, 1645).

Plymouth to send forth their 40 men with all speed to lie at Seekonk lest any danger should befall it before the rest were ready, it lying next the enemy; and there to stay till the Massachusetts should join with them. Also Connecticut and New Haven forces were to join together and march with all speed, and the Indian confederates of those parts with them. All which was done accordingly, and the soldiers of this place were at Seekonk, the place of their rendezvous, eight or ten days before the rest were ready. They were well armed all, with snaphance pieces,[2] and went under the command of Captain |266| Standish; those from other places were led likewise by able commanders, as Captain Mason for Connecticut, etc. And Major Gibbons was made general over the whole, with such commissions and instructions as was meet.

Upon the sudden dispatch of these soldiers the present necessity requiring it, the deputies of the Massachusetts Court being now assembled immediately after the setting forth of their 40 men, made a question whether it was legally done without their Commission. It was answered that howsoever it did properly belong to the authority of the several jurisdictions (after the war was agreed upon by the Commissioners, and the number of men) to provide the men and means to carry on the war; yet in this present case the proceeding of the Commissioners and the commission given was as sufficient as if it had been done by the General Court. First, it was a case of such present and urgent necessity as could not stay the calling of the Court or Council. 2. In the Articles of Confederation, power is given to the Commissioners to consult, order and determine all affairs of war, etc. And the word *determine* comprehends all acts of authority belonging thereunto. 3. The Commissioners are the judges of the necessity of the expedition. 4. The General Court have made their own Commissioners their sole counsel for these affairs. 5. These counsels could not have had their due effect except they had power to proceed in this case, as they have done; which were to make the Commissioners' power and the main end of the Confederation to be frustrate, and that merely for observing a cere-

[2] A snaphance was a light flintlock musket, a more advanced type of weapon than the matchlock, which required a stand to support it.

mony. 6. The Commissioners having sole power to manage the war for number of men, for time, place, etc., they only know their own counsels and *determinations*, and therefore none can grant commission to act according to these but themselves.

All things being thus in readiness, and some of the soldiers gone forth and the rest ready to march, the Commissioners thought it meet before any hostile act was performed to cause a present to be returned, which had been sent to the Governor of the Massachusetts from the Narragansett sachems, but not by him received, but laid up to be accepted or refused as they should carry themselves and observe the covenants. Therefore they, violating the same, and standing out thus to a war, it was again returned by two messengers and an interpreter. And further to let know that their men already sent to Uncas, and other where sent forth, have hitherto had express order only to stand upon his and their own defense, and not to attempt any invasion of the Narragansetts' country. And yet, if they may have due reparation for what is past and good security for the future, it shall appear they are as desirous of peace and shall be as tender of the Narragansetts' blood as ever. If therefore Pessacus, Janemo [3] with other sachems will without further delay come along with you to Boston, the Commissioners do promise and assure them, they shall have free liberty to come and return without molestation or any just grievance from the English. But deputies will not now serve, nor may the preparations in hand be now stayed, or the directions given recalled, till the forementioned sagamores come and some further order be taken. But if they will have nothing but war, the English are providing and will proceed accordingly.

Pessacus, Mixanno and Witowash, three principal sachems of the Narragansett Indians, and Aumsequen,[4] deputy for the Nian-

[3] Pessacus, better known under the name of Canonicus, was a Narragansett sachem, brother of Miantonomo; Janemo (spelled Innemo by Bradford), better known as Ninigret, was a Niantic sachem.

[4] Mixanno was the eldest son and heir of Canonicus; he married the "Old Queen," a sister of Ninigret. Witowash is the same Narragansett sachem as Weetowish, who signed the Narragansetts' agreement above. Aumsequen is otherwise unknown to fame. See Howard M. Chapin *Sachems of the Narragansetts* (Rhode Island Historical Society, 1931).

tics, with a large train of men, within a few days after came to Boston. And to omit all other circumstances and debates that passed between them, and the Commissioners, they came to this conclusion following.[5]

|268| This treaty and agreement betwixt the Commissioners of the United Colonies and the sagamores and deputy of Narragansetts and Niantic Indians, was made and concluded, Benedict Arnold being interpreter, upon his oath; Sergeant Collicott, and an Indian his man being present; and Josias and Cutshamakin, two Indians acquainted with the English language, assisting therein; who opened and cleared the whole treaty and every article to the sagamores and deputy there present.

And thus was the war at this time stayed and prevented. |269|

[5] See Appendix XII, Official Documents, No. 6.

CHAPTER XXXVI

Anno Dom: 1646 [*A Noted Pirate in Plymouth*]

About the middle of May this year came in three ships into this harbor, in warlike order. They were found to be men of war. The captain's name was Cromwell, who had taken sundry prizes from the Spaniards in the West Indies; he had a commission from the Earl of Warwick. He had aboard his vessels about 80 lusty men, but very unruly, who after they came ashore, did so distemper themselves with drink as they became like madmen, and though some of them were punished and imprisoned, yet could they hardly be restrained. Yet in the end they became more moderate and orderly. They continued here about a month or six weeks, and then went to the Massachusetts, in which time they spent and scattered a great deal of money among the people, and yet more sin I fear than money, notwithstanding all the care and watchfulness that was used towards them to prevent what might be.[1]

In which time one sad accident fell out. A desperate fellow of the company fell a-quarreling with some of his company. His captain commanded him to be quiet and surcease his quarreling, but he would not, but reviled his captain with base language and in the end half drew his rapier and intended to run at his captain; but he closed with him and wrested his rapier from him and gave him a box on the ear. But he would not give over, but still as-

[1] Thomas Cromwell, whom Governor Winthrop in his *Journal* for 1646 describes as a man "ripped out of his mother's belly, and never sucked, nor saw father nor mother, nor they him," had come to Boston as a common sailor around 1636. Subsequently he entered the service of a Captain Jackson who was pirating around the Caribbean, using the Earl of Warwick's island of Old Providence off the coast of Nicaragua as base. He was now bringing two prizes, cedar-built "frigates" of 60 and 80 tons, according to Winthrop, to Boston for sale; but was forced into Plymouth by a northwest gale after rounding Cape Cod. Governor Winthrop regarded this diversion as a special providence "for the comfort and help of that town, which was now almost deserted." At Boston, where Capt. Cromwell arrived 10 June, he presented Governor Winthrop with a fine piece of loot, a sedan chair worth £50, said to have belonged to the Viceroy of Mexico. Winthrop hadn't much use for a sedan chair in Boston, but it came in handy as a propitiatory gift to Monsieur d'Aunay, when that lord of Acadia demanded £8000 damages for the help given by the Bay Colony to his rival La Tour.

saulted his captain; whereupon he took the same rapier as it was in the scabbard and gave him a blow with the hilt, but it lit on his head and the small end of the bar of the rapier hilt pierced his skull, and he died a few days after. But the captain was cleared by a council of war. This fellow was so desperate a quarreler, as the captain was fain many times to chain him under hatches from hurting his fellows, as the company did testify. And this was his end.

This Captain Thomas Cromwell set forth another voyage to the West Indies from the Bay of the Massachusetts, well manned and victualed, and was out three years, and took sundry prizes and returned rich unto the Massachusetts. And there died the same summer, having got a fall from his horse, in which fall he fell on his rapier hilt and so bruised his body as he shortly after died thereof, with some other distempers which brought him into a fever. Some observed that there might be something of the hand of God herein; that as the forenamed man died of the blow he gave him with the rapier hilt, so his own death was occasioned by a like means.

[*Winslow's Final Departure*]

This year Mr. Edward Winslow went into England, upon this occasion: some discontented persons under the government of the Massachusetts sought to trouble their peace and disturb, if not innovate, their government by laying many |270| scandals upon them, and intended to prosecute against them in England by petitioning and complaining to the Parliament.[2] Also, Samuel Gorton and his company made complaints against them.[3] So as they made

[2] This was the Remonstrance and Petition to the General Court of 6 May 1646, to which Robert Child was the first signer. S. E. Morison *Builders of the Bay Colony* chap. viii.

[3] Samuel Gorton, one of the most persistent and amusing of all troublemakers in early New England, eventually the founder of a sect, was expelled from four colonies before founding his own at Warwick, R. I. His virtual banishment from Plymouth took place in 1638, according to him, for defending a young widow whom the Court wished to deport; according to Winslow, Gorton was expelled for abusing his landlord (the Rev. Ralph Smith) and trying to start a revolt against the civil authorities. Bradford's failure to notice the event in chap. xxix above, or elsewhere, is inexplicable. There are several biographies of Gorton and he is noticed by all historians of the colonies, notably by Channing and Andrews.

choice of Mr. Winslow to be their agent to make their defense, and gave him commission and instructions for that end. In which he so carried himself as did well answer their ends and cleared them from any blame or dishonour, to the shame of their adversaries. But by reason of the great alterations in the State, he was detained longer than was expected, and afterwards fell into other employments there; so as he hath now been absent this four years, which hath been much to the weakening of this government, without whose consent he took these employments upon him.[4]

Anno 1647. And Anno 1648.[5]

[4] Winslow never did return to New England. Oliver Cromwell appointed him, with Admiral Penn and General Venable, a joint head of the expeditionary force that captured Jamaica in 1655, and he died on the return voyage. His portrait, painted in England in 1651, now hangs in Pilgrim Hall, Plymouth; it is the only one extant of a Pilgrim Father.

[5] There are no entries under this heading. It is followed by two blank leaves. The list of *Mayflower* passengers (Appendix XIII) begins on the verso of a third.

APPENDICES

APPENDIX I

A Late Observation as it Were, by the Way, Worthy to be Noted

Full little did I think that the downfall of the Bishops, with their courts, canons and ceremonies, etc. had been so near, when I first began these scribbled writings (which was about the year 1630 and so pieced up at times of leisure afterward) or that I should have lived to have seen or heard of the same. But it is the Lord's doing, and ought to be marvelous in our eyes! [1] "Every plant which mine heavenly Father hath not planted" (saith our Saviour) "shall be rooted up." Matthew xv.13. "I have snared thee, and thou art taken, O Babel (Bishops), and thou wast not aware; thou art found, and also caught, because thou hast striven against the Lord." Jeremiah 1.24. But will they needs strive? Against the truth, against the servants of God, what, and against the Lord Himself? Do they provoke the Lord to anger? Are they stronger than He? 1 Corinthians x.22. No, no! They have met with their match. "Behold, I come unto thee, O proud man, saith the Lord God of hosts; for thy day is come, even the time that I will visit thee." Jeremiah 1.31. May not the People of God now say, and these poor people among the rest, "The Lord hath brought forth our righteousness; come, let us declare in Zion the work of the Lord our God." Jeremiah li.10. "Let all flesh be still before the Lord, for He is raised up out of His holy place." Zechariah ii.13.

In this case, these poor people may say (among the thousands of Israel) "When the Lord brought again the captivity of Zion, we were like them that dream." Psalm cxxvi.1. "The Lord hath done great things for us, whereof we rejoice." Verse 3. "They that sow in tears, shall reap in joy. They went weeping and carried precious seed, but they shall return with joy and bring their sheaves." Verses 5, 6.

Do you not now see the fruits of your labours, O all ye servants of the Lord? That have suffered for His truth, and have been faithful witnesses of the same, and ye little handful amongst the rest, the least amongst the thousands of Israel? [2] You have not

[1] Psalm cxviii.23. These and subsequent quotations in this Appendix are from the Geneva Bible.

[2] Micah v.2.

only had a seed time, but many of you have seen the joyful harvest; should you not then rejoice? Yea, and again rejoice, and say, "Hallelujah! Salvation, and glory, and honour, and power be to the Lord our God, for true and righteous are His judgments." Revelation xix.1, 2.

But thou wilt ask, "What is the matter? What is done?" Why, art thou a stranger in Israel that thou shouldest not know what is done? Are not those Jebusites overcome that have vexed the people of Israel so long, even holding Jerusalem till David's days and been as thorns in their sides, so many ages; and now began to scorn that any David should meddle with them? [3] They began to fortify their tower, as that of the old Babylonians; but those proud Anakims are thrown down, and their glory laid in the dust.[4] The tyrannous Bishops are ejected, their courts dissolved, their canons forceless, their service cashiered, their ceremonies useless and despised, their plots for popery prevented, and all their superstitions discarded and returned to Rome from whence they came, and the monuments of idolatry rooted out of the land. And the proud and profane supporters and cruel defenders of these, as bloody papists and wicked atheists, and their malignant consorts, marvelously overthrown. And are not these great things? Who can deny it?

But who hath done it? Who, even He that sitteth on the white horse, who is "called Faithful and true, and judgeth and fighteth righteously," Revelation xix.11. whose garments are "dipped in blood, and His name was called the Word of God," (verse 13) "for He shall rule them with a rod of iron; for it is He that treadeth the winepress of the fierceness and wrath of God Almighty. And He hath upon His garment, and upon His thigh a name written, The King of Kings, and Lord of Lords." Verses 15, 16.

Anno Domini 1646. Hallelujah!

[3] 2 Samuel v.6–9. [4] Joshua xi.21–2.

APPENDIX II

Correspondence with the Virginia Company, and Francis Blackwell's Unfortunate Voyage, 1618–19

[Manuscript ff. 22–6]

The Copy of a Letter Sent to Sir John Wolstenholme [1]

RIGHT WORSHIPFUL:

With due acknowledgment of our thankfulness for your singular care and pains in the business of Virginia, for our and, we hope, the common good, we do remember our humble duties unto you, and have sent enclosed, as is required, a further explanation of our judgments in the three points specified by some of His Majesty's Honourable Privy Council. And though it be grievous unto us that such unjust insinuations are made against us, yet we are most glad of the occasion of making our just purgation unto so honourable personages. The declarations we have sent enclosed, the one more brief and general, which we think the fitter to be presented; the other something more large, and in which we express some small accidental differences, which if it seem good unto you and other of our worshipful friends you may send instead of the former. Our prayers unto God is that your Worship may see the fruit of your worthy endeavours, which on our parts we shall not fail to further by all good means in us. And so praying that you would please with the convenientest speed that may be, to give us knowledge of the success of the business with His Majesty's Privy Council, and accordingly what your further pleasure is, either for our direction or furtherance in the same, so we rest

Your Worship in all duty,
JOHN ROBINSON
WILLIAM BREWSTER

Leyden, January 27
Anno 1617 Old Style [2]

The First Brief Note was This.

Touching the ecclesiastical ministry, namely of pastors for teaching, elders for ruling, and deacons for distributing the church's con-

[1] Sir John Wolstenholme—whose name was probably pronounced "Worssenham," as Bradford spells it—was one of the greater merchant adventurers of the period; an incorporator of the East India Company and member of the Council for Virginia.

[2] In the English calendar. The New Style date, as used in the Netherlands, would have been 6 Feb. 1618.

tribution, as also for the two sacraments, baptism and the Lord's Supper, we do wholly and in all points agree |23| with the French Reformed Churches, according to their public confession of faith.

The oath of Supremacy we shall willingly take if it be required of us, and that convenient satisfaction be not given by our taking the oath of Allegiance.

John Robinson
William Brewster

The Second was This.

Touching the ecclesiastical ministry, etc. as in the former, we agree in all things with the French Reformed Churches,[3] according to their public confession of faith; though some small differences be to be found in our practices, not at all in the substance of the things, but only in some accidental circumstances.

1. As first, their ministers do pray with their heads covered; ours uncovered.
2. We choose none for Governing Elders but such as are able to teach; which ability they do not require.
3. Their elders and deacons are annual, or at most for two or three years; ours perpetual.
4. Our elders do administer their office in admonitions and excommunications for public scandals, publicly and before the congregation; theirs more privately and in their consistories.
5. We do administer baptism only to such infants as whereof the one parent at the least is of some church, which some of their churches do not observe; though in it our practice accords with their public confession and the judgment of the most learned amongst them.

Other differences worthy mentioning we know none in these points. Then about the oath, as in the former.

Subscribed,
John Robinson
William Brewster

Part of Another Letter from Him that Delivered These

London. February 14
1617[18]

Your letter to Sir John Worstenholme I delivered almost as soon as I had it, to his own hands, and stayed with him the opening and read-

[3] See footnote 6, chap. xvi, above.

ing. There were two papers enclosed, he read them to himself, as also the letter, and in the reading he spake to me and said, "Who shall make them?" viz. the ministers. I answered his Worship that the power of making was in the Church, to be ordained by the imposition of hands by the fittest instruments they had. It must either be in the Church or from the Pope, and the Pope is Antichrist. "Ho!" said Sir John, "what the Pope holds good (as in the Trinity) that we do well to assent to. But," said he, "we will not enter into dispute now." And as for your letters he would not show them at any hand, lest he should spoil all. He expected you should have been of the Archbishop's mind for the calling of ministers, but it seems you differed. I could have wished to have known the contents of your two enclosed, at which he stuck so much, especially the larger. I asked his Worship what good news he had for me to write tomorrow. He told me very good news, for both the King's Majesty and the bishops have consented. He said he would go to Mr. Chancellor, Sir Fulke Greville, as this day, and next week I should know more. I met Sir Edwin Sandys on Wednesday night. He wished me to be at the Virginia Court the next Wednesday, where I purpose to be. Thus loath to be troublesome at present, I hope to have somewhat next week of certainty concerning you. I commit you to the Lord. Yours,

SABINE STARESMORE [4]

|24| These things being long in agitation, and messengers passing to and again about them, after all their hopes they were long delayed by many rubs that fell in the way. For at the return of these messengers into England they found things far otherwise than they expected. For the Virginia Council was now so disturbed with factions and quarrels amongst themselves as no business could well go forward. The which may the better appear in one of the messenger's letters as followeth:

[*Robert Cushman to the Leyden Congregation*]

TO HIS LOVING FRIENDS, etc.

I had thought long since to have writ unto you, but could not effect that which I aimed at, neither can yet set things as I wished; yet,

[4] Signed "S. B." in the manuscript but identified by Prince with a copy in a now lost letter book of Bradford's as Sabine Staresmore, a member of the Pilgrim Church at Leyden who did not emigrate. The paragraph that follows is Bradford's.

notwithstanding, I doubt not but Mr. B. hath written to Mr. Robinson. But I think myself bound also to do something, lest I be thought to neglect you. The main hindrance of our proceedings in the Virginia business is the dissensions and factions (as they term it) amongst the Council and Company of Virginia, which are such, as that ever since we came up no business could by them be dispatched. The occasion of this trouble amongst them is for that a while since, Sir Thomas Smith, repining at his many offices and troubles, wished the Company of Virginia to ease him of his office in being Treasurer and Governor of the Virginia Company. Whereupon the Company took occasion to dismiss him, and chose Sir Edwin Sandys Treasurer and Governor of the Company, he having 60 voices, Sir John Worstenholme 16 voices, and Alderman Johnson 24. But Sir Thomas Smith, when he saw some part of his honour lost, was very angry and raised a faction to cavil and contend about the election, and sought to tax Sir Edwin with many things that might both disgrace him and also put him by his office of Governor. In which contentions they yet stick and are not fit nor ready to intermeddle in any business; and what issue things will come to, we are not yet certain. It is most like Sir Edwin will carry it away, and if he do, things will go well in Virginia; if otherwise, they will go ill enough. Always we hope in some two or three Courts' days things will settle. Mean space [5] I think to go down into Kent and come up again about fourteen days or three weeks hence, except either by these aforesaid contentions or by the ill tidings from Virginia we be wholly discouraged, of which tidings I am now to speak.

Captain Argall [6] is come home this week (he upon notice of the intent of the Council came away before Sir George Yeardley came there, and so there is no small dissension); but his tidings are ill, though his person be welcome. He saith Mr. Blackwell's ship came not there till March, but going towards winter they had still northwest winds which carried them to the southward beyond their course. And the master of the ship and some six of the mariners dying, it seemed they could not find the bay till after long seeking and beating about. Mr. Blackwell is dead and Mr. Maggner, the Captain. Yea, there are dead, he saith, 130 persons, one and other in that ship;

[5] I.e., in the meantime.

[6] Samuel Argall, a famous early settler of Virginia, who broke up the French settlements at Mount Desert and Port Royal in 1613. In 1617–19 he became Deputy Governor of Virginia, but returned to England prematurely to answer various charges; later he became a member of the Council for New England.

it is said there was in all an 180 persons in the ship, so as they were packed together like herrings; they had amongst them the flux, and also want of fresh water, so as it is here rather wondered at that so many are alive, than that so many are dead. The merchants here say it was Mr. Blackwell's fault to pack so many in the ship; yea, and there were great mutterings and repinings amongst them, and upbraiding of Mr. Blackwell for his dealing and disposing of them, when they saw how he had disposed of them and how he insulted over them. Yea, the streets at Gravesend rung of their extreme quarrelings, crying out one of another, "Thou hast brought me to this," and "I may thank thee for this." Heavy news it is, and I would be glad to hear how far it will discourage. I see none here discouraged much, |25| but rather desire to learn to beware by other men's harms and to amend that wherein they have failed.

As we desire to serve one another in love, so take heed of being enthralled by any imperious person, especially if they be discerned to have an eye to themselves. It doth often trouble me to think that in this business we are all to learn and none to teach; but better so than to depend upon such teachers as Mr. Blackwell was. Such a stratagem he once made for Mr. Johnson and his people at Emden, which was their subversion. But though he there cleanlily yet unhonestly plucked his neck out of the collar, yet at last his foot is caught. Here are no letters come; the ship Captain Argall came in is yet in the west parts. All that we hear is but his reports; it seemeth he came away secretly. The ship that Mr. Blackwell went in will be here shortly. It is as Mr. Robinson once said—he thought we should hear no good of them.

Mr. B.[7] is not well at this time; whether he will come back to you or go into the north, I yet know not. For myself, I hope to see an end of this business ere I come, though I am sorry to be thus from you. If things had gone roundly forward, I should have been with you within these fourteen days. I pray God direct us and give us that spirit which is fitting for such a business. Thus having summarily pointed at things which Mr. Brewster, I think, hath more largely writ of to Mr. Robinson, I leave you to the Lord's protection.

London, May 8 — Yours in all readiness, etc.
Anno 1619 — ROBERT CUSHMAN

[7] Elder Brewster; he was "wanted by the police" for having published prohibited books in Leyden. See 1912 ed. Bradford I 89 note.

[*Bradford's comments follow*]

A word or two by way of digression touching this Mr. Blackwell. He was an elder of the church at Amsterdam, a man well known of most of them. He declined from the truth with Mr. Johnson and the rest, and went with him when they parted asunder in that woeful manner which brought so great dishonour to God, scandal to the truth, and outward ruin to themselves in this world. But I hope, notwithstanding, through the mercies of the Lord, their souls are now at rest with him in the heavens and that they are arrived in the haven of happiness; though some of their bodies were thus buried in the terrible seas, and others sunk under the burthen of bitter afflictions. He with some others had prepared for to go to Virginia. And he, with sundry godly citizens being at a private meeting (I take it a fast) in London, being discovered, many of them were apprehended, whereof Mr. Blackwell was one. But he so glozed with the bishops and either dissembled or flatly denied the truth which formerly he had maintained. And not only so but very unworthily betrayed and accused another godly man who had escaped, that so he might slip his own neck out of the collar and to obtain his own freedom brought others into bonds. Whereupon he so won the bishops' favor (but lost the Lord's) as he was not only dismissed but in open court the archbishop gave him great applause and his solemn blessing to proceed in his voyage.[8] But if such events follow the bishops' blessing, happy are they that miss the same. It is much better to keep a good conscience and have the Lord's blessing, whether in life or death.

But see how the man thus apprehended by Mr. Blackwell's means writes to a friend of his:

[*Sabine Staresmore to John Carver*]

RIGHT DEAR FRIEND AND CHRISTIAN BROTHER, MR. CARVER:

I salute you and yours in the Lord, etc. As for my own present condition, I doubt not but you well understand it ere this by our brother Masterson, who should have tasted of the same cup had his

[8] Nobody has ever been able to find anything about this tragic voyage except what is related in Bradford.

place of residence and his person been as well known as myself. Somewhat I have written to Mr. Cushman how the matter still continues. I have petitioned twice to Mr. Sheriff, and once to my Lord Cooke,[9] and have used such reasons to move them to pity, that if they were not overruled by some others, I suppose I should soon gain my liberty, as that I was a young man living by my credit, |26| indebted to divers in our city, living at more than ordinary charges in a close and tedious prison, besides great rents abroad, all my business lying still, my only servant lying lame in the country, my wife being also great with child. And yet no answer till the lords of His Majesty's Council gave consent. Howbeit, Mr. Blackwell, a man as deep in this action as I, was delivered at a cheaper rate, with a great deal less ado; yea, with an addition of the Archbishop's blessing. I am sorry for Mr. Blackwell's weakness, I wish it may prove no worse. But yet he and some others of them, before their going, were not sorry but thought it was for the best that I was nominated, not because the Lord sanctifies evil to good, but that the action was good, yea for the best. One reason I well remember he used was, because this trouble would increase the Virginia Plantation, in that now people began to be more generally inclined to go; and if he had not nominated some such as I, he had not been free, being it was known that divers citizens besides themselves were there. I expect an answer shortly what they intend concerning me. I purpose to write to some others of you, by whom you shall know the certainty. Thus not having further at present to acquaint you withal, commending myself to your prayers, I cease and commit you and us all to the Lord.

From my chamber in Wodstreet Compter.[1]

September 4 Your friend, and brother in bonds,
Anno 1618 Sabine Staresmore

But thus much by the way, which may be of instruction and good use.[2]

[9] Sir Edward Coke, who had been dismissed from the Chief Justiceship in 1616.

[1] A prison in London.

[2] Bradford's comment.

APPENDIX III

Correspondence of June 1620 between the Leyden Committee and their Agents in London, on the Agreement with the Adventurers

[Manuscript ff. 31–4]

Another Letter from Sundry of Them at the same Time

To Their Loving Friends John Carver and Robert Cushman, These, etc.

Good brethren, after salutations, etc. We received divers letters at the coming of Mr. Nash and our pilot,[1] which is a great encouragement unto us, and for whom we hope after times will minister occasion of praising God. And indeed, had you not sent him, many would have been ready to faint and go back, partly in respect of the new conditions which have been taken up by you (which all men are against), and partly in regard of our own inability to do any one of those many weighty businesses you refer to us here. For the former whereof, whereas Robert Cushman desires reasons for our dislike, promising thereupon to alter the same, or else saying we should think he hath no brains, we desire him to exercise them therein, referring him to our pastor's former reasons, and them to the censure of the godly wise. But our desires are that you will not entangle yourselves and us in any such unreasonable courses as those are; viz. that the merchants should have the half of men's houses and lands at the dividend, and that persons should be deprived of the two days in a week agreed upon, yea every moment of time for their own Particular; by reason whereof we cannot conceive why any should carry servants for their own help and comfort, for that we can require no more of them than all men one of another. This we have only by relation from Mr. Nash, and not from any writing of your own, and therefore hope you have not proceeded far in so great a thing without us. But requiring you not to exceed the bounds of your commission, which was to proceed upon the things or conditions agreed upon and expressed in writing (at your going over about it) we leave it; not without marveling that yourself, as you write, knowing how small a thing troubleth our consultations, and how few, as you fear,

[1] Thomas Nash, a member of the Leyden congregation who did not emigrate, and Robert Coppin, who piloted the *Speedwell* from Delftshaven to Southampton and was afterwards transferred to the *Mayflower*.

understands the business aright, should trouble us with such matters as these are, etc.

Salute Mr. Weston from us, in whom we hope we are not deceived. We pray you make known our estate unto him, and if you think good, show him our letters; at least tell him that, under God, we much rely upon him and put our confidence in him. And, as yourselves well know, that if he had not been an adventurer with us, we had not taken it in hand; presuming that if he had not seen means to accomplish it he would not have begun it. So we hope in our extremity he will so far help us as our expectation be no way made frustrate concerning him. Since therefore, good brethren, we have plainly opened the state of things with us in this matter, you will, etc.

Thus beseeching the Almighty, who is all sufficient to raise us out of this depth of difficulties, to assist us herein; raising such means by His providence and fatherly care for us, His poor children and servants, as we may with comfort behold the hand of our God for good towards us in this our business which we undertake in His name and fear, we take leave and remain

Your perplexed, yet hopeful brethren,
Samuel Fuller
Edward Winslow
William Bradford
Isaac Allerton [2]

June 10, New Style
Anno 1620

A Letter of Robert Cushman's to Them [3]

Brethren, I understand by letters and passages that have come to me that there are great discontents and dislikes of my proceedings amongst you. Sorry I am to hear it, yet content to bear it, as not doubting but that partly by writing and more principally by word when we shall come together, I shall satisfy any reasonable man. I have been persuaded |32| by some, especially this bearer, to come and clear things unto you; but as things now stand I cannot be absent one day, except I should hazard all the voyage. Neither conceive I any great good would come of it. Take then, brethren, this as a step to give you content.

First, for your dislike of the alteration of one clause in the conditions. If you conceive it right, there can be no blame lie on me at all,

[2] Initials only in the ms., names supplied by Prince from one of Bradford's letter-books which has perished.

[3] Undated, but evidently a reply to the above.

for the articles first brought over by John Carver were never seen of any of the Adventurers here except Mr. Weston; neither did any of them like them because of that clause, nor Mr. Weston himself after he had well considered it. But as at the first there was £500 withdrawn by Sir George Ferrar[4] and his brother upon that dislike; so all the rest would have withdrawn, Mr. Weston excepted, if we had not altered that clause. Now, whilst we at Leyden conclude upon points, as we did, we reckoned without our host, which was not my fault. Besides, I showed you by a letter the equity of that condition, and our inconveniences, which might be set against all Mr. Robinson's inconveniences; that without the alteration of that clause we could neither have means to get thither nor supply whereby to subsist when we were there. Yet notwithstanding all those reasons, which were not mine but other men's wiser than myself, without answer to any one of them; here cometh over many querimonies and complaints against me, of lording it over my brethren and making conditions fitter for thieves and bondslaves than honest men, and that of my own head I did what I list. And at last a paper of reasons framed against that clause in the conditions, which as they were delivered me open, so my answer is open to you all. And first, as they are no other but inconveniences, such as a man might frame twenty as great on the other side, and yet prove nor disprove nothing by them; so they miss and mistake both the very ground of the article and nature of the project.

For, first, it is said that if there had been no division of houses and lands, it had been better for the poor. True, and that showeth the inequality of the condition; we should more respect him that ventur-

[4] Probably a mistake for John Ferrar, merchant and deputy treasurer of the Virginia Company at this time, eldest son of Sir Nicholas Ferrar, merchant, one of the leading figures in the Virginia Company, who died in April 1620. John's brothers were Nicholas Ferrar, who succeeded him as deputy treasurer and subsequently became vicar of Little Gidding and a famous mystic (see T. S. Eliot's *Four Quartets*), and William Ferrar, who emigrated to Virginia in 1618. The elder Ferrar, much interested in the conversion and education of the Indian children, left by will £300 for that purpose. It may well be that this explains why we find in the *Records of the Virginia Company* for 16 Feb. 1620 (I 310–11) Sir John Wolstenholme (another Virginia friend of the Pilgrims) proposing that "John Peirce and his Associates"—the grantees of the second Patent for the Pilgrim Colony—be entrusted with £500 given by an anonymous donor for bringing up and educating 30 "Infidells' Children" given as hostages by Opechancanough. But it is more likely that the Company tried to place this responsibility on Peirce & Co. because the existing colonists were reluctant to take charge of these poor little wretches.

eth both his money and his person, than him that ventureth but his person only.

2. Consider whereabout we are, not giving alms but furnishing a storehouse. No one shall be poorer than another for seven years, and if any be rich none can be poor. At the least, we must not in such business cry, "Poor, poor, mercy, mercy!" Charity hath its life in wrecks, not in ventures; you are by this most in a hopeful pity of making; therefore complain not before you have need.[5]

3. This will hinder the building of good and fair houses, contrary to the advice of politics.[6] Answer: So we would have it; our purpose is to build for the present such houses as, if need be, we may with little grief set afire and run away by the light. Our riches shall not be in pomp but in strength; if God send us riches we will employ them to provide more men, ships, munition, etc. You may see it amongst the best politics that a commonweal is readier to ebb than to flow, when once fine houses and gay clothes come up.

4. The Government may prevent excess in building. Answer: But if it be on all men beforehand resolved on to build mean houses, the Governor's labour is spared.

5. All men are not of one condition. Answer: If by condition you mean wealth, you are mistaken. If you mean by condition qualities, then I say he that is not content his neighbour shall have as good a house, fare, means etc. as himself, is not of a good quality. Secondly, such retired persons as have an eye only to themselves are fitter to come where catching is, than closing, and are fitter to live alone than in any society, either civil or religious.

6. It will be of little value, scarce worth £5. Answer: True, it may be not worth half £5. |33| If then so small a thing will content them, why strive we thus about it and give them occasion to suspect us to be worldly and covetous? I will not say what I have heard since these complaints came first over.

7. Our friends with us that adventure mind not their own profit, as did the old Adventurers. Answer: Then they are better than we, who for a little matter of profit are ready to draw back, and it is more apparent. Brethren, look to it, that make profit your main end; repent of this, else go not lest you be like a Jonas to Tarshish. Secondly,

[5] I.e., charity should not be expected to enter into a business deal and the Leyden committee's complaints of the conditions may make a wreck of their enterprise.

[6] I.e., writers on political theory. Cushman, like Bradford, had probably been reading Jean Bodin *de Republica,* whose gibes at the communistic "conceits" of Plato are reflected in Bradford's remarks in chapter xiv, above.

though some of them mind not their profit, yet others do mind it; and why not as well as we? Ventures are made by all sorts of men and we must labour to give them all content if we can.

8. It will break the course of community, as may be showed by many reasons. Answer: That is but said, and I say again, it will best foster communion, as may be showed by many reasons.

9. Great profit is like to be made by trucking, fishing, etc. Answer: As it is better for them, so for us; for half is ours, besides our living still upon it; and if such profit in that way come, our labour shall be the less on the land and our houses and lands must and will be of less value.

10. Our hazard is greater than theirs. Answer: True, but do they put us upon it, do they urge or egg us? Hath not the motion and resolution been always in ourselves? Do they any more than in seeing us resolute if we had means, help us to means upon equal terms and conditions? If we will not go, they are content to keep their moneys. Thus I have pointed at a way to loose those knots, which I hope you will consider seriously and let me have no more stir about them.

Now further, I hear a noise of slavish conditions by me made; but surely this is all that I have altered, and reasons I have sent you. If you mean it of the two days in a week for particular, as some insinuate, you are deceived; you may have three days in a week for me if you will. And when I have spoken to the Adventurers of times of working, they have said they hope we are men of discretion and conscience, and so fit to be trusted ourselves with that. But indeed the ground of our proceedings at Leyden was mistaken, and so here is nothing but tottering every day, etc.

As for them of Amsterdam, I had thought they would as soon have gone to Rome as with us, for our liberty is to them as rat's bane, and their rigour as bad to us as the Spanish Inquisition.[7] If any practice of mine discourage them, let them yet draw back; I will undertake they shall have their money again presently paid here. Or if the company think me to be the Jonas, let them cast me off before we go. I shall be content to stay with good will, having but the clothes on my back; only let us have quietness and no more of these clamours. Full little did I expect these things which now are come to pass, etc.

Yours,

R. Cushman

[7] Apparently some of the English Puritans at Amsterdam, with whom the Robinson congregation had broken some years before (see chap. iii above), proposed to join them now, and were not wanted.

[*The following is by Bradford*]

But whether this letter of his ever came to their hands at Leyden I well know not; I rather think it was stayed by Mr. Carver and kept by him, forgiving offense. But this which follows was there received, both which I thought pertinent to recite.

Another of his to the Foresaid, June 11, 1620

Salutations, etc.

I received your letter yesterday, by John Turner, with another the same day from Amsterdam by Mr. W. savouring of the place whence it came. And indeed the many discouragements I find here, together with the demurs and retirings there, had made me to say I would give up my accounts to John Carver, and at his coming acquaint him fully with all courses and so leave it quite, with only the poor clothes on my back. But gathering up myself, by further consideration, |34| I resolved yet to make one trial more, and to acquaint Mr. Weston with the fainted state of our business. And though he hath been much discontented at something amongst us of late which hath made him often say that, save for his promise, he would not meddle at all with the business any more; yet considering how far we were plunged into matters and how it stood both on our credits and undoing, at the last he gathered up himself a little more, and coming to me two hours after, he told me he would not yet leave it.

And so advising together we resolved to hire a ship, and have took liking of one till Monday, about 60 last—for a greater we cannot get except it be too great—but a fine ship it is.[8] And seeing our near friends there are so straight-laced, we hope to assure her without troubling them any further. And if the ship fall too small, it fitteth well that such as stumble at straws already may rest them there awhile, lest worse blocks come in the way ere seven years be ended. If you had beaten this business so thoroughly a month ago, and writ to us as now you do, we could thus have done much more conveniently. But it is as it is. I hope our friends there, if they be quitted of the ship hire, will be induced to venture the more. All that I now require is that salt and nets may there be bought, and for all the rest we will here provide it. Yet if that will not be, let them but stand for it a month or two, and we will take order to pay it all. Let Mr. Rein-

[8] Not the *Mayflower;* one last = 12 bbl. cargo capacity.

holds [9] tarry there and bring the ship to Southampton. We have hired another pilot here, one Mr. Clarke,[1] who went last year to Virginia with a ship of kine.

You shall hear distinctly by John Turner, who I think shall come hence on Tuesday night. I had thought to have come with him, to have answered to my complaints, but I shall learn to pass little for their censures; and if I had more mind to go and dispute and expostulate with them than I have care of this weighty business, I were like them who live by clamours and jangling. But neither my mind nor my body is at liberty to do much, for I am fettered with business and had rather study to be quiet,[2] than to make answer to their exceptions. If men be set on it, let them beat the air; I hope such as are my sincere friends will not think but I can give some reason of my actions. But of your mistaking about the matter and other things tending to this business, I shall next inform you more distinctly. Mean space, entreat our friends not to be too busy in answering matters before they know them. If I do such things as I cannot give reasons for, it is like you have set a fool about your business and so turn the reproof to yourself and send another and let me come again to my combs.[3] But setting aside my natural infirmities, I refuse not to have my cause judged, both of God and all indifferent men, and when we come together, I shall give account of my actions here. The Lord, who judgeth justly without respect of persons,[4] see into the equity of my cause and give us quiet, peaceable and patient minds in all these turmoils, and sanctify unto us all crosses whatsoever. And so I take my leave of you all, in all love and affection.

Your poor brother,

June 11, 1620 ROBERT CUSHMAN

I hope we shall get all here ready in fourteen days.

[9] Reynolds, master of the *Speedwell.*

[1] John Clarke, of Rotherhithe, had sailed to Virginia in 1610. Next year, when a Spanish caravel visited the Chesapeake, Clarke went on board as pilot; when the English detained some Spaniards who came ashore, the caravel carried Clarke to Spain, where he was imprisoned for four years. After his release he was employed by the Virginia Company to carry Irish cattle to Virginia, and in one of these voyages was associated with Christopher Jones. He was selected as master's mate and one of the pilots of the *Mayflower*.

[2] 1 Thessalonians iv.11.

[3] Cushman was a wool comber by trade.

[4] 1 Peter 1.17.

APPENDIX IV

The Rev. John Robinson's Farewell Letters to John Carver, July 1620

[Manuscript ff. 39–41]

MY DEAR BROTHER, I received enclosed in your last letter the note of information, which I shall carefully keep and make use of as there shall be occasion. I have a true feeling of your perplexity of mind and toil of body, but I hope that you who have always been able so plentifully to administer comfort unto others in their trials, are so well furnished for yourself, as that far greater difficulties than you have yet undergone (though I conceive them to have been great enough) cannot oppress you; though they press you, as the Apostle speaks.[1] The spirit of a man (sustained by the Spirit of God) will sustain his infirmity; I doubt not so will yours.[2] And the better much when you shall enjoy the presence and help of so many godly and wise brethren, for the bearing of part of your burthen, who also will not admit into their hearts the least thought of suspicion of any the least negligence, at least presumption, to have been in you, whatsoever they think in others.

Now what shall I say or write unto you and your good wife my loving sister? [3] Even only this: I desire, and always shall, unto you from the Lord, as unto my own soul. And assure yourself that my heart is with you, and that I will not forslow [4] my bodily coming at the first opportunity. I have written a large letter to the whole, and am sorry I shall not rather speak than write to them; and the more, considering the want of a preacher, which I shall also make some spur to my hastening after you. I do ever commend my best affection unto you, which if I thought you made any doubt of, I would express in more and the same more ample and full words.

And the Lord in whom you trust and whom you serve ever in this business and journey, guide you with His hand, protect you with His wing, and show you and us His salvation in the end, and bring us in the meanwhile together in the place desired, if such be His good will, for His Christ's sake. Amen.

Yours, etc.

July 27, 1620 JOHN ROBINSON

[1] 2 Corinthians i.8 and Acts xviii.5.

[2] Proverbs xviii.14.

[3] Mrs. Carver, who died shortly after the Governor, in 1621.

[4] I.e., be slow or dilatory about. But Robinson never did come.

This was the last letter that Mr. Carver lived to see from him. The other follows:

Loving and Christian Friends, I do heartily and in the Lord salute you all as being they with whom I am present in my best affection, and most earnest longings after you. Though I be constrained for a while to be bodily absent from you. I say constrained, God knowing how willingly and much rather than otherwise, I would have borne my part with you in this first brunt, were I not by strong necessity held back for the present. Make account of me in the meanwhile as of a man divided in myself with great pain, and as (natural bonds set aside) having my better part with |40| you. And though I doubt not but in your godly wisdoms you both foresee and resolve upon that which concerneth your present state and condition, both severally and jointly, yet have I thought it but my duty to add some further spur of provocation unto them who run already; if not because you need it, yet because I owe it in love and duty. And first, as we are daily to renew our repentance with our God, especially for our sins known, and generally for our unknown trespasses; so doth the Lord call us in a singular manner upon occasions of such difficulty and danger as lieth upon you, to a both more narrow search and careful reformation of your ways in His sight; lest He, calling to remembrance our sins forgotten by us or unrepented of, take advantage against us, and in judgment leave us for the same to be swallowed up in one danger or other. Whereas, on the contrary, sin being taken away by earnest repentance and the pardon thereof from the Lord, sealed up unto a man's conscience by His Spirit, great shall be his security and peace in all dangers, sweet his comforts in all distresses, with happy deliverance from all evil, whether in life or in death.

Now, next after this heavenly peace with God and our own consciences, we are carefully to provide for peace with all men what in us lieth, especially with our associates. And for that, watchfulness must be had that we neither at all in ourselves do give, no, nor easily take offense being given by others. Woe be unto the world for offenses, for though it be necessary (considering the malice of Satan and man's corruption) that offenses come, yet woe unto the man, or woman either, by whom the offense cometh, saith Christ, Matthew xviii.7. And if offenses in the unseasonable use of things, in themselves indifferent, be more to be feared than death itself (as the Apostle teacheth, 1 Corinthians ix.15) how much more in things simply evil, in which neither honour of God nor love of man is thought worthy to be regarded. Neither yet is it sufficient that we keep ourselves by the grace of God from giving offense, except withal we be armed against the taking of them when they be given by others. For how unperfect and lame is the work of grace in that person who wants charity to cover a multitude of offenses, as the Scriptures speak! [5]

Neither are you to be exhorted to this grace only upon the common grounds of Christianity, which are, that persons ready to take offense either want charity to cover offenses, or wisdom duly to weigh human frailty; or lastly, are gross, though close hypocrites as Christ our Lord teacheth (Matthew vii.1, 2, 3), as indeed in my own experience few or none have been found which sooner give offense than such as easily take it. Neither have they ever proved sound and profitable members in societies, which have nourished this touchy humor.

But besides these, there are divers motives provoking you above others to great care and conscience this way: As first, you are many of you strangers, as to the persons so to the infirmities one of another, and so stand in need of more watchfulness this way, lest when such things fall out in men and women as you suspected not, you be inordinately affected with them; which doth require at your hands much wisdom and charity for the covering and preventing of incident offenses that way. And, lastly, your intended course of civil community will minister continual occasion of offense, and will be as fuel for that fire, except you diligently quench it with brotherly forbearance. And if taking of offense causelessly or easily at men's doings be so carefully to be avoided, how much more heed is to be taken that we take not offense at God Himself, which yet we certainly do so oft as we do murmur at His providence in our crosses, or bear impatiently such afflictions as wherewith He pleaseth to visit us. Store up, therefore, patience against that evil day, without which we take offense at the Lord Himself in His holy and just works.

A fourth thing there is carefully to be provided for, to wit, that with your common employments you join common affections truly bent upon the general good, avoiding as a deadly |41| plague of your both common and special comfort all retiredness of mind for proper advantage, and all singularly affected any manner of way. Let every man repress in himself and the whole body in each person, as so many

[5] 1 Peter iv.8.

rebels against the common good, all private respects of men's selves, not sorting with the general conveniency. And as men are careful not to have a new house shaken with any violence before it be well settled and the parts firmly knit, so be you, I beseech you, brethren, much more careful that the house of God, which you are and are to be, be not shaken with unnecessary novelties or other oppositions at the first settling thereof.

Lastly, whereas you are become a body politic, using amongst yourselves civil government, and are not furnished with any persons of special eminency above the rest, to be chosen by you into office of government; let your wisdom and godliness appear, not only in choosing such persons as do entirely love and will promote the common good, but also in yielding unto them all due honour and obedience in their lawful administrations, not beholding in them the ordinariness of their persons, but God's ordinance for your good; not being like the foolish multitude who more honour the gay coat than either the virtuous mind of the man, or glorious ordinance of the Lord. But you know better things, and that the image of the Lord's power and authority which the magistrate beareth,[6] is honourable, in how mean persons soever. And this duty you both may the more willingly and ought the more conscionably to perform, because you are at least for the present to have only them for your ordinary governors, which yourselves shall make choice of for that work.

Sundry other things of importance I could put you in mind of, and of those before mentioned in more words, but I will not so far wrong your godly minds as to think you heedless of these things, there being also divers among you so well able to admonish both themselves and others of what concerneth them. These few things therefore, and the same in few words I do earnestly commend unto your care and conscience, joining therewith my daily incessant prayers unto the Lord, that He who hath made the heavens and the earth, the sea and all rivers of waters, and whose providence is over all His works, especially over all His dear children for good, would so guide and guard you in your ways, as inwardly by His Spirit, so outwardly by the hand of His power, as that both you and we also, for and with you, may have after matter of praising His name all the days of your and our lives. Fare you well in Him in whom you trust, and in whom I rest.

[6] Romans xiii.4. This paragraph is sometimes said to have inspired the drafting of the Mayflower Compact.

An unfeigned wellwiller of your happy success in this hopeful voyage,

JOHN ROBINSON

This letter, though large, yet being so fruitful in itself and suitable to their occasion, I thought meet to insert in this place.

APPENDIX V

Letters that Came in the Charity, *in March* 1624

[Manuscript ff. 110–11, 113–15]

[*From James Sherley*, 25 *January* 1623/24]

MOST WORTHY AND LOVING FRIENDS, Your kind and loving letters I have received, and render you many thanks, etc. It hath pleased God to stir up the hearts of our Adventurers to raise a new stock for the setting forth of this ship, called the *Charity*, with men and necessaries, both for the plantation and the fishing, though accomplished with very great difficulty. In regard we have some amongst us which undoubtedly aim more at their own private ends and the thwarting and opposing of some here, and other worthy instruments [1] of God's glory elsewhere, than at the general good, and furtherance of this noble and laudable action. Yet again we have many other, and I hope the greatest part, very honest Christian men, which I am persuaded their ends and intents are wholly for the glory of our Lord Jesus Christ in the propagation of His gospel and hope of gaining those poor savages to the knowledge of God. But, as we have a proverb, One scabbed sheep may mar a whole flock, so these malcontented persons and turbulent spirits do what in them lieth, to withdraw men's hearts from you and your friends; yea even from the general business, and yet under show and pretence of godliness and furtherance of the Plantation. Whereas the quite contrary doth plainly appear, as some of the honester-hearted men (though of late of their faction) did make manifest at our late meeting. But what should I trouble you or myself with these restless opposers of all goodness, and I doubt will be continual disturbers of our friendly meetings and love.

On Thursday, the 8th of January we had a meeting about the articles between you and us, where they would reject that which we in our late letters pressed you to grant—an addition to the time of our joint stock. And their reason which they would make known to us was, it troubled their conscience to exact longer time of you than was agreed upon at the first. But that night they were so followed and crossed of their perverse courses, as they were even wearied and offered to sell their adventures and some were willing to buy. But I, doubting they would raise more scandal and false reports, and so divers ways do us more hurt by going off in such a fury than they

[1] He means Mr. Robinson (Bradford).

could or can by continuing Adventurers amongst us, would not suffer them.

But on the 12th of January we had another meeting; but in the interim divers of us had talked with most of them privately, and had great combats and reasoning, pro and con. But at night when we met to read the general letter, we had the lovingest and friendliest meeting that ever I knew,[2] and our greatest enemies offered to lend us £50. So I sent for a pottle of wine (I would you could do the like) which we drank friendly together.[3] Thus God can turn the hearts of men when it pleaseth Him, etc. Thus, loving friends, I heartily salute you all in the Lord, hoping ever to rest,

Yours to my power,
Jan. 25, 1623[24] JAMES SHERLEY

|111| *Another Letter* [from Robert Cushman]

BELOVED SIR, etc.

We have now sent you, we hope, men and means to settle these three things, viz. fishing, salt making, and boat making. If you can bring them to pass to some perfection, your wants may be supplied. I pray you bend yourself what you can to settle these businesses. Let the ship be fraught away as soon as you can, and sent to Bilbao. You must send some discreet man for factor, whom once more you must also authorize to confirm the conditions; if Mr. Winslow could be spared, I could wish he came again.

This ship carpenter is thought to be the fittest man for you in the land, and will no doubt do you much good. Let him have an absolute command over his servants and such as you put to him. Let him build you two ketches, a lighter, and some six or seven shallops, as soon as you can. The salt man is a skillful and industrious man; put some to him that may quickly apprehend the mystery of it. The preacher we have sent is (we hope) an honest plain man, though none of the most eminent and rare. About choosing him into office, use your own lib-

[2] But this lasted not long; they had now provided Lyford and others to send over (Bradford).

[3] It is worthy to be observed, how the Lord doth change times and things; for what is now more plentiful than wine? And that of the best, coming from Malaga, the Canaries, and other places, sundry ships lading in a year. So as there is now more cause to complain of the excess and the abuse of wine, through men's corruption, even to drunkenness, than of any defect or want of the same. Witness this year 1646. The good Lord lay not the sins and unthankfulness of men to their charge in this particular (Bradford).

erty and discretion; he knows he is no officer amongst you, though perhaps custom and universality may make him forget himself. Mr. Winslow and myself gave way to his going, to give content to some here, and we see no hurt in it, but only his great charge of children.

We have took a patent for Cape Ann, etc. I am sorry there is no more discretion used by some [4] in their letters hither. Some say you are starved in body and soul; others, that you eat pigs and dogs that die alone; others, that the things here spoken of, the goodness of the country, are gross and palpable lies; that there is scarce a fowl to be seen or a fish to be taken, and many such like. I would such discontented men were here again, for it is a misery when the whole state of a plantation shall be thus exposed to the passionate humors of some discontented men. And for myself I shall hinder, for hereafter, some that would go, and have not better composed their affections; mean space it is all our crosses, and we must bear them.

I am sorry we have not sent you more and other things; but in truth we have run into so much charge to victual the ship, provide salt and other fishing implements, etc., as we could not provide other comfortable things as butter, sugar, etc. I hope the return of this ship and the *James* will put us in cash again. The Lord make you full of courage in this troublesome business, which now must be stuck unto, till God give us rest from our labours. Farewell in all hearty affection.

Your assured friend,
January 24, 1623[24] ROBERT CUSHMAN

|113| *His [5] Letter to the Governor*

MY LOVING AND MUCH BELOVED FRIEND, whom God hath hitherto preserved, preserve, and keep you still to His glory, and the good of many; that His blessing may make your godly and wise endeavours answerable to the valuation which they there have, and set upon the same. Of your love to and care for us here, we never doubted; so are we glad to take knowledge of it in that fullness we do. Our love and care to and for you is mutual, though our hopes of coming |114| unto you be small, and weaker than ever. But of this at large in Mr. Brewster's letter, with whom you, and he with you mutually, I know, communicate your letters, as I desire you may do these, etc.

Concerning the killing of those poor Indians, of which we heard at first by report, and since by more certain relation. Oh, how happy a

[4] This was John Oldham and his like (Bradford).

[5] Rev. John Robinson's.

thing had it been, if you had converted some before you had killed any! Besides, where blood is once begun to be shed, it is seldom staunched of a long time after. You will say they deserved it. I grant it; but upon what provocations and invitements by those heathenish Christians?[6] Besides, you being no magistrates over them were to consider not what they deserved but what you were by necessity constrained to inflict. Necessity of this, especially of killing so many (and many more, it seems, they would, if they could) I see not. Methinks one or two principals should have been full enough, according to that approved rule, The punishment to a few, and the fear to many. Upon this occasion let me be bold to exhort you seriously to consider of the disposition of your Captain, whom I love, and am persuaded the Lord in great mercy and for much good hath sent you him, if you use him aright. He is a man humble and meek amongst you, and towards all in ordinary course. But now if this be merely from an humane spirit, there is cause to fear that by occasion, especially of provocation, there may be wanting that tenderness of the life of man (made after God's image) which is meet. It is also a thing more glorious, in men's eyes, than pleasing in God's or convenient for Christians, to be a terrour to poor barbarous people. And indeed I am afraid lest, by these occasions, others should be drawn to affect a kind of ruffling course in the world.

I doubt not but you will take in good part these things which I write, and as there is cause, make use of them. It were to us more comfortable and convenient that we communicated our mutual helps in presence; but seeing that cannot be done, we shall always long after you, and love you, and wait God's appointed time. The Adventurers, it seems, have neither money nor any great mind of us, for the most part. They deny it to be any part of the covenants betwixt us that they should transport us, neither do I look for any further help from them, till means come from you. We here are strangers in effect to the whole course, and so both we and you (save as your own wisdoms and worths have interested you further) of principals intended in this business, are scarce accessories, etc.

My wife, with me, re-salutes you and yours. Unto Him who is the same to His in all places, and near to them which are far from one another, I commend you and all with you, resting,

Yours truly loving,

Leyden, December 19, 1623 JOHN ROBINSON

[6] Mr. Weston's men (Bradford).

His to Mr. Brewster

Loving and Dear Friend and Brother: That which I most desired of God in regard of you, namely the continuance of your life and health, and the safe coming of these sent unto you; that I most gladly hear of, and praise God for the same. And I hope Mrs. Brewster's weak and decayed state of body will have some repairing by the coming of her daughters, and the provisions in this and former ships I hear is made for you. Which makes us with more patience bear our languishing state, and the deferring of our desired transportation—which I call desired rather than hoped for, whatsoever you are borne in hand by any others.

For first, there is no hope at all, that I know or can conceive of, of any new stock to be raised for that end; so that all must depend |115| upon returns from you, in which are so many uncertainties as that nothing with any certainty can thence be concluded. Besides, howsoever for the present the Adventurers allege nothing but want of money, which is an invincible difficulty; yet if that be taken away by you, others without doubt will be found. For the better clearing of this, we must dispose the Adventurers into three parts, and of them some five or six (as I conceive) are absolutely bent for us, above any others; other five or six are our bitter professed adversaries; the rest, being the body, I conceive to be honestly minded and lovingly also toward us. Yet such as have others (namely the forward preachers) nearer unto them than us, and whose course, so far as there is any difference, they would rather advance than ours.

Now what a hanck [7] these men have over the professors, you know. And I persuade myself that, for me, they of all others are unwilling I should be transported, especially such of them as have an eye that way themselves, as thinking if I come there, their market will be marred in many regards.[8] And for these adversaries, if they have but half the wit to their malice, they will stop my course when they see it intended, for which this delaying serveth them very opportunely. And as one restive jade can hinder, by hanging back, more than two or three can (or will at least, if they be not very free) draw forward, so will it be in this case. A notable experiment of this they gave in your messenger's presence, constraining the company to promise that none of the money now gathered should be expended or employed to the help of any of us towards you.

[7] Restraint, influence.

[8] He means that others, like Lyford, want his job.

Now, touching the question propounded by you, I judge it not lawful for you (being a ruling Elder, as Romans xii.7 and 8, and 1 Timothy v.17 opposed to the Elders that teach and exhort and labour in the Word and doctrine, to which the sacraments are annexed), to administer them, nor convenient if it were lawful. Whether any learned man will come unto you or not, I know not; if any do, you must *consilium capere in arena.*[9]

Be you most heartily saluted, and your wife with you, both from me and mine. Your God and ours, and the God of all His, bring us together if it be His will, and keep us in the meanwhile, and always to His glory, and make us serviceable to His Majesty, and faithful to the end. Amen.

Your very loving brother,

Leyden, December 20, 1623 JOHN ROBINSON

[9] Take counsel on the spot.

APPENDIX VI

Correspondence with the Dutch at Manhattan, 1627

[Manuscript, ff. 149–51]

[*Isaack de Rasieres to Bradford*]

Edele, Erenfeste, Wijze Voorzienige Heren, de Gouverneur en Raeken in New Plymouth residerende; onze zeer Goede vrienden. De Directeur en de Raad van Nieuw-Nederland wensen Un Edelen Erenfesten en wijzen, voorzienigen geluk, gelukzaligheid in Christi Jesu onze Heer; met goede voorspoed en gezondheid, naar ziel en lichaam. Amen.[1]

The rest I shall render in English, leaving out the repetition of superfluous titles: [2] |150|

We have often before this wished for an opportunity or an occasion to congratulate you and your prosperous and praiseworthy undertakings and government of your colony there. And the more, in that we also have made a good beginning to pitch the foundation of a colony here, and seeing our native country lies not far from yours, and our forefathers divers hundred years ago have made and held friendship and alliance with your ancestors, as sufficiently appears by the old contracts and intercourses confirmed under the hands of kings and princes in the point of war and traffic, as may be seen and read by all the world in the old chronicles. The which are not only by the King now reigning confirmed, but it hath pleased His Majesty upon mature deliberation to make a new covenant, and to take up arms with the States General of our dear native country against our common enemy the Spaniards, who seek nothing else but to usurp and overcome other Christian kings' and princes' lands, that so he might obtain and possess his pretended monarchy over all Christendom, and so to rule and command after his own pleasure over the consciences of so many hundred thousand souls, which God forbid.

[1] The orthography of some of these words differs from the modern way of spelling them; and we have no means of ascertaining the accuracy of Bradford's copy from the original letter. This passage may be rendered thus:

"Noble, worshipful, wise, and prudent Lords, the Governor and Councillors residing in New Plymouth, our very dear friends: The Director and Council of New Netherland wish to your Lordships, worshipful, wise and prudent, happiness in Christ Jesus our Lord, with prosperity and health, in soul and body. Amen."

[2] Bradford's statement.

And also seeing it hath some time since been reported unto us by some of our people that by occasion came so far northward with their shallop, and met with sundry of the Indians, who told them that they were within half a day's journey of your Plantation, and offered their service to carry letters unto you; therefore we could not forbear to salute you with these few lines, with presentation of our good will and service unto you in all friendly kindness and neighbourhood. And if it so fall out that any goods that come to our hands from our native country may be serviceable unto you, we shall take ourselves bound to help and accommodate you therewith, either for beaver or any other wares or merchandise that you should be pleased to deal for. And if in case we have no commodity at present that may give you content, if you please to sell us any beaver or otter or such like commodities as may be useful for us for ready money, and let us understand thereof by this bearer in writing (whom we have appointed to stay three or four days for your answer); when we understand your minds therein, we shall depute one to deal with you at such place as you shall appoint.

In the meantime, we pray the Lord to take you, our honoured good friends and neighbours, into His holy protection.

By the appointment of the Governor and Council, etc.

Isaack de Rasieres, Secrectaris

From the Manhatas, in the fort Amsterdam,
March 9, Anno 1627 [3]

To this they returned answer as followeth, on the other side: |151|

[*Bradford and Council to the Dutch Governor*]

To the Honoured, etc.

The Governor and Council of New Plymouth Wisheth, etc.

We have received your letters, etc. wherein appeareth your good wills and friendship towards us, but is expressed with over-high titles, more than belongs to us or is meet for us to receive. But for your good will and congratulations of our prosperity in these small beginnings of our poor colony, we are much bound unto you and with many thanks do acknowledge the same, taking it both for a great honour done unto us, and for a certain testimony of your love and good neighbourhood.

[3] New Style; 27 Feb. 1626/27 in the English calendar.

Now these are further to give your Worships to understand that it is to us no small joy to hear that His Majesty hath not only been pleased to confirm that ancient amity, alliance and friendship, and other contracts formerly made and ratified by his predecessors of famous memory; but hath himself (as you say) strengthened the same with a new union, the better to resist the pride of that common enemy the Spaniard, from whose cruelty the Lord keep us both, and our native countries. Now forasmuch as this is sufficient to unite us together in love and good neighbourhood in all our dealings; yet are many of us further obliged by the good and courteous entreaty we have found in your country, having lived there many years with freedom and good content, as also many of our friends do to this day. For which we, and our children after us, are bound to be thankful to your nation and shall never forget the same, but shall heartily desire your good and prosperity as our own forever.

Likewise for your friendly tender and offer to accommodate and help us with any commodities or merchandise you have or shall come to you, either for beaver, otters or other wares, it is to us very acceptable, and we doubt not but in short time we may have profitable commerce and trade together. But for this year we are fully supplied with all necessaries, both for clothing and other things. But hereafter it is like we shall deal with you if your rates be reasonable. And therefore when you please to send to us again by any of yours, we desire to know how you will take beaver by the pound and otters by the skin. And how you will deal per cent for other commodities, and what you can furnish us with. As likewise what other commodities from us may be acceptable unto you, as tobacco, fish, corn or other things, and what prices you will give, etc.

Thus hoping that you will pardon and excuse us for our rude and imperfect writing in your language, and take it in good part because |152| for want of use we cannot so well express that we understand, nor happily understand everything so fully as we should. And so we humbly pray the Lord for His mercy sake that He will take both us and you into His keeping and gracious protection.

By the Governor and Council of New Plymouth,
Your Worships' very good friends and neighbours, etc.

New Plymouth, March 19

APPENDIX VII

Letters of Sherley and Hatherley to Bradford and Others, 1627–1635

[Manuscript, ff. 156, 164, 166–70, 183–4, 194–5, 207]

Another letter of his, that should have been placed before.[1] |156|

Most Worthy and Beloved Sir, I have received your letter of the 14th of June last, by your and my loving friend Mr. Allerton, wherein it pleaseth you to express more thankfulness than I have deserved; I confess my desire is much larger than my power, to do you and those good friends with you, the good I would. We cannot but take notice how the Lord hath been pleased to cross our proceedings and caused many disasters to befall us therein. I conceive the only reason to be, we or many of us aimed at other ends than God's glory. But now I hope that cause is taken away. The bargain being fully concluded, as far as our powers will reach and confirmed under our hands and seals, to Mr. Allerton and the rest of his and your copartners. But for my own part, I confess as I was loath to hinder the full confirming of it, being the first propounder thereof at our meeting; so on the other side, I was as unwilling to set my hand to the sale, being the receiver of most part of the adventures, and a second causer of much of the engagements. And one more threatened, being most envied and aimed at, if they could find any step to ground their malice on, than any other whosoever. I profess I know no just cause they ever had, or have so to do; neither shall it ever be proved that I have wronged them, or any of the Adventurers, wittingly or willingly, one penny in the disbursing of so many pounds in those two years' trouble. No, the sole cause why they malign me (as I and others conceived) was that I would not side with them against you, and the going over of the Leyden people; but as I then cared not, so now I little fear what they can do, yet charge and trouble I know they may cause me to be at. And for these reasons I would gladly have persuaded the other four to have sealed to this bargain and left me out, but they would not. So, rather than it should fail, Mr. Allerton having taken

[1] This is written on fol. 154 v. of the ms., which Bradford evidently meant to number 155 as the next leaf is 156. The salutation, the first sentence and the year, come from Bradford's *Letter Book,* printed in Massachusetts Historical Society *Collections* 1st ser. III 49–51. Ford, however, thinks that the true date is 1626 (1912 ed. Bradford II 37 *n*).

so much pains, I have sealed with the rest; with this proviso and promise of his, that if any trouble arise here, you are to bear half the charge. Wherefore now I doubt not but you will give your generality good content, and settle peace amongst yourselves, and peace with the natives; and then no doubt but the God of Peace will bless your going out and your returning, and cause all that you set your hands unto to prosper; the which I shall ever pray the Lord to grant if it be His blessed will.

Assuredly, unless the Lord be merciful to us, and the whole land in general, our estate and condition is far worse than yours. Wherefore if the Lord should send persecution or trouble here (which is much to be feared) and so should put into our minds to fly for refuge, I know no place safer than to come to you, for all Europe is at variance one with another, but chiefly with us.[2] Not doubting but to find such friendly entertainment as shall be honest and conscionable, notwithstanding what hath lately passed. For I profess in the word of an honest man, had it not been to procure your peace and quiet from some turbulent spirits here, I would not have sealed to this last deed, though you would have given me all my adventure and debt ready down. Thus desiring the Lord to bless and prosper you, I cease ever resting,

Your faithful and loving friend to my power,

December 27, 1627 JAMES SHERLEY

|164| *A Letter of Mr. Sherley's to the Governor*

May 25, 1629

SIR, etc. Here are now many of your and our friends from Leyden coming over, who though for the most part be but a weak company, yet herein is a good part of that end obtained which was aimed at, and which hath been so strongly opposed by some of our former Adventurers. But God hath His working in these things, which man cannot frustrate. With them we have also sent some servants in the ship called the *Talbot* that went hence lately; but these come in the *Mayflower*.[3] Mr. Beauchamp and myself, with Mr. Andrews and Mr.

[2] England was nominally at peace, but the Thirty Years' War had been going on for nine years, and the Spanish and Imperial armies under Tilly had beaten the Protestants in Germany and Denmark to their knees. Many English Puritans, fearing lest it be their turn next, were preparing to emigrate to New England.

[3] Not the famous *Mayflower*. This one and *Talbot* were sent over by the Massachusetts Bay Company in 1629.

Hatherley,[4] are with your love and liking joined partners with you, etc.

Your deputation we have received, and the goods have been taken up and sold by your friend and agent Mr. Allerton, myself having been near three months in Holland at Amsterdam and other parts in the Low Countries.

[*Letter of* 8 *March* 1629/30] [5]

I see further the agreement you have made with the generality, in which I cannot understand but you have done very well both for them and you, and also for your friends at Leyden. Mr. Beauchamp, Mr. Andrews, Mr. Hatherley and myself do so like and approve of it as we are willing to join with you, and God directing and enabling us, will be assisting and helpful to you the best that possibly we can. Nay, had you not taken this course, I do not see how you should accomplish the end you first aimed at, and some others endeavoured these years past. We know it must keep us from the profit which otherwise by the blessing of God and your endeavours might be gained. For most of those that come in May, and these now sent, though I hope honest and good people, yet not like to be helpful to raise profit, but rather, nay certain, must some while be chargeable to you and us; at which it is likely, had not this wise and discreet course been taken, many of your generality would have grudged.

Again, you say well in your letter and I make no doubt but you will perform it, that now being but a few on whom the burthen must be, you will both manage it the better and set to it more cheerfully, having no discontents nor contradiction but so lovingly to join together in affection and counsel, as God no doubt will bless and prosper your honest labours and endeavours. And therefore in all respects I do not see but you have done marvelously discreetly and advisedly, and no doubt but it gives all parties good content; I mean [those] that are reasonable and honest men, such as make conscience of giving the best satisfaction they be able for their debts, and that

[4] Timothy Hatherley, merchant of London, was one of the Adventurers who signed the agreement of 15 Nov. 1626. He had come to Plymouth in 1623 but returned the same year; in 1632 he emigrated to Boston and became a freeman of the Bay Colony, but owned land at Scituate and represented Plymouth in the New England Confederation.

[5] Second letter (Bradford). The letter of 8 March 1629/30 evidently begins here.

regard not their own particular so much as the accomplishing of that good end for which this business was first intended, etc.

Thus desiring the Lord to bless and prosper you and all yours, and all our honest endeavours, I rest

Your unfeigned and ever loving friend,
London, March 8, 1629[30] JAMES SHERLEY

|166| [*Sherley and Hatherley to Bradford,* 19 *March* 1629/30]

MOST WORTHY AND LOVING FRIENDS, etc. Some of your letters I received in July, and some since by Mr. Peirce, but till our main business, the patent, was granted, I could not settle my mind nor pen to writing. Mr. Allerton was so turmoiled about it, as verily I would not nor could not have undergone it, if I might have had a thousand pounds; but the Lord so blessed his labours, even beyond expectation in these evil days, as he obtained the love and favour of great men in repute and place. He got granted from the Earl of Warwick and Sir Ferdinando Gorges all that Mr. Winslow desired in his letters to me, and more also, which I leave to him to relate.[6] Then he sued to the King to confirm their grant and to make you a corporation, and so to enable you to make and execute laws in such large and ample manner as the Massachusetts Plantation hath it. Which the King graciously granted, referring it to the Lord Keeper to give order to the solicitor to draw it up, if there were a precedent for it. So the Lord Keeper furthered it all he could, and also the solicitor. But as Festus said to Paul, "With no small sum of money obtained I this freedom." [7] For by the way many riddles must be resolved and many locks must be opened with the silver, nay the golden key. Then it was to come to the Lord Treasurer, to have his warrant for freeing the custom for a

[6] This was the Warwick Patent from the Council for New England, dated 13 January 1629/30, upon which the authority and bounds of the Plymouth Colony ultimately rested. The original is preserved in the Registry of Deeds, Plymouth; the gist of it is printed in William MacDonald *Select Charters* pp. 51–3. It includes a confirmation and enlargement of the Pilgrims' Maine grant, to 15 miles on each side of the Kennebec from its junction with the Cobbosseecontee to the rippling at Nequamke, about 6 miles down-river from the Taconic falls.

[7] Acts xxii.28; but it was a Roman centurion, not Festus, who said it. Thomas Coventry, the Lord Keeper on whose favor Sherley counted to obtain a royal charter, had been a member of the Virginia Company and was much interested in colonization. But, for reasons unknown, the Plymouth Colony never did obtain its royal charter.

certain time; but he would not do it but referred it to the Council table. And there Mr. Allerton attended day by day when they sat, but could not get his petition read. And by reason of Mr. Peirce his staying with all the passengers at Bristol, he was forced to leave the further prosecuting of it to a solicitor.

But there is no fear nor doubt but it will be granted, for he hath the chief of them to friend. Yet it will be marvelously needful for him to return by the first ship that comes from thence. For if you had this confirmed, then were you complete and might bear such sway and government as were fit for your rank and place that God hath called you unto, and stop the mouths of base and scurrilous fellows that are ready to question and threaten you in every action you |167| do. And besides, if you have the custom free for 7 years inward and 21 outward, the charge of the Patent will be soon recovered, and there is no fear of recovering it.

But such things must work by degrees; men cannot hasten it as they would. Therefore we (I write in the behalf of all our partners here) desire you to be earnest with Mr. Allerton to come, and his wife to spare him this one year more to finish this great and weighty business which we conceive will be much for your good, and I hope for your posterity and for many generations to come.

This much of this letter. It was dated the March 19, 1629.

[*Bradford inserted the second part of this letter on folios* 167–9.]

I see what you write in your letters concerning the overcoming and paying of our debts, which I confess are great and had need to be carefully looked unto; yet no doubt but we joining in love may soon overcome them. But we must follow it roundly and to purpose, for if we peddle out the time of our trade others will step in and nose us. But we know that you have that acquaintance and experience in the country as none have the like. Wherefore, friends and partners, be no way discouraged with the greatness of the debt, etc. but let us not fulfil the proverb to bestow 12*d* on a purse and put 6*d* |168| in it. But as you and we have been at great charge and undergone much for settling you there, and to gain experience; so as God shall enable us, let us make use of it. And think not with £50 a year sent you over, to raise such means as to pay our debts. We see a possibility of good if you be well supplied and fully furnished, and chiefly if you lovingly agree. I know I write to godly and wise men, such as have learned to bear one another's infirmities and rejoice at anyone's prosperities. And if I were able I would press this the more, because it is hoped by some of your enemies that you will fall out one with another, and so overthrow your hopeful business. Nay, I have heard it credibly reported that some have said that till you be disjointed by discontents and fractions amongst yourselves, it boots not any to go over in hope of getting or doing good in those parts. But we hope better things of you, and that you will not only bear one with another but banish such thoughts and not suffer them to lodge in your breasts. God grant you may disappoint the hopes of your foes and procure the hearty desire of yourselves and friends in this particular. |169|

I am to acquaint you that we have thought good to join with one Edward Ashley (a man I think that some of you know) but it is only of that place whereof he hath a patent in Mr. Beauchamp's name.[8] And to that end have furnished him with large provisions, etc. Now if you please to be partners with us in this, we are willing you shall. For after we heard how forward Bristol men (and as I hear some able men of his own kindred) have been, to stock and supply him hoping of profit, we thought it fitter for us to lay hold of such an opportunity and to keep a kind of running plantation, than others who have not borne the burthen of settling a plantation, as we have done. And he on the other side, like an understanding young man, thought it better to join with those that had means by a plantation to supply and back him there, rather than strangers that look but only after profit. Now it is not known that you are partners with him but only we four, Mr. Andrews, Mr. Beauchamp, myself and Mr. Hatherley, who desired to have the Patent in consideration of our great loss we have already sustained in settling the first Plantation there. So we agreed together to take it in our names. And now, as I said before, if you please to join with us, we are willing you should; Mr. Allerton had no power from you to make this new contract, neither was he

[8] This was the Muscongus Patent, granted by the Council for New England 13 March 1629/30, to John Beauchamp of London and Thomas Leverett of Boston, Lincs. It included Muscongus Sound and the land between Pemaquid Point and the Penobscot River. Very little if anything was done about settling this region until after 1715 when President Leverett of Harvard College, grandson of Thomas Leverett, had it confirmed to him and took in Samuel Waldo and other partners. Under this Waldo Propriety, as it came to be called, Waldo County and other adjacent parts of Maine were settled. The original Muscongus Patent is in the Massachusetts Historical Society.

willing to do anything therein without your consent and approbation.

Mr. William Peirce is joined with us in this, for we thought it very convenient, because of landing Ashley and his goods there, if God please, and he will bend his course accordingly. He hath a new boat with him and boards to make another, with four or five lusty fellows, whereof one is a carpenter. Now in case you are not willing in this particular to join with us, fearing the charge and doubting the success, yet thus much we entreat of you, to afford him all the help you can, either by men, commodities or boats; yet not but that we will pay you for anything he hath. And we desire you to keep the accounts apart, though you join with us; because there is, as you see, other partners in this than the other. So for all men's wages, boats' hire, or commodities which we shall have of you, make him debtor for it; and what you shall have of him, make the Plantation or yourselves debtor for it to him, and so there will need no mingling of the accounts.

And now, loving friends and partners, if you join in Ashley's patent and business, though we have laid out the money and taken up much to stock this business and the other, yet I think it conscionable and reasonable that you should bear your shares and proportion of the stock. If not by present money yet by securing us for so much as it shall come to, for it is not barely the interest that is to be allowed and considered of, but also the adventure. Though I hope in God by His blessing and your honest endeavours, it may soon be paid, yet the years that this partnership holds is not long, nor many. Let all therefore lay it to heart and make the best use of the time that possibly we can, and let every man put to his shoulder and the burthen will be the lighter. I know you are so honest and conscionable men as you will consider hereof |170| and return such an answer as may give good satisfaction. There is none of us that would venture as we have done, were it not to strengthen and settle you, more than our own particular profit.

There is no likelihood of doing any good in buying the debt for the purchase, I know some will not abate the interest and therefore let it run its course. They are to be paid yearly and so I hope they shall according to agreement. The Lord grant that our loves and affections may still be united and knit together. And so we rest your ever loving friends,

James Sherley
Bristol, March 19, 1629[30] Timothy Hatherley

|183| *Some parts of Mr. Sherley's letters about these things, in which the truth is best manifested.*

Sir: Yours I have received by our loving friends, Mr. Allerton and Mr. Hatherley who, blessed be God, after a long and dangerous passage with the ship *Angel*, are safely come to Bristol. Mr. Hatherley is come up, but Mr. Allerton I have not yet seen; we thank you, and are very glad you have dissuaded him from his Spanish voyage, and that he did not go on in these designs he intended. For we did all utterly dislike of that course, as also of the fishing that the *Friendship* should have performed; for we wished him to sell the salt and were unwilling to have him undertake so much business; partly for the ill success we formerly had in those affairs, and partly being loath to disburse so much money. But he persuaded us, this must be one way that must repay us; for the Plantation would be long in doing of it. Nay, to my remembrance, he doubted you could not be able, with the trade there, to maintain your charge and pay us. And for this very cause he brought us on that business with Edward Ashley, for he was a stranger to us, etc.

For the fishing ship, we are sorry it proves so heavy, and will be willing to bear our parts. What Mr. Hatherley and Mr. Allerton have done, no doubt but themselves will make good.[9] We gave them no order to make any composition, to separate you and us in this or any other. And I think you have no cause to forsake us, for we put you upon no new thing, but what your agent persuaded us to, and you by your letters desired. If he exceed your order, I hope you will not blame us, much less cast us off, when our moneys be laid out, etc. But I fear neither you nor we have been well dealt withal, for sure,

[9] They were too short in resting on Mr. Hatherley's honest word, for his order to discharge them from the *Friendship's* account, when he and Mr. Allerton made the bargain with them; and they delivered them the rest of the goods, and thereby gave them opportunity also to receive all the freight of both voyages, without seeing an order to have such power under their hands in writing, which they never doubted of, seeing he affirmed he had power; and they both knew his honesty, and that he was specially employed for their agent at this time. And he was as short in resting on a verbal order from them, which was now denied when it came to a particular of loss; but he still affirmed the same. But they were both now taught how to deal in the world, especially with merchants, in such cases. But in the end this light upon these here also, for Mr. Allerton had got all into his own hand, and Mr. Hatherley was not able to pay it, except they would have utterly undone him, as the sequel will manifest (Bradford's note on fol. 182 v.).

as you write, half £4000, nay a quarter, in fitting commodities, and in seasonable time would have furnished you better than you were. And yet for all this, and much more I might write, I dare not but think him honest and that his desire and intent was good; but the wisest may fail. Well, now that it hath pleased God to give us hope of meeting, doubt not but we will all endeavour to perfect these accounts just and right, as soon as possibly we can. And I suppose you sent over Mr. Winslow, and we Mr. Hatherley, to certify each other how the state of things stood; we have received some content upon Mr. Hatherley's return, and I hope you will receive good content upon Mr. Winslow's return.

Now I should come to answer more particularly your letter, but herein I shall be very brief. The coming of the *White Angel* on your account could not be more strange to you, than the buying of her was to us; for you gave him commission [1] that what he did you would stand to. We gave him none, and yet for his credit and your sakes, paid what bills he charged on us, etc. For that I writ she was to act two parts, fishing and trade; believe me I never so much as thought of any particular trade, nor will side with any that doth, if I conceive it may wrong you. For I ever was against it, using these words: "They will eat up and destroy the General."

Other things I omit as tedious and not very pertinent. This was dated November 19, 1631.

In another letter bearing date the 24th of this month, being an answer to the general letter, he hath these words: |184|

For the *White Angel*, against which you write so earnestly and say we thrust her upon you contrary to the intent of the buyer, herein we say you forget yourselves and do us wrong. We will not take upon us to divine what the thoughts or intents of the buyer was, but what he spake we heard and that we will affirm, and make good against any that oppose it. Which is, that unless she were bought and such a course taken, Ashley could not be supplied; and again, if he were not supplied, we could not be satisfied [of] what we were out for you. And further, you were not able to do it. And he gave some reasons which we spare to relate, unless by your unreasonable re-

[1] This commission is abused. He never had any for such, as they well knew; neither had they any to pay this money, nor would have paid a penny, if they had not pleased for some other respect (Bradford).

fusal you will force us, and so hasten that fire which is a-kindling too fast already, etc.

Out of another of his, bearing date January 2, 1631

We purpose to keep the *Friendship* and the *White Angel* for the last year voyages on the general account, hoping together they will rather produce profit than loss and breed less confusion in our accounts and less disturbance in our affections.

As for the *White Angel*, though we laid out the money and took bills of sale in our own names, yet none of us had so much as a thought (I dare say) of dividing from you in anything this year, because we would not have the world (I may say Bristol) take notice of any breach betwixt Mr. Allerton and you, and he and us, and so disgrace him in his proceedings on in his intended voyage. We have now let him the ship at £30 per month by charter-party, and bound him in a bond of £1000 to perform covenants and bring her to London, if God please. And what he brings in her for you shall be marked with your mark, and bills of lading taken and sent in Mr. Winslow's letter, who is this day riding to Bristol about it. So in this voyage we deal and are with him as strangers.

He hath brought in three books of accounts; one for the Company, another for Ashley's business, and the third for the *White Angel* and *Friendship*. The books, or copies, we purpose to send you, for you may discover the errours in them better than we. We can make it appear how much money he hath had of us, and you can charge him with all the beaver he hath had of you. The total sum, as he hath put it is £7,103 17*s* 1*d*. Of this he hath expended and given to Mr. Vines and others, about £543 odd money, and then by your books you will find whether you had such and so much goods as he chargeth you withal. And this is all that I can say at present concerning these accounts. He thought to dispatch them in a few hours, but he and Straton and Fogge[2] were above a month about them. But he could not stay till we had examined them, for losing his fishing voyage which I fear he hath already done, etc.

We bless God who put both you and us in mind to send each to other, for verily had he run on in that desperate and chargeable course one year more, we had not been able to support him. Nay, both he and we must have lain in the ditch and sunk under the burthen, etc. Had there been an orderly course taken and your business

[2] Two of the original Adventurers who decided not to continue.

better managed, assuredly (by the blessing of God) you had been the ablest plantation that, as we think or know, hath been undertaken by Englishmen, etc.

Thus far of these letters of Mr. Sherley.

[*Sherley to Bradford, 24 June 1633, fol. 194*]

Loving Friends, my last was sent in the *Mary and John* by Mr. William Collier, etc. I then certified you of the great and uncomfortable and unseasonable loss you and we had in the loss of Mr. Peirce his ship the *Lyon*. But the Lord's holy name be blessed, who gives and takes as it pleaseth Him; His will be done, Amen. I then related unto you that fearful accident or rather judgment the Lord pleased to lay on London Bridge by fire, and therein gave you a touch of my great loss. The Lord I hope will give me patience to bear it, and faith to trust in Him and not in these slippery and uncertain things of this world.

I hope Mr. Allerton is near upon safe with you by this, but he had many disasters here before he could get away. Yet the last was a heavy one. His ship, going out of the harbor at Bristol, by stormy weather was so far driven on the shore as it cost him above £100 before she could be got off again. Verily his case was so lamentable as I could not but afford him some help therein, and so did some mere strangers to him. Besides, your goods were in her and if he had not been supported he must have broke off his voyage and so loss could not have been avoided on all sides. When he first bought her, I think he had made a saving match if he had then sunk her and never set her forth. I hope he sees the Lord's hand against him, and will leave off these voyages. I think we did well in parting with her. She would have been but a clog to the account from time to time, and now though we shall not get much by way of satisfaction, yet we shall lose no more. And now, as before I have writ, I pray you finish all the accounts and reckonings with him there; for here he hath nothing but many debts that he stands engaged to many men for. Besides, here is not a man that will spend a day or scarce an hour about the accounts but myself, and that business will require more time and help than I can afford. I shall not need to say any more. I hope you will do that which shall be best and just; to which add mercy and consider his intent, though he failed in many particulars which now cannot be helped, etc.

Tomorrow or next day at furthest, we are to pay £300 and Mr. Beauchamp is out of the town, yet the business I must do. Oh, the grief and trouble that man Mr. Allerton hath brought upon you and us! I cannot forget it, and to think on it draws many a sigh from my heart and tears from my eyes. And now the Lord hath visited me with another great loss, yet I can undergo it with more patience. But this I have foolishly pulled upon myself, etc.

And in another he hath this passage: [8]

By Mr. Allerton's fair propositions and large |195| promises I have overrun myself. Verily, at this time grief hinders me to write and tears will not suffer me to see; wherefore, as you love those that ever loved you and that Plantation, think upon us. Oh what shall I say of that man who hath abused your trust and wronged our loves! But now to complain is too late; neither can I complain of your backwardness, for I am persuaded it lies as heavy on your hearts as it doth on our purses or credits. And had the Lord sent Mr. Peirce safe home, we had eased both you and us of some of those debts. The Lord I hope will give us patience to bear these crosses. And that great God whose care and providence is everywhere, and specially over all those that desire truly to fear and serve Him; direct, guide, prosper and bless you so as that you may be able (as I persuade myself you are willing) to discharge and take off this great and heavy burthen which now lies upon me for your sakes. And I hope in the end for the good of you and many thousands more. For had not you and we joined and continued together, New England might yet have been scarce known, I am persuaded; not so replenished and inhabited with honest English people as now it is. The Lord increase and bless them, etc.

So, with my continual prayers for you all, I rest

Your assured loving friend,

June 24, 1633 JAMES SHERLEY

[*Sherley to Bradford*, 7 *September* 1635, *fol.* 207]

Your letter of the 22nd July 1634 by your trusty and our loving friend Mr. Winslow I have received, and your large parcel of beaver and otter skins (blessed be our God); both he and it came safely to us and we have sold it in two parcels: the skin at 14*s* a pound and

[8] Bradford's interposition.

some at 16; the coat at 20*s* the pound. The accounts: I have not sent you them this year; I will refer you to Mr. Winslow to tell you the reason of it. Yet be assured that none of you shall suffer by the not having of them, if God spare me life. And whereas you say the six years are expired that the people put the trade into your and our hands for, for the discharge of that great debt which Mr. Allerton needlessly and unadvisedly ran you and us into, yet it was promised it should continue till our disbursements and engagements were satisfied. You conceive it is done; we feel and know otherwise, etc. I doubt not but we shall lovingly agree, notwithstanding all that hath been written on both sides about the *White Angel.* We have now sent you a letter of attorney thereby giving you power in our names (and to shadow it the more we say for our uses) to obtain what may be of Mr. Allerton towards the satisfying of that great charge of the *White Angel.* And sure he hath bound himself, though at present I cannot find it; but he hath often affirmed with great protestations that neither you nor we should lose a penny by him, and I hope you shall find enough to discharge it so as we shall have no more contesting about it. Yet, notwithstanding his unnatural and unkind dealing with you, in the midst of justice remember mercy and do not all you may do, etc. Set us out of debt and then let us reckon and reason together, etc.

Mr. Winslow hath undergone an unkind imprisonment, but I am persuaded it will turn much to all your good, I leave him to relate particulars, etc.

Your loving friend,

London, Sept. 7, 1635 JAMES SHERLEY

APPENDIX VIII

Governor Winthrop's Letters on the Pequot War

[Manuscript ff. 220–2, 224–6]

[*To Bradford*, 20 *May* 1637]

SIR: The Lord having disposed as that your letters to our late Governor is fallen to my lot to make answer unto, I could have wished I might have been at more freedom of time and thoughts also that I might have done it more to your and my own satisfaction. But what shall be wanting now may be supplied hereafter. For the matters which from yourself and Council were propounded and objected to us, we thought not fit to make them so public as the cognizance of our General Court. But as they have been considered by those of our Council, this answer we think fit to return unto you.

1. Whereas you signify your willingness to join with us in this war against the Pequots, though you cannot engage yourselves without the consent of your General Court, we acknowledge your good affection towards us (which we never had cause to doubt of) and are willing to attend your full resolution when it may most seasonably be ripened.

2. Whereas you make this war to be our people's, and not |221| to concern yourselves otherwise than by consequence, we do in part consent to you therein. Yet we suppose that in case of peril you will not stand upon such terms as we hope we should not do towards you; and withal we conceive that you look at the Pequots and all other Indians as a common enemy, who though he may take occasion of the beginning of his rage, from some one part of the English, yet if he prevail, will surely pursue his advantage, to the rooting out of the whole nation. Therefore when we desired your help, we did it not without respect to your own safety, as ours.

3. Whereas you desire we should be engaged to aid you upon all like occasions, we are persuaded you do not doubt of it; yet as we now deal with you as a free people, and at liberty, so as we cannot draw you into this war with us otherwise than as reason may guide and provoke you; so we desire we may be at the like freedom when any occasion may call for help from us. And whereas it is objected to us that we refused to aid you against the French, we conceive the case was not alike; yet we cannot wholly excuse our failing in that matter.

4. Whereas you object that we began the war without your privity, and managed it contrary to your advice, the truth is that our first

intentions being only against Block Island, and the enterprise seeming of small difficulty, we did not so much as consider of taking advice or looking out for aid abroad. And when we had resolved upon the Pequots, we sent presently or not long after to you about it; but the answer received, it was not seasonable for us to change our counsels except we had seen and weighed your grounds, which might have outweighed our own.

5. For our people's trading at Kennebec, we assure you to our knowledge it hath not been by any allowance from us; and what we have provided in this and like cases at our last Court, Mr. Edward Winslow can certify you.

6. And whereas you object to us that we should hold trade and correspondency with the French, your enemies, we answer, you are misinformed; for besides some letters which hath passed between our late Governor and them, to which we were privy, we have neither sent nor encouraged ours to trade with them. Only one vessel or two for the better conveyance of our letters, had license from our Governor to sail thither.[1]

Divers other things have been privately objected to us by our worthy friend, whereunto he received some answer; but most of them concerning the apprehensions of particular discourtesies or injuries from some particular persons amongst us. It concerns not us to give any other answer to them than this: that if the offenders shall be brought forth in a right way, we shall be ready to do justice as the case shall require. In the meantime we desire you to rest assured that such things are without our privity, and not a little grievous to us.

Now for the joining with us in this war, which indeed concerns us no otherwise than it may yourselves, viz. the relieving of our friends and Christian |222| brethren, who are now first in the danger. Though you may think us able to make it good without you (as, if the Lord please to be with us, we may) yet three things we offer to your consideration, which we conceive may have some weight with you.

First, that if we should sink under this burden, your opportunity of seasonable help would be lost in three respects: 1. You cannot recover us or secure yourselves there, with three times the charge and hazard which now ye may. 2. The sorrows which we should lie under (if through your neglect) would much abate of the acceptableness of your help afterwards. 3. Those of yours who are now full of

[1] But by this means they did furnish them, and have still continued to do (Bradford).

courage and forwardness would be much damped and so less able to undergo so great a burden.

The second thing is this, that it concerns us much to hasten this war to an end before the end of this summer; otherwise the news of it will discourage both your and our friends from coming to us next year. With what further hazard and loss it may expose us unto, yourselves may judge.

The third thing is this, that if the Lord shall please to bless our endeavours, so as we end the war or put it in a hopeful way without you, it may breed such ill thoughts in our people towards yours as will be hard to entertain such opinion of your good will towards us, as were fit to be nourished among such neighbours and brethren as we are. And what ill consequences may follow on both sides, wise men may fear and would rather prevent than hope to redress.

So with my hearty salutations to yourself and all your council, and other our good friends with you, I rest

Yours most assured in the Lord,
JOHN WINTHROP

Boston, the 20th of the 3rd month, 1637

[*To Bradford* 28 *July* 1637, *fol.* 224]

WORTHY SIR: I received your loving letter and am much provoked to express my affections towards you, but straitness of time forbids me. For my desire is to acquaint you with the Lord's great mercies towards us in our prevailing against His and our enemies, that you may rejoice and praise His name with us. About eighty of our men, having coasted along towards the Dutch Plantation (sometimes by water but most by land) met here and there with some Pequots whom they slew or took prisoners. Two sachems they took and beheaded and not hearing of Sassacus, the chief sachem, they gave a prisoner his life to go and find him out. He went and brought them word where he was; but Sassacus, suspecting him to be a spy, after he was gone, fled away with some twenty more to the Mohawks; so our men missed of him. Yet dividing themselves and ranging up and down as the providence of God guided them (for the Indians were all gone save three or four and they knew not whither to guide them or else would not) upon the 13th of this month they light upon a great company of them; viz. 80 strong men and 200 women and children in a small Indian town fast by a hideous swamp, which they all slipped into before our men could get to them. Our captains were not then come together, but there was Mr. Ludlow and Captain Mason, with some ten |225| of their men, and Captain Patrick with some twenty or more of his, who, shooting at the Indians, Captain Trask with fifty more came soon in at the noise. Then they gave order to surround the swamp, it being about a mile about. But Lieutenant Davenport and some twelve more, not hearing that command, fell into the swamp among the Indians. The swamp was so thick with shrub-wood and so boggy withal that some of them stuck fast and received many shot. Lieutenant Davenport was dangerously wounded about his armhole, and another shot in the head, so as, fainting, they were in great danger to have been taken by the Indians. But Sergeant Riggs and Jeffery and two or three more rescued them and slew divers of the Indians with their swords.

After they were drawn out, the Indians desired parley and were offered by Thomas Stanton, our interpreter, that if they would come out and yield themselves, they should have their lives, all that had not their hands in the English blood; whereupon the sachem of the place came forth, and an old man or two and their wives and children, and after that some other women and children. And so they spake two hours, till it was night. Then Thomas Stanton was sent into them again, to call them forth; but they said they would sell their lives there, and so shot at him so thick as if he had not cried out and been presently rescued, they had slain him. Then our men cut off a place of the swamp with their swords, and cooped the Indians into so narrow a compass as they could easier kill them through the thickets. So they continued all the night, standing about twelve foot one from another, and the Indians, coming close up to our men, shot their arrows so thick as they pierced their hat brims and their sleeves and stockings and other parts of their clothes. Yet so miraculously did the Lord preserve them, as not one of them was wounded, save those three who rashly went into the swamp. When it was near day, it grew very dark, so as those of them which were left dropped away between our men, though they stood but twelve or fourteen foot asunder; but were presently discovered and some killed in the pursuit.

Upon searching of the swamp the next morning, they found nine slain, and some they pulled up, whom the Indians had buried in the mire; so as they do think that of all this company not twenty did escape, for they after found some who died in their flight of their wounds received. The prisoners were divided, some to those of the

River, and the rest to us; of these we send the male children to Bermuda,[2] by Mr. William Peirce, and the women and maid children are disposed about in the towns. There have been now slain and taken in all, about 700. The rest are dispersed; and the Indians in all quarters so terrified as all their friends are afraid to receive them. Two of the sachems of Long Island came to Mr. Stoughton and tendered themselves to be tributaries under our protection. And two of the Nipmuc sachems have been with me to seek our friendship. Among the prisoners we have the wife and children of Mononoto, a woman of a very modest countenance and behaviour. It was by her mediation that the two English |226| maids were spared from death, and were kindly used by her; so that I have taken charge of her. One of her first requests was that the English would not abuse her body, and that her children might not be taken from her. Those which were wounded were fetched off soon by John Gallup, who came with his shallop in a happy hour, to bring them victuals, and to carry their wounded men to the pinnace where our chief surgeon was, with Mr. Wilson, being about eight leagues off. Our people are all in health (the Lord be praised) and although they had marched in their arms all the day and had been in fight all the night, yet they professed they found themselves so fresh as they could willingly have gone to such another business.

This is the substance of that which I received, though I am forced to omit many considerable circumstances. So, being in much straitness of time (the ships being to depart within this four days, and in them the Lord Lee and Mr. Vane) I here break off; and with hearty salutes to, etc., I rest

Yours assured,

The 28th of the 5th month, 1637 JOHN WINTHROP

The captains report we have slain 13 sachems, but Sassacus and Mononoto are yet living.

[2] But they were carried to the West Indies (Bradford). These unfortunates, 2 boys and 15 women, were taken to Old Providence.

APPENDIX IX

Terminating the Undertakers' Agreement with their London Partners, 1641

[Manuscript ff. 236–40]

[*Sherley to Bradford*, 18 *May* 1641]

Sir: My love remembered, etc. I have writ so much concerning the ending of accounts betwixt us, as I profess I know not what more to write, etc.

If you desire an end, as you seem to do, there is as I conceive but two ways; that is to perfect all accounts from the first to the last, etc. Now if we find this difficult and tedious, having not been so strict and careful as we should and ought to have done, as for my own part I do confess I have been somewhat too remiss, and do verily think so are you, etc. I fear you can never make a perfect account of all your petty voyages out and home, too and again, etc.[1] So then the second way must be by biding or |237| compounding; and this way, first or last, we must fall upon, etc. If we must war at law for it, do not you expect from me, neither will I from you, but to cleave the hair; and then I dare say the lawyers will be most gainers, etc. Thus let us set to the work, one way or other and end, that I may not always suffer in my name and estate. And you are not free; nay, the gospel suffers by your delaying and causeth the professors of it to be hardly spoken of that you, being many and now able, should combine and join together to oppress and burden me, etc. Fear not to make a fair and reasonable offer, believe me I will never take any advantage to plead it against you or to wrong you, or else let Mr. Winslow come over, and let him have such full power and authority as we may end by compounding; or else the account so well and fully made up as we may end by reckoning.

Now, blessed be God, the times be much changed here. I hope to see many of you return to your native country again and have such freedom and liberty as the Word of God prescribes. Our bishops were never so near a downfall as now. God hath miraculously confounded them and turned all their popish and Machiavellian plots and projects on their own heads, etc. Thus you see what is fit to be done concerning our particular grievances, I pray you take it seri-

[1] This was but to pretend advantage, for it could not be done, neither did it need (Bradford).

ously into consideration. Let each give way a little that we may meet, etc.

Be you and all yours kindly saluted, etc. So I ever rest

Your loving friend,

Clapham, May 18, 1641 JAMES SHERLEY |238|

Articles of Agreement Made and Concluded upon the 15th Day of October, 1641, etc.

IMPRIMIS: Whereas there was a partnership for divers years agreed upon between James Sherley, John Beauchamp and Richard Andrews of London, merchants, and William Bradford, Edward Winslow, Thomas Prence, Myles Standish, William Brewster, John Alden and John Howland, with Isaac Allerton, in a trade of beaver skins and other furs arising in New England; the term of which said partnership being expired and divers sums of money in goods adventured into New England by the said James Sherley, John Beauchamp, and Richard Andrews. And many large returns made from New England by the said William Bradford, Edward Winslow, etc. And difference arising about the charge of two ships, the one called the *White Angel* of Bristol, and the other the *Friendship* of Barnstaple, and a voyage intended in her, etc., which said ships and their voyages the said William Bradford, Edward Winslow, etc. conceive do not at all appertain to their accounts of partnership: And whereas the accounts of the said partnership are found to be confused and cannot orderly appear (through the default of Josias Winslow, the bookkeeper); And whereas the said W. B. etc. have received all their goods for the said trade from the foresaid James Sherley, and have made most of their returns to him, by consent of the said John Beauchamp and Richard Andrews; And whereas also the said James Sherley hath given power and authority to Mr. John Atwood, with the advice and consent of William Collier of Duxbury, for and on his behalf to put such an absolute end to the said partnership, with all and every accounts, reckonings, dues, claims, demands, whatsoever, to the said James Sherley, John Beauchamp and Richard Andrews, from the said W. B., etc. for and concerning the said beaver trade and also the charge the said two ships and their voyages made or pretended whether just or unjust, from the world's beginning to this present, as also for the payment of a purchase of £1800 made by Isaac Allerton for and on the behalf of the said W. B., Ed. W., etc., and of the joint stock, shares, lands and adventures, whatsoever in New England aforesaid, as appeareth by a deed bearing date the 6th of November 1627; and also for and from such sum and sums of money or goods as are received by William Bradford, Thomas Prence and Myles Standish for the recovery of dues by accounts betwixt them, the said James Sherley, John Beauchamp and Richard Andrews, and Isaac Allerton, for the ship called the *White Angel.*

Now the said John Atwood with advice and counsel of the said William Collier, having had much communication and spent divers days in agitation of all the said differences and accounts with the said W. B., E. W., etc., and the said W. B., E. W. etc. have also with the said bookkeeper spent much time in collecting and gathering together the remainder of the stock of partnership for the said trade and whatsoever hath been received or is due by the said attorneyship before expressed, and all, and all manner of goods, debts and dues thereunto belonging, as well those debts that are weak and doubtful |239| and desperate as those that are more secure, which in all do amount to the sum of £1400 or thereabout; and for more full satisfaction of the said James Sherley, John Beauchamp and Richard Andrews, the said W. B. and all the rest of the abovesaid partners, together with Josias Winslow the bookkeeper, have taken a voluntary oath that within the said sum of £1400 or thereabout is contained whatsoever they know, to the utmost of their remembrance.

In consideration of all which matters and things before expressed, and to the end that a full, absolute and final end may be now made, and all suits in law may be avoided, and love and peace continued, it is therefore agreed and concluded between the said John Atwood, with the advice and consent of the said William Collier for and on the behalf of the said James Sherley, to and with the said W. B. etc. in manner and form following: viz. that the said John Atwood shall procure a sufficient release and discharge under the hands and seals of the said James Sherley, John Beauchamp and Richard Andrews to be delivered fair and unconcealed to the said William Bradford, etc. at or before the last day of August next ensuing the date hereof; whereby the said William Bradford, etc., their heirs, executors and administrators and every of them shall be fully and absolutely acquitted and discharged of all actions, suits, reckonings, accounts, claims and demands whatsoever concerning the general stock of beaver trade, payment of the said £1800 for the purchase, and all demands, reckonings and accounts, just or unjust, concerning the two ships *White Angel* and *Friendship* aforesaid, together with whatsoever hath been received by the said William Bradford of the goods or estate of Isaac Allerton, for the satisfaction of the accounts of the said ship called the *White Angel*, by virtue of a letter of attorney to him, Thomas Prence and Myles Standish, directed from the said James Sherley, John Beauchamp and Richard Andrews for that purpose as aforesaid.

It is also agreed and concluded upon between the said parties to these presents that the said W. B., E. W., etc. shall now be bound in £2400 for payment of £1200 in full satisfaction of all demands as aforesaid, to be paid in manner and form following, that is to say, £400 within two months next after the receipt of the aforesaid releases and discharges, £110 whereof is already in the hands of John Winthrop, Senior, of Boston, Esquire, by the means of Mr. Richard Andrews aforesaid; and 80 pounds' weight of beaver now deposited into the hands of the said John Atwood, to be both in part of payment of the said £400, and the other £800 to be paid by £200 per annum, to such assigns as shall be appointed, inhabiting either in Plymouth or Massachusetts Bay, in such goods and commodities and at such rates as the country shall afford at the time of delivery and payment. And in the meantime, the said bond of £2400 to be deposited into the hands of the said John Atwood.

And it is agreed upon, by and between the said parties to these presents, that if the said John Atwood shall not or cannot procure such said releases and discharges as aforesaid from the said James Sherley, John Beauchamp and Richard Andrews at or before the last day of August next ensuing the date hereof, that then the said John Atwood shall at the said day precisely redeliver, or cause to |240| be delivered unto the said W. B., E. W., etc. their said bond of £2400, and the said 80 pounds' weight of beaver, or the due value thereof without any fraud or further delay. And for performance of all and singular the covenants and agreements herein contained and expressed, which on the one part and behalf of the said James Sherley are to be observed and performed, shall become bound in the sum of £2400 unto them, the said William Bradford, Edward Winslow, Thomas Prence, Myles Standish, William Brewster, John Alden and John Howland. And it is lastly agreed upon between the said parties that these presents shall be left in trust, to be kept for both parties, in the hands of Mr. John Rayner, teacher, of Plymouth. In witness whereof, all the said parties have hereunto severally set their hands, the day and year first above written.

JOHN ATWOOD
WILLIAM BRADFORD
EDWARD WINSLOW, etc.

In the presence of EDMUND FREEMAN
WILLIAM THOMAS
WILLIAM PADDY
NATHANIEL SOUTHER

APPENDIX X

Opinions of Three Ministers on Unnatural Vice, 1642

[Manuscript ff. 244–8]

[*Answers of the Rev. John Rayner*]

Question: What sodomitical acts are to be punished with death, and what very fact (*ipso facto*) is worthy of death; or, if the fact itself be not capital, what circumstances concurring may make it capital?

Answer: In the judicial law (the morality whereof concerneth us) it is manifest that carnal knowledge of man or lying with man as with woman, *cum penetratione corporis*, was sodomy, to be punished with death; what else can be understood by Leviticus xviii.22 and xx.13 and Genesis xix.5?

Secondly, it seems also that this foul sin might be capital, though there was not *penetratio corporis* but only *contactus* and *fricatio usque ad effusionem seminis*, for these reasons: |245|

1. Because it was sin to be punished with death (Leviticus xx.13) in the man who was lyen withal, as well as in him that lieth with him. Now his sin is not mitigated where there is not penetration, nor augmented where it is; whereas it's charged upon the women that they were guilty of this unnatural sin as well as men (Romans i.26, 27). The same thing doth further appear,

2. Because of that proportion betwixt this sin and bestiality, wherein if a woman did stand before or approach to a beast for that end, to lie down thereto (whether penetration was or not) it was capital, Leviticus xviii.23 and xx.16.

3. Because something else might be equivalent to penetration where it had not been; viz. the forementioned acts with frequency and long continuance with a high hand, utterly extinguishing all light of nature. Besides, full intention and bold attempting of the foulest acts may seem to have been capital here, as well as coming presumptuously to slay with guile was capital. Exodus xxi.14.

Yet it is not so manifest that the same acts were to be punished with death in some other sins of uncleanness, which yet by the law of God were capital crimes; besides other reasons:—

1. Because sodomy and also bestiality is more against the light of nature than some other capital crimes of uncleanness, which reason is to be attended unto as that which most of all made this sin capital;

2. Because it might be committed with more secrecy and less suspicion, and therefore needed the more to be restrained and suppressed by the law;

3. Because there was not the like reason and degree of sinning against family and posterity in this sin as in some other capital sins of uncleanness.

2. Question: How far a magistrate may extract a confession from a delinquent to accuse himself of a capital crime, seeing *nemo tenetur prodere seipsum*? [1]

Answer: A magistrate cannot without sin neglect diligent inquisition into the cause brought before him. Job xxix.16. Proverbs xxiv.11, 12 and xxv.2.

Secondly, if it be manifest that a capital crime is committed, and that common report or probability, suspicion or some complaint (or the like), be of this or that person, a magistrate ought to require, and by all due means to procure from the person (so far already bewrayed) a naked confession of the fact. As appears

[1] "No man is required to incriminate himself." In the Leigh case in Elizabeth's reign, the accused, who refused to answer under oath before the Court of High Commission, was released by a common law court because (wrote Coke) *Nemo tenetur se ipsum prodere*. But the classic case, with which the Pilgrim Fathers were doubtless familiar because the victim had done exactly what William Brewster had—printed Puritan books in Holland—was John Lilburne's. Hauled before Star Chamber in 1637, Lilburne refused to incriminate himself. He was whipped down the Strand from the Fleet prison to Palace Yard, and then imprisoned until the Long Parliament ordered him released in Nov. 1640. When William Penn and his friend Mead were tried in 1670 for tumultuous assembly and Mead was asked an incriminating question he replied: "It is a maxim in your own law, *Nemo tenetur accusare seipsum*, which if it be not true Latin, I am sure it is true English. . . ." Edmund H. Morgan in 34 *Minnesota Law Review* (Dec. 1949) pp. 7–10. The same right is incorporated in the Federal Bill of Rights (1791) Art. V. The bearing of this ancient right on the U. S. Senate crime investigation of 1951 was discussed in *New York Times Magazine* 22 April 1951 p. 20.

by that which is moral and of perpetual equity, both in the case of uncertain murder, Deuteronomy xxi.1–9; and slander, Deuteronomy xxii.13–21. For, though *nemo tenetur prodere seipsum,* yet by that which may be known to the magistrate by the forenamed means, he is bound thus to do or else he may betray his country and people to the heavy displeasure of God: Leviticus xviii.24, 25, Joshua xxii.18, Psalm cvi.30. Such as are innocent to the sinful, base, cruel lusts of the profane, and such as are delinquents, and others with them, into the hands of the stronger temptations and more boldness, and hardness of heart, to commit more and worse villainy, besides all the guilt and hurt he will bring upon himself.

Thirdly, to inflict some punishment merely for this reason, to extract a confession of a capital crime, is contrary to the nature of vindictive justice, which always hath respect to a known crime committed by the person punished; and it will therefore, for anything which can before be known, be the provoking and forcing of wrath, as compared to the wringing of the nose (Proverbs xxx.33) which is as well forbidden the fathers of the country as of the family (Ephesians vi.4) as producing many sad and dangerous effects. That an oath *ex officio* for such a purpose is no due means, hath been abundantly proved by the godly learned, and is well known.

3. Question: In what cases of capital crimes one witness with other circumstances shall be sufficient to convince? Or is there no conviction without two witnesses?

Answer: In taking away the life of man, one witness alone will not suffice; there must be two, or that which is *instar.*[2] The texts are manifest: Numbers xxxv.30, Deuteronomy xvii.6 and xix.15.

Secondly, There may be conviction by one witness, and something that hath the force of another, as the evidency of the fact done by such an one, and not another; unforced confession when there was no fear or danger of suffering for the fact, handwritings acknowledged and confessed.

JOHN RAYNER |246|

[2] The equivalent.

Mr. Partridge[3] *his Writing, in Answer to the Questions.*

What is that sodomitical act which is to be punished with death?

Though I conceive probable that a voluntary effusion of seed *per modum concubitus* of man with man, as of a man with woman, though *in concubitu* there be not *penetratio corporis*, is that sin which is forbidden, Leviticus xviii: 22, and adjudged to be punished with death, Leviticus xx.13 because, though there be not *penetratio corporis*, yet there may be *similitudo concubitus muliebris*, which is that the law specifieth; yet I dare not be con[fident].

1. Because Genesis xix.5 the intended act of the Sodomites (who were the first noted masters of this unnatural art of more than brutish filthiness) is expressed by carnal copulation of man with woman; "Bring them out unto us, that we may know them."

2. Because it is observed among the nations where this unnatural uncleanness is committed, it is with penetration of the body;

3. Because, in the judicial proceedings of the judges in England, the indict[ment] so run (as I have been informed).

Question: How far may a magistrate extract a confession of a capital crime from a suspected and an accused person?

Answer: I conceive that a magistrate is bound, by careful examination of circumstances and weighing of probabilities, to sift the accused; and by force of argument to draw him to an acknowledgment of the truth. But he may not extract a confession of a capital crime from a suspected person by any violent means, whether it be by an oath imposed, or by any punishment inflicted or threatened to be inflicted, for so he may draw forth an acknowledgment of a crime from a fearful innocent. If guilty, he shall be compelled to be his own accuser when no other can, which is against the rule of justice.

Question: In what cases of capital crimes one witness with other circumstances shall be sufficient to convict? Or is there no conviction without two witnesses?

[3] The Rev. Ralph Partridge, of Duxbury. A sizar at Trinity College, Cambridge, he took his M.A. in 1623 and for several years was curate of a parish in Kent. Emigrating to Boston in 1636, he was ordained pastor of the church in Duxbury, 1638, and continued there until his death in 1658.

Answer: I conceive that, in the case of capital crimes, there can be no safe proceedings unto judgment without two witnesses, as Numbers xxxv.30, Deuteronomy xix.15, except there can some evidence be produced as available and firm to prove the fact as a witness is; then one witness may suffice, for therein the end and equity of the law is attained. But to proceed unto sentence of death upon presumptions, where probably there may *subesse falsum*, though there be the testimony of one witness, I suppose it cannot be a safe way; better for such a one to be held in safe custody for further trial, I conceive.

RALPH PARTRIDGE

The Answer of Mr. Charles Chauncy
An contactus et fricatio usque ad seminis effusionem sine penetratione corporis sit sodomia morte plectenda?

Question: The question is, What sodomitical acts are to be punished with death, and what very fact committed (*ipso facto*) is worthy of death, or if the fact itself be not capital, what circumstances concurring may make it capital? The same question may be asked of rape, incest, bestiality, unnatural sins, presumptuous sins. These be the words of the first question. The answer unto this I will lay down (as God shall direct by His Word and Spirit) in these following conclusions:

1. That the judicials of Moses that are appendances to the moral law, and grounded on the law of nature, or the Decalogue, are immutable and perpetual, which all orthodox divines acknowledge. See the authors following: Luther, tome I (Wittenberg) fol. 435 and fol. 7; Melancthon in *Locis Communibus*, loco de conjugio; Calvin lib. iv *Institutio* cap. 20 sect. 15; Junius *de Politiae Mosis* theses 29 and 30; Henry Bullinger *Decades* iii sermo 8; Wolf. Musculus *Locis Communibus* in *sexti praecepti explicatione*; Bucer *de Regno Christi* lib. ii cap. 17; Theo. Beza vol. I *de Haereticis Puniendis* p. 154; Zanchi *in tertium Decalogi praeceptum*; Ursinus part 4 *Explicatio Catecheticae*; Joh. Piscator *in Aphorismis, loco de Lege Dei*, aphor. 17.[4] And more might be

[4] All these works and the extracts quoted from them are taken from Wilhelm Zepper (Zepperus) *Legum Mosaicarum Forensium Explanatio* (2nd ed., Herborn 1614, copy in Harvard Law School Library) lib. I cap. xii, with which

added. I forbear, for brevity's sake, to set down their very words. This being the constant and general opinion of the best divines, I will rest in this as undoubtedly true, though much more might be said to confirm it.

2. That all the sins mentioned in the question were punished with death by the judicial law of Moses, as adultery, Leviticus xx.10, Deuteronomy xxii.22, Ezekiel xvi.38, John viii.5, which is to be understood not only of double adultery, when as both parties are married (as some conceive) but whosoever (besides her husband) lies with a married woman, whether the man be married or not, as in the place Deuteronomy xxii.22; or whosoever, being a married man, lieth with another woman (besides his wife) as Peter Martyr saith [in his] *Loci Communes*, which in divers respects makes the sin worse on the married man's part. For the Lord in this law hath respect as well to public honesty (the sin being so prejudicial to the church and state) as the private wrongs (saith Junius). So incest is to be punished with death, Leviticus xx.11–22. Bestiality likewise, Leviticus xx.15, Exodus xxii.19. Rapes in like manner, Deuteronomy xxii.25. Sodomy in like sort, Leviticus xviii.22 and xx.13. And all presumptuous sins, Numbers xv.30, 31.

3. That the punishment of these foul sins with death is grounded on the law of nature and is agreeable to the moral law: (1) because the reasons annexed show them to be perpetual, Deuteronomy xxii.22: "So shalt thou put away evil." Incest, bestiality, are called confusion and wickedness. (2) Infamy to the whole human nature, Leviticus xx.13, Leviticus xviii.23. Rapes are as murder, Deuteronomy xxii.25. Sodomy is an abomination, Leviticus xviii.22. |247| No holier and juster laws can be devised by any man or angel than have been by the Judge of all the world, the wisdom of the Father, by whom kings do reign, etc. (3) Because, before the giving of the Law, this punishment was anciently practiced, Genesis xxvi.11, 29, xxxix.20, and even by the heathen, by the very light of nature, as Peter Martyr shows.

Bradford's text has been collated. The long quotation from Zepper himself is on pp. 86–7, but I have been unable to find the Abulentis and Paraeus extracts. Chauncy had a horrible handwriting, and Bradford made rather wild work of his Latin. The second word of the Ursinus title, for instance, Bradford writes as "contra" and runs it along with the Piscator work as one book.

(4) Because the land is defiled by such sins, and spews out the inhabitants, Leviticus xviii.24, 25, and that in regard of those nations that were not acquainted with the law of Moses. (5) All the divines above specified consent in this, that the unclean acts punishable with death by the law of God are not only the gross acts of uncleanness by way of carnal copulation, but all the evident attempts thereof, which may appear by those several words that are used by the Spirit of God, expressing the sins to be punished with death; as, the discovering of nakedness, Leviticus xviii.6–19, which is *retegere pudenda*, as parts *per euphemismum* (saith Junius) or *detegere ad cubandum* (saith Willet), to uncover the shameful parts of the body (saith Ainsworth); which, though it reaches to the gross acts, yet it is plain it doth comprehend the other foregoing immodest attempts, as *contactum, fricationem*, etc.

4. Likewise the phrase of lying with, so often used, doth not only signify carnal copulation but other obscure acts preceding the same, is implied in Paul's word ἀρσενοκοῖται, 1 Corinthians vi.9, men lying with men; 1 Timothy i.10, men defiling themselves with mankind; men burning with lust towards men, Romans 1.27 and Leviticus xviii.22; sodomy and sin going after strange flesh, Jude verses 7, 8; and lying with mankind as with a woman, Leviticus xviii.22. Abulentis says that it signifies *omnes modus quibus masculus masculo abutatur*, changing the natural use into that which is against nature, Romans i.26; *arrogare sibi cubare*, as Junius well translates Leviticus xx.15; to give consent to lie withal, so approaching to a beast and lying down thereto, Leviticus xx.16 *ob solum conatum* (saith Willet) or for going about to do it. Add to this a notable speech of Zepperus *de legibus* (who hath enough to end controversies of this nature, lib. 1 he saith:—"*In crimine adulterii voluntas*" (understanding manifest) "*sine effectu subsecuto de jure attenditur*"; and he proves it out of good laws in these words: "*Solicitatores alienarum nuptiarum itemque matrimoniorum interpellatores, et si effectu sceleris potiri non possunt, propter voluntatem tamen perniciosae libidinis, extra ordinem puniuntur. Nam generale est quidem affectum sine effectu non puniri; sed contrarium observatur in atrocioribus, et horum similibus.*"

5. In concluding punishments from the judicial law of Moses that is perpetual, we must often proceed by analogical proportion and interpretation, as *a paribus similibus, minore ad majus*, etc.; for there will still fall out some cases, in every commonwealth, which are not in so many words extant in Holy Writ, yet the substance of the matter in every kind (I conceive under correction) may be drawn and concluded out of the Scripture by good consequence of an equivalent nature. As, for example, there is no express law against destroying conception in the womb by potions, yet by analogy with Exodus xxi.22, 23, we may reason that life is to be given for life. Again, the question *an contactus et fricatio*, etc., and methinks that place Genesis xxxviii.9 in the punishment of Onan's sin may give some clear light to it. It was (saith Pareus) *beluina crudelitas quam Deus pari loco cum parricidio habuit, nam semen corrumpere, quic fuit aliud quam hominem ex semine generandum occidere propterea juste a Deo occisus est.* Observe his words. And again, *Discamus quantopere Deus abominetur omnem seminis genitalis abusum, illicitam effusionem, et corruptionem*, etc., very pertinent in this case. That also is considerable, Deuteronomy xxv.11, 12. God commanded that if any wife drew nigh to deliver her husband out of the hand of him that smiteth him, etc., her hand should be cut off; yet such a woman in that case might say much for herself, that what she did was in trouble and perplexity of her mind, and in her husband's defense; yet her hand must be cut off for such impurity (and this is moral, as I conceive). Then we may reason from the less to the greater, what grievous sin in the sight of God it is, by the instigation of burning lusts, set on fire of hell, to proceed to *contactum et fricationem ad emissionem seminis*, etc., and that *contra naturam*, or to attempt the gross acts of unnatural filthiness. Again, if that unnatural lusts of men with men, or woman with woman, or either with beasts, be to be punished with death, than *a pari* natural lusts of men towards children under age are so to be punished.

6. *Circumstantiae variant vis e actiones* (saith the lawyers) and circumstances in these cases cannot possibly be all reckoned up; but God hath given laws for those causes and cases that are of greatest moment, by which others are to be judged of, as in the difference betwixt chance medley, and wilful murder. So in the

sins of uncleanness it is one thing to do an act of uncleanness by sudden temptation, and another to lie in wait for it, yea to make a common practice of it; this mightily augments and multiplies the sin. Again, some sins of this nature are simple, others compound, as that is simple adultery or incest, or simple sodomy; but when there is a mixture of divers kinds of lust, as when adultery and sodomy *et perditio seminis* go together in the same act of uncleanness, this is capital, double and triple. Again, when adultery or sodomy is committed by professors or church members, I fear it comes too near the sin of the priest's daughters, forbidden and commanded to be punished, Leviticus xxi.9, besides the presumption of the sins of such. Again, when uncleanness is committed with those whose chastity they are bound to preserve, this comes very near the incestuous copulation, I fear; but I must hasten to the other questions. |248|

2. Question the second, upon the point of examination, how far a magistrate may extract a confession from a delinquent to accuse himself in a capital crime, seeing *nemo tenetur prodere seipsum.*

Answer: The words of the question may be understood of extracting a confession from a delinquent either by oath or bodily torment. If it be meant of extracting by requiring an oath (*ex officio* as some call it), and that in capital crimes, I fear it is not safe, nor warranted by God's Word, to extract a confession from a delinquent by an oath in matters of life and death. 1. Because the practice in the Scriptures is otherwise, as in the case of Achan, Joshua vii.19: "Give, I pray thee, glory to the Lord God of Israel, and make a confession to him, and tell me how thou hast done." He did not compel him to swear. So when as Jonathan's life was endangered, 1 Samuel xiv.43, "Saul said unto Jonathan, Tell me what thou hast done." He did not require an oath. And notable is that, Jeremiah xxxviii.14. Jeremiah was charged by Zedekiah who said, "I will ask thee a thing, hide it not from me," and Jeremiah said, "If I declare it unto thee, wilt thou not surely put me to death?" implying that, in case of death, he would have refused to answer him. 2. Reason shows it, and experience, Job ii.4: "Skin for skin," etc. It is to be feared that those words "whatsoever a man hath" will comprehend also the conscience of an oath, and the fear of God, and all care of religion. Therefore for laying a snare before the guilty, I think it ought not to be done. But now, if the question be meant of inflicting bodily torments to extract a confession from a malefactor, I conceive that in matters of highest consequence, such as do concern the safety or ruin of states or countries, magistrates may proceed so far to bodily torments, as racks, hot irons, etc. to extract a confession, especially where presumptions are strong; but otherwise by no means. God sometimes hides a sinner till his wickedness is filled up.

Question 3. In what cases of capital crimes, one witness with other circumstances shall be sufficient to convict, or is there no conviction without two witnesses?

Answer: Deuteronomy xix.15. God hath given an express rule that in no case one witness shall arise in judgment, especially not in capital cases. God would not put our lives into the power of any one tongue. Besides, by the examination of more witnesses agreeing or disagreeing, any falsehood ordinarily may be discovered; but this is to be understood of our witness of another. But if a man witness against himself, his own testimony is sufficient, as in the case of the Amalekite, 2 Samuel i.16. Again, when there are sure and certain signs and evidences by circumstances, there needs no witness in this case, as in the business of Adonijah desiring Abishag the Shunamite to wife, that thereby he might make way for himself unto the kingdom, 1 Kings ii.23, 24. Again, probably by many concurring circumstances, if probability may have the strength of a witness, something may be this way gathered, methinks, from Solomon's judging betwixt the true mother and the harlot, 1 Kings iii.25. Lastly, I see no cause why in weighty matters, in defect of witnesses and other proofs, we may not have recourse to a lot, as in the case of Achan (Joshua vii.16), which is a clearer way in such doubtful cases (it being solemnly and religiously performed) than any other that I know, if it be made the last refuge. But all this under correction.

The Lord in mercy direct and prosper the desires of His servants that desire to walk before Him in truth and righteousness in the administration of justice, and give them wisdom and largeness of heart.

CHARLES CHAUNCY

APPENDIX XI

Conclusion of Business with London Partners, 1642–3
[Manuscript ff. 250–3]

Mr. Sherley's to Mr. Atwood [1]

MR. ATWOOD, my approved loving friend, Your letter of the 18 of October last I have received, wherein I find you have taken a great deal of pains and care about that troublesome business betwixt our Plymouth partners and friends, and us here, and have deeply engaged yourself, for which compliments and words are no real satisfaction, etc. For the agreement you have made with Mr. Bradford, Mr. Winslow, and the rest of the partners there, considering how honestly and justly I am persuaded they have brought in an account of the remaining stock, for my own part I am well satisfied and so, I think, is Mr. Andrews; and I suppose will be Mr. Beauchamp, if most of it might accrue to him, to whom the least is due, etc. And now for peace sake, and to conclude as we began, lovingly and friendly, and to pass by all failings of all, the conclude is accepted of; I say this agreement that you have made is condescended unto, and Mr. Andrews hath sent his release to Mr. Winthrop, with such directions as he conceives fit. And I have made bold to trouble you with mine, and we have both sealed in the presence of Mr. Weld and Mr. Peters [2] and some others, and I have also sent you another for the partners there to seal to me. For you must not deliver mine to them except they seal and deliver one to me. This is fit and equal, etc.

Yours to command in what I may or can,

June 14, 1642 JAMES SHERLEY

[1] John Atwood, a freeman of Plymouth Colony, appears to have had some special dealings with the London partners.

[2] The Rev. Hugh Peter, Thomas Weld and William Hibbens were sent by the Bay Colony on a mission to England in the summer of 1641, in the hope of obtaining something to ease the effects of the depression in New England economy, playing up the need for funds for Harvard College and for the conversion of the Indians. *New Englands First Fruits* (1643) was their promotion pamphlet. They did rather well, especially for the College, their big shot being the £100 scholarship fund from Lady Mowlson (Anne Radcliffe). S. E. Morison *Founding of Harvard College* 303–14, and Raymond P. Stearns "The Weld-Peter Mission to England," Colonial Society of Massachusetts *Transactions* XXXII 179–306. These letters show, and Winthrop tacitly admits, that the three Massachusetts men "pulled a fast one" on Plymouth, consenting to the London partners' unjust claim of £1200, and getting three fourths of it for the Bay Colony.

His to the Partners as Followeth

Loving Friends, Mr. Bradford, Mr. Winslow, Mr. Prence, Captain Standish, Mr. Brewster, Mr. Alden and Mr. Howland: give me leave to join you all in one letter concerning the final end and conclude of that tedious and troublesome business, and I think I may truly say uncomfortable and unprofitable to all, etc. It hath pleased God now to put us upon a way to cease all suits, and disquieting of our spirits, and to conclude with peace and love, as we began. I am contented to yield and make good what Mr. Atwood and you have agreed upon; and for that end have sent to my loving friend, Mr. Atwood, an absolute and general release unto you all, and if there want anything to make it more full, write it yourselves and it shall be done, provided that all you, either jointly or severally, seal the like discharge to me. And for that end I have drawn one jointly and sent it to Mr. Atwood with that I have sealed to you. Mr. Andrews hath sealed an acquittance also and sent it to Mr. Winthrop, with such directions as he conceived fit and, as I hear, hath given his debt, which he makes £544, unto the gentlemen of the Bay.

Indeed, Mr. Weld, Mr. Peters and Mr. Hibbens have taken a great deal of pains with Mr. Andrews, Mr. Beauchamp and myself, to bring us to agree; and to that end we have had many meetings and spent much time about it. But as they are very religious and honest gentlemen, yet they had an end that they drove at and laboured to accomplish. (I mean not any private end, but for the general good of their Patent.) It had been very well you had sent one over.

Mr. Andrews wished you might have one third part of the £1200 and the Bay two thirds; but then we three must have agreed together, which were a hard matter now. But Mr. Weld, Mr. Peters and Mr. Hibbens and I have agreed, they giving you bond so to compose with Mr. Beauchamp as to procure his general release, and free you from all trouble and charge that he may put you to. Which indeed is nothing, for I am persuaded Mr. Weld will in time gain him to give them all that is due to |251| him, which in some sort is granted already. For though his demands be great, yet Mr. Andrews hath taken some pains in it, and makes it appear to be less than I think he will consent to give them for so good an use; so you need not fear that for taking bond there to save you harmless, you be safe and well.

Now our accord is that you must pay to the gentlemen of the Bay £900. They are to bear all charges that may any way arise concerning the free and absolute clearing of you from us three. And you to have the other £300, etc.

Upon the receiving of my release from you, I will send you your bonds for the purchase money. I would have sent them now, but I would have Mr. Beauchamp release as well as I, because you are bound to him in them. Now I know if a man be bound to twelve men, if one release it is as if all released, and my discharge doth cut them off. Wherefore doubt you not but you shall have them and your commission, or anything else that is fit. Now you know there is two years of the purchase money that I would not own, for I have formerly certified you that I would but pay seven years, but now you are discharged of all, etc.

Your loving and kind friend in what I may or can,

June 14, 1642 JAMES SHERLEY

The copy of his release is as followeth:

Whereas divers questions, differences and demands have arisen and depended between William Bradford, Edward Winslow, Thomas Prence, Myles Standish, William Brewster, John Alden and John Howland, gentlemen, now or lately inhabitants or resident at New Plymouth in New England, on the one party; and James Sherley of London merchant and others on th' other part, for and concerning a stock and partable trade of beaver and other commodities, and freighting of ships, as the *White Angel*, *Friendship* or others, and the goods of Isaac Allerton which were seized upon by virtue of a letter of attorney made by the said James Sherley and John Beauchamp and Richard Andrews, or any other matters concerning the said trade either here in Old England or there in New England or elsewhere, all which differences are since by mediation of friends composed, compromised, and all the said parties agreed. Now know all men by these presents that I, the said James Sherley, in performance of the said compromise and agreement have remissed, released and quit-claimed and do by these presents remiss, release and for me, mine heirs, executors and administrators, and for every of us for ever quit-claim unto the said William Bradford, Edward Winslow, Thomas Prence, Myles Standish, William Brewster, John Alden and John Howland and every of them, their and every of their heirs, executors and administrators, all and all manner of actions, suits, debts, accounts, reckonings, commissions, bonds, bills, specialties, judgments, executions, claims, challenges, differences, and demands whatsoever, with or against the said William Bradford, Edward Winslow, Thomas Prence, Myles Standish, William Brewster, John Alden, and John Howland or any of them, ever I had, now have or in time to come can, shall, or may have for any matter, cause or thing whatsoever from the beginning of the world until the day of the date of these presents.

In witness whereof I have hereunto put my hand and seal, given the second day of June, 1642 and in the eighteenth year of the reign of our sovereign lord King Charles, etc.

Sealed and delivered JAMES SHERLEY
in the presence of THOMAS WELD
HUGH PETERS
WILLIAM HIBBENS
ARTHUR TIRREY, Scribe
THOMAS STURGES, his servant

[*Richard Andrews to Edmund Freeman, fol.* 252]

MR. FREEMAN: My love remembered unto you, etc. I then certified the partners how I found Mr. Beauchamp and Mr. Sherley in their particular demands, which was according to men's principles of getting what they could; although the one will not show any account, and the other a very unfair and unjust one. And both of them discouraged me from sending the partners my account, Mr. Beauchamp especially. Their reason, I have cause to conceive, was that although I do not, nor ever intended to, wrong the partners or the business, yet if I gave no account I might be esteemed as guilty as they in some degree at least, and they might seem to be the more free from taxation in not delivering their accounts; etc. Who have both of them charged the account with much interest they have paid forth, and one of them would likewise for much interest he hath not paid forth, as appeareth by his account, etc. And seeing the partners have now made it appear that there is £1200 remaining due between us all, and that it may appear by my account I have not charged the business with any interest but do forgive it unto the partners above £200; if Mr. Sherley and Mr. Beauchamp, who have between them wronged the business so many hundred pounds both in principal and interest likewise, and have therein wronged me as well and as much as any of the partners, yet if they will not make and deliver fair and true accounts of the same, nor be content to take what by computation is more than can be justly due to either, that is to Mr. Beauchamp £150 as by Mr. Allerton's account, and Mr. Sherley's account, on oath in Chancery. And though there might be nothing due to Mr. Sherley, yet he requires £100, etc.

I conceive, seeing the partners have delivered on their oaths the sum remaining in their hands, that they may justly detain the £650 which may remain in their hands after I am satisfied, until Mr. Sherley and Mr. Beauchamp will be more fair and just in their ending, etc. And as I intend, if the partners fairly end with me, in satisfying in part and engaging themselves for the rest of my said £544 to return back for the poor my part of the land at Scituate. So likewise I intend to relinquish my right and interest in their dear Patent, on which much of our money was laid forth, and also my right and interest in their cheap purchase, the which may have cost me first and last £350. But I doubt whether other men have not charged or taken on account what they have disbursed in the like case, which I have not charged, neither did I conceive any other durst so do, until I saw the account of the one and heard the words of the other. The which gives me just cause to suspect both their accounts to be unfair;[3] for it seemeth they consulted one with another about some particulars therein, therefore I conceive the partners ought the rather to require just accounts from each of them before they part with any money to either of them, for merchants understand how to give an account. If they mean fairly they will not deny to give an account for they keep memorials to help them to give exact accounts in all particulars, and memorial cannot forget his charge if the man will remember.

I desire not to wrong Mr. Beauchamp or Mr. Sherley, nor may be silent in such apparent probabilities of their wronging the partners, and me likewise, either in denying to deliver or show any account, or in delivering one very unjust in some particulars and very suspicious in many more, either of which, being from understanding merchants, cannot be from weakness or simplicity, and therefore the more unfair.

So commending you and yours and all the Lord's people unto the gracious protection and blessing of the Lord, and rest your loving friend,

April 7, 1643 RICHARD ANDREWS

[3] This he means of the first adventures, all which were lost as hath before been shown; and what he here writes is probable at least (Bradford).

[*Sherley to the Plymouth Partners*, 27 *April* 1643, *fol.* 253]

Loving Friends, Mr. Bradford, Mr. Winslow, Captain Standish, Mr. Prence and the rest of the partners with you; I shall write this general letter to you all, hoping it will be a good conclude of a general but a costly and tedious business I think to all, I am sure to me, etc. I received from Mr. Winslow a letter of the 28th of September last, and so much as concerns the general business I shall answer in this, not knowing whether I shall have opportunity to write particular letters, etc. I expected more letters from you all, as some particular writes, but it seemeth no fit opportunity was offered. And now, though the business for the main may stand, yet some particulars is altered. I say my former agreement with Mr. Weld and Mr. Peters, before they could conclude or get any grant of Mr. Andrews, they sought to have my release; and thereupon they sealed me a bond for a £110. So I sent my acquittance, for they said without mine there would be no end made (and there was good reason for it). Now they hoped, if they ended with me, to gain Mr. Andrews' part as they did wholly to a pound (at which I should wonder, but that I observe some passages) and they also hoped to have gotten Mr. Beauchamp's part. And I did think he would have given it them, but if he did well understand himself and that account he would give it, for his demands make a great sound. But it seemeth he would not part with it, supposing it too a great a sum, and that he might easily gain it from you.[4] Once he would have given them £40 but now they say he will not do that, or rather I suppose they will not take it; for if they do, and have Mr. Andrews's, then they must pay me their bond of £110 three months hence. Now it will fall out far better for you, that they deal not with Mr. Beauchamp, and also for me if you be as kind to me as I have been and will be to you. And that thus, if you pay Mr. Andrews, or the Bay men by his order, £544 which is his full demand, but if looked into perhaps might be less. The man is honest, and in my conscience would not wittingly do wrong, yet he may forget as well as other men, and Mr. Winslow may call to mind wherein he forgets—but sometimes it is good to buy peace.

The gentlemen of the Bay may abate £100 and so both sides have more right and justice than if they exact all, etc. Now if you send me £150, then say Mr. Andrews' full sum and this, it is near £700. Mr. Beauchamp he demands £400; and we all know that if a man de-

[4] This was a mystery to them, for they heard nothing hereof from any side the last year, till now the conclusion was past and bonds given (Bradford).

mands money he must show wherefore and make proof of his debt, which I know he can never make good proof of one hundred pound due unto him as principal money. So till he can, you have good reason to keep the £500 etc. This I protest I write not in malice against Mr. Beauchamp, for it is a real truth; you may partly see it by Mr. Andrews making up his account, and I think you are all persuaded I can say more than Mr. Andrews concerning that account. I wish I could make up my own as plain and easily, but because of former discontents I will be sparing till I be called, and you may enjoy the £500 quietly till he begin. For let him take his course here or there, it shall be all one; I will do him no wrong; and if he have not one penny more, he is less loser than either Mr. Andrews or I. This I conceive to be just and honest, the having or not having of his release matters not. Let him make such proof of his debt as you cannot disprove, and according to your first agreement you will pay it, etc.

Your truly affectioned friend,

London, April 27, 1643 James Sherley

APPENDIX XII

OFFICIAL DOCUMENTS

1. *Order of the Privy Council, on Complaint of Sir Christopher Gardiner,* et al.[1] [190 v.]

At the Court at Whitehall, the 19 January 1632[33]

PRESENT

Lord Privy Seal	Lord Cottington
Earl of Dorset	Mr. Treasurer
Lord Viscount Falkland	Mr. Vice Chamberlain
Lord Bishop of London	Mr. Secretary Coke

Mr. Secretary Windebank

WHEREAS His Majesty hath lately been informed of great Distraction and much Disorder in that Plantation in the parts of America called New England, which if they be true and suffered to run on, would tend to the great Dishonour of this kingdom and utter ruin of that Plantation. For prevention whereof, and for the orderly settling of Government according to the intention of those Patents which have been granted by His Majesty and from his late Royal Father King James, it hath pleased His Majesty that the Lords and others of his most Honourable Privy Council should take the same into consideration. Their Lordships in the first place thought fit to make a Committee of this Board to take examination of the matters informed. Which committees having called divers of the principal Adventurers in that Plantation and heard those that are complainants against them. Most of the things informed being denied and resting to be proved by parties that must be called from that place, which required a long expense of time. And at present their Lordships finding the Adventurers were upon dispatch of men, victuals and merchandise for that

[1] This is a correct transcription of the Records of the Privy Council, with minor verbal differences, according to Ford in 1912 ed. Bradford II 142–4. Thomas Morton, Philip Ratcliffe and perhaps others also complained; Sir Richard Saltonstall, Matthew Cradock and John Humfry replied. The real reason for this to-do was the desire of Sir Ferdinando Gorges and others of the Council for New England to get some profit from the rapid settlement taking place in New England, by having the charter of the Massachusetts Bay Company canceled. This report was laid before the King, who said "he would have them severely punished who did abuse his Governor and the Plantation," according to Winthrop.

place, all which would be at a stand if the Adventurers should have discouragement or take suspicion that the State here had no good opinion of that Plantation. Their Lordships, not laying the fault or fancies (if any be) of some particular men upon the General Government or Principal Adventurers (which in due time is further to be inquired into) have thought fit in the meantime to declare that the appearances were so fair and hopes so great that the Country would prove both beneficial to this Kingdom and profitable to the particular Adventurers, as that the Adventurers had cause to go on cheerfully with their undertakings; and rest assured, if things were carried, as was pretended when the Patents were granted, and accordingly as by the Patents it is appointed, His Majesty would not only maintain the Liberties and Privileges heretofore granted, but supply anything further that might tend to the Good Government, Prosperity and Comfort of his people there of that place, etc.

William Trumball

2. *Royal Commission for Regulating Plantations,* 28 *April* 1634 [2]

CHARLES by the grace of GOD King of England, Scotland, France, and Ireland, Defender of the Faith, ETC.

To the most Reverend father in Christ, our well beloved and faithful counsellor William, by divine Providence Archbishop of Canterbury, of all England Primate and Metropolitan; Thomas Lord Coventry, Keeper of our Great Seal of England; the most Reverent father in Christ our well beloved and most faithful counselor, Richard, by divine Providence Archbishop of York, Primate and Metropolitan; our well beloved and most faithful cousins and counselors, Richard Earl of Portland, our High Treasurer of England; Henry Earl of Manchester, Keeper of our Privy Seal; Thomas, Earl of Arundel and Surrey, Earl Marshal of England; Edward Earl of Dorset, Chamberlain of our most dear consort the Queen; and our beloved and faithful councillors, Francis Lord Cottington, Councillor and Undertreasurer of our Exchequer; Sir Thomas Edmonds knight, Treasurer of our household; Sir Henry Vane knight, comptroller of the same household; Sir John Cook knight, one of our Privy Secretaries, And Francis Windebank knight, another of our Privy Secretaries, Greeting.

[2] This document Bradford copied onto the reverse of ff. 200–1.

Whereas very many of our subjects and of our late father's of beloved memory, our sovereign lord James, late King of England, by means of license royal, not only with desire of enlarging the territories of our empire but chiefly out of a pious and religious affection, and desire of propagating the gospel of our Lord Jesus Christ, with great industry and expenses have caused to be planted large colonies of the English nation in divers parts of the world altogether unmanured and void of inhabitants, or occupied of the barbarous people that have no knowledge of divine worship. We being willing to provide a remedy for the tranquility and quietness of those people, and being very confident of your faith and wisdom, justice and provident circumspection, have constituted you, the aforesaid Archbishop of Canterbury, Lord Keeper of the Great Seal of England, the Archbishop of York, etc. and any five or more of you, our Commissioners. And to you and any five or more of you, we do give and commit power for the government and safety of the said colonies drawn, or which out of the English nation into those parts hereafter shall be drawn, to make laws, constitutions and ordinances pertaining either to the public state of these colonies or the private profit of them. And concerning the lands, goods, debts and succession in those parts, and how they shall demean themselves towards foreign princes and their people, or how they shall bear themselves towards us and our subjects, as well in any foreign parts whatsoever or on the seas in those parts or in their return sailing home or which may pertain to the clergy government, or to the cure of souls among the people there living, and exercising trade in those parts, by designing out congruent portions arising in tithes, oblations and other things there, according to your sound discretions in political and civil causes, and by having the advice of two or three bishops for the settling, making and ordering of the business for the designing of necessary ecclesiastical and clergy portions, which you shall cause to be called and taken to you. And to make provision against the violation of those laws, constitutions and ordinances, by imposing penalties and mulcts, imprisonment if there be cause and that the quality of the offense do require it, by deprivation of member or life, to be inflicted. With power also (our assent being had) to remove and displace the governors or rulers of those colonies for causes which to you shall seem lawful and others in their stead to constitute. And require an account of their rule and government, and whom you shall find culpable, either by deprivation from their place or by imposition of a mulct upon the goods of them in those parts to be levied, or banishment from those provinces in which they have been governor or otherwise to cashier according to the quantity of the offense. And to constitute judges and magistrates political and civil, for civil causes and under the power and form which to you, five or more of you, shall seem expedient. And judges and magistrates and dignities to causes ecclesiastical, and under the power and form which to you, five or more of you, with the bishops vicegerents (provided by the Archbishop of Canterbury for the time being) shall seem expedient; and to ordain courts, pretorian and tribunal, |201 v| as well ecclesiastical as civil, of judgments; to determine the forms and manner of proceedings in the same, and of appealing from them in matters and causes as well criminal as civil, personal, real and mixed, and to their seats of justice, what may be equal and well ordered and what crimes, faults or excesses of contracts or injuries ought to belong to the ecclesiastical court, and what to the civil court and seat of justice.

Provided, nevertheless, that the laws, ordinances and constitutions of this kind, shall not be put in execution before our assent be had thereunto in writing under our signet, signed at least; and this assent being had and the same publicly proclaimed in the provinces in which they are to be executed, we will and command that those laws, ordinances, and constitutions, more fully to obtain strength and be observed, and shall be inviolably of all men whom they shall concern.

Notwithstanding, it shall be for you, or any five or more of you, (as is aforesaid) although those laws, constitutions and ordinances shall be proclaimed with our royal assent, to change, revoke and abrogate them and other new ones, in form aforesaid, from time to time frame and make as aforesaid; and to new evils arising, or new dangers, to apply new remedies as is fitting, so often as to you it shall seem expedient.

Furthermore, you shall understand that we have constituted you, and every five or more of you, the aforesaid Archbishop of Canterbury; Thomas Lord Coventry, Keeper of the Great Seal of England; Richard Bishop of York, Richard Earl of Portland, Henry Earl of Manchester, Thomas Earl of Arundel and Surrey, Edward Earl of Dorset, Francis Lord Cottington, Sir Thomas Edmonds knight, Sir Henry Vane knight, Sir Francis Windebank knight, our Commissioners to hear and determine according to your sound discretions all manner of complaints either against those colonies or their rulers or governors, at the instance of the parties grieved, or at their accusation brought concerning injuries from hence or from thence between them and their members to be moved and to call the parties before you. And to the parties or to their procurators from hence or from thence being heard, the full complement of justice to be exhibited. Giving unto you or any five or more of you power that if you shall find any of the colonies aforesaid or any of the chief rulers upon the jurisdictions of others by unjust possession or usurpation or one against another making grievance or in rebellion against us, or withdrawing from our allegiance, or our commandments not obeying, consultation first with us in that case had, to cause those colonies or the rulers of them for the causes aforesaid, or for other just causes, either to return to England or to command them to other places designed, even as according to your sound discretions it shall seem to stand with equity and justice or necessity. Moreover, we do give unto you and any five or more of you power and special command over all the charters, letters patents and rescripts royal of the regions, provinces, islands or lands in foreign parts, granted for rising colonies, to cause them to be brought before you. And the same being received, if anything surreptitiously or unduly have been obtained, or that by the same privileges, liberties and prerogatives hurtful to us or to our crown or to foreign princes, have been prejudicially suffered or granted, the same being better made known unto you, five or more of you, to command them according to the laws and customs of England to be revoked, and to do such other things which to the profit and safeguard of the aforesaid colonies and of our subjects resident in the same, shall be necessary. And therefore we do command you that about the premises at days and times which for these things you shall make provision, that you be diligent in attendance as it becometh you; giving in precept also and firmly enjoining we do give command to all and singular chief rulers of provinces into which the colonies aforesaid have been drawn, or shall be drawn, and concerning the colonies themselves, and concerning others that have been interest therein, that they give attendance upon you and be observant and obedient unto your warrants in those affairs, as often as and even as in our name they shall be required, at their peril.

In testimony whereof we have caused these our letters to be made patent.

Witness ourself at Westminster the 28th day of April, in the tenth year of our reign.

By writ from the Privy Seal,

Anno Domini 1634 Willies

3. *The Agreement of the Bounds Betwixt Plymouth and Massachusetts.*[3] 9 *June* 1640 |232|

Whereas there were two commissions granted by the two jurisdictions, the one of Massachusetts Government, granted unto John Endecott gent., and Israel Stoughton gent.; the other of New Plymouth Government, to William Bradford governor, and Edward Winslow gent.; and both these for the setting out, settling and determining of the bounds and limits of the lands between the said jurisdictions, whereby not only this present age but the posterity to come may live peaceably and quietly in that behalf. And forasmuch as the said commissioners on both sides have full power so to do, as appeareth by the records of both jurisdictions, we therefore, the said commissioners above named, do hereby with one consent and agreement conclude, determine and by these presents declare:

That all the marshes at Cohasset that lie of the one side of the river next to Hingham shall belong to the jurisdiction of Massachusetts Plantation, and all the marshes that lie on the other side of the river next to Scituate shall belong to the jurisdiction of New Plymouth, excepting 60 acres of marsh at the mouth of the river on Scituate side next to the sea, which we do hereby agree, conclude and determine shall belong to the jurisdiction of the Massachusetts.

And further, we do hereby agree, determine and conclude, that the bounds of the limits between both the said jurisdictions are as followeth; viz., from the mouth of the brook that runneth into Cohasset marshes (which we call by the name of Bound Brook) with a straight and direct line to the middle of a great pond that lieth on the right hand of the upper path or common way that leadeth between Weymouth and Plymouth, close to the path as we |233| go along, which was formerly named (and still we desire may be called) Accord Pond,[4] lying about five or six miles from Weymouth southerly, and from thence with a straight line to the southernmost part of Charles River[5] and three miles southerly inward into the country,

[3] Also printed in *Plymouth Colony Records* IX 1. Bradford, in copying it, modestly omitted the *Esq*^{r}. after his name.

[4] Bound Brook is the stream that flows over a ledge of rocks into Cohasset Harbor; the place where the main road (Justice Cushing Highway) crosses it is marked. Accord Pond is in the south part of Hingham; the old "Common Way" in the main is followed by the present Route 3.

[5] Which is Charles River may still be questioned (Bradford). And still was being questioned two centuries later! In 1642 the Bay sent Nathaniel Woodward and Solomon Saffry (described as "skillful artists" and "mathematicians" by

according as is expressed in the patent granted by His Majesty to the Company of the Massachusetts Plantation. Provided always and never the less concluded and determined by mutual agreement between the said commissioners, that if it fall out that the said line from Accord Pond to the southernmost part of Charles River, and three miles southerly as is before expressed, straiten or hinder any part of any plantation begun by the Government of New Plymouth, or hereafter

---

Massachusetts authorities, as "a pair of obscure sailors" by the Rhode Islanders) to find the source of the Charles. Leaving the main stream at a point in Medway, they ascended a southward-flowing tributary known at different eras as Jack's Pasture Brook, Stop River and Mill River, to its source in the pond once called Wrentham, later Whitney, and now Lake Pearl. From that they pushed three miles south and drove in a stake, since called the "Woodward and Saffry Station" on the plain which gives its name to the present town of Plainville. They took a solar observation and declared the latitude of this station to be 41°55′ N. In reality it was 42°01′30″, slightly north and about 1 mile east of Burnt Swamp Corner (lat. 42°01′08.35″ N, long. 71°22′54.51″ W), which determines the present NE corner of Rhode Island. An 18th-century copy of Woodward and Saffry's survey is reproduced in 1912 ed. Bradford II 280, but a much clearer sketch from it is in Clarence W. Bowen *Boundary Disputes of Connecticut* (1883) p. 19.

Next, on 9 May 1664 a committee of five from the Bay Colony and Plymouth (Constant Southworth and Josiah Winslow being the Plymouth representatives) met at Dedham, followed the former route up the Charles and Mill Rivers to Lake Pearl, and then stretched a much more generous 3 miles southward to "a white oak in a plain full of trees," which they marked. This station, since called the Angle Tree Bound, was marked by a tall granite shaft in 1790. The Joint Commission of 1664 laid out a line W past Sneech Pond until it hit the Nipmuck (Blackstone) River, returned to the Angle Tree, and then pushed ENE through the woods to Accord Pond. They missed the pond by half a mile, made a fresh start from a black oak halfway down that pond's western shore, and returned through the woods to the Angle Tree (*Massachusetts Bay Records* IV Part 2 pp. 115–16). This "Old Colony Line," as it was called, became the boundary between the Massachusetts Bay and Plymouth Colonies; it is still the boundary between Norfolk County on the north and Bristol and Plymouth Counties on the south. Since either the Angle Tree or the Woodward and Saffry Station was supposed to fix the northern boundaries of Rhode Island and Connecticut, both colonies claimed that they had been cheated by Massachusetts taking Lake Pearl for the source of the Charles River, which really rises in the town of Hopkinton near Hayden Row. Rhode Island, however, consented to have the line run about as Massachusetts claimed, in 1718 and 1726. After interminable squabbles about which colony should tax the border towns, the subject was finally threshed out before the Supreme Court of the United States in the case of Rhode Island vs. Massachusetts, in 1846, 4 Howard or 45 U. S. Reports 591–640. Justice McLane, delivering the opinion of the Court, declared in effect that if Rhode Island had originally been cheated, she had been cheated so long ago that the well-established boundary should not be upset.

to be begun within ten years after the date of these presents, that then notwithstanding the said line, it shall be lawful for the said Government of New Plymouth to assume on the northerly side of the said line, where it shall so entrench as aforesaid, so much land as will make up the quantity of eight miles square, to belong to every such plantation begun, or to [be] begun as aforesaid; which we agree, determine and conclude to appertain and belong to the said Government of New Plymouth.

And whereas the said line, from the said brook which runneth into Cohasset saltmarsh (called by us Bound Brook and the pond called Accord Pond) lieth near the lands belonging to the townships of Scituate and Hingham, we do therefore hereby determine and conclude that if any divisions already made and recorded by either the said townships do cross the said line, that then it shall stand and be of force according to the former intents and purposes of the said towns granting them, the marshes formerly agreed on excepted. And that no town in either jurisdiction shall hereafter exceed, but contain themselves within the said lines expressed.

In witness whereof we the commissioners of both jurisdictions do by these presents indented, set our hands and seals the ninth day of the fourth month in 16th year of our sovereign lord King Charles, and in the year of our Lord 1640.

William Bradford, Governor — John Endecott
Edward Winslow — Israel Stoughton

4. *Surrender of the Patent to the Body of Freemen, March* 1641 [6]

Whereas William Bradford and divers others the first instruments of God in the beginning of this great work of plantation, together with such as the all-ordering hand of God in His providence soon added unto them, have been at very great charges to procure the lands, privileges and freedoms from all entanglements, as may appear by divers and sundry deeds, enlargements of grants, purchases, and payments of debts, etc.; by reason whereof the title, to the day of these presents, |234| remaineth in the said William Bradford, his heirs, associates, and assigns. Now for the better settling of the estate of the said lands contained in the grant or Patent, the said Wil-

[6] Also printed in *Plymouth Colony Records* II 10, with a more elaborate preamble deriving Bradford's title from the Council for New England and from "His Majesty our dread sovereign Charles, by the grace of God King of England, Scotland, France and Ireland, etc." The date is 2 March 1640/41.

liam Bradford, and those first instruments termed and called in sundry orders upon public record, the Purchasers, or Old Comers, witness two in special, the one bearing date the 3rd of March, 1639, the other in December the 1st, anno 1640, whereunto these presents have special relation and agreement. And whereby they are distinguished from other the freemen and inhabitants of the said corporation.[7]

Be it known unto all men, therefore, by these presents, that the said William Bradford for himself, his heirs, together with the said Purchasers, do only reserve unto themselves, their heirs and assigns those three tracts of land mentioned in the said resolution, order and agreement bearing date the first of December 1640; viz. first, from the bounds of Yarmouth, three miles to the eastward of Namskaket, and from sea to sea, cross the neck of land. The second of a place called Acoughcus, which lieth in the bottom of the bay adjoining to the west side of Point Peril, and two miles to the western side of the said river, to another place called Acushnet River, which entereth at the western end of Nacata, and two miles to the eastward thereof, and to extend eight miles up into the country. The third place, from Sowamsett River to Pawtucket River, with Cawsumsett Neck which is the chief habitation of the Indians and reserved for them to dwell upon, extending into the land eight miles through the whole breadth thereof.[8] Together with such other small parcels of

[7] The General Court voted 5 March 1639/40 to pay the 58 Purchasers or Old Comers £300 for the surrender of the Patent, and that they reserve some ungranted land for themselves; these parcels were confirmed on 1 Dec. 1640; see *Plymouth Colony Records* XI. The Purchasers or Old Comers were those of the Colony who bought out the Adventurers' interest in the Plantation at the expiration of seven years—see chap. xviii above—together with others later admitted to the body. Their names are printed in *Plymouth Colony Records* II 177 and 1912 ed. Bradford II 285–6.

[8] The Warwick Patent of 13 Jan. 1630 from the Council for New England granted the entire territory of the Colony to "William Bradford, his heirs, associates and assigns." He promptly took in the "Old Comers" or "Purchasers" who had been regarded as proprietors of the land under the Peirce Patent, and they could have continued as sole proprietors of the soil, had they so chosen. Instead, they regarded themselves as trustees for the community, which recognized their generosity in the renunciation of special privilege by the grant of the three Reserved Tracts. No. 1 on Cape Cod extended from Bound Brook or Quivet Creek (the present Dennis-Brewster boundary) on the west to a point just east of Allen's Harbor or Harwichport; the northern bound was near the southern part of Eastham; it embraced South Orleans and the greater part of Harwich and Brewster (William C. Smith *History of Chatham* pp. 45–7). Tract No. 2 comprised Dartmouth, Fairhaven, New Bedford and Little Compton,

lands as they or any of them are personally possessed of or interested in, by virtue of any former titles or grant whatsoever. And the said William Bradford doth by the free and full consent, approbation and agreement of the said Old Planters or Purchasers, together with the liking, approbation and acceptation of the other part of the said Corporation, surrender into the hands of the whole Court, consisting of the Freemen of this Corporation of New Plymouth, all that other right and title, power, authority, privileges, immunities and freedoms granted in the said Letters Patents by the said right Honourable Council for New England. Reserving his and their personal right of freemen, together with the said Old Planters aforesaid, except the said lands before excepted, declaring the freemen of this Corporation, together with all such as shall be legally admitted into the same, his associates. And the said William Bradford for him, his heirs and assigns, do hereby further promise and grant to do and perform whatsoever further thing or things, act or acts, which in him lieth, which shall be needful and expedient for the better confirming and establishing the said premises as by counsel learned in the laws shall be reasonably advised and devised, when he shall be thereunto required.

In witness whereof, the said William Bradford hath in public Court surrendered the said Letters Patents actually into the hands and power of the said Court, binding himself, his heirs, executors, administrators and assigns to deliver up whatsoever specialties are in his hands, that do or may concern the same.

5. *Constitution of the New England Confederation,* 19 *May* 1643 |257|

Articles of Confederation between the Plantations under the Government of the Massachusetts, the Plantations under the Government of New Plymouth, the Plantations under the Government of

---

R. I. No. 3 comprised Swansea, Rehoboth, Seekonk and Attleboro, Mass., and East Providence, Cumberland and part of Pawtucket, R. I. (R. LeBaron Bowen *Early Rehoboth* I 50). The grantees of all three tracts organized as proprietary bodies, extinguished Indian titles, granted free land titles to early settlers, and either divided up or sold the rest; most of the proprietors soon sold out their interests to a small group. Governor Bradford and his son Major William were particularly interested in the third tract, bordering on Rhode Island. It was also claimed by the Bay Colony, but the New England Confederation adjudged it to Plymouth in 1644.

Connecticut, and the Government of New Haven, with the Plantations in combination therewith.[9]

Whereas we all came into these parts of America with one and the same end and aim, namely to advance the kingdom of our Lord Jesus Christ and to enjoy the Liberties of the Gospel in purity with peace. And whereas in our settling by a wise Providence of God we are further dispersed upon the Seacoasts and Rivers than was at first intended, so that we cannot according to our desires with conveniency communicate in one government and jurisdiction; and whereas we live encompassed with people of several Nations and strange languages which hereafter may prove injurious to us and our posterity; and forasmuch as the Natives have formerly committed sundry insolencies and outrages upon several Plantations of the English, and have of late combined themselves against us; and seeing, by reason of those[1] distractions in England (which they have heard of) and by which they know we are hindered from that humble way of seeking advice or reaping those comfortable fruits of protection which at other times we might well expect; we therefore do conceive it our bounden duty without delay to enter into a present Consociation amongst ourselves for mutual help and strength in all our future concernments. That as in Nation and Religion, so in other respects, we be and continue One, according to the tenor and true meaning of the ensuing Articles.

1. Wherefore it is fully Agreed and Concluded by and between the Parties or Jurisdictions above named, and they jointly and severally do by these presents agree and conclude, That they all be and henceforth be called by the name of THE UNITED COLONIES OF NEW ENGLAND.

2. The said United Colonies for themselves and their posterities do jointly and severally hereby enter into a firm and perpetual League of Friendship and Amity for offense and defense, mutual advice and succour upon all just occasions, both for preserving and propagating the truth [and liberties] of the Gospel and for their own mutual safety and welfare.

[9] Also printed, from this text, in *Old South Leaflet* No. 169. Another text, in *New Haven Colonial Records 1653–65* p. 562, is reprinted in William MacDonald *Select Charters* p. 94. The minutes of the Commissioners' meetings are in *Plymouth Colony Records* Vols. IX, X. A good brief account of this interesting experiment in federalism is the chapter by Constance McL. Green in A. B. Hart *Commonwealth History of Massachusetts* (1927) Vol. I.

[1] The New Haven official text above noted has "the sad" instead of "those"; there are other minor differences that are entered here in square brackets.

3. It is further agreed, That the Plantations which at present are or hereafter shall be settled with[in] the limits of the Massachusetts, shall be forever under the [Government of the] Massachusetts and shall have peculiar Jurisdiction among themselves in all cases [2] as an entire body; and that Plymouth, Connecticut and New-Haven shall, each of them, [in all respects] have like peculiar Jurisdiction and Government within their limits. And in reference to the Plantations which already are settled or shall hereafter be erected, or shall settle within [any of] their limits, respectively, provided that no other Jurisdiction shall hereafter be taken in, as a distinct head or Member of this Confederation, nor shall any other, [either] Plantation or Jurisdiction in present being, and not already in combination or under the Jurisdiction of any of these Confederates, be received by any of them, nor shall any two of the Confederates join in one Jurisdiction without consent of the rest, which consent to be interpreted as is expressed in the Sixth Article ensuing.

4. It is [also] by these Confederates agreed, That the charge of all just wars, whether offensive or defensive, upon what part or Member of this Confederation soever they fall, shall, both in men, provisions and all other disbursements be borne by all the parts of this Confederation, in different proportions according to their different abilities, in manner following. Namely, that the Commissioners for each Jurisdiction, from time to time as there shall be occasion, bring a true account and number of all the males in every Plantation, or any way belonging to or under their several Jurisdictions, of what quality or condition soever they be, from 16 years old to 60, being inhabitants there. And that according to the different numbers which from time to time shall be found in each Jurisdiction upon a true and just account, the service of men and all charges of the war be borne by the poll: each Jurisdiction or Plantation being left to their own just course and custom of rating themselves and people according to their different estates, with due respects to their qualities and exemptions amongst themselves, though the Confederation take no notice of any such privilege. And that, according to their different charge of each Jurisdiction and Plantation, the whole advantage of the war (if it please God [so] to bless their endeavours), whether it be in lands, goods or persons, shall be proportionably divided among the said Confederates.

5. It is further agreed, That if these Jurisdictions or any Plantation under or in combination with them be invaded by any en-

[2] These three words omitted in New Haven text.

emy whomsoever, upon notice and request of any three |258| Magistrates of that Jurisdiction of [so] invaded, the rest of the Confederates, without any further meeting or expostulation, shall forthwith send aid to the Confederate in danger, but in different proportion; namely, the Massachusetts, an hundred men sufficiently armed and provided for such a service and journey, and each of the rest forty-five so armed and provided, or any lesser number, if less be required, according to this proportion. But if such Confederate in danger may be supplied by their next Confederate, not exceeding the number hereby agreed, they may crave help there and seek no further for the present; the charge to be borne as in this Article is expressed. And at their return to be victualed and supplied with powder and shot for their journey (if there be need) by that Jurisdiction which employed or sent for them. But none of the Jurisdictions to exceed these numbers till by a meeting of the Commissioners for this Confederation a greater aid appear necessary. And this proportion to continue till upon knowledge of greater numbers in each Jurisdiction, which shall be brought to the next meeting, and some other proportion be ordered. But in [any] such case of sending men for present aid, whether before or after such order or alteration, it is agreed that at the meeting of the Commissioners for this Confederation that the cause of such war or invasion be duly considered; and if it appear that the fault lay in the parties so invaded, that then that Jurisdiction or Plantation make just satisfaction, both to the invaders whom they have injured, and bear all the charges of the war themselves, without requiring any allowance from the rest of the Confederates towards the same. And further, that if any Jurisdiction see any danger of any invasion approaching and there be time for a meeting, That in such a case three Magistrates of that Jurisdiction may summon a meeting at such convenient place as themselves shall think meet, to consider and provide against the threatened danger. Provided, when they are met, they may remove to what place they please. Only, whilst any of these four Confederates have but three Magistrates in their Jurisdiction, their [a] request or summons from any two of them shall be accounted of equal force with the three mentioned in both the clauses of this Article, till there be an increase of Magistrates there.

6. It is also agreed, That for the managing and concluding of all affairs proper and concerning the whole Confederation, two Commissioners shall be chosen by and out of each of these four Jurisdictions: namely, two for the Massachusetts, two for Plymouth, two for Connecticut and two for New-Haven, being all in church fellowship

with us, which shall bring full power from their several General Courts respectively to hear, examine, weigh and determine all affairs of war or peace, leagues, aids, charges and numbers of men for war, divisions of spoils and whatsoever is gotten by conquest; receiving of more Confederates or Plantations into Combination with any of the Confederates, and all things of like nature which are the proper concomitants or consequences of such a Confederation, for amity, offense and defense; not intermeddling with the Government of any of the Jurisdictions which by the third Article is preserved entirely to themselves. But if these eight Commissioners, when they meet, shall not all agree, yet it concluded, That any six of the eight agreeing shall have power to settle and determine the business in question. But if six do not agree, that then such Propositions, with their Reasons so far as they have been debated, be sent and referred to the four General Courts; viz. the Massachusetts, Plymouth, Connecticut and New-Haven. And if at all the said General Courts the business so referred be concluded, then to be prosecuted by the Confederates and all their Members. It was further agreed that these eight Commissioners shall meet once every year, besides extraordinary meetings (according to the Fifth Article) to consider, treat and conclude of all affairs belonging to this Confederation; which meeting shall ever be the first Thursday in September. And that the next meeting after the date of these presents, which shall be accounted the second meeting, shall be at Boston in the Massachusetts, the third at Hartford, the fourth at New-Haven, the fifth at Plymouth, [the sixth and seventh at Boston; and then Hartford, New-Haven and Plymouth,] and so in course successively, if in the meantime some middle place be not found out and agreed on which may be commodious for all the Jurisdictions.

7. It is further agreed, That at each meeting of these eight Commissioners, whether ordinary or extraordinary, they all six of them agreeing as before may choose a President out of themselves, whose office and work shall be to take care and direct for order and a comely carrying on of all proceedings in the present meeting. But he shall be invested with no such power or respect as by which he shall hinder the propounding or progress of any business, or any way cast the scales otherwise than in the precedent Article is agreed. |259|

8. It is also agreed, That the Commissioners for this Confederation hereafter at their meetings, whether ordinary or extraordinary, as they may have commission or opportunity, do endeavour to frame and establish Agreements and Orders in general cases of a civil nature wherein all the Plantations are interested, for the preserving of

peace amongst themselves and preventing (as much as may be) all occasions of war or difference with others. As about the free and speedy passage of justice in every Jurisdiction, to all the Confederates equally as to their own, not [3] receiving those that remove from one Plantation to another without due Certificate, how all the Jurisdictions may carry [it] towards the Indians, that they neither grow insolent nor be injured without due satisfaction, lest war break in upon the Confederates through such miscarriages. It is also agreed that if any Servant run away from his Master into another of these Confederated Jurisdictions, That in such case, upon the Certificate of one Magistrate in the Jurisdiction out of which the said Servant fled, or upon other due proof, the said Servant shall be delivered either to his Master, or any other that pursues and brings such Certificate or proof. And that upon the escape of any Prisoner whatsoever or fugitive for any Criminal Cause, whether breaking Prison or getting from the Officer or otherwise escaping, upon the Certificate of two Magistrates of the Jurisdiction out of which the escape is made that he was a prisoner or such an offender at the time of the escape, the Magistrates, or some of them, of that Jurisdiction where for the present the said Prisoner or fugitive abideth, shall forthwith grant such a Warrant as the case will bear, for the apprehending of any such person and the delivering of him into the hands of the Officer or other person who pursues him. And if there be help required for the safe returning of any such offender, then it shall be granted to him that craves the same, he paying the charges thereof.

9. And for that the justest wars may be of dangerous consequence, especially to the smaller Plantations in these United Colonies, it is agreed, That neither the Massachusetts, Plymouth, Connecticut nor New-Haven, nor any [of the] Members of any of them shall at any time hereafter begin, undertake or engage themselves or this Confederation, or any part thereof in any war whatsoever (sudden exigents with the necessary consequents thereof excepted, which are also to be moderated as much as the case will permit) without the consent and agreement of the forementioned eight Commissioners, or at the least six of them, as in the Sixth Article is provided. And that no charge be required of any of the Confederates in case of a defensive war, till the said Commissioners have met and approved the justice of the war, and have agreed upon the sum of money to be levied; which sum is then to be paid by the several Confederates in proportion to the Fourth Article.

[3] "Not" is omitted in the New Haven text.

10. That in extraordinary occasions, when meetings are summoned by three Magistrates of any Jurisdiction, or two as in the Fifth Article, if any of the Commissioners come not, due warning being given or sent, it is agreed that four of the Commissioners shall have power to direct a war which cannot be delayed, and to send for due proportions of men out of each Jurisdiction, as well as six might do if all met. But not less than six shall determine the justice of the war or allow the demands or bills of charges or cause any levies to be made for the same.

11. It is further agreed, That if any of the Confederates shall hereafter break any of these present Articles, or be any other ways injurious to any one of the other Jurisdictions, such breach of Agreement or injury shall be duly considered and ordered by the Commissioners for the other Jurisdictions, that both peace and this present Confederation may be entirely preserved without violation.

12. Lastly, this perpetual Confederation and the several Articles [and Agreements] thereof being read and seriously considered, both by the General Court for the Massachusetts and by the Commissioners for Plymouth, Connecticut and New-Haven, were fully allowed and confirmed by three of the forenamed Confederates; namely, the Massachusetts, Connecticut and New-Haven. Only the Commissioners for Plymouth, having no commission to conclude, desired respite till they might advise with their General Court. Whereupon it was agreed and concluded by the said Court of the Massachusetts and the Commissioners for the other two confederates that if Plymouth consent then the whole treaty as it stands in these present articles is and shall continue firm and stable without alteration.[4] But if Plymouth come not in, yet the other three Confederates do by these presents |260| confirm the whole Confederation and the Articles thereof. Only in September next, when the second meeting of the Commissioners is to be at Boston, new consideration may be taken of the Sixth Article, which concerns number of Commissioners for meeting and concluding the affairs of this Confederation to the satisfaction of the Court of the Massachusetts and the Commissioners for the other two Confederates, but the rest to stand unquestioned. In the testimony whereof, the General Court of the Massachusetts by their Secretary, and the Commissioners for Connecticut and New Haven, have subscribed these present articles this 19th of the third month, commonly called May, Anno Domini 1643.

[4] These sentences about Plymouth's adhesion differ in the New Haven text, but the sense is the same.

At a meeting of the Commissioners for the Confederation held at Boston the 7th of September, it appearing that the General Court of New Plymouth, and the several townships thereof, have read and considered and approved these Articles of Confederation, as appeareth by commission from their General Court bearing date the 29th of August, 1643, to Mr. Edward Winslow and Mr. William Collier to ratify and confirm the same on their behalves, we therefore the Commissioners for the Massachusetts, Connecticut and New-Haven, do also for our several governments subscribe unto them.

JOHN WINTHROP, Governor of the Massachusetts
THOMAS DUDLEY — THEOPHILUS EATON
GEORGE FENWICK — EDWARD HOPKINS
THOMAS GREGSON

6. *Treaty between the New England Confederation and the Narragansetts, 27 August* 1645. |267|

It was agreed betwixt the Commissioners of the United Colonies and the forementioned sagamores and Niantic deputy, that the said Narragansett and Niantic sagamores

1. Should pay or cause to be paid at Boston to the Massachusetts Commissioners the full sum of 2000 fathom of good white wampum, or a third part of black wampumpeag, in four payments; namely, 500 fathom within 20 days, 500 fathom within 4 months, 500 fathom at or before next planting time, and 500 fathom within 2 years next after the date of these presents; which 2000 fathom the Commissioners accept for satisfaction of former charges expended.

2. The foresaid sagamores and deputy, on the behalf of the Narragansett and Niantic Indians, hereby promise and covenant that they upon demand and proof satisfy and restore unto Uncas, the Mohegan sagamore, all such captives, whether men, or women, or children, and all such canoes as they or any of their men have taken, or as many of their own canoes in the room of them full as good as they were, with full satisfaction for all such corn as they or any of their men have spoiled or destroyed of his or his men's since last planting time; and the English Commissioners hereby promise that Uncas shall do the like.

3. Whereas there are sundry differences and grievances betwixt Narragansett and Niantic Indians, and Uncas and his men, (which in Uncas his absence cannot now be determined) it is hereby agreed that Narragansett and Niantic sagamores either come them-

selves or send their deputies to the next meeting of the Commissioners for the Colonies, either at New Haven in September 1646 or sooner (upon convenient warning if the said Commissioners do meet sooner), fully instructed to declare and make due proof of their injuries and to submit to the judgment of the Commissioners in giving or receiving satisfaction. And the said Commissioners, not doubting but Uncas will either come himself or send his deputies in like manner furnished, promising to give a full hearing to both parties with equal justice, without any partial respects according to their allegations and proofs.

4. The said Narragansett and Niantic sagamores and deputies do hereby promise and covenant to keep and maintain a firm and perpetual peace, both with all the English United Colonies and their successors; and with Uncas the Mohegan sachem and his men; with Ousamequin, Pomham, Socanoket, Cutshamakin, Shoanan, Passaconaway,[5] and all other Indian sagamores and their companies who are in friendship with or subject to any of the English; hereby engaging themselves that they will not at any time hereafter disturb the peace of the country by any assaults, hostile attempts, invasions or other injuries to any of the United Colonies or their successors, or to the aforesaid Indians either in their persons, buildings, cattle, or goods, directly or indirectly, nor will they confederate with any other against them. And if they know of any Indians or others that conspire or intend hurt against the said English or any Indians subject to or in friendship with them, they will without delay acquaint and give notice thereof to the English Commissioners or some of them. Or if any questions or differences shall at any time hereafter arise or grow betwixt them and Uncas or any Indians before mentioned, they will, according to former engagements (which they hereby confirm and ratify) first acquaint the English and crave their judgments and advice therein, and will not attempt or begin any war or hostile invasion till they have liberty and allowance from the Commissioners of the United Colonies so to do.

5. The said Narragansetts and Niantic sagamores and deputies do hereby promise that they will forthwith deliver and restore all such Indian fugitives or captives which have at any time fled from

[5] Ousamequin is another name of Massasoit, the Pilgrims' faithful ally. Pomham or Pumham, the sachem of Shawomet, the region above Warwick, R. I., was slain in King Philip's War. Socanoket or Socononoco was the sachem of Pawtuxet. Cutshamakin, a sachem of the Massachusetts, had been an ally of the English in the Pequot War. Passaconaway, sachem of the middle Merrimac region, has attained a certain immortality in Whittier's "Bridal of Pennacook."

any of the English, and are now living or abiding amongst them, or give due satisfaction for them to the Commissioners for the Massachusetts; and further, that they will, without more delays, pay or cause to be paid a yearly tribute a month before harvest, every year after this at Boston to the English Colonies, for all such Pequots as live amongst them, according to the former treaty and agreement made at Hartford, 1638. Namely, one fathom of white wampum for every Pequot man and half a fathom for each Pequot youth, and one hand length for each male child. And if Weequashcook refuse to pay this tribute for any Pequots with him, the Narragansetts' sagamores promise to assist the English against him. And they further covenant that they will resign and yield up the whole Pequot country, and every part of it to the English colonies as due to them by conquest.

6. The said Narragansett and Niantic sagamores and deputy do hereby promise and covenant that within fourteen days they will bring and deliver to the Massachusetts Commissioners on the behalf of the colonies |268| four of their children; viz. Pessacus his eldest son, the son [of] Tassaquanawit, brother to Pessacus, Awashawe his son, and Ewanghos' son a Niantic, to be kept as hostages and pledges by the English, till both the forementioned 2000 fathom of wampum be paid at the times appointed, and the differences betwixt themselves and Uncas be heard and ordered; and till these articles be underwritten at Boston by Janemo and Wipetock.

And further, they hereby promise and covenant that if at any time hereafter any of the said children shall make escape or be conveyed away from the English before the premises be fully accomplished, they will either bring back and deliver to the Massachusetts Commissioners the same children, or if they be not to be found, such and so many other children to be chosen by the Commissioners for the United Colonies or their assigns, and that within 20 days after demand. And in the meantime until the said four children be delivered as hostages, the Narragansett and Niantic sagamores and deputy do freely and of their own accord leave with the Massachusetts Commissioners as pledges for present security, four Indians, namely, Witowash, Pummash, Iawashoe, Waughwamino, who also freely consent and offer themselves to stay as pledges till the said children be brought and delivered as abovesaid.

7. The Commissioners for the United Colonies do hereby promise and agree that at the charge of the United Colonies the four Indians now left as pledges shall be provided for and that the four children to be brought and delivered as hostages shall be kept and

maintained at the same charge. That they will require Uncas and his men, with all other Indian sagamores before named, to forbear all acts of hostility against the Narragansetts and Niantic Indians for the future. And further, all the promises being duly observed and kept by the Narragansett and Niantic Indians and their company, they will at the end of two years restore the said children delivered as hostages, and retain a firm peace with the Narragansetts and Niantic Indians and their successors.

8. It is fully agreed by and betwixt the said parties that if any hostile attempt be made while this treaty is in hand, or before notice of this agreement (to stay further preparations and directions) can be given, such attempts and the consequences thereof shall on neither part be accounted a violation of this treaty, nor a breach of the peace here made and concluded.

9. The Narragansetts and the Niantic sagamores and deputy hereby agree and covenant to and with the Commissioners of the United Colonies that henceforth they will neither give, grant, sell or in any manner alienate any part of their country nor any parcel of land therein either to any of the English or others without consent or allowance of the Commissioners.

10. Lastly they promise that if any Pequot or other be found and discovered amongst them who hath in time of peace murdered any of the English, he or they shall be delivered to just punishment.

In witness whereof the parties above named have interchangeably subscribed these presents, the day and year above written.

John Winthrop, President	George Fenwick
Herbert Pelham	Edward Hopkins
Thomas Prence	Theophilus Eaton
John Browne	Stephen Goodyear

Pessacus his mark
Mixanno his mark
Witowash his mark
Aumsequen his mark (the Niantic deputy)
Abdas his mark
Pummash his mark
Cutshamakin his mark

APPENDIX XIII

PASSENGERS IN THE MAYFLOWER[1]

(indicates Signers of the Mayflower Compact)*[2]

The names of those which came over first, in the year 1620, and were by the blessing of God the first beginners and in a sort the foundation of all the Plantations and Colonies in New England; and their families.

8 * Mr. John Carver, Katherine his wife, Desire Minter, and two manservants, * John Howland, Roger Wilder. William Latham, a boy, and a maidservant and a child that was put to him[3] called Jasper More.

6 * Mr. William Brewster, Mary, his wife, with two sons, whose names were Love and Wrestling. And a boy was put to him called Richard More, and another of his brothers. The rest of his children were left behind and came over afterwards.

5 * Mr. Edward Winslow, Elizabeth his wife and two menservants called * George Soule and Elias Story; also a little girl was put to him called Ellen, the sister of Richard More.

2 * William Bradford and Dorothy his wife, having but one child, a son left behind who came afterward.

6 * Mr. Isaac Allerton and Mary his wife, with three children, Bartholomew, Remember and Mary. And a servant boy John Hooke.

[1] Bradford writes these in two columns, starting on the reverse of the third unnumbered leaf after the unfilled heading for 1647 and 1648, and continuing on both sides of the next two leaves. The numerals, which he enters on the left of each group, show the number of passengers in each family. I have followed the generally accepted spelling of these names as given in Charles E. Banks *The English Ancestry and Names of the Pilgrim Fathers* (1929). Readers who are interested in establishing a pedigree should apply to the Society of Mayflower Descendants, 9 Walnut Street, Boston.

[2] These are not given in Bradford but in Nathaniel Morton's *New Englands Memoriall* (1669). Some authorities think that Morton merely copied the text of the Compact from Bradford's *History* and picked out from the list of passengers those whom he thought would have been likely to have signed. I think that the differences between Morton's text and Bradford's indicate that Morton had access to the original document with the signatures.

[3] I.e., assigned to him to take charge of and bring up, as an apprentice or servant.

* Mr. Samuel Fuller and a servant called William Button.
2 His wife was behind, and a child which came afterwards.

2 * John Crackston and his son John Crackston.

2 * Captain Myles Standish and Rose his wife.

* Mr. Christopher Martin and his wife and two servants,
4 Solomon Prower and John Langmore.

* Mr. William Mullins and his wife and two children, Jo-
4 seph and Priscilla; and a servant, Robert Carter.

* Mr. William White and Susanna his wife and one son
6 called Resolved, and one born a-shipboard called Peregrine, and
two servants named William Holbeck and Edward Thompson.

* Mr. Stephen Hopkins and Elizabeth his wife, and two
children called Giles and Constanta, a daughter, both by a for-
8 mer wife. And two more by this wife called Damaris and
Oceanus; the last was born at sea. And two servants called * Edward Doty and * Edward Lester.

* Mr. Richard Warren, but his wife and children were
1 left behind and came afterwards.

* John Billington and Ellen his wife, and two sons, John
4 and Francis.

* Edward Tilley and Ann his wife, and two children that
4 were their cousins, Henry Sampson and Humility Cooper.

3 * John Tilley and his wife, and Elizabeth their daughter.

* Francis Cooke and his son John; but his wife and other
2 children came afterwards.

* Thomas Rogers and Joseph his son; his other children
2 came afterwards.

3 * Thomas Tinker and his wife and a son.

2 * John Rigsdale and Alice his wife.

* James Chilton and his wife, and Mary their daughter;
3 they had another daughter that was married, came afterward.

3 * Edward Fuller and his wife, and Samuel their son.

* John Turner and two sons; he had a daughter came
3 some years after to Salem, where she is now living.

* Francis Eaton and Sarah his wife, and Samuel their son,
3 a young child.

* Moses Fletcher, * John Goodman, * Thomas Williams,
* Digory Priest, * Edmund Margesson, * Peter Browne, * Rich-
10 ard Britteridge, * Richard Clarke, * Richard Gardiner, * Gilbert
Winslow.

* John Alden was hired for a cooper at Southampton
1 where the ship victualed, and being a hopeful young man was
much desired but left to his own liking to go or stay when he
came here; but he stayed and married here.

* John Allerton and * Thomas English were both hired,
the latter to go master of a shallop here, and the other was re-
2 puted as one of the company but was to go back (being a seaman) for the help of others behind. But they both died here before the ship returned.

There were also other two seamen hired to stay a year
2 here in the country, William Trevor, and one Ely. But when
their time was out they both returned.

These being about a hundred souls, came over in this first ship and began this work, which God of His goodness hath hitherto blessed. Let His holy name have the praise.

And seeing it hath pleased Him to give me to see thirty years completed since these beginnings, and that the great works of His providence are to be observed, I have thought it not unworthy my pains to take a view of the decreasings and increasings of these persons and such changes as hath passed over them and theirs in this thirty years.[4] It may be of some use to such as come after; but however I shall rest in my own benefit. I will therefore take them in order as they lie.

Mr. Carver and his wife died the first year, he in the spring, she in the summer. Also, his man Roger and the little boy Jasper died before either of them, of the common infection. Desire Minter returned to her friend and proved not very well

[4] Bradford evidently wrote this in 1650.

and died in England. His servant boy Latham, after more than 20 years' stay in the country, went into England and from thence to the Bahama Islands in the West Indies; and there with some others was starved for want of food. His maidservant married and died a year or two after, here in this place. His servant John Howland married the daughter of John Tilley, Elizabeth, and they are both now living and have ten children, now all living, and their eldest daughter hath four children; and their
15 second daughter one, all living, and other of their children marriageable. So 15 are come of them.

Mr. Brewster lived to very old age; about 80 years he was when he died, having lived some 23 or 24 years here in the coun-
4 try. And though his wife died long before, yet she died aged. His son Wrestling [5] died a young man unmarried. His son Love lived till this year 1650 and died and left four children, now living.
2 His daughters which came over after him are dead but have left sundry children alive. His eldest son [6] is still living and hath nine or ten children; one married who hath a child or two.

Richard More's brother [7] died the first winter, but he is
4 married and hath four or five children, all living.

Mr. Edward Winslow his wife died the first winter, and
2 he married with the widow of Mr. White and hath two children living by her, marriageable, besides sundry that are dead.

One of his servants died, as also the little girl, soon after
8 the ship's arrival. But his man, George Soule, is still living and hath eight children.

William Bradford his wife died soon after their arrival,
4 and he married again and hath four children, three whereof are married.

Mr. Allerton his wife died with the first, and his servant John Hooke. His son Bartle [8] is married in England but I know
8 not how many children he hath. His daughter Remember is married at Salem and hath three or four children living. And his

[5] Bradford spells it *Wrastle* which was doubtless how the name was pronounced.

[6] Jonathan, eldest son of William Brewster.

[7] Jasper, who was "put to" the Carver family.

[8] Diminutive for Bartholomew.

daughter Mary is married here and hath four children. Himself married again with the daughter of Mr. Brewster and hath one son living by her, but she is long since dead. And he is married again and hath left this place long ago. So I account his increase to be eight, besides his sons in England.

Mr. Fuller his servant died at sea; and after his wife came
2 over he had two children by her, which are living and grown up
to years; but he died some fifteen years ago.

John Crackston died in the first mortality, and about some five or six years after his son died, having lost himself in the woods; his feet became frozen, which put him into a fever of which he died.

Captain Standish his wife died in the first sickness and he
4 married again and hath four sons living and some are dead.

Mr. Martin, he and all his died in the first infection, not long after the arrival.

Mr. Mullins and his wife, his son and his servant died the
first winter. Only his daughter Priscilla survived, and married
15 with John Alden; who are both living and have eleven children.
And their eldest daughter is married and hath five children.

Mr. White and his two servants died soon after their landing. His wife married with Mr. Winslow, as is before noted. His
7 two sons are married and Resolved hath five children, Peregrine
two, all living. So their increase are seven.

Mr. Hopkins and his wife are now both dead, but they
lived above twenty years in this place and had one son and four
daughters born here. Their son became a seaman and died at Bar-
badoes, one daughter died here and two are married; one of
5 them hath two children, and one is yet to marry. So their increase which still survive are five. But his son Giles is married
4 and hath four children.

12 His daughter Constanta is also married and hath twelve
children, all of them living and one of them married.

Mr. Richard Warren lived some four or five years and
had his wife come over to him, by whom he had two sons before
[he] died, and one of them is married and hath two children. So
4 his increase is four. But he had five daughters more came over

with his wife, who are all married and living, and have many children.

John Billington, after he had been here ten years, was ex-
8 ecuted for killing a man, and his eldest son died before him but
his second son is alive and married and hath eight children.

Edward Tilley and his wife both died soon after their arrival, and the girl Humility, their cousin, was sent for into Eng-
7 land and died there. But the youth Henry Sampson is still living
and is married and hath seven children.

John Tilley and his wife both died a little after they came ashore. And their daughter Elizabeth married with John Howland and hath issue as is before noted.

Francis Cooke is still living, a very old man, and hath seen
his children's children have children. After his wife came over
with other of his children; he hath three still living by her, all
8 married and have five children, so their increase is eight. And his
4 son John which came over with him is married, and hath four
children living.

Thomas Rogers died in the first sickness but his son Jo-
6 seph is still living and is married and hath six children. The rest
of Thomas Rogers' came over and are married and have many
children.

Thomas Tinker and his wife and son all died in the first sickness.

And so did John Rigsdale and his wife.

James Chilton and his wife also died in the first infection,
10 but their daughter Mary is still living and hath nine children; and
one daughter is married and hath a child. So their increase is ten.

Edward Fuller and his wife died soon after they came
4 ashore, but their son Samuel is living and married and hath four
children or more.

John Turner and his two sons all died in the first sickness. But he hath a daughter still living at Salem, well married and approved of.

Francis Eaton his first wife died in the general sickness. And he married again and his second wife died, and he married

4 the third and had by her three children. One of them is married
and hath a child. The others are living but one of them is an
idiot. He died about 16 years ago. His son Samuel who came
1 over a sucking child, is also married and hath a child.

Moses Fletcher, Thomas Williams, Digory Priest, John Goodman, Edmund Margesson, Richard Britteridge, Richard Clarke, all these died soon after their arrival in the general sickness that befel. But Digory Priest had his wife and children sent hither afterwards, she being Mr. Allerton's sister. But the rest left no posterity here.

Richard Gardiner became a seaman and died in England or at sea.

Gilbert Winslow, after divers years' abode here, returned into England and died there.

Peter Browne married twice. By his first wife he had two
6 children who are living and both of them married; and the one
of them hath two children. By his second wife he had two more.
He died about sixteen years since.

Thomas English and John Allerton died in the general sickness.

John Alden married with Priscilla, Mr. Mullins's daughter, and had issue by her as is before related.

Edward Doty and Edward Lester, the servants of Mr. Hopkins. Lester, after he was at liberty, went to Virginia and there died. But Edward Doty by a second wife hath seven children, and both he and they are living.

Of these hundred persons which came first over in this first ship together, the greater half died in the general mortality, and most of them in two or three months' time. And for those which survived, though some were ancient and past procreation, and others left the place and country, yet of those few remaining are sprung up above 160 persons in this thirty years, and are now living in this present year 1650, besides many of their children which are dead and come not within this account.

And of the old stock, of one and other, there are yet living this present year, 1650, near thirty persons. Let the Lord have the praise, who is the High Preserver of men.

[Bradford himself died 9 May 1657. The following entries are in two later hands.]

Twelve persons living of the old stock this present year, 1679.

Two persons living that came over in the first ship 1620, this present year 1690: Resolved White and Mary Cushman the daughter of Mr. Allerton.

And John Cooke the son of Francis Cooke that came in the first ship, is still living this present year, 1694.

And Mary Cushman is still living this present year, 1698.[9]

[9] Mary (Allerton) Cushman, who was born in 1616, died in 1699, last survivor of the *Mayflower's* passengers.

FINIS

INDEX

B. means William Bradford. The list of Mayflower *passengers in Appendix XIII is not indexed. Ships' names are in* italics. *Familiar quotations from this History will be found at the end of the alphabetical index.*

QUOTATIONS

A NOTE ON THE TYPE

This book was set on the Linotype in Janson, a recutting made direct from the type cast from matrices (now in possession of the Stempel foundry, Frankfurt am Main) made by Anton Janson some time between 1660 and 1687.

Of Janson's origin nothing is known. He may have been a relative of Justus Janson, a printer of Danish birth who practiced in Leipzig from 1614 to 1635. Some time between 1657 and 1668 Anton Janson, a punch-cutter and type-founder, bought from the Leipzig printer Johann Erich Hahn the type-foundry that had formerly been a part of the printing house of M. Friedrich Lankisch. Janson's types were first shown in a specimen sheet issued at Leipzig about 1675. Janson's successor, and perhaps his son-in-law, Johann Karl Edling, issued a specimen sheet of Janson types in 1689. His heirs sold the Janson matrices in Holland to Wolffgang Dietrich Erhardt.

Typography and binding designs are by W. A. Dwiggins.